The Canonica

Crossing Disciplinary and Cultural Boundaries

149

Internationale Forschungen zur
Allgemeinen und
Vergleichenden Literaturwissenschaft

Begründet von Alberto Martino und in Verbindung mit

Francis Claudon (Université Paris-Est Créteil Val de Marne) – Rüdiger Görner
(Queen Mary, University of London) – Achim Hölter (Universität Wien) –
Klaus Ley (Johannes Gutenberg-Universität Mainz) – John A. McCarthy
(Vanderbilt University) – Alfred Noe (Universität Wien) – Manfred Pfister
(Freie Universität Berlin) – Sven H. Rossel (Universität Wien)

herausgegeben von

Norbert Bachleitner

(Universität Wien)

Redaktion: Paul Ferstl und Rudolf Pölzer

Anschrift der Redaktion:
Institut für Vergleichende Literaturwissenschaft, Sensengasse 3A , A-1090 Wien

The Canonical Debate Today
Crossing Disciplinary and Cultural Boundaries

Edited by
Liviu Papadima,
David Damrosch
and Theo D'haen

Amsterdam - New York, NY 2011

Cover photo: Vlad A. Arghir

Cover design: Pier Post

Le papier sur lequel le présent ouvrage est imprimé remplit les prescriptions de "ISO 9706:1994, Information et documentation - Papier pour documents - Prescriptions pour la permanence".

The paper on which this book is printed meets the requirements of " ISO 9706:1994, Information and documentation - Paper for documents - Requirements for permanence".

Die Reihe "Internationale Forschungen zur Allgemeinen und Vergleichenden Literaturwissenschaft" wird ab dem Jahr 2005 gemeinsam von Editions Rodopi, Amsterdam – New York und dem Weidler Buchverlag, Berlin herausgegeben. Die Veröffentlichungen in deutscher Sprache erscheinen im Weidler Buchverlag, alle anderen bei Editions Rodopi.

From 2005 onward, the series "Internationale Forschungen zur Allgemeinen und Vergleichenden Literaturwissenschaft" will appear as a joint publication by Editions Rodopi, Amsterdam – New York and Weidler Buchverlag, Berlin. The German editions will be published by Weidler Buchverlag, all other publications by Editions Rodopi.

ISBN: 978-90-420-3281-1
E-Book ISBN: 978-90-420-3282-8
© Editions Rodopi B.V., Amsterdam - New York, NY 2011
Printed in The Netherlands

Printed by Printforce, the Netherlands

TABLE OF CONTENTS

Liviu Papadima

Introduction

A Can(n)on in Need Is a Can(n)on Indeed

According to dictionaries, a 'cannon' is a device usually employed to break walls, whereas the slightly shorter word 'canon' seems to imply the opposite. Built out of fragile and composite raw materials such as rules, norms, measurements, conventions, names, judgments, beliefs, contentions, and much more, with the help of sophisticated machineries that include exegesis, gossip, salons, universities, magazines, academies, encyclopedias, and publishing houses, aesthetic canons are meant to make objects of art endure. Obviously, not all of them – just the ones supposed to deserve it. How is it possible to decide in a legitimate, acceptable way, on such a delicate matter?

Let us imagine a world with just a couple of dozen artists of all times: writers, painters, musicians, and so on. In this world, the sheer idea of an aesthetic canon would be considered a bizarre fantasy. Fortunately, this is not the case. We need canons – if we really need them – because we need to choose.

Raising immaterial or even material walls – libraries, museums, theaters, concert halls –, canons, past and present as well, are a matter of choice: value per square meter. But value itself, the core of all canons, is a highly controversial notion. Some would say that it is arbitrary, that it depends on our individual needs – the rest is either pretence or politics. Others would blame it, even worse, for being circumstantial; meaning that agreement upon value is controlled by the particular context in which this agreement is reached. From this point of view, politics becomes a central issue – it is no longer 'the rest', maybe just all there is to canon formation.

That is why most often canons resemble fortresses, both protective and defying strongholds, both vulnerable and menacing citadels. Many of them exhibit, above the entrance, the more or less conspicuous coat of arms of some local landlord.

'*Der Zeit ihre Kunst. Der Kunst ihre Freiheit*' – is written under the gilded dome of the Sezession building in Vienna. In order to render this highly problematic equation functional, time has to build and demolish simultaneously. 'To every epoch, its canons. To every canon, its cannons.'

What does the present-day battlefield of canonical encounters look like, after the fierce campaigns fought in the late sixties and during the eighties?

What is the impact of recent changes – in terms of (cultural) politics, literary production, and distribution, the status and mission of academic institutions etc. – on the structure and orientation of literary studies, reconsidering both their past and their future prospects? What are the gains and the losses, the opportunities and the perils, enhanced by the current tendencies to blur or even to suppress vertical as well as horizontal boundaries – between literary and literature-related genres, between aesthetic levels, between cultural communities? These were some of the major questions addressed by the participants in the international conference 'National Literatures in the Age of Globalization: The Issue of the Canon' organized at the end of 2008 by the Faculty of Letters, of the University of Bucharest. The papers delivered and the accompanying discussions at this meeting gave an impetus to the construction of the present volume. This explains why the primarily theoretical purport of this collective work is enhanced by a special focus, mainly in the last section of the volume, on the dynamics of Romanian literature.

I would like to emphasize from the very beginning that the arrangement of the materials in three separate sections does not impede at all the dialogue among essays with different main topics. The various streams of ideas which irrigate the surface and the depth of the volume across individual contributions are a natural consequence of the thick intertwining of the matters under discussion.

Not only do intersecting ideas and opinions bring the individual essays closer to each other, but they also outline a common approach, shared by most of the contributors. Instead of assertiveness, they would prefer to highlight the intricacies and even the paradoxes of the problems dealt with.

The first section is dedicated to the literary canon as such: its dilemmas in the contemporary world, especially related to endeavors to identify common denominators capable of (re)shaping the identity of European culture as a whole; its troublesome connection to theoretical thinking; its historical links to contiguous fields like fine arts and religion and their present-day relevance; its sensitivity to changes in sexuality and in politics; its possible affinity with other explanatory frames of cultural evolution; and, last but not least, the alleged criteria of canon formation, put under the scrutiny of on-going criticism.

The debates on canons of Dutch-language literature in recent years give *Theo D'haen* the opportunity to sketch a suggestive picture – tinted with a dash of charming irony – of the surprising, apparently highly idiosyncratic complications which arise when the task of canon formation is assumed rigidly. The comparison with the similar phenomenon, viewed on a larger scale, starting with the 1920s, in the United States – undoubtedly the most notorious example – reveals illuminating common traits. The most spectacular one is that the process of canon building is oriented not only towards the past, but also towards the future. Very often canons are rooted in a societal 'ideal', in a collective project, much the same way that 'imagined communities' are born. We may learn a lot from the American experience, Theo D'haen suggests, especially about the particular hindrances to the attempts to construe – and construct – a European canon. The road towards such a daring, yet unavoidable enterprise is blocked not only by the feebleness of mutual contacts among the national cultures in Europe, but also by the absence of a 'European dream' comparable to the American one(s).

Rodica Mihăilă's essay completes and deepens Theo D'haen's discussion of the American canon. The author insists on the two final stages of canon building in the United States, the multicultural and the transnational one, as they reveal an evolution that might be considered symptomatic by/for the entire world. Canons have been always used not only to evince artistic 'peaks', but also to circumscribe the 'territories' which support their ascent. As aesthetic hierarchies are gradually levelled, the traditional implosive cultural – i.e., roughly speaking, national – geographies turn into explosive 'imaginary geographies'. 'American literature read as world literature, obsessed by the world and fully engaged in the world' – is this merely a new hypostasis of the already acknowledged 'American exceptionalism', or is it the premonition of a planetary 'new order' in the literary field, among others?

According to Theo D'haen, a successful European literary canon 'might serve as the catalyst for a newly emerging "world" literature'. The inverted commas, referring to the already obsolete notion of 'world literature', are significant. *William Franke* also underlines the contemporary necessity to rethink the notion of 'universality', the one which laid the foundation of *Weltliteratur* in Goethe's time. The 'transhistorical communicability of value', a basic prerequisite for writings to enter the canon, does not necessarily lead to the positing of landmarks beyond time and space, but rather to 'a universality that can be apprehended always only *in the making*', which 'might be more accurately called *omni*versality'. The redefined concept would no longer operate by exclusion, but 'rather by inclusion potentially with no restrictions', in the same paradoxical way in which theory, designed to forge and reshape concepts, is 'never merely theory. It is always also, at the same time, a practice'.

Quite in the same line with William Franke and with Theo D'haen runs *Caius Dobrescu*'s suggestion of a 'federalist phenomenology' aiming at the construction of a European literary canon. In order to 'promote supranational context-free "cold" values and at the same time preserve the "warmth" of a context-bound communal memory', the trumpeted 'celebration of diversity' will not suffice. A European canon should rather bring to light the 'European-ness', 'as a genuine and innerly-cohesive event of consciousness'. Therefore, it should be inclusive, by means of relevance, rather than exclusive, by means of abstract value hierarchies. Dobrescu's view of 'value-as-experience' mirrors Franke's idea of 'universality *in the making*'. The phenomenological stand brings to the foreground works that have hall-marked deeply and persistently the intellectual life of the continent – the intellectualization of emotions, the exploration, and the exploitation of the Greco-Roman heritage, utopian thinking, alternative patterns of processing experience, and the interplay of various identities. A phenomenological approach also favors writings and writers who could aid to the construction of an imagology of Europe, perceived either by insiders or by outsiders.

Delia Ungureanu's comprehensive overview of criteria involved in critical controversies over the canon – Harold Bloom, Frank Kermode, Robert Alter, Geoffrey Hartman, John Guillory –, deployed under the provocative motto 'Is it necessary to have a literary canon today?', reaches the conclusion that 'the literary canon is not only useful nowadays, but also necessary'.

A survey of the canon both in visual arts and in literature enables *Adina Ciugureanu* to detect the (relatively) concurrent courses of both forms of artistic representation, although there may seem to be little in common between the perspectives of the two theorists the author of the essay mainly relies upon, Michel Foucault and Harold Bloom. The same difficulty is encountered by *Simona Drăgan* in her explicit attempt to compare the *episteme* model elaborated by Foucault in *Les mot et les choses* and the sequence of 'ages' identified by Bloom in *The Western Canon*. As a matter of fact, the very scarce, passing citations of the former by the latter are invariably polemical and deprecatory. Nevertheless, in spite of the blatant, admitted differences between the two thinkers, 'what suggests a strange similarity between them is this curious, *coincidental four-age division*' of the 'archeology of knowledge' and the panorama of the Western literary canon.

Zakaria Fatih's essay reminds the reader of the constant overlapping of literary studies and theological scholarship – e.g. in hermeneutics, the practice of interpretation of exemplary texts, be they secular, as Homer's epics, or sacred, as The Bible. Religious canon building has its closest counterpart in literature in the attempts at shaping the notion of the 'classics' – illustrated, in Fatih's paper, by the criticism of Saint-Beuve, T. S. Eliot and Kermode. These 'critics have relied, consciously or otherwise, on tools that have been used to define the religious canon; they also considered the corpus of literary classics as limited and sacred as if it were a body of Scriptures' – states Fatih. Is this position, overtly – and sometimes radically – exclusive, still defendable faced with the much more generous, but somehow vague, visions of inclusive canonicity, that prevail in present times? The cross-reading of the contributions in this respect may prompt further reflections on the inclusion-exclusion dialectics of canon formation.

A case study by *Frédéric Canovas* is meant 'to retrace the emergence of Cocteau's written and visual discourse on homosexuality as well as his original role as a homosexual role model and perhaps the first global figure of what was going to become a new literary canon: the gay canon.' The essay focuses mainly on the most difficult task Cocteau had to face throughout his life in order to be able to freely and convincingly affirm his own vision of homosexual identity: parting with André Gide.

Magda Răduță scrutinizes the evolution of the literary field in the decade before and in the year after the collapse of communism in Romania. She finds that exceptional political circumstances, such as the rise and fall of a radical dictatorship, trigger unexpected effects in the literary community, such as the fact that, by the end of the '70s, the older, authoritative critics warmly encouraged the younger writers who rebelled against their generation, or that the abrupt end of the regime immediately put its former enemies among the writers under pressure to choose between an ethical and an aesthetical position regarding both the past and the future.

The studies collected in the second section of the volume deal with the present situation of comparative literature and the historical roots of discipline separation in the humanities.

'World literature is often regarded today as a global phenomenon, sometimes even seen as a cultural expression of an emerging "world system"' – states *David Damrosch* in the opening of his essay. The trouble is that this 'global phenomenon' – a 'work in progress', one may say – is perceived in strikingly different ways from various points of the globe, in various institutional contexts. Moreover, even in the same place and in the same milieu, localism and globalism may confront each other, generating contradictory vectors of perception. In the United States, David Damrosch remarks, comparatism is simultaneously Americentric – in the American anthologies of world literature, for example – and Amerifugal – e.g. in the contents of specialized periodicals. Analyzing the scholarly comparatist practices in India and China, Damrosch recommends a multicentric view on world literature, sustained by 'a double movement, both inward and outward', enabling the strengthening of the links to one's own culture, on the one hand, and the widening of the scope of inquiry to the 'varieties of comparatist practice' on the other hand.

Scrutinizing a rich set of definitions of the term 'globalization', *Dumitru Radu Popa* argues that the reality referred to by this 'buzzword', 'even a treacherous word' is not as recent a phenomenon as one may believe. The author refuses to take the idea of globalization as a skeleton key to open all the either alluring or disquieting doors of the future, parallel to the refusal of the current 'exceptionalist' image of the present – itself not an utterly new state of mind. Instead, Popa supports an invigorating and balanced view of the changes comparative literature has been undergoing in contemporary times, neither as an agonizing discipline, nor as the awaited savior of mankind.

Oana Fotache adds to the discussion of the relationship between globalization and literary studies an analysis of the various meanings the notion of 'global literature' has acquired in different cultural and academic fields: literary sociology, postcolonial and diaspora studies, popular culture and, last but not least, comparative literature. Contrasting 'global literature' with the more familiar concept of 'world literature', Fotache proposes that the former 'gestures towards its general readership', whereas the latter 'is a matter of critical response and canon'. Roughly speaking, 'global' points to present time, while 'world literature' is oriented towards the past. The two related notions may be regarded as the result of a continuously gliding focus, with the 'present' permanently turning into the 'past', giving thus a profitable theoretical insight in the ambivalent process of canon formation and preservation.

Although she is an academic deeply involved in the advances of interdisciplinary cultural studies in Romania, *Mihaela Irimia* advocates the status of disciplinarity in researching literature. In her opinion, the specific disciplines of literary studies derive from a long-term process, comprising 'the emergence, sedimentation and institutionalization of *literature* and the accreditation of the *classic modern canon*', both phenomena described 'as embedded in (cultural) history'. Following the path of what is called 'the long modernity', Irimia notes that 'In the mid-1700s the disciplines, like the literary canon, come into being as they are still with us, albeit undergoing sea changes like never before'.

Stefan H. Uhlig pushes the history of disciplinarity in literary studies a step further. Mainly interested, in the first part of his essay, in the metamorphoses of intersecting and competing notions such as 'literature', 'letters' and 'poetry', Uhlig argues that a crucial phase is the first half of the 19th century, when German and English universities 'largely start to teach the subject "literature" by way of, or indeed through literary history', while American and Scottish colleges (and, in their own fashion, the French universities, too) choose rhetoric as the appropriate frame for teaching literature. One of the consequences of the fact that the German and English approach gradually won out over the alternative choice was the modeling of *literature* as 'an overwhelmingly descriptive, academic concept quite unlike, say, *poetry* or *rhetoric*'.

The contributions gathered in the third section of the volume pinpoint multiple facets of the contemporary obsession with 'borders': the ups and downs of the allegedly 'high' versus 'low' or 'popular' forms of art, the paradoxes of value assessments when cultures with different value criteria or frames of reference come within touching distance of each other, and the cultural politics and strategies to promote the 'marginals'.

Elaine Martin then discusses 'the potential demise of (serious) literature – and, with it, of the very concept of a canon – due to both the growing hegemony of image media over text media and the overwhelming rise of popular culture as a whole'. Although experts in literature may still indulge in skepticism about the (sudden) overthrow of the written word by the image – a sort of apocalypse already prophesied decades ago – they can no longer ignore what is happening under their very eyes: the worldwide decrease of reading, the amalgamation of media – the symbiotic relation between literary works and film, the graphic novel etc. –, and the expressive forms facilitated by the new technologies – self-publishing, blogging and so on. Is this development a menace or a new opportunity for comparatists?

Ion Manolescu backs up Elaine Martin's advocacy of popular culture in more polemical terms. Deploring Romanian literary critics' and historians' lack of interest in the remarkable achievements of some of their country-fellows, creators of comics, Manolescu blames their 'blindness' on the (hidden) criteria of canonicity they operate with, firmly disavowing these criteria as 'prejudices': the elitist prejudice, the prejudice of the closed canon and the prejudice of undisputed aesthetic authority of 'high' genres.

A momentous situation of failed intercultural dialogue is studied by *Alexandra Vrânceanu*. The Romanian writer Panait Istrati was highly appreciated in France, where he lived as an expatriate between the two World Wars, while Romanian critics of the time either ignored his writings, or harshly rejected them. At the same time, the novelist, playwright and poet Camil Petrescu, the champion of Romanian Modernism, contemporary to Istrati, remained practically unknown to both critics and readers in France, in spite of the close relations connecting the two cultures at that time. The explanation, according to Vrânceanu, lies in the dissymmetry of these relations. The Romanian authors and critics were willing to enter the mainstream, which meant, at that time, French Modernism (above all, Proust), while French readers and critics expected from Romanian authors rather crude stories and exoticism.

Ileana Orlich's essay deals with Camil Petrescu's best known novel, *The Bed of Procrustes*. The complementary enigmas of the two main male characters of the novel – an old-fashioned poet fallen in love with a trivial and frivolous prostitute and a fashionable young intellectual and sportsman, unable to nourish a love affair in which he seems to be deeply entangled – are considered tokens of the crisis of masculinity also recognizable, in a psychoanalytical reading, in the writings of Baudelaire, Pound and Eliot.

Roumiana Stantcheva draws attention to the perils raised by the strategies often used by literary critics belonging to 'central' cultures in their endeavor to promote authors and writings stemming from 'peripheral' cultures. Their attempts to describe and evaluate such works by means of comparisons that bring the unfamiliar closer to the familiar – i.e. famous reference points of the Western canon – run the risk of stereotyping and leveling, in the extreme, of absorbing the richness of cultural diversity into one single pattern.

What are the most effective cultural politics to employ in order for the literary products of less-known cultures to reach a larger international audience? According to *Cristina Balinte*, one should emphasize affinities with broader, regional cultural frames and stimulate exchange programs conceived according to mutual interests.

Ioana Both criticizes the premises underlying the current strategies to promote the creation of the most celebrated Romanian poet Mihai Eminescu. According to Ioana Both, the highly apologetic, self-centered presentations of Eminescu as an epiphany of 'Romanian-ness' are less convincing than a reader-oriented comparative approach 'which would put him in the company of consecrated and accessible names from universal literature.'

Translated anthologies are a powerful means of widening cultural awareness, expanding the boundaries inherent to the process of canon formation. *Mădălina Vatcu* shows in her contribution how such literary collective volumes can miss the target, however, when they are biased by inner political demands. This is the case of most of the anthologies of Romanian literature translated into French during the communist period.

Teachers of literature tend to recommend both extensive and intensive reading to their students, in spite of the fact that reading fiction has become a rather obsolete activity nowadays. Although we are convinced that it is worth spending a lot of time with books, we encounter serious difficulties in making our point clear. What is literature meant for? Should it please? Is it meant to open our eyes towards the world we live in and towards our own selves? Should it mould our souls? Is it meant to refine our minds, our thinking? Should it expand our limited existence? Is it meant to unite different people or does it separate people in emphasizing differences, between individuals, between cultures?

Canons, disciplines and cultural borders are all spectres of our inquietude about the fate of literary reading. Recurrent in our daily questions, they continuously challenge us to find provisional answers.

For the time being, allow me to express my gratitude to Oana Fotache from the Faculty of Letters, Bucharest, to Mihaela Doagă from the Faculty of Foreign Languages and Literatures, Bucharest and to Florin Bican, from the National Book Center of the Romanian Cultural Institute, Bucharest, who selflessly and expertly helped the present volume take shape.

I. CANONS AND CONTEXTS

Theo D'haen

How Many Canons Do We Need? World Literature, National Literature, European Literature

Taking my initial cue from a debate on canons of Dutch-language literature as recently conducted in the Dutch and Flemish media, I move on to a more general discussion of the nature of canons and the uses to which they are put. I then relate this to presently ongoing re/considerations of national, European, and world literature, with particular attention to the issue of a/the European canon(s) in the light of an expanding and integrating European Union.

Canons are all the rage in Holland and Belgium these days.[1] During the months of October through December 2008 a series of four public lectures on canons was held at the Brussels Museum for Fine Arts, one of the most prestigious locations to speak at in Belgium. These lectures addressed, respectively, the literary canon, the cultural canon, the science canon, and the European canon. All lectures were given by extremely eminent Dutch literary historians or, in one case, a prominent scientist. Two of the speakers were, or had been, Presidents of the KNAW or Royal Dutch Academy of Sciences. It is surely not a coincidence that all of these speakers were Dutch, even if the event itself was held in Brussels, capital not only of Europe, nor even of Belgium, but also of Flanders, the northern-most, and Dutch-speaking region of the linguistically divided kingdom of Belgium. There is a well-known Belgian expression, shared by French-speaking Walloons and Dutch-speaking Flemings alike, that when it pours in Paris it drizzles in Brussels. As far as canons are concerned, the same thing seems to be true for Amsterdam and Brussels – perhaps, cheekily mixing metaphors, we might say that when the canon roars in Amsterdam the report is heard in Brussels. And how it does roar in Amsterdam! An historical canon of The Netherlands was commissioned in 2005 by the then Minister of Education from the Royal Dutch Academy of Sciences, and put together by an august committee of

---

[1] Parts of this article earlier appeared as 'Working the American Canon: Reflections of a Canon-Watcher,' in *Rewriting the Dream: Reflections on the Changing American Literary Canon*, ed. by W.M. Verhoeven, Costerus New Series 83 (Amsterdam/Atlanta: Rodopi, 1992), pp. 233-44. I am grateful to the editor and the publishers for granting me permission to re-use, in modified form, the relevant paragraphs.

historians presided over by the then President of the Academy, himself the most celebrated historian of medieval Dutch literature, and one of the speakers at the Brussels series of events. This canon was officially presented to the Minister in 2006. But there now is also a Science Canon, likewise put together under the auspices of the Academy, with a new President presiding, and presented to the new Minister of Education in 2008. This was since turned into a popular cartoon version by 'Fokke & Sukke,' a celebrated pair of cartoonists that started their career for the Leyden University weekly *Mare* back in the late 1990s. And there is an 'Amsterdam Canon,' celebrating that famous city. Over the last year or so ever more cities in The Netherlands have been following the Amsterdam example. All these canons draw the line at fifty items – apparently, this is where the 'ordinary' Dutchman's capacity for memory is deemed to be exhausted.

The number fifty was retained in the Flemish version of the canon, and here we also move into the field of literature. The Flemish weekly *Knack* early in 2008 appealed to authors, literary scholars, critics, secondary school teachers, librarians, publishers and booksellers, for suggestions as to what they deemed the fifty most important Flemish books. These were to figure as input to a joint Dutch-Flemish list, in essence a Dutch-language canon. The Dutch are at work on similar list. An official Dutch-Flemish committee is at work on the joint list. Now this immediately brings out a problem inherent to all canons: if that joint list would again number 50 items, as is likely, each of the separate Dutch and Flemish lists would have to be cut to make room for the other party's candidates in the amalgamated version. But how to do this? Do we take the first twenty-five items on each list and join these, round and round, to make up a new list of fifty? Then who gets to start, and thus number one on the list? Or do we choose more items from the Dutch list, as there are more Dutchmen than Flemings, and presumably (in fact: certainly) also more Dutch books than Flemish books? If so, how many more? Or do we choose according to 'objective' importance of the works concerned, with the (unlikely) risk that, say, 40 Flemish books come out on top, and there is only room for 10 Dutch books at the bottom of the list; or vice versa? Or, again, does the order in which we choose the books perhaps change when we start amalgamating the two initial lists, and could a book that occupies a lower position in its original list actually be rated higher if we consider it from a joint perspective? Or should we not rank at all, and simply list fifty titles *ex aequo*? I will return to these questions at the end of my talk. By the way, the solution to this problem, at least as far as the Dutch-Flemish problem is concerned, is easy and simple, according to the first speaker in the Brussels series, Geert Buelens, Professor of Modern Dutch literature at Utrecht University in The Netherlands, but a Fleming himself. He proposes to have three lists: a Dutch one, a Flemish one, and a Dutch-language one. The latter would then be composed, quite naturally, of works that 'evidently belong to the core literary heritage of both regions,' whereas the national canons would equally obviously tilt towards more national concerns. Although this at first sight seems an obvious solution, it in fact still leaves open the question of the joint list as I briefly raised it before, though it may now have become somewhat less acute, as each community is also granted its own list. In fact, Buelens speaks of listing writers rather than titles, unlike the weekly *Knack*. He is also not very clear as to whether he sees the joint list as containing at least a number of the same titles as the national lists, or whether he sees the three lists as not sharing any names or titles. The latter, of course, would with one sleight of hand raise the number of 'canonized' books, or their authors, to one hundred and fifty – an inflationary gesture if ever I saw one, but perhaps also a smart move in a global literary context where every "'iterature' were to be granted, say, a list of fifty; again, I will come back to this. A more obvious possibility, it seems to me, is that the joint list be different from the 'national' lists in that it would, by necessity, not only not contain a number of works itemized in these national lists, but also in that it might contain items that are not listed in either national canon.

Of course, all these constraints and conjectures only hold true if we accept the 'magical' number of fifty as in any way binding. In fact, the Flemish daily *De Standaard* came up with a much shorter list of only fourteen of what it called 'immortals,' and an additional list of eight 'perhaps' immortals or 'runners-up.' *De Standaard* arrived at its restricted list or lists via a very simple procedure: it compared the various lists on Flemish literature circulating in academe, and retained only those names that featured either unanimously or repeatedly. It is significant that only nineteenth- and twentieth-century authors were considered for the *De Standaard* list or lists, as prior to the nineteenth century, and *a fortiori* before the middle of the seventeenth century, the differentiation into Dutch (as distinct from 'Dutch-language') and Flemish literature is virtually meaningless. In fact, 'Flemish' literature can be said to have been an invention of the nineteenth century, and this for political, economic and social as much as for cultural reasons. And the same goes for 'Dutch' literature in the seventeenth century. Again, I will come back to a number of the issues thus raised.

It is interesting to read how in all publications surrounding the canon debate in Holland and Belgium there is reference to popular culture in the form of the 'top fifty', etc. In the publicity announcement to the series in Brussels the question was actually raised whether 'canonization is a noble form of caring for past monuments, a remedy to the lessened attention to our icons, or quite simply the literary equivalent to the golden spikes best-player-of-the-year election in football.' Such remarks, but in a much more strident tone, also featured in the debate on the American canon in the 1980s and 1990s. Take, for instance, an article with the mock-arch title 'Paradise Tossed: The Fall of Literary Standards,' by the columnist Jonathan Yardley in *The*

Washington Post of 11 January 1988. Yardley rages against what he calls 'the vigilantes of the English department,' 'the new professoriat,' 'the young Turks' he sees at work undermining all in literature that has made America great. Ridiculing what he calls 'careerists and political schemers' he claims that present-day English departments are out to replace James, and Faulkner, and Hemingway with Louis L'Amour, a popular writer of westerns. As Yardley himself puts it: 'Makes you want to rush right back to college, doesn't it? To hell with Shakespeare and Milton, Emerson and Faulkner! Let's boogie! Let's take courses in the writers who really matter, the writers whom the WASPish old guard sneers at. Let's get relevant, with courses on Gothic novels, bodice-ripper romances, westerns, detective stories.' Although Yardley does not specifically mention this, he is not only taking aim at popular culture here, but also at multiculturalism via his use of the verb 'boogie,' with its direct reference to black music, and the implied savage contrast to the 'civilized' canon of 'true' literature. As such, he is obviously taking position in the so-called Culture wars raging in American academe in the last quarter of the twentieth century. To most European literary historians and critics this debate is undoubtedly much better known than the Dutch debate on the issue. However, and this is a point I will return to, these same literary historians and critics most probably know the American canon debate not only better than the Dutch one, but probably also better than that in any other European country, perhaps even better than that in their own country, if such a debate is being conducted there. If there is not, my bet is that very soon there will be, for reasons I hope to outline before long. First, however, I turn to the American debate.

In the 1980s, the 'canon' became a hotly debated issue, especially – though not exclusively – with regard to American literature.[2] In *Fragments against our ruins: Canons in de Anglistiek*, my inaugural lecture at Leyden University in 1988, I briefly tried to sketch, for a Dutch public, some of the issues involved by examining a number of anthologies of American literature, from *The American Tradition in Literature* in its first (1956) and third (1967) editions, over the first (1979) and second (1985) editions of the *Norton Anthology of American Literature*, to *The Harper American*

---

[2]   The list of relevant publications by now has become almost endless; a useful early survey is Jan Gorak, *The Making of the Modern Canon: Genesis and Crisis of a Literary Idea* (London & Atlantic Highlands, NJ: The Athlone Press, 1991). Gorak points out that the term 'canon' has a very long and complicated history, going back to the original Greek meaning of 'standard' or 'measure' and in the course of history allowing for such widely divergent applications as the Aristotelian notion of designating a flexible set of rules framed according to circumstances to Saint Augustine's fixed and closed set of sacred texts as the basis for exegesis, explanation, and teaching. It is the latter sense that eventually filtered into our modern investments of the term. Applied to literature, though, the application of the term, as we now do, to a particular and privileged set of literary works, was preceded by its use with reference to a set of rules to be applied *to* literary works, the so-called 'canons of criticism' or 'laws' governing the propriety of a specific genre.

Literature from 1987.[3] I traced a movement from a fairly narrow canon, focusing upon a limited range of authors, mostly men, mostly of WASP-origin, mostly fitting the parameters of a Leavisian 'Great Tradition' or a New Critical paradigm, to a very open selection, comprising texts about the New World drawn from English, French, Spanish, and Italian sources, Indian creation myths and reports of encounters with white men, and a wide range of texts by women, blacks, Asian-Americans, Chicanos and other Spanish-speaking Americans, and Native Americans. At the same time, I noted a change in approach from purely text-centered close-reading to an avowed ambition 'to show how celebrated and less-heralded works of literature illuminate each other and enable us to appreciate the diverse achievements that have shaped a distinctively American culture' (*Harper*, p. xxviii). These changes, I argued, were a response to changes in the demographic make-up of the United States, to changes in the political and ideological climate of the country, to shifts in literary theory affecting American academe throughout the 1970s and 1980s, and to shifts in power relations within the profession of academic scholarship in American literary studies during the same period. Most of these changes could be labeled with the headings 'pluralism' and 'multiculturalism.'

That the developments I traced in 1988 have only accelerated since then is borne out by more recent anthologies such as *The Heath Anthology of American Literature*, first published in 1990,[4] and the newer versions of the *Norton Anthology of American Literature*. In their preface, 'To the Reader', the editors of *The Heath Anthology of American Literature* narrate how the idea for a new anthology came to them in the turbulent year 1968. They sketch how at that time 'large numbers of teachers and scholars of all ethnic backgrounds began to question the "canon" of American literature –that is, the list of works and authors believed to be sufficiently important to read, study, write about, teach – and thus transmit to the next generation of readers' (p. xxxiii). The problem, as the then prospective editors of what would eventually become *The Heath Anthology of American Literature* saw it, was 'how to provide teachers and students with a textbook that truly displayed the enormous richness of the cultures of America' (p. xxxiv). In order to overcome this problem, they adopted a number of principles. First, 'because [they] want[ed] students to be able to gain a sense of the formal and historical cross-currents which helped shape individual works within a given period, [they] provide[d] a much richer selection of authors from each time

---

[3]   Theo D'haen, *Fragments against our ruins: Canons in de Anglistiek* (Amsterdam: De Arbeiderspers, 1988).

[4]   *The Heath Anthology of American Literature*, ed. by Paul Lauter (Lexington, Mass.: D.C. Heath and Company, 1990).

frame than is available in any other anthology' (pp. xxxiv-xxxv). They believed that

> reading this *range* of writers offers opportunities for drawing stimulating comparisons and contrasts between canonical and non-canonical figures, between female and male, between one ethnic writer and another. It allows us to study the diverse and changing cultures of America, not only a narrow group of authors (p. xxxv).

Second, they included many 'reasonably familiar but undervalued authors' (p. xxxv) or less-known works by relatively well-known writers. Third, they let themselves be guided by 'how a text engages concerns central to the period in which it was written as well as to the overall development of American culture' (p. xxxv). As such, they think their selections 'reflect an effort, which [they] believe appropriate and important, to reconnect literature and its study with the society and culture of which it is fundamentally a part' (p. xxxvi). In line with this effort, many of the works they have chosen 'treat issues and subjects that have often been downplayed, even avoided: such topics include household labor in poems of the colonial period, child abuse [...], sexuality, including homosexuality [...], the forms of affirmation as well as the experience of racial violence in minority communities' (p. xxxvi). Still, the 'traditional analyses of familiar themes, such as what it means to be "American"' (p. xxxvi), have not been spurned. At variance with confirmed usage in earlier anthologies, though, the editors of *The Heath Anthology of American Literature* have not confined themselves to selections by well-known writers on this issue, such as Franklin, Crevecoeur, Emerson, or Henry Adams. Instead, they have amplified their selections to also take in pronouncements on the theme by 'those who begin on the margin of American society, as slaves, immigrants, or "native" Americans', and for whom their marginality 'only intensifies' the question of what it means to be American (p. xxxvi). And then follows the roll-call to substantiate these claims:

> This selection includes material by 109 women of all races, 25 individual Native American authors (as well as 17 texts from tribal origins), 53 African-Americans, 13 Hispanics (as well as 12 texts from earlier Spanish originals and two from French), and 9 Asian-Americans. We have also included significant selections from Jewish, Italian, and other ethnic traditions. (pp. xxxvi-xxxvii)

I have dwelt to such length on this anthology because in its day it was the clearest demonstration that the guiding principle in establishing an American 'canon' at that time, at least with part of the profession in the United States itself, was no longer 'the formal scrutiny of isolated texts' (p. xxxix) by 'a narrow group of authors' (p. xxxv) – 'perhaps a dozen "major" writers' (p. xxxiii) –, but rather 'to study the diverse and changing cultures of America' (p. xxxv) via 'analyses which depend upon an examination of [...] historical contexts' (p. xxxix). As all the material included, moreover, was proposed or suggested by 'the profession at large' (p. xxxviii) via a very large scale direct mail consulting effort, and was put together by an unusually large board of editors selected on the basis of fair representation of race, gender, regional provenance, and kind of institution, this surely must have been the most 'democratic' of anthologies of American literature until then, both as to content and genesis. To varying degrees, all anthologies after *The Heath Anthology* of 1990 have continued the trend, with the *Norton Anthology of American literature*, in its 2003 sixth, full five-volume, edition, containing, for early American literature, next to the familiar selections from John Smith, William Bradford, John Winthrop and Anne Bradstreet, texts by Spanish and French explorers, native creation and trickster tales, early Dutch settlers, etc. Likewise, *Volume E, Literature since 1945*, contains generous selections from most ethnic literatures, next to only a few texts by white postmodernists.

If the widening of the American canon is amply and convincingly testified to, then, by recent anthologies, the question remains *why* this widening has taken place when it did, and what the implications are for American scholars and teachers, as for their counterparts abroad. At first sight, a deep contradiction seems to rule this late twentieth-century battle of the books. The new open 'reconstructed' canon is lauded for its democratic qualities, implying that the earlier one was not democratic, but elitist or repressive. Yet that canon, foregrounding the American Renaissance authors, Twain, James, T.S. Eliot, Hemingway, Scott Fitzgerald, Faulkner, down to Saul Bellow and Bernard Malamud, was propounded by the liberal humanist academic and intellectual establishment that in America traditionally stands for democracy, for the defense of the economically and politically weak, for the immigrants and minorities, the supporters of F.D. Roosevelt and J.F. Kennedy, the archetypal 'D/democrats'? It is time here for a little historical excursus, a contextualizing of 'the American canon' according to the recipe also advocated in *The Heath Anthology of American Literature*.

The 'classic' American literary canon emerged in the 1920s as a result of the same kinds of shifts that are now breaking up this very same canon: demographic, political and ideological, literary theoretical, and professional. Only then these shifts made not for pluralism or multiculturalism, but for centralism and cultural 'Unitarianism.' Paul Lauter has chronicled how the institutionalization of American literature as an academically acceptable discipline, the rise of the professoriate as a result of the professionalization of learning in the United States, the ascendancy of formal aesthetic criticism along New Critical lines and the periodization of literary study, all led to a restricted canon favoring white, male authors from a predominantly middle-class and North-Eastern background, whereas an earlier American canon – largely that of nineteenth- and early twentieth-century reading societies and magazines – had been much wider, comprising a fair share of women and blacks.[5] The 'classic' canon was presented as 'timeless' and as representing the highest achievement of American literature coinciding with the deepest-felt definition of what it meant to be American. This 'Americanness' was then further defined as an ideal in opposition to what its proponents saw as the massification and commercialization of actual American life and culture. The result was an elite canon holding out democratic individualism as the ultimate goal for all Americans. Given the abstraction of this ideal condition, differences of race and gender could conveniently be disregarded. The avowed 'masterpieces' of American literature showed the way toward self-fulfillment for *all* Americans, and consequently considerations of 'representation' in the sense of 'representativeness' were besides the question. It is not difficult to discern a clear parallel here to the teleological ideals at the same time ruling also other areas of American life and culture: the 'American dream' of success and the political melting-pot. In practice, the insistence on the ideal led to the deferral of concrete steps toward achieving that ideal. In fact, it could be said that American literature, as defined by the 'classic' canon, and American society at large, functioned in counterbalance, the former providing relief and solace for the political and economic reality of the latter, but at the same time also channeling feelings of disaffection via education into the ideal rather than the actual realm.

For a number of reasons the 'concordia discors' just sketched broke down in the 1960s. To begin with, the teleological logic of 'America' came crashing down around the ears of Americans in the 1960s and the decades following with the Vietnam war, with its political and military defeat, the moral and political divisions it engendered, and the subsequent relative political, economic and military decline of the United States. Paul Kennedy, in *The Rise and Fall of the Great Powers* already argued in the late 1980s that there was no reason for the feeling already becoming prevalent then in the United States that they were losing their grip on the world, because the superiority they enjoyed throughout the 1950s and 1960s was not so much the result – or not solely the result, as Americans like to believe – of the United States' own inner resources and strength but rather of the disarray in which the other major powers had been thrown by World War II, and that the shifting situation as of the 1990s merely signals a return to more 'normal'

---

[5]   Paul Lauter, 'Race and Gender in the Shaping of the American Literary Canon: A Case Study from the Twenties,' in *Canons and Contexts* (New York/Oxford: Oxford University Press, 1991), pp. 22-47; for illuminating insights into the beginning of academic literary professionalism in the United States see also Gerald Graff and Michael Warner, eds., *The Origins of Literary Studies in the United States: A Documentary Anthology* (New York and London: Routledge, 1989); for historical surveys of the profession see Gerald Graff, *Professing Literature: An Institutional History* (Chicago and London: The University of Chicago Press, 1987), and (older, radical, but still illuminating) Richard Ohmann, *English in America: A Radical View of the Profession* (New York: Oxford University Press, 1976).

global power relations.[6] Still, the fact remains that to Americans it felt, and undoubtedly feels even more so now, as if for the first time in their history they were, or are, no longer God's or History's chosen country where things can only go better than ever before or anywhere else. With the teleological lid off American exceptionalism, attention shifted from deferred ideal individual fulfillment to the remedying of existing injustices and inequalities. In particular, this provided an opening for airing the grievances of those groups in American society that, for one reason or another, had been excluded from fully sharing in the economic and political boons of actual America, but whose claims had hitherto been dismissed as irrelevant or perhaps even 'unfair' or 'non-American' by the hegemonic 'American ideology' of ideal individualism. As this ideology, under the guise of extreme individualism, was in fact tailor-made to further the interests of the group of WASP-males or, by extension, white (heterosexual) males, it is not surprising to find that the groups now claiming a greater stake in actual America structured themselves along lines of race and gender. It will also not come as a surprise that the crisis of the 'American ideology' also meant the end of the 'classic' American canon upholding this ideology.

As Emerson put it, 'The experience of each new age requires a new confession, and the world seems always waiting for its poet'. A new age, then, also required a new canon. And just as the classic canon served as an instrument – willy-nilly – to uphold the old consensus, the shaping of the new canon was now seen as a battle-ground for social and political contention. As Lauter, who has been among those most responsible for firing the canon-debate in the first place, and who has been instrumental in giving it shape over the years, put it himself in 1991,

> From my perspective, education – like other cultural institutions – is an arena for struggle, and what is decided there significantly affects the political economy and important social arrangements. [...] What has come to be called 'the question of the canon' is one front in this cultural battle, a particularly vital one. By 'canon' I mean the set of literary works, the grouping of significant philosophical, political, and religious texts, the particular accounts of history generally accorded cultural weight within a society. How one defines a cultural canon obviously shapes collegiate curricula and research priorities, but it also helps to determine precisely whose experiences and ideas become central to academic study. [...] debating the canon turns out to be a symbolic way of arguing a variety of other social and political issues – basically, who has power and how it is exercised (pp. viii-x).

With the demise of the old pieties, the question became 'what next'. As Lauter has suggested, there were three answers possible. One was to re-assert the value of the 'classic' canon, regardless of changes, in the name of 'humanity' and of 'American values'. This was the tack taken, albeit with

---

[6] Paul Kennedy, *The Rise and Fall of the Great Powers: Economic Change and Military Conflict From 1500 to 2000* (London: Unwin Hyman, 1988).

varying arguments, by Allan Bloom, and E.D. Hirsch.[7] Perhaps now the best-known, and certainly the most eloquent defender of this position is Harold Bloom, with his *The Western Canon*. Harold Bloom defends 'aesthetic value' against the onslaught of what he labels the 'current School of Resentment,' the cardinal principle of which, he claims, 'can be stated with particular bluntness: what is called aesthetic value emanates from class struggle' (Bloom 1994: 22). Or again: 'Whatever the Western Canon is, it is not a program for social salvation' (*ibid.* 28). For Bloom, the canon finally serves only the purpose of helping the individual reflect upon him- or herself in the company of the sharpest minds on paper. What these best minds are, Bloom argues, is determined by themselves: only those authors survive, and for Bloom a canon is also a 'kind of survivor's list' (*ibid.* 36), that are recognized by other survivors in the continual struggle for eminence marked by what Bloom in an earlier book called *The Anxiety of Influence*.[8] That conservative forces in the US are using the Western Canon in the service of their political ideals even now transpires from an article in *The New York Times* of 22 September 2008, which reports on initiatives to create programs and centers at various American institutions of higher learning to 'restore what conservative and other critics see as leading casualties of the campus culture wars of the 1980s and '90s: the teaching of Western culture and a triumphal interpretation of American history.'[9] According to the article, 'the programs and centers differ in emphasis, with some concentrating on American democratic and capitalist institutions and others on the Western canon, the great books often derided during the culture wars as the history of "dead white men "'. A second solution consisted in accumulating ever more specialized knowledge on historically proven texts. This is the road of theory, trying to safeguard a space for itself by out-professionalizing even the most specialized of professions. Especially during the 1970s this was a much-traveled road, one that has been analyzed at length by a.o. John Guillory in *Cultural Capital: The Problem of Literary Canon Formation*.[10] The third solution, obviously the one Lauter supports, was to redraw the canon in order to let in those excluded before, and to reorient the study of literature along the

---

[7]   Allan Bloom, *The Closing of the American Mind* (New York: Simon & Schuster, 1987); and E.D. Hirsch, Jr., *Cultural Literacy* (Boston: Houghton Mifflin Company, 1987).

[8]   Harold Bloom, *The Anxiety of Influence: A Theory of Poetry* (New York: Oxford University Press, 1973).

[9]   'Conservatives Try New Tack on Campuses', The *New York Times*, 22 September 2008.

[10]   John Guillory, *Cultural Capital: The Problem of Literary Canon Formation* (Chicago and London: The University of Chicago Press, 1993).

lines advocated in the preface to *The Heath Anthology of American Literature*. It is not for nothing that Lauter acted as coordinating editor of that anthology.

Lauter had likewise been instrumental in firing the debate over the canon in academic circles: among other things, he organized the first MLA session on the canon at the Chicago convention of 1973 (Lauter 1991:7) and in 1983 he edited *Reconstructing American Literature: Courses, Syllabi, Issues*, which carried on its very cover the injunction: 'so that the work of Frederick Douglass, Mary Wilkins Freeman, Agnes Smedley, Zora Neale Hurston and others is read with the work of Nathaniel Hawthorne, Henry James, William Faulkner, Ernest Hemingway and others'.[11] The very term 'reconstructing' was taken up again by Sacvan Bercovitch in *Reconstructing American Literary History*, a path-breaking volume on canon-formation and shifts in American literature.[12] Bercovitch is also the general editor of the *New Cambridge History of American Literature*, which runs along 'reconstructed' lines. And Lauter himself, in his preface, calls *The Heath Anthology of American Literature* a 'reconstructed' anthology. It is clear, then, that in all these instances the canon had come to be seen as a factor – both a reflection of and an actor in – in the changing power relationships within the US. That it was indeed experienced as such is shown by the stir caused, both in academic circles and in the popular press, by the changes in the humanities curriculum giving wider exposure to a 'reconstructed' canon at prestigious Stanford University that led to the eruption of the already mentioned Culture Wars in the US. This may also explain the heavy barrage of critical fire the Modern Language Association came in for from the more conservative sectors of the popular press for advocating a reconstructed canon, as in its 1990 volume *Redefining American Literary History*.[13] A 1991 MLA survey on the issue, however, proved that a majority of the profession, at least in principle, had accepted the changes.[14] Interestingly, though, some scholars, such as Werner Sollors and Henry Louis Gates, Jr., whose work has contributed significantly toward the reconstruction of the canon, at the same time, started voicing a mounting unease with some of the tenets, and most

---

[11] Paul Lauter, ed., *Reconstructing American Literature: Courses, Syllabi, Issues* (Old Westbury, NY: The Feminist Press, 1983).

[12] Sacvan Bercovitch, ed., *Reconstructing American Literary History* (Cambridge, Mass.: Harvard University Press, 1986).

[13] A. LaVonne Brown Ruoff and Jerry Ward, eds., *Redefining American Literary History* (New York: The Modern Language Association of America, 1990).

[14] 'MLA Survey Casts Light on Canon Debate', *MLA Newsletter* 23, 4 (Winter 1991), 12-14.

particularly with the persistent ethnicization, underlying that same process.[15] Gates, in fact, closed his 'Introduction' to his 1992 *Loose Canons: Notes on the Culture Wars,* with 'Today, the mindless celebration of difference for its own sake is no more tenable than the nostalgic return to some monochrome homogeneity. My hope is to have contributed, however stumblingly, to the search for a middle way.' (p. xix).

It is customary in the United States to look for the rationale behind the 'question of the canon' at developments that are purely internal to that country itself. In a 1984 paper, reprinted in his 1991 collection of essays called *Canons and Contexts*, and prefiguring his preface to *The Heath Anthology of American Literature*, Lauter says that:

> The question of the canon grows directly from the impact of the social movements of the 1960s on the profession. They asked of our courses, our texts, our research, 'Where are the blacks? Where are the women?'(7).

However natural such a way of looking at the question may be for an American, for us, outsiders and Europeans, the import of the debate reaches beyond the confines of the United States.

If for Americans the increased emphasis given to Asian-American writers or to Chicano authors may merely seem to be a response to the changing demographic reality of their country, to an European observer what is being signaled here is a turning away, in literary and cultural matters, as in matters economic and political, from Europe as the hitherto historically privileged partner or interlocutor of the United States. By writing its own citizens of Asian-American or Spanish-language background larger into its own literary past and present than had until then been the case the United States, by a dialectic of culture, economics and politics, is adjusting to a new world order in which its relations to the Pacific Rim countries and to Latin America loom ever larger, and those with Western Europe concomitantly smaller. Further, though the rise of pluralism and multiculturalism, and the shaping of a new canon, in the United States may well be the result of shifting power relations in that country between sexes, genders and ethnicities during the 1970s and 1980s, we notice comparable developments elsewhere too. For instance, what passes for multiculturalism in the United States goes under the heading of post-colonialism in much of the rest of the world. Continuing a little in this vein, if we consider 'America' not as a monolith with a monolithic literature, but as an ever shifting constellation of regional entities and ethnic

---

[15] See for instance Werner Sollors' 'Introduction' to *The Invention of Ethnicity* (New York: Oxford University Press, 1989) and Henry Louis Gates, Jr., 'Good-bye, Columbus? Notes on the Culture of Criticism', *American Literary History* 3, 4 (Winter 1991), 711-27; for a wider discussion of the issues involved see Lawrence J. Oliver, 'Deconstruction or Affirmative Action: The Literary-Political Debate over the "Ethnic Question"', *American Literary History* 3, 4 (Winter 1991), 792-808.

communities with many literatures contending with each other, we are looking at something that rather resembles the European situation. As such, the lessons learned from 'reconstructing' the unified American canon may come in handy when Europe too, after the successive enlargements of first the European Communities and later the European Union, may well enter a search for a 'European canon' to fit the continent. This might become increasingly relevant as our 'European' classrooms become more and more mixed in terms not just of gender but also of ethnicity with the opening up of the European Union's internal borders, and with the increasing popularity of Europe as a continent to immigrate to rather than from; in short, when the Europe of the nation states begins to resemble a 'United States of Europe'.

It is here, however, that I have to pull up short, and turn back to my Dutch and Flemish examples. Because even though obviously there are resemblances or parallels between the American situation and the Dutch/Flemish, and by extension the European one, there are also huge differences. To begin with, if in the US the campus culture wars were triggered by a discontent with the rigidity of a canon generally upheld as all-'American' and as embodied in then current educational materials such as anthologies and literary histories, yet no longer corresponding to the real make-up of the country, nor with shifting ideological stances, in Europe, even though the issue of multiculturalism is very much alive in the educational field, it is not the immediate cause for the upsurge in interest in canons. In Holland, for instance, but this also goes for most other European nations I am sure, the problem is not that a too rigid canon needs to be 'opened up', as is the case, or at least the saying, in the United States. The problem rather is that there is no canon, or that at least is the popular, and finally also the official perception of things. Why this is so has a number of causes.

An important cause is certainly the aftermath of 1968, with education largely turning away from learning from memory and instilling knowledge to imparting skills and, in the case of literature, emphasizing pupils' immediate emotional reactions to texts. By the early years of the twenty-first century a number of events shocked the Dutch, who are usually very critical of any kind of authority but who at the same time and for the longest time were also rather satisfied with what they saw as their own, and their country's role in history, and which they themselves liked to see as that of a 'pilot country' (*Nederland gidsland*), in the vanguard of social developments internationally when it comes to issues such as tolerance (politically, sexually, individually, etc. including a relaxed drugs legislation), into sudden doubts as to their own identity. These events included, among other things, the murders of the rightwing politician Pim Fortuyn and of the leftwing film-maker Theo van Gogh. These events, or the possibility of them happening, were all at once blamed on a lack of historical awareness with the younger generations, not only those of Dutch descent, from which issued the murderer of Fortuyn, but also the second- and third-generation descendants of mostly North African Maghreb and Turkish migrant workers that had come to the Netherlands in the 1960s and 1970s, and from which issued the murderer of Van Gogh. The remedy was seen to lie in a re-affirmation of 'Dutch' values, Dutch history, etc. The variety of canons that emerged in the early years of the new millennium served this very purpose. As Herman Pleij, professor of Dutch literary history at the University of Amsterdam, put it in his talk in the Brussels series on canons, they satisfy a 'hunger for certainties'. They allow for the re-building, perhaps even the re-invention, of what Benedict Anderson has famously called an 'imagined community', the 'communitas' of which was perceived to have been lost; in short, they make for the recovery of a particular collective identity.[16] That such identity indeed often rests on processes of invention was demonstrated by Eric Hobsbawm and Terence Ranger, in a book published in the same year as Anderson's.[17] If we want to look at Pleij's 'hunger for certainties' in the popular sphere, suffice it to point toward the rage for the election of the 'greatest' national politician, scientist, artist, etc. that ran, or in some cases still runs, through most European countries. What issues from these contests is a counterpart, by popular vote, to the canons engineered by committees of experts. Together, they are a source of renewed pride in 'one's own'.

The need for the re-affirmation of a group's or a nation's collective identity through a call for the return of canons is also fueled in Holland, Belgium, and probably the rest of Europe, through the continuous, some say the relentless, unification of the continent with the creation of a European Union. Robert Schumann, one of the founding fathers of what eventually became the European Union, at the end of his life famously declared that if he had to start the process of European unification all over again he would begin with culture rather than economics. The still relatively recent Dutch and French rejections of a proposal for a European Constitution, and the even more recent Irish rejection of a modified proposal, are widely seen to have confirmed Schumann's suspicion that the cultural dimension was and to a large degree still is lacking in the European project. At the same time, harmonization proceeds apace on all other levels of European life: political, economic, social. Each European country, and this is true *a fortiori* for the smaller among them, increasingly becomes part of a much larger whole in which it risks losing part, or most, of its decision-making and -taking power. At the same time the lack of a 'European dream', comparable to that nebulous American concept, prevents Europe's citizens from identifying

---

[16]   Benedict Anderson, *Imagined Communities: Reflections on the Origins and Spread of Nationalism* (London and New York: Verso, 1991) (1983).

[17]   Eric Hobsbawm and Terence Ranger, eds., *The Invention of Tradition* (Cambridge: Cambridge University Press, 1983).

whole-heartedly with Europe. The result, as in the Dutch, French and Irish cases, but undoubtedly also in other European countries, is a citizen's revolt that takes the dual form of a rejection of further integration, and a re-affirmation of national or local identities. Of course, to a large extent what is happening on the European level also happens elsewhere under the impact of globalization. We could then say that the re-affirmation of local identities via local or national canons is an instance of 'glocalization', i.e. the translation of global impact factors on the local level, and this often in the form of resistance to globalization, but at the same time on a global level, with in this case each country or in some cases linguistic or cultural community, pursuing the same common path towards diversification.

This brings me quite naturally from the national, Dutch, Belgian or other, level to the European one. Just a moment ago I intimated that the EU lacks the cultural 'glue' to make good on its promise of 'unity in diversity' as the road to a larger Andersonian 'imagined community'. For some, though, such glue already is operative on the levels of language, with various forms of 'eurospeak', 'translationese', 'commissionese', 'tourist English', or "Eurenglish', and popular culture, with the Eurovision song festival and the European Champions' (soccer) League. In fact, 'culture' as a unifying factor can be thought of as stretching from the most popular forms, such as popular music, over television series widely screened around Europe, such as *Morse, Der Alte, Tatort,* or *Mankell,* popular literary forms such as detectives and thrillers, to 'high' literature. Occasionally, the most popular and the most elevated are surprisingly thrown together, as in the case of poetry, which, I am told, seems to be gaining an umpteenth lease on life via blogs, or avant-garde film, which does the same via video, digital recording, YouTube, etc. It may just be, then, that my perception of a lack of common culture in Europe is simply the result of advanced age and a definite out-of-touchness with what is 'really' going on in my own backyard. If this is really the case, 'Europe' is in better shape than I thought. In general though, it seems to me that for the majority of the popular as well as the official opinion there is a definite lack of European identification 'machinery' on the 'higher' cultural level.

One such identification generator might of course be a European canon of literature. Such an undertaking has been advocated before, notably by Douwe Fokkema in an article published in the *European Review* in 1993, and titled, appropriately, 'A European Canon of Literature?'. It is telling that Fokkema phrases his title as a question rather than an affirmation. Fokkema reviews some of the issues of canons and canon making, but does not really offer very much concrete advice for the creation of a European canon. On the one hand he upholds that on the academic level it is precisely the historical formation of canons that should be the object of research, as historical data in the history of European taste judgment, etc. On the other hand he recognizes that on the level of practical teaching, especially when it comes to secondary school and university, what is needed is a curriculum based on a canon. In this regard he feels strongly that 'If European culture is to be more than a diversity of regional cultures, some thought must be given to the question of what that larger European culture may comprise' (Fokkema 27). I agree with Fokkema, but I also immediately see a number of problems arising. Obviously, any study of literature in Europe, or even 'for' Europe, as was the title of an ESF-LIU (European Science Foundation/Linköping University) Conference I organized, together with a number of colleagues from the HERMES consortium, in Vadstena, Sweden, in May 2007, should respect the diversity in unity of Europe's many cultures and literatures.[18] If at the Conference mentioned we advocated a turn, then, from the mono-disciplinary study of national literatures to some form of 'comparative literature' embracing a wider European geography, we did so in order not to promote older or established forms of comparative literature, traditionally sticking to Europe's 'major' literatures, or at most to a combination of one 'minor' literature (usually one's own) and some 'major' one, but rather to push for more integrative versions of the discipline, ensuring more equitable and democratic coverage. To this end I personally think that a European policy of active promotion of wide-scale translation, and open access to electronic resources, is indispensable. Ideally, this would make for equal access to all literatures in all languages of the European Union, and beyond, and hence for an 'open' canon of European literature. It would also facilitate the re-organization of the teaching of literature in Europe from national literature departments into comparative literature departments 'new style', which might then usefully be re-labeled departments of 'European literature'. Ironically, the continuous retrenchment European higher education has been subjected to for the last few decades, especially so in the humanities, by the reduction of staff for the separate literatures may have actually already helped point the way. Such a 'European literature' ideally should also not study individual manifestations in single linguistic or national settings, but should instead concentrate on processes of translation and dissemination, of works, genres, styles, theories, and methodologies.

It should also be clear, though, that any such 'European literature' cannot be subservient to an 'imperial Europe'. Hence, there can be no such thing as

---

[18] I wish here to acknowledge the input of these colleagues, Helena Buescu (Lisbon), Harald Hendrix (Utrecht), Svend-Erik Larsen (Aarhus), Timothy Mathews (University College London), and Ansgar Nünning (Giessen), in some of the paragraphs to follow. The responsibility for these paragraphs, of course, rests with me. These same paragraphs, in somewhat altered form, also feature as 'Introduction' to Theo D'haen and Iannis Goerlandt, eds., *Literature for Europe?* (Amsterdam and New York: Rodopi, 2009), the volume resulting from the ESF-LIU Vadstena Conference.

'a' European literary history. Instead, any such history should rather be a history of histories, histories written and to be written, an archeology of histories, a genealogy of histories, a reflection on ideal histories, and on the impossibilities of such histories. In other words, it should rather be a reflection on what 'a' European literary history cannot do. In this regard the input of the view of the outsider, say the 'postcolonial view', on Europe's literary history is of crucial importance, whether that of Europe's distant selves, such as the US, Latin America, or any of the settler colonies, or of its near or distant 'others', Africa, the Near or Middle East, India, China, Japan. As such, a 'new' European literature might serve as the catalyst for a newly emerging 'world' literature. 'Europe', then, should also in the literary realm be considered, with Jürgen Habermas, an 'unfinished project', an 'imaginative construct', or, in the words of Zygmunt Bauman, 'an unfinished adventure', or yet again, with the title of a recent book by Rodolphe Gasché, 'an infinite task'.[19] Such an open attitude, then, also with regard to its own being, should be part and parcel of any methodology of 'European' literature.

As far as the content of our teaching goes, what would in first instance be needed might be a reshuffling rather than a making over. For instance, we might highlight matters of migration and dissemination, of European experience, by foregrounding, next to Joyce, Canetti and other masters' of exile when discussing Modernism or the first half of the twentieth century. As such, we would also be turning European literature once again into an 'instrument for life', i.e. life in present-day Europe, not the nostalgic Europe of memory – even though the study of that memory should be a part of our 'new' European literature too. As literature is uniquely equipped to present or represent those aspects of life not addressed anywhere else, its input is vital to any Europe of the future that tries to take into account the aspirations and fears, the anxieties and desires of its citizens. This would also put 'literature' in its new dispensation back on the map as a 'useful' discipline, and thus help us to overcome what is widely perceived as a crisis of the discipline. Literary experience might thus provide some unexpected input for actual policy-making, an input that would be ignored at the peril of the wider European community without conflict we are all aiming at.

However, in order to achieve all this, we need the proper instruments, and in the present state of affairs this means that, more often than not, we have to turn to... American anthologies, not of European Literature but of 'World Literature'. Why is this so? Because most of our students, in fact probably

---

[19]   Jürgen Habermas, 'Modernity – An Incomplete Project', in *Modernism/Postmodernism*, ed. by Peter Brooker (London: Longman, 1992), pp. 125-38. Zygmunt Bauman, *Europe: An Unfinished Adventure* (Cambridge: Polity Press, 2004). Rodolphe Gasché, *Europe, or the Infinite Task* (Stanford: Stanford University Press, 2009).

most of us ourselves, at best master, next to our native tongue, only one or two foreign languages. In most cases, and increasingly so around Europe, by far and away the foreign language most commonly used is English. Pending the massive program of translation I called for earlier, a burden so huge, in terms of work as well as expenditure, that in all probability it would have to be shouldered by a central instance such as the European Commission, we will therefore be reduced to using anthologies in English. For reasons of scale, though, such anthologies in practice at present are only produced for the American market, and particularly for courses on World Literature. Or I should say: were produced, because with the shifts in American education that I sketched earlier gaining increasing momentum, the American idea of 'world literature', which until the rise of multiculturalism basically equaled European literature, progressively grows away from Europe, and comes to include more and more non-European material. Ironically, then, when 'Europe' is in need of the kind of anthologies produced for the longest time in the US under the heading of 'world literature', and which essentially served to boost the 'cultural capital', in the sense given to that term by Pierre Bourdieu and after him in the American context by John Guillory in his book with the same title, of the recipients of an American 'liberal education', this kind of anthology, because no longer profitable in the US, in both the cultural and the 'real' capital sense, risks being fazed out! In one sense, this situation is a wry illustration of the measure to which European education, or at least the practical teaching of literature from a supra-national, and in this case even a specifically 'European', point of view has become dependent upon its American counterpart. Another instance is that of literary history, where for a 'canonical' description of European literature we are condemned to something like Harold Bloom's *The Western Canon*, idiosyncratic as it is. In the context, this would risk allying us with the forces of conservatism.[20] In the European context, however, a little 'Eurocentrism' perhaps is not 'out of place'? Twisting Emerson's words from 'The American Scholar' somewhat, we might say that 'we have listened too long to the scholarly muses of America', and launch a call for 'self-reliance' at least in this matter.

Finally, let me try to answer the question that serves as my title: 'how many canons do we need?' As a 'global' citizen there is a lot to be said for a canon of world literature. As members of a particular national or linguistic community, we obviously also need canons on these levels. But I would say we need also yet another canon on that intermediate level, between world and national literature, of 'European' literature. To bring this about will be a long and arduous task, but I think it is one fit for a younger generation of European scholars. To end with a reference to yet another American writer,

---

[20]   See for instance the article 'Conservatives Try New Tack on Campus', *The New York Times*, 22 September 2008.

this time Walt Whitman in the 'Preface' to *Leaves of Grass*, it is also one commensurate with the age, and perhaps ultimately 'commensurate with a people'.

WORKS CITED

Bloom, Harold, *The Western Canon: The Books and School of the Ages* (New York: Riverhead Books, 1994)

Fokkema, Douwe, 'A European Canon of Literature?', *European Review* 1/1 (1993), 21-29

Gates, Henry Louis Jr., *Loose Canons: Notes on the Culture Wars* (New York: Oxford University Press, 1992)

Lauter, Paul, ed., *Reconstructing American Literature: Courses, Syllabi, Issues* (Old Westbury, NY: The Feminist Press, 1983)

—. ed., *The Heath Anthology of American Literature*. Lexington (Mass.: D.C. Heath and Company, 1990)

—. 'Race and Gender in the Shaping of the American Literary Canon: A Case Study from the Twenties', in *Canons and Contexts* (New York/Oxford: Oxford University Press, 1991)

Rodica Mihăilă

Opening the Boundaries of National Literatures:
From a Multicultural to a Transnational Literary Canon.
The American Challenge

The paper is an inquiry into the changes taking place in the literary field under the double impact of globalization and the reconfiguration of the academic disciplines and a comment on the way in which the fluid boundaries of the field and the eroding boundaries of the nation reflect on the process of literary canon formation. Based on the example of recent approaches to American literature in a global context, the first stage of the process is seen as being marked by the gradual shift from a multicultural to a transnational canon, which attempts to destabilize the nation-centered field by enfolding both its inside and its outside. The transnational canon is a relational one, highlighting such elements as the relation between the local and the global, the particular and the universal and the relation between identity, culture and geography, identities by affiliation, hybridity, cultural translation and the circulation of aesthetic forms.

Since the collapse of communism and the creation of the World Wide Web in the opening years of the 1990s, America has been regarded as the main agent of globalization and in various contexts, 'cultural globalization' has become almost synonymous with 'Americanization'. Recent changes in America's global role, especially in the wake of 9/11, have invited an increasing number of studies which view America not only as main agent, but also as object of globalization. American literature is no exception.

My comments on the transformation and opening of the boundaries of national literatures in the age of globalization are therefore based on an inquiry into the canonical revisions of American literature operated by the ascendency in the reconceptualization of the United States, first, of multiculturalism and next, of transnationalism, as two important steps leading slowly but steadily to the dissociation of the boundaries of American literature from the contours of the U.S. national borders. An important question raised by such an inquiry is whether the erosion of the boundaries between the national and the global may be another case of American exceptionalism or a direction of change to be taken, sooner or later, by all national literatures. Undoubtedly, the unique combination of America's extraordinary racial and ethnic diversity, its multilingualism, its perennial rejuvenation fuelled up by the enduring attraction of the American dream and its leading role in the contemporary world that has made this dissociation possible, can hardly apply to many other nations, even more so in the case of countries like Romania, for instance, which have made every effort to re-define and re-assert their national identities after the collapse of communism.

My essay addresses the question by discussing the list of Romanian translations from American literature published by two leading Publishing Houses starting with the year 2000. The conclusion points to the relative resistance of ex-communist countries not so much to the transnational as to the multicultural canon as a result of the rise of various post-Cold War forms of nationalism and the cultural mistranslation of American multiculturalism in close association with the idea of 'political correctness' and memories of Marxist norms applied to literature. If not exactly a model, American literature's opening to the world is at least a major challenge.

From the very beginning, the forging of American literature and its emancipation from the tyranny (imitation) of English models was a nationalist project, born in rejection of 'the courtly Muses of Europe' (Emerson) as an expression of democratic consciousness and of the uniqueness of the American experience (Parrington, Matthiesen).[1] The classical canon institutionalized only after World War II by the monumental *Literary History of the United States*, ed. by Robert Spiller (1948), was largely inspired by the postwar nationalist ethos; it was Eurocentric and oriented toward dead white English male writers (DWEM) whose work substantiated in one way or another the ideological consensus over (the American national identity and) America's exceptionalism and met the aesthetic standards imposed by the formalism and organicism of New Criticism.

The first blows to the nation-based paradigm of American literature came in the 1970s following what Bercovitch called the great 'disensus' brought to light by the radicalism and the social and political upheaval of the explosive sixties under the banners of the civil rights, the feminist and the anti-war movements. The wave of European poststructuralism that reached the American shores in the seventies offered theoretical grounding to a Euro-, male-centered model of national identity that evinced power relations of domination and marginalization of minorities on the basis of their difference of race, class, gender, ethnicity or sexual orientation. The identity politics grounded in strong radical multiculturalism generated fierce culture wars all through the 1980s and, under the impact of nation-wide students' protests,

---

[1]   The first history of American literature, *The Cambridge History of American Literature*, 4 vols, ed. by W.P.Trent and others (Cambridge: Cambridge University Press, 1917-1921), treated American literature as an appendix of English literature, and well into the 1920s American literature was still the Cinderella of the English Departments (Renker 352).

had immediate effects on the Academy, among them, wider access to education, a new pedagogy, the re-configuration of disciplines and the creation of new academic fields such as cultural studies, ethnic studies and queer studies, curricular reforms and canon revisions.

As for the effects on literature, they were spectacular: by the turn of the century the American literary stage had been taken by women authors, African-American and emergent literatures. The ensuing multicultural canon was not only an expansion but also a re-valuation of the classical one, which challenged the old Eurocentric, male-centered model. As such, it was institutionalized in the 1980s by *The Columbia Literary History of the United States* ed. by Emory Elliott (1988), the nine volume project of the *Cambridge History of American Literature* ed. by Sacvan Bercovich, and the path-breaking *Heath Anthology of American Literature* ed. by Paul Lauter (1989). But, as Lockard and Sandell rightly observe in their recent comments on 'National Narratives and the Politics of Inclusion': 'While multiculturalism and the politics of recognition have provided an important corrective to the normative whiteness and maleness of American literature, they do not always significantly revise the parameters of the canon or the nation'.[2]

By the end of the century multiculturalism had turned 'weak'. Already appropriated by the neo-liberal rhetoric, it was mainstreamed as the new kind of identity that the United States tested for the 21st century world, thus re-enforcing the idea of American exceptionalism.

While radical, 'strong' multiculturalism had an effect of ghettoization of various minorities on the basis of their difference, weak multiculturalism acts as a sort of 'multicultural nationalism'[3], which puts forward a homogenized and universalist image of America, minimizing the complexity of the power relations established between and among various social groups while validating the boundaries of the nation. In other words, far from opening the boundaries of the nation, multiculturalism, be it strong or weak, re-inscribes American literature within the limits of the nation, even though it challenges some of the assumptions that lie at the nation's foundation.

If the end of the Cold War and the New World Order made the opening of the nation's boundaries possible, the accelerated pace of globalization and America's new being in the world made it impossible to avoid. If the example of Kosovo and the 9/11 evidence of the US frontier vulnerability,

---

[2]   Joe Lockard and Jillian Sandell, 'National Narratives and the Politics of Inclusion: Historicizing American Literature Anthologies', *Pedagogy: Critical Approaches to Teaching Literature, Language, Composition, and Culture*, 2, 8 (2008), 227-254 (p. 248).

[3]   Minoo Moallem and Iain A. Boal, 'Multicultural Nationalism and the Poetics of Inauguration', in *Between Woman and Nation: Nationalism, Transnational Feminism, and the State*, ed. by Caren Kaplan, Norma Alarcon, and Minoo Moallem (Durham N.C.: Duke University Press, 1999), 248.

placed the age of post-nationalism in a not so near future, the gradual fluidization of the boundaries of the nation's 'imagined community' made transnationalism a key element in the dynamics of today's world.

Drawing on the tradition of postcolonial and border studies, the rise of transnationalism as a category of cultural analysis all through the 90s has marked a turning point in American cultural and literary studies.[4] Similarly, the response of American writers to the conditions of globalization and the challenges of transnationalism has performed a major change on the literary scene reflected in an emerging transnational literary canon, which goes beyond the limitations of the postmodernist and the multicultural one.

As in the case of the multicultural canon, the formation of a transnational canon has equally implied expansion and re-valuation. The dynamics of canon formation shows that American literature changes spectacularly when read in a transnational perspective, across the borders of the nation and beyond the tropes of exceptionalism, that is, when read as hemispheric, multilingual, planetary or world literature (Levander and Levine, Sollors, Spivak, Dimock) and it also highlights the dramatic change in post-Cold War American literature produced by the massive infusion of new writers who are migrants or belong to the first generation of migrants' children born in the US, as Rachel Adams rightly argues in her obituary of postmodernism ('The Ends of America, the Ends of Postmodernism').[5] The originality of these new-comers' voices is given by the surprising and imaginative ways in which they address current issues of globalization and bring to American literature 'a new set of genealogical, geographic, and temporal referents', as they explore specific circumstances of globalization, flows of people, images and ideas across national borders, cross-roads of identities, cultures and economies, faces of hybridization and acculturation. Among these writers are Jhumpa Lahiri, Sandra Cisneros, Chang Rae Lee, Junot Diaz, Ruth Ozecki, Jessica Hagedorn, Gish Jen, Bharati Mukherjee, Susan Choi, Oscar Hijuelos, Edwidge Danticat, Jamaica Kincaid, and many others' (Adams, 251). And undoubtedly, the list is much longer if we add European migrants from former communist countries.

A recent example of change is the 2008 Pulitzer Prize winner, *The Brief Wondrous Life of Oscar Wao*, the first novel of the Dominican-American writer Junot Diaz. The book is a major attempt to rewrite both the Dominican and the American history from the vantage point of their interconnectedness

---

[4]   Among the books that marked the opening of a transnational perspective all through the 1990s see *Cultures of U.S. Imperialism* (1993), eds. Donald Pease and Amy Kaplan, *The Cultures of Globalization* (1998), eds. Jameson and Miyioshi and *Post-Nationalist American Studies* (2000), ed. John Carlos Rowe.

[5]   Rachel Adams, 'The Ends of America, the Ends of Postmodernism', *Twentieth-Century Literature*, 53, 3 (Fall 2007), 248-272.

(Oscar de Leon is a first-generation Dominican-American) and to show, using Dominican examples, the mechanism by which the national borders are subtly destabilized by the multi-racial and multi-ethnic Dominican identities of mixed Taíno, African and Spanish descent. Significantly, the long epigraph at the beginning of the book, which is taken from Derek Walcott, ends with the following lines:

> *I am just a red nigger who love the sea,*
> *I had a sound colonial education,*
> *I have Dutch, nigger, and English in me,*
> *And either I'm nobody, or I'm a nation.*

The unifying element in the experience of various nationalities and generations interwoven in the texture of the book is the threat of *fukú*, a looming curse, a pervasive sense of doom associated with the European discovery of the New World. The destabilization of borders at the level of the nation is performed at the linguistic level as well starting with the simple sentence, in which the multitude of interfering cultures, languages and nations is reflected in the rapid shift from one language to another, from high to low culture, from a chiselled expression to a rough one.

Applying transnationalism as a category of cultural analysis to an inquiry into the gradual globalization of American literature engages both physical and imagined geographies.

Appadurai explains cultural globalization as a complex process of de- and re-territorialization (Deleuze and Guatari) which describes the flows of ideas, people, images, and beliefs across the boundaries of specific territories, or 'scapes' as he calls them.[6] Drawing on Appadurai, Paul Giles addresses the question of national literatures in the globalization age by investigating the relationship between 'American literature and physical space'/geography through the lenses of 'various kinds of deterritorializing forces that had been gathering pace since the Reagan years.[7]

He starts from the assumption that the geographical borders of literature cannot be taken as a given that remains unchanged over the centuries and he describes the instabilities in the relationship between American literature and geography, among them deterritorialization, as particular 'terrains' subjected to various kinds of 'mutation and controversy' (p. 39). To superimpose current geographical (national) borders on the boundaries of literature, in

---

[6]   Arjun Appadurai, *Modernity at Large. Cultural Dimensions of Globalization* (Minneapolis, London: University of Minnesota Press, 1996), p. 53.

[7]   Paul Giles, *Virtual Americas: Transnational Fictions and the Transatlantic Imaginary* (Durham: Duke University Press, 2002), p. 51.

other words, to cast literature in a national frame means to overlook or
deliberately obscure such instabilities. This happened in what Giles calls 'the
nationalist phase' of American literature and culture, from the end of the
Civil War in 1865 to the end of Jimmy Carter's presidency, in 1980. Since
the Reagan years, when the U.S. took a leading position in the newly
emerged global networks of exchange, the process of de- and re-
territorialization has provided the main grounds for debates over the national
identity and the reconceptualization of America, marking in Giles's opinion
the beginning of the 'current transnational phase' (p. 55).

Giles studies the dynamics of the deterritorialization of American
literature and comes to the conclusion that the most provocative aspect of
American literature in 'the era of transnationalism' is 'how it represents ways
in which these pressures of deterritorialization are being internalized and
understood affectively' (p. 53).

In this respect, a relevant example is offered by Leslie Marmon Silko's
novel *Almanac of the Dead* (1991), a most ambitious attempt to rewrite the
history of America from the standpoint of the Native American communities
of the Arizona region and to provide literally and through narrative substance
a 'Five Hundred Year Map' of the whole territory from Laguna Pueblo
Reservation to Mexico City seen in the context of the Aztec civilization and
the Apache wars. With Tucson at its center, the American Southwest is a site
of intersections of cultures and clash of civilizations, the U.S.-Mexico border
is rendered irrelevant, as flows of people and cultures have crossed the land
for centuries, and 'the familiar national narrative of the United States', as
Giles observes, is rendered 'contingent and reversible' (p. 54).

Before being an exemplary writer in the transnational canon, Silko, like
many other writers ignored or marginalized in the traditional canon of
American literature on the basis of their difference of class, race, gender or
ethnicity, took center stage in the multicultural canon. The reading of her
novel as a redrawing of 'the map of the United States in space as well as
time' from the vantage point of a Native-American, reconfirms, in my
opinion, the relationship between multiculturalism and transnationalism as
two forms and phases of the deterritorialization of American literature, and
two necessary steps in opening the borders of a nation-bound literary canon.

Inspired and inspiring as Giles' deterritorialization thesis may be, it fails
to consider the role of multiculturalism as a form of deterritorialization that
put an end to the nationalist phase of American literature and opened the road
for transnationalism.

As Silko's novel proves, viewing American literature through the lens of
transnationalism requires what Rachel Adams calls 'creative mapping', that
is, mapping which replaces the contours of the nation with 'alternative
geographical frames', among them, 'the Caribbean, the Americas, the Black,

the trans- or circum-Atlantic, the Pacific Rim, continents, hemispheres, and worlds' (p. 268) or replaces them with imagined geographies. [8]

Paula Moya and Ramon Saldivar introduce a form of creative mapping grounded in what they call 'trans-American imaginary', which is, they argue, 'transnational to the degree that American fiction must be seen as a heterogeneous grouping of overlapping but distinct discourses that refer to the U.S. in relation to a variety of national entities'[9] and, at the same time, 'imaginary to the extent that it figures a very real but fundamentally different syntax of codes, images, and icons, as well as the tacit assumptions, convictions, and beliefs that seek to bind together the varieties of American national discourses' (p. 2). Moya and Saldivar are right when they conclude that the trans-American imaginary offers an 'interpretive framework' to American literature that reveals its heterogeneity and diversity, but their alternative framework 'that yokes together North and South America instead of New England and England' (p. 2) leaves out much of the heterogeneity and diversity grounded in the relationship between the Old and the New Worlds. In other words, the boundaries of literature have distanced themselves from those of the nation, but remain confined to hemispheric limits.

A more comprehensive form of creative mapping in today's transnational world calls for a more inclusive definition of transnational spaces, as for instance, the one put forward by the contributors to *Transnational Spaces* (2004).[10] In their usage of the term, transnational spaces are produced from various positionalities by people with various backgrounds and include 'the material geographies of labour migration', 'the trading in transnational goods and services' as well as 'the symbolic and imaginary geographies through which we attempt to make sense of our increasingly transnational world (p. 3). These 'complex, multidimensional' spaces may be 'multiply inhabited' temporarily or permanently. For instance, a person inhabits a transnational space temporarily when visiting an ethnic theme park and permanently, when living in an ethnic transnational community.

---

[8] Adams gives several examples of critics who proposed the use of alternative geographical frames, among them: Jane C. Desmond and Virginia R. Dominguez; Claire Fox and Claudia Sadowski-Smith; Paul Giles; Paul Gilroy; Gregory S. Jay; Amy Kaplan and Donald Pease; John Muthyala; Carolyn Porter; Joseph Roach; John Carlos Rowe, Jose David Saldivar, and Doris Sommer. I add to Adams' list, Caroline Levander and Robert Levine, editors of *Hemispheric American Studies* (2008).

[9] Paula M.L.Moya and Ramon Saldivar, 'Fictions of the Trans-American Imaginary', *MFS Modern Fiction Studies*, 49, 1 (Spring 2003), 1-18 (p. 1).

[10] *Transnational Spaces*, ed. by Peter Jackson, Philip Crang and Claire Dwyer (London: Routledge, 2004).

Such an all-inclusive definition of transnational spaces echoes Appadurai's imaginary geography, with its 'multiple worlds that are constituted by the historically situated imaginations of persons and groups spread around the globe' and its five 'scapes' (ethnoscapes, mediascapes, technoscapes, financescapes, and ideoscapes) corresponding to the main global cultural flows (Appadurai, p. 33). In such definitions the transnational opens to, or rather turns into the global.

A breakthrough in theorizing the globalization of American literature has been offered by Way Chee Dimock's book *Through Other Continents. American Literature across Deep Time.*[11] Starting from the observation that alternative geographical and temporal frames seem to have already influenced our reading of American literature, Way Chee Dimock places American literature in the much wider spatial and temporal frame offered by the world and its global history; she redraws its map with an eye to 'other continents and other time frames' that seem to interfere in the act of reading (p. 8).

Dimock grounds her re-mapping of American literature in the concept of 'deep time' that binds together space and time, continents and ages. In her definition, deep time 'gives us a set of coordinates at once extended and embedded, as fine-grained as it is long-lasting, operating both above and below the plane of the nation. The subnational and the transnational come together here in a loop' (p. 23).

In a review of Dimock's book, Djelal Kadir explains the way in which the concept functions as a new interpretive frame for American literature or as an instrument of remapping it: 'Deep time [...] reaches beyond history as locally constituted and nationally constructed into a trans-historic, trans-continental temporality that de-defines US national literary culture and re-defines it as global phenomenon [...] or as part of a global legacy of human history'.[12]

Viewed from such a perspective that highlights the marks left on it by old civilizations, American literature is removed from the national or English-language context and reconceived on a planetary scale. 'Deep time' casts fresh light even on canonical writers such as Thoreau, Emerson, Margaret Fuller, Henry James, Ezra Pound, and Robert Lowell.

The idea of a new transnationalism, part of a long discussed project to internationalize the study of American writing that Dimock's book proposed, was resumed and further detailed a year later in *Shades of the Planet. American Literature as World Literature* (2007), a book she edited together with Lawrence Buell, which put together the contributions of several leading

---

[11]   Wai Chee Dimock, *Through Other Continents. American Literature across Deep Time* (Princeton and Oxford: Princeton University Press, 2006).

[12]   Djelal Kadir, '*Through Other Continents: American Literature Across Deep Time (review)*', *Comparative Literature Studies*, 3, 45 (2008), 370-372 (p. 371).

representatives of the field.[13] The term 'planet', borrowed from Spivak's *Death of a Discipline* (2003), designates the complex mechanism that makes the 'enfolding' possible.[14]

For, as Spivak explains, the global, with its homogenizing effects, generates alienation, while 'planetarity' provides the grounds for commonality, 'inscribing collective responsibility' (p. 102).

Focussing on 'the enfolding of the outside and the inside' (p. 9) of American literature, the contributors trace in it other continents and cultures as they bring together writers, genres and experiences across time and space. American literature is read as world literature, obsessed by the world and fully engaged in the world.

If the nation-based approach to American literature has been blamed for an implicit or explicit re-affirmation of American exceptionalism, provocative and attractive as the 'planetary' thesis may be, seeing American literature as 'planetary' is, ironically, another way of reinforcing the idea of exceptionalism with the same arguments with which it was meant to be dismantled.

In his provocative book *What is World Literature?* David Damrosch investigates various ways in which literature changes when it moves from the national into the global, but significantly, he does so by 'concentrating particularly (though not exclusively) on world literature as it has been construed over the past century in a specific cultural space, that of the formerly provincial and now metropolitan United States'.[15] World literature is no longer perceived as 'a set canon of texts' (p. 281), but as a mode of circulation and reading, in which translation plays an important part (p. 4).

When reversing the direction of Damrosch's argument based on circulation, reading and translation as shaping elements of the circuit linking the national and the global, we can see how American literature turns into

---

[13]   *Shades of the Planet. American Literature as World Literature*, ed. by Way Chee Dimock, Lawrence Buell (Princeton and Oxford: Princeton University Press, 2008).

[14]   Drawing the distinction between the global and the planetary, Spivak explains: 'The globe is on our computers. No one lives there. It allows us to think that we can aim to control it. The planet is in the species of alterity, belonging to another system; and yet we inhabit it, on loan. It is not really amenable to a neat contrast with the globe [...] When I invoke the planet, I think of the effort required to figure the (im)possibility of this underived intuition' – Gayatri Chakravorty Spivak, *Death of a Discipline* (New York: Columbia University Press, 2003), p. 72. 'To be human is to be intended toward the other [...] If we imagine ourselves as planetary subjects rather than global agents, planetary creatures rather than global entities, alterity remains underived from us; it is not our dialectical negation, it contains us as much as it flings us away' (p. 73).

[15]   David Damrosch, *What is World Literature?* (Princeton and Oxford: Princeton University Press, 2003), pp. 27-8.

world literature by a double process of absorption and expansion, which started in the 'provincial' stage of American culture reaching a climax in the age when 'metropolitan United States' is placed at the center of the globalization process.

Multicultural and transnational, American literature is in the unique position of being produced by a culture that contains and is contained in the larger world and more than ever before, in the globalization age, its multiculturalism and transnationalism turn it into a challenge for all national literatures.

How would the literatures of the countries formerly in the Soviet sphere of influence respond to the American challenge, when for many of those countries the re-evaluation and re-assertion of their national identities in a reconfigured Europe has been a top issue on their agenda of democracy building?

Eschewing the vastness of the research area involved even in a tentative reply, in order to supply an illustration in support of my conclusions I have conducted a statistical analysis of the American titles published by two leading Romanian publishing houses, *Polirom* and *Humanitas*, from 2000 to 2006, and from 2006 to the present, rating the writers as canonical or non-canonical, in accordance with the pedagogical canon proposed by *The Norton Anthology of American Literature*, a standard anthology, updated regularly and widely used by many universities around the world.[16]

A major remark refers to the fact that the Romanian publishers have largely ignored the voices of the multicultural canon. Whatever the reasons, their failure to keep pace with the changes on the American literary scene illustrates the biased Romanian response to the American idea of multiculturalism and culture wars and draws attention to certain shaping forces behind the process of cultural translation.

In the six-year interval from 2000 to 2006,[17] out of a total of 292 translations from foreign literatures published by *Polirom*, 72 are by American authors (35 authors). Out of the total of 35 writers, 25 are canonical, only three are 19th century writers and all the four translations

---

[16]   Seven editions of *The Norton Anthology of American Literature* have come out since its first publication: 1979, 1985, 1989, 1994, 1999, 2002, 2007.

[17]   I first published the statistics for this time interval in my essay 'The Literary Canon as Space of Transition. The Case of American Literature in Romanian Translation', in *New/Old Worlds. Spaces of Transition*, Rodica Mihăilă and Irina Pană (Bucharest: Univers Enciclopedic, 2007), pp. 492-512. Expanding the area of my research to the subsequent time-interval, I detected several inaccuracies in my early estimates. From 2000 through 2005, Polirom published 72 titles from the works of 35 American writers, not 59 titles from 22 writers as I mentioned in my earlier version. Likewise, the number of women writers translated was 6 not 3. Humanitas published 20 titles by 15 American writers, among them 3 minor women writers, not 14 titles by 11 American white male writers as mentioned in my 2007 version.

from their work are reprints: Poe (*The Masque of the Red Death* and *The Mystery of Marie Roget*), Hawthorne (*House of the Seven Gables*) and Henry James (*Daisy Miller*); two are modernists: Faulkner (4 reprints) and Fitzgerald (3 reprints) and the other 30, including Nabokov (4 titles), are postwar/contemporary writers—among them no African-American and only six women, three of them canonical writers: Flannery O'Connor, Sylvia Plath and Amy Tan, the latter being also the only representative of ethnic literatures.

During the same period, *Humanitas* issued two collections of literary translations: 'Cartea de pe noptieră' ('The book on the bedside table') and 'Raftul Întâi' ('Shelf no. 1') with a total of 169 titles, out of which 20 titles by 15 American writers: no African-American, no writer from other racial or ethnic groups and only three minor women writers.

A survey of the translations published by the same two publishers since 2006 demonstrates that the translation policy has not changed much.

Out of a total of 145 translations from foreign literatures published by *Polirom*, 55 are by American authors (33 authors). Among the 33 authors, 16 are canonical and only two are from the 19th century, the two translations from their work being reprints: Poe (*Călătorii imaginare*, transl. by Liviu Cotrău) and Melville (*Moby Dick,* transl. by Petre Solomon); three are modernists, and 29 are postwar/contemporary writers—among them no African-American and only two women: Asian-American Amy Tan and Anita Diamant, a Jewish-American journalist and minor writer.

During the same period *Humanitas* added 'Raftul Denisei' ('Denisa's shelf') to the two already existing collections of literary translations mentioned above. Out of a total of 141 translations from foreign literatures, 35 are from American literature (23 authors). Among the 23 American authors there is only one 19th century writer (Melville), the other twenty-two being postwar/ contemporary writers; eighteen started publishing after 1990, three are canonical (Nabokov, Updike, Vonnegut), six are women (Berberova, Kleinbaum, Jones, Pachett, Krauss, Tyler, and Yalom, with Tyler the only reputed writer and Yalom the only ethnic one). No African-American, no writer from other racial or ethnic groups.

The resistance to the U.S. multicultural canon, especially the absence of African-American literature, is disquieting, but, at the same time, symptomatic of the cautionary Romanian response to the idea of American multiculturalism. Marked as this response has been by the Marxist connotations of political correctness, the communist experience of a 'politicized canon' and the danger of Marxist-Leninist norms applied to literature (Martin 310), it points to the Romanian cultural (mis)translation of the American idea of multiculturalism and culture wars and it also points to the conflict in Romanian culture between a tradition of viewing world literature as 'a form of detached engagement with worlds beyond our own place and time' to use Damrosch's definition (p. 281) and the increasing pressures of globalization on the translation market and the fate of literature. There is no doubt that American literature as world/planetary literature is not and cannot be a heterotopic space, but its very opening to the world could be – and in many respects really is – a challenge for the contemporary world.

WORKS CITED

Adams, Rachel, 'The Ends of America, the Ends of Postmodernism', *Twentieth-Century Literature*, 53, 3 (Fall 2007), 248-272

Appadurai, Arjun, *Modernity at Large. Cultural Dimensions of Globalization* (Minneapolis, London: University of Minnesota Press, 1996)

Damrosch, David, *What is World Literature?* (Princeton and Oxford: Princeton University Press, 2003)

Desmond, Jane C., and Virginia R. Dominguez, 'Resituating American Studies in a Critical Internationalism', *American Quarterly*, 48 (Fall 1996), 475-90

Dimock, Wai Chee, *Through Other Continents. American Literature across Deep Time* (Princeton and Oxford: Princeton University Press, 2006)

— & Lawrence Buell, eds., *Shades of the Planet. American Literature as World Literature* (Princeton and Oxford: Princeton University Press, 2008)

Fox, Claire, and Claudia Sadowski-Smith, 'Theorizing the Hemisphere: Inter-Americas Work at the Intersection of American, Canadian, and Latin American Studies', *Comparative American Studies*, 2, 1 (March 2004), 5-38

Giles, Paul, *Virtual Americas: Transnational Fictions and the Transatlantic Imaginary* (Durham: Duke University Press, 2002)

—. 'The Deterritorialization of American Literature, in *Shades of the Planet. American Literature as World Literature*, ed. by Dimock and Buell (Princeton and Oxford: Princeton University Press, 2008) (New Brunswick, New Jersey: Rutgers University Press, 2008), 39-61

Gilroy, Paul, *The Black Atlantic: Modernity and Double Consciousness* (Cambridge: Harvard University Press, 1993)

Jackson, Peter, Philip Crang and Claire Dwyer, eds., *Transnational Spaces* (London: Routledge, 2004)

Jay, Gregory S., 'The End of American Literature', *College English*, 53, 3 (March 1991), 264-81

Kadir, Djelal, '*Through Other Continents: American Literature Across Deep Time (review)*', *ComparativeLiterature Studies*, 3, 45 (2008), 370-372

Kaplan, Amy and Donald Pease, eds., *Cultures of United States Imperialism* (Durham: Duke University Press, 1993)

Levander, Caroline F. and Robert S. Levine, eds., *Hemispheric American Studies* (New Brunswick, New Jersey, and London: Rutgers University Press, 2008)

Lockard, Joe and Jillian Sandell, 'National Narratives and the Politics of Inclusion: Historicizing American Literature Anthologies', *Pedagogy: Critical Approaches to Teaching Literature, Language, Composition, and Culture*, 2, 8 (2008), 227-254

Matthiessen, F.O., *American Renaissance. Art and Expression in the Age of Emerson and Whitman* (London: Oxford University Press, 1941)

Moallem, Minoo and Iain A. Boal, 'Multicultural Nationalism and the Poetics of Inauguration', in *Between Woman and Nation: Nationalism, TransnationalFeminism, and the State*, ed. by Caren Kaplan, Norma Alarcon, and Minoo Moallem (Durham N.C.: Duke University Press, 1999)

Moya, Paula M.L. and Ramon Saldivar, 'Fictions of the Trans-American Imaginary', *MFS Modern Fiction Studies*, 49, 1 (Spring 2003), 1-18

Muthyala, John, 'Reworlding America: The Globalization of American Studies', *Cultural Critique*, 47 (Winter 2001), 91-119

Parrington, Vernon Louis, *Main Currents in American Thought: An Interpretation of American Literature from the Beginning to 1920*, 2 vols (New York: Harcourt, Brace, 1927-1930)

Porter, Carolyn, 'What We Know That We Don't Know: Remapping American Literary Studies', *American Literary History*, 6, 3 (Fall 1994), 467-526

Renker, Elizabeth, 'Resistance and Change: The Rise of American Literature Studies', *American Literature*, 64, 2 (June 1992), 347-365

Roach, Joseph, *Cities of the Dead: Circum-Atlantic Performance* (New York: Columbia University Press, 1996)

Rowe, John Carlos, 'Nineteenth-Century US Literary Culture and Transnationality', *PMLA*, 188, 1 (Jan. 2003), 78-89

—. ed., *Post-Nationalist American Studies* (Berkeley: University of California Press, 2000)

Saldivar, Jose David, *Border Matters: Remapping American Cultural Studies* (Berkeley: University of California Press, 1997)

Sollors, Werner, *Multilingual America: Transnationalism, Ethnicity and the Languages of American Literature* (New York: NYU Press, 1998)

Spivak, Gayatri Chakravorty, *Death of a Discipline* (New York: Columbia University Press, 2003)

William Franke

The Canon Question and the Value of Theory: Towards a New (Non-) Concept of Universality

Recent decades have witnessed the emergence of a new concept of universality based not on the categorical thinking of a general concept but rather on the open-ended reaching out towards communication with others and connection in all directions on behalf of something that remains conceptually undefined—or always newly to be defined. This is a new understanding of universality, and it has been introduced and concretely worked out in relation to myriad literatures and discourses and peoples and nations and cultures. It issues in recognition of the exemplarity of works that are received as having something to say far beyond their original contexts of production. Such universality is the basis of a dynamic literary canon, and the process of its formation is guided by the work of theory as a malleable koiné of cross-cultural discourse. A canon in this sense lives and grows by transforming itself from age to age and demonstrates how values can become 'universal'.

The wide diffusion of theoretical awareness about literature has taught us to view the canon not as a thing, like a stone monument rising out of the desert sands or a bronze plaque with names engraved on it, but as an ongoing historical process. It is not as if the literary canon went unchallenged for thousands of years until critics suddenly woke up in 1968 and declared the need for a change. The canon throughout history has been continually forged and re-forged on new and different bases, and not without struggle and conflict: it has been constituted by recurrent, hard-fought negotiations issuing in periodic and sometimes precipitous change. Nevertheless, the presupposition of any theoretical debate over the canon is that claims concerning values communicated in and through literature can be intelligible to other peoples and perspectives — in other periods and in other cultural contexts — than those in which they originate, or in other words that they are capable of being understood and validated transhistorically.

Such transhistorical communicability of value is a minimum requirement for any work's being recognized as canonical. This constitutes universality in a sense far different from that represented by static categories held to be true in all times and places: it is a universality that can be apprehended always only *in the making*, never as a finished product but as in the process of being forged. Such universality exists as discourse in the present being communicated into new and emerging situations and contexts and thereby making contact and connecting with other discourses in unrestricted ways and in all directions. Such universality might be more accurately called *omni*versality. This essay aims to elicit such a notion in its emergence from discussion concerning the canon in contemporary literary theory. To ground this notion, it will be helpful to start with a telescoped retrospective in an outline sketch (however summary!) of the metamorphoses of conceptions of the literary canon since antiquity.

The Alexandrian critics of the Hellenistic age, signally Aristarchus (c. 217-145 B.C.) and his pupil Apollodorus (born c. 180 B.C.), began to establish a canon of ancient Greek classics. Their doing so was steered by their own philosophically reflective standpoint, imposing allegorical interpretations that completely transformed and distorted the intentions of the literature, including Homer and the Greek tragedians, that they interpreted and evaluated. A few centuries later, the Romans from Horace to Quintilian elaborated a canon of Latin authors imitating Greek models selected and sorted and hierarchized according to a very different taste. Late in the life of the Roman Empire, Augustine and Jerome, among other fathers of the Church, excised and exorcized the authors canonized by classical pagan tradition in filtering them through Christian doctrine. Meanwhile, a new canon of Christian literature also emerged. The medieval *accessus ad auctores* ushered in further selections and revisions, partly reflecting the rise of new vernacular literatures that began making their own new claims to canonicity.

Renaissance Humanism sought to return behind patristic mediations to the classical texts themselves and at the same time disparaged popular medieval literature in comparison to their classical models. The *querelles des anciens et des modernes* revolved around open strife between different canons and particularly around differences over whether modern works needed to be based on ancient models in order to rank as canonical. Enlightenment criticism later rejected Latin influences and exemplary authors, such as had guided the Renaissance Humanists, and returned to their Greek progenitors as more original: Homer rather than Vergil, Pindar rather than Horace, Sophocles rather than Seneca. Romantic critics gave the canon a wholly different twist and emphasis with their valorization of nationhood and of the genius of the folk as the matrix of genuine literary creativity. In all these transitions, myriad works were re-evaluated; some were posthumously rediscovered and belatedly canonized, while others were un-canonized. Some were de-canonized and re-canonized several times over.[1]

Nearer to our own time of epochal shifts, some time in the 1970s, there began a concerted outcry against the canon of literary classics perceived as immobile and oppressive. This provoked reactions such as Allan Bloom's *The Closing of the American Mind* (1987) and E.D. Hirsch's *Cultural*

---

[1]   In this historical sketch, I have followed Willems, as well as Grosse.

Literacy: What Every American Needs to Know (1987) against what was later called 'canon bashing' (David Bromwich). Thus arose the especially heavy debates of the years 1987-91.[2] After a great deal of difficult discussion and oftentimes bitter strife and fighting, universities saw some deep-cutting reconfigurations of the reading lists for their courses in general culture and humanities. However, while the dissatisfaction with a static canon of classics has been effective in bringing about change, the question remains as to what constitutes literary value and why any particular selection of texts should be held up and prized as deserving of study, as exemplary of worthwhile learning and culture. Since literary theory has been such a crucial catalyst in the revision and revaluation of the literary canon, it is logical to look to theory for guidance in illuminating the grounds for canonicity of the more dynamic type that theoretical reflection and questioning have ushered in and established in our institutions of higher learning.

At first glance, however, theory seems to have far more to offer of a purely negative nature, undermining whatever norms and standards may hitherto have been applied in assessing and conferring literary value. Especially recent developments in theory seem to preempt and render vain any efforts to establish stable and valid criteria for evaluating literary art. The eminent literary theorist Terry Eagleton, in his essay 'The Rise of English', the opening chapter of his widely read *Literary Theory* (1983), exposes the political motives for mystifications that declare aesthetic value timeless and universal. According to Eagleton, the canon of English literature has taken over from religion in sanctioning these sorts of illusions that direct people's attention away from the divisive class interests that otherwise threaten to discomfit society and upset its forcibly imposed order. The canon of superior literature exalted as timelessly true, universally valid and meaningful, shows up thus as a political construct serving a ruling elite.

Providing some empirical substantiation for this point of view, Richard Ohmann's 'The Shaping of a Canon: U.S. Fiction, 1960-75' documented concretely how 'aesthetic value arises from class conflict' and is dictated in indirect ways by the interests of 'monopoly capital' and the common values and beliefs of the professional-managerial classes. In concluding that '[t]he values and beliefs of a small group of people played a disproportionate role in deciding what novels would be widely read in the United States',[3] Ohmann stressed that "the emergence of these novels has been a process saturated with class values and interests, a process inseparable from the broader

---

[2]   Recent history leading to current debate is treated by Grimm and in Gorak. See also *South Atlantic Quarterly*, 98, 1 (1990).

[3]   Ohmann, Richard, 'The Shaping of a Canon: U.S. Fiction, 1960-75', in *Politics of Letters* (Middletown, Conn.: Wesleyan University Press, 1987), p. 70.

struggle for position and power in our society, from the institutions that mediate that struggle, as well as from legitimation of and challenges to the social order (p. 69).

More general philosophical grounds for undermining claims to canonical authority are adduced by another prestigious literary theorist, Barbara Hernstein Smith. The canon pretends to be based on disinterested aesthetic value, but according to Smith there can be no such thing. It is impossible even to define what aesthetic value is except in terms of other pragmatic use-values from which it is supposed to be independent. In her *Contingencies of Value* (1988), Smith insists on the contingent character of all aesthetic value against the Kantian aesthetics of disinterestedness as founding a universally valid standard of taste. And she is voicing convictions that have been very widely shared and have spear-headed a great part of the new initiatives in criticism that have emerged under the aegis of theory in recent decades. Theory, seen from this angle, would seem to be naturally biased against any canon and against any claims for enduring, more-than-contingent values.

However, oftentimes attacks on the canon are predicated paradoxically on what turns out to be just the opposite assumption: they assume the validity of canonicity in general and its foundation in authoritative and enduring values even in the very attempt to challenge and change the canon's specific contents. Detractors from 'the' canon, like Chinua Achebe in 'An Image of Africa: Racism in Conrad's *Heart of Darkness*' attacking Joseph Conrad as a racist and challenging his right to be honored as a classic author on grounds of political incorrectness, may be recognized as having an important and very practical impact. But it is not really against the canon as such, against *any* canon that they are arguing. They are actually assuming the concept of a canon and assuming its legitimacy, but disputing prevailing views about which works should be accorded the honor of being included in it. This is appropriate, for the canon is an open and evolving body of works. Yet these arguments are not so much against the canon and its claim to universal validity as against certain results that the process of canonization has produced: they fall rather within the negotiations aimed at deciding which works will be valorized as canonical.

The complaint against the existing canon as invidious and exclusionary, as elitist and the instrument of domination, as represented by critics such as Paul Lauter and Lillian Robinson, usually presupposes that a canon could also work in a more even-handed and socially-progressive manner. What is being attacked is the imposition of a certain race's or gender's or class's literature as canonical. Generally, such protests are motivated not by objection to the idea of canonicity as such, but rather by a desire to participate in this claim and to have it work *for* rather than against one's own constituency. A more fundamental issue can be raised as to whether canonizing certain literary works and canonizing literature per se as a privileged mode of cultural expression is not itself inextricably ideological, political, and merely an enforcement of political and cultural power and not at all about appreciating ideals such as beauty and cultivating aesthetic taste or other generally valid values. All these softer, subjective phenomena may be unmasked as screens for asserting the interests of empowered groups and applying oppressive measures to control others. They are deployed to engender the consensus necessary for civil society by covering over breaches caused by conflicting material interests within society.

Some attempts have been made to use purely socio-ethnic and -economic parameters in selecting works to read, and so give up the effort to make distinctions of literary value. Ngugi wa Thiong'o, Taban Lo Liyong, and Henry Owuor-Anymba in 'On the Abolition of the English Department' (1968) argued for changing the criterion for inclusion from excellence to representativity. This indeed directly challenges Matthew Arnold's idea of literature, articulated in his famous definition of culture, as the best of what has been thought and written. Yet it is doubtful whether value judgments can or should be avoided in selecting works to study as literature. If in the interest of being fair to all contenders no real distinctions of merit are made, then it becomes really arbitrary — from an aesthetic or artistic point of view — which works are selected as representative. Without at least this prospect of selecting works for their intrinsic worth, we will soon forget what we are reading for or why we are reading literature at all. The difficult business of evaluating what is excellent and worthwhile, with all the contentiousness that this must entail, can perhaps not be avoided. Any selection results in some kind of canon, and as E. Dean Kolbas points out, 'the very concept of a canon necessarily involves qualitative judgment, because to be canonical also means to be exemplary'.[4]

The more radical critiques and rethinkings of the canon are not those that wish to retain its authority in order to invest other works and traditions, those of their own choice, with the privileges thought to have been held to date too exclusively by an unjustifiably small circle of elites. Challenges of the latter type have sometimes been effective in actually changing the canon, making many more women and non-Western and non-elite writers staples in courses at elite universities. But this would hardly have been possible without the searching theoretical questioning that forced recognition of the relativity and changeability of any possible canon — its necessarily dynamic mutability. Theory has proved invaluable for opening to investigation every aspect of the literary canon and every settled assumption about it. However, the unrestricted scope of its corrosive effect reaches to dissolving the category of the literary itself into ideological mists.

---

[4]   E. Dean Kolbas, *Critical Theory and the Literary Canon* (Boulder, Colorado: Westview Press, 2001).

Indeed the prestige of literature as such has itself been subjected to severe questioning, and the privilege accorded literary writings in public instruction and cultural institutions has been challenged head on. Why should texts labeled literary be elevated above others as having enduring value beyond the pragmatic use-value accorded to instruction manuals, research data, and news reports? Such 'distinctions', to use Pierre Bourdieu's term, have ideological implications.[5] These implications have been exposed forcefully, for example, by Raymond Williams's analysis in *Marxism and Literature* (1977) of the rise of a modern concept of literature in the 18th century as a special category of creative, imaginative writing in correlation with the rise of a new bourgeois middle class and its 'sensibility' in response to industrial capitalism.

Consequently, there has been a tendency to impugn the status of literature as canonical, to challenge its cultural authority per se, without distinction and without questioning which works are worthy of canonical status and which are not. Yet even if the literary as such has no definable content that is constant across cultures, its characteristic freedom of form as a genre of unrestricted invention and creativity suits it to serve in the transit of contents and concepts from culture to culture. To this extent, literature surely can be a force conducive to social dynamism. Although we have seen literature attacked for political reasons as associated inevitably with conservative ideologies, this ignores the key role that literature has also played in radical and revolutionary movements. Indeed, the early twentieth century modernist literary avant-gardes such as futurism and Dada wished to destroy libraries together with museums and the established institutions of society in general.

The attack on literature has been part and parcel of the wholesale attacks on all forms of cultural authority since 1968. Yet again these are typically bids to lay claim to cultural authority on behalf of parties representing themselves as disenfranchised. The more radical challenges deny the possibility of such authority altogether, and this is where the most searching theoretical reflection is apt to lead. René Wellek's essay, 'The Attack on Literature', examines a variety of political and ideological reasons why literature per se has been denigrated in recent decades and then proposes that '[m]uch more serious and interesting is the attack on literature which is basically motivated by a distrust of language'.[6] Roland Barthes, for example, characterizes literature as 'a system of deceptive signification', and Maurice Blanchot prophesies the 'disappearance of literature' by its reduction to

---

[5]   In addition to Bourdieu, *La distinction,* see Guillory, who uses Bourdieu's thinking to reflect on the impact of the institutionalization of literary theory on the formation of literary canons.

[6]   René Wellek, *The Attack on Literature and Other Essays* (Chapel Hill: University of North Carolina Press, 1982), p. 5.

silence (p. 7). Wellek himself then points out that '[l]ess apocalyptically, literature and writing have been seen as a transitory form of human communication to be replaced by the media of the electronic age' (p. 8). These are challenges to literary value per se. Indeed if context and motives of social power alone are decisive in determining which books and which kinds of discourse are treasured and kept, then texts are emptied of all intrinsic value and are canonized on only extrinsic grounds. The canon is considered to be a matter only of consolidated power, not of merit or aesthetic value.

Lately, it is not only literature but theory itself that has come under attack, and for similar reasons: the literature of theory, too, is viewed as privileging Western, white, bourgeois, phallogocentric discourse as normative and as in a position to judge all others. Voices from the margins identifying with minorities object to theory and the sort of exclusionary drawing of boundaries around the appropriate object of literary criticism, thereby establishing the canon, with which it is complicit. But this is rather too gross a generalizing view itself, and it ignores how theoretical work has actually highlighted the historical contingencies that go into making up the canon. The critics of the canon sometimes write as if it were a centrally organized conspiracy, whereas history shows the process to be much more complicated and aleatory than that. Beyond all deliberate manipulations, what effectively establishes a literary canon in the collective mind of a culture is more like an 'invisible hand', the result of incalculably complex interactions of myriad individual, intentional efforts at the micro-level (Winko, 'Literatur-Kanon als *invisible hand*-Phenomen').

Paradoxically, this linking of the canon question with that of the justification for theory is key to illuminating and even to 'justifying' them both. Theory, like the canon, has come under fire, yet both these challenges are reflexes in which theoretical reflection turns back on itself and turns into self-questioning and self-limitation or even self–liquidation. The questioning of literature and theory alike is an eminently theoretical activity. Whether theory is valorized or impugned, it is in any case actively deployed by such critique, and to that extent whatever is said depends on and assumes the value nd validity of theoretical reflection as such. Likewise, the challenge to the canon belongs to the vocation of theory: this challenge is itself theoretical and cannot flourish without theoretical methods and instruments. Canonicity too is a theoretical — and originally theological — construct, and even the attack against the canon is a further manifestation of the self-reflexive and even self-subversive powers of critical reflection or theory.[7]

Even the argument 'Against Theory' of Walter Benn Michaels and Steven Knapp is in its own way an eminently theoretical argument. It takes a general

---

[7]   Most helpful here are Cancik and Trowitzisch.

position against theoretical criticism on philosophical grounds. The reason is basically that no matter what reasons are given the argument is first of all a practice that cannot account for itself theoretically except by producing and promulgating more beliefs that remain, however, always practical positions of belief rather than theoretically justified truths. The pretense of stepping — or of attempting to step — outside of one's practical commitments in order to ground them in some belief-neutral theory is exposed as bad faith. Even the highly pragmatist Stanley Fish succumbs to this temptation in presenting a general theory of how theory as such has no practical consequences. But then does not the same hold for Knapp and Michaels's own argument? As an intervention into literary-theoretical debate, it has a practical point to make. It ought not, however, to be believed as a theory, and therefore its prescription that the theoretical enterprise be ended has no general validity. It may be implemented by those it happens to serve in strategic or pragmatic ways, but it is not justified and prescriptive on any universalizable grounds. It must not be allowed *theoretical* credibility or validity.

Theory is inevitably reductive inasmuch as it abstracts from the infinite complications of practice. It does, nevertheless, open a space for negotiations between different points of view because theory places certain of these practical assumptions into question. Our practical critical assumptions are indeed different and sometimes even incommensurable. The value of theory is the stimulus it provides to opening up the parameters of our discussions. It has no positive doctrine to offer: it is a facilitator, for theory projects a forum for discussion where none could previously be supposed because there is no self-evident practical intersection between disparate fields like modern anthropology and ancient Greek tragedy (Girard) or between the history of seventeenth-century religious conflicts and the use of signs by poets and artists in the early twentieth century avant-garde movements (Barthes). Theory invites to such hybrid discussions. Having no fixed framework of references of its own, it opens up an in-between space for comparison that might otherwise never be discovered. In opening up this space of free play, where boundaries and definitions are set in motion, theory behaves like literature—free from constraints of fixed frameworks and set fields of objects, free to reconstruct them in creative and imaginative ways.[8]

In this vein, which opens to indetermination as a peculiar virtue, Gerald Graff, in 'Taking Cover in Coverage', makes a case for featuring theory in the literature curriculum. Although he acknowledges the many conflicts with which theory is fraught, he maintains that the conflicts need not be resolved in order for theory to be taught. According to Graff, theory should catalyze exchange rather than become one more specialization. It is currently

---

[8]   Bissel gathers together a number of suggestive essays on this head.

threatened with compartmentalization according to various disciplines, whereas it is suited by its nature to play a role between departments, fostering reflection on connections and contextualization. Rather than being consigned to the well-defined precincts of a special discipline, theory should be central to all the different specializations represented within academic departments, 'not by putting theory specialists in charge but by recognizing that *all* their members are theorists'.[9]

Insight into the contingency of all value judgments is actually theoretical insight — perhaps *the* essential theoretical insight. It is judgment that distances itself from immediate belief in any judgment — even in itself as concrete, determinate judgment. For theory is itself dependent on contingencies in reaching any of its judgments. They come about in certain historical conjunctures as the result of a whole set of contingent conditions and biases.

Theory etymologically means 'seeing' (from Greek *theorein*). As such, it objectifies and knows, even while stepping back into a position of detachment. Sight is traditionally the sense that affords knowledge at a distance and in detachment from what is known. However, while in principle theoretical knowledge is an objective and, to that extent, absolute knowing, as practiced it is relative; it is always a particular endeavor at theorizing that realizes one angle of vision in a determinate set of circumstances. Theoretical formulations cannot help positing themselves as having some sort of general validity, but their actual impact depends rather on their opening possibilities for communication between positions that in themselves seem to exclude one another. By taking a more objective view it becomes possible to recognize commonalities between alternatives that appear to be mutually exclusive. The significance of theory, accordingly, is in the possibilities it opens for negotiating relationships and making connections across what are apparently entrenched divisions and impermeable boundaries.

Theory has enabled and promoted the discovery of diversity and multiplicity of literatures and cultures through its insight into the contingency of purportedly universal norms and supposedly enduring or even unchanging standards. A theoretical perspective relativizes the motives for any particular viewpoint — that is what the objectifying, distancing look of theory is apt to do. It relativizes its object, that is, uproots it from its natural ground, detaches it from its unconscious assumptions, and places it in contexts in which it must negotiate complicated relations and sustain conflicts. While the object of the theoretical gaze is thus relativized, the gaze itself seems to reveal truth — though only until it too is taken as object for further theoretical reflection. The pretense to objective knowledge, which is indeed objectionable for all

---

[9]   Gerald Graff, 'Taking Cover in Coverage', in *Critical Reasoning in Contemporary Culture*, ed. by Richard A. Talaska (Albany: SUNY Press, 1992), p. 201.

the reasons that have been urged against the whole historical edifice of Western thought as metaphysics, pertains to first-order formulations of theory, but not to the life of theory as an ongoing process of self-critical reflection. Theory relativizes — only to turn, in turn, into a normative discourse itself: yet it is at the same time the capacity and the drive to subject its own new discourse to critical scrutiny. It is in its dynamic working rather than in any achieved results or static precepts that theory has its meaning and importance. The theoretical outlook distances from concrete claims and motivations, thereby relativizing them and opening up alternatives and catalyzing mutations.

Theory in the literal sense entails stepping back to see the field as a whole rather than being embroiled in contentions from a given position that obstructs one's outlook and restricts seeing. A theoretical position is presumably disengaged from all practical standpoints, and to this extent 'objective'. This is illusory, of course, yet as an ideal it can be efficacious in loosening the strangle-hold of apparently self-evident dogmas. Hence the rather piquant paradox that theoretical detachment is practically useful and even necessary, although it is strictly and rigorously — that is, in principle or in theory — impossible. This is all theory can do. It has no positive, prescriptive value, as Knapp and Michaels insist. Yet such an activity of detached analysis and evaluation does have practical consequences, even if it cannot control and prescribe them. It fundamentally changes how literature, and consequently life, is viewed. Although it cannot impose any specific values, it frees and complicates literary value, exposing it as not given but as negotiated, as not natural but instituted.

Theory is thus never merely theory. It is always also, at the same time, a practice. Distancing and objectifying is always dialectically related to taking a position and manifesting one's positionality in ways that escape conscious control. As a moment of detached reflection, theory is a necessary and enlightened way to deal especially with the differences and conflicts that inevitably arise in all human affairs. This is why the view against theory, that 'theory is nothing else but the attempt to escape practice',[10] is far too reductive. Just as this pragmatic attack uses a theoretical tone and form of statement to try and convince us that it is right, so other theories are to be evaluated always also in terms of their meaning as practiced. This is an insight traditionally found at the heart of hermeneutics — the theory of interpretation. Knapp and Michaels conclude, 'Our thesis has been that no one can reach a position outside practice, that theorists should stop trying, and that the theoretical enterprise should therefore be abandoned' (p. 30). Yet

---

[10]   Steven Knapp and Walter Benn Michaels, 'Against Theory', in *Against Theory: Literary Studies and the New Pragmatism*, ed. by W.J.T. Mitchell (Chicago: University of Chicago Press, 1982), p. 30.

striving to achieve objectivity, to stand outside the limitations of one's current point of view, is crucial for the attempt to meet with others and interact with their practices so as to compromise and cooperate with them rather than only blindly playing out the conflicts between our different, apparently incompatible practices.

From Matthew Arnold to Italo Calvino, theory has been extolled for its capacity of rendering practice indirect, and thereby of escaping from the typically deadlocked, polarized impasses of the political scene and its embattled institutions. Theory is necessary in order to see past the blinders of one's own practice and to see a little more than one does when one focuses on doing alone. According to Arnold, 'A polemical practical criticism makes men blind even to the ideal imperfection of their practice, makes them willingly assert its ideal perfection, in order the better to secure it against attack; and clearly this is narrowing and baneful for them. If they were reassured on the practical side, they might be brought to entertain speculative considerations of ideal perfection, and their spiritual horizon would thus gradually widen'.[11] In other words, try to see the other's point of view, determined as it is by a different practical angle and exigency that you do not share but can theoretically approximate and hypothetically adopt. That is how new, creative possibilities can emerge, in order to negotiate conflicts in creative ways, preserving what is valuable on both sides rather than surrendering to the logic of triumph of one over the other and consequent fortification and rigidifying of the one and erasure of the other.

The value of theory is demonstrated consistently by its weaning us away from too positivistic a view of literature and its value. We see how value is produced through relations negotiated in social fields rather than being inherent in the nature of linguistic products themselves. This outlook is enshrined in the basic structuralist insight into the relativity of linguistic significance dictated by the diacritical nature of the linguistic sign (Saussure). From this insight rises the great tidal wave of theoretical rethinkings that have rocked the latter half of the twentieth century and continue their stir on into the present millennium. Such insight is effectively shown to dwell diffusely in a great variety of subsequent theoretical movements, many of them political in inspiration, for example, by Homi Bhabha's analyses of the mutual implications of nation and narration. Theory furnishes a more flexible outlook on the choices we make as to what to value in literature and which literary works to canonize. Certainly the intensive questioning of the canon in recent decades has been possible only on the basis of the theoretical ferment that opened up perspectives on literature and culture to reassessment and re-

---

[11]   Matthew Arnold, 'The Function of Criticism at the Present Time', in *Lectures and Essays in Criticism*, ed. by R. H Super (Ann Arbor: University of Michigan Press, 1962), p. 271.

negotiation. The foundations of our cultural institutions and literary canons were challenged by free theoretical reflection which, in part, undermined theory and theoretical foundations and made the practical claims of literature paramount. Theory is a self-subverting discourse. Its vocation is to call everything, and ultimately itself, into question. That is what makes it so invaluable, even and perhaps especially to those to whom it is objectionable.

Why has theory evolved since 1968, over the '70s, '80s and '90s, away from the ostensibly disinterested and universal researches of structuralism, of hermeneutics, even of deconstruction and other forms of 'high theory', towards ever more concrete forms representing specific groups and identities according to race, class, gender? This, too, is the work of theory. It is a necessary consequence of the self-critique to which Western epistemologies of universal and necessary knowledge were subjected. It is the distancing movement of theory that has brought out the ethnocentric, class- and gender-interested character of traditional, elite Western culture and its epistemological models and methods. The rejection of theory is itself a theoretical gesture par excellence: it is the further pursuit and fulfillment of critical reason which has been the soul and inspiration of Western thinking since the first discovery of Logos over two and a half millennia ago in the speculatively theoretical texts of Parmenides and Heraclitus. With respect to the canon, the challenges and struggles over selection of texts are the continuation of the very process in which, historically, canon formation consists. There may be good theoretical arguments for the rejection of canonicity altogether, but this very penchant for self-critique and self-annihilation has been the most characteristic gesture of Western culture all along. This impulse is embodied quintessentially today in theory — together with the antitheory that it engenders.

It must be conceded that the relativizing discourse of theory can sometimes be experienced as stultifying and dis-empowering for particular political agendas. Barbara Christian speaks out against theory, or against the 'race for theory', as she puts it, since there is and has always been a dynamic type of theoretical reflection antithetical to Western logic at work in the narrative and gnomic forms of the colored peoples, especially black, third world women, in whose name she speaks. This is another kind of 'race' and another kind of theory that resists all expropriating generalization of its specific differences. Against the neutralizing tendencies of theory in general that would reduce new and emergent literatures to silence and non-existence, strong assertion of life requires unquestioning self-confidence and the projection — be they only mirages — of one's identity and ideology. Theory with its dissolution of myths is not helpful for waging wars either of repression or of liberation: the two are, in fact, inextricably linked in a theoretical perspective, however diametrically opposite, like good and evil, they are in the practical perspective of those who feel the duty to fight for what they deem right. And culture wars are no exception.

On the other hand, in another obvious paradox, the claims of difference and of race, of racial and gender difference, are being asserted against generalizing, presumably theoretical discourses thanks to the thought of difference which emerged on the wider critical scene emblematically with Jacques Derrida and the theory revolution spearheaded by the many theoretical movements influenced by deconstruction. These include the New Historicism and Cultural Studies. With varying degrees of acknowledgment of this indebtedness, Cornell West and Henry Louis Gates, as well as bell hooks, have attempted to incorporate theory into projects of showing specific racial differences as relevant to general philosophical thinking. Hence the motto: 'race matters'.

Such a theoretical viewpoint has seemed to entail the demise of any and all appeals to universal values. It would seem that no standard, no 'canon' for measuring literary merit and thereby establishing the enduring value of literary works is possible in such a perspective. Indeed no work has value simply on the basis of its intrinsic qualities alone, but only as a function of what these qualities can mean *to someone* in some concrete historical context. However, this can still be value of a universal nature, where universality is a matter not of fixed properties or even of definable content but rather of communication without restrictions, of opening outward towards encounter with readers in other times and places and in other cultures.

Although it is never over, history finds some way of deciding what is to be valued and credited with enduring worth, and the condition of this recognition and hence the criterion of canonicity cannot but be some form of communicability, a power to transmit and translate oneself and one's own meaning into other contexts and further matrices of significance. This is the universality not of a changeless Platonic idea but of discourse in action, a universality of which the content cannot be isolated and settled once and for all because it is constantly being re-negotiated and can only be discovered in its emergence as it transmigrates from one form of instantiation to another. This is universality in a performative sense: cross-cultural, transhistorical communication of value that is demonstrated in being enacted. Not without reason, then, theoretical reflection on literature has led to a new and acute sensitivity to the importance of 'crossing borders' in validating literary and cultural values.

In recent decades, we have in effect witnessed the emergence of a new concept, or rather non-concept, of universality based not on the categorical thinking of a general concept but on the open-ended reaching out towards communication with others and connection in all directions of what remains conceptually undefined — or always newly to be defined. The concept is based on a cutting, a 'cept' or incision. It works by exclusion. The concept of *anthropos* as *zôon échòn lógon* cuts out and excludes all those beings which are not living or not logical, not endowed with reason. The new universality discovered through literary theory particularly in contemplating the canon works rather by inclusion potentially without restrictions; it is universal precisely in its unlimited openness to new connections and aggregation. This is a new understanding of universality, and it has been introduced and concretely worked out in relation to myriad literatures and discourses and peoples and nations and cultures. It issues in recognition of the exemplarity of works that are received as having something to say far beyond the original contexts of their production. Safeguarding and promoting this recognition is the work of theory as a malleable *koiné* of cross-cultural discourse. Such transfusion across cultures demonstrates how an idea of universal value, such as is enshrined in the concept of canonicity, lives and grows by transforming itself from age to age.

WORKS CITED

Achebe, Chinua, 'An Image of Africa: Racism in Conrad's *Heart of Darkness'*, *The Massachusetts Review*, XVIII/4 (1977), 782-794

Alter, Robert, *Canon and Creativity: Modern Writing and the Authority of Scripture* (New Haven: Yale University Press, 2000)

Arnold, Heinz Ludwig, ed., *Literarische Kanonbildung. Text + Kritik. Zeitschrift für Literatur. SONDERBAND* (München: R. Boorberg Verlag GmbH & Co, 2002)

Arnold, Matthew, 'The Function of Criticism at the Present Time', in *Lectures and Essays in Criticism*, ed. by R. H Super (Ann Arbor: University of Michigan Press, 1962)

Barthes, Roland, *Le Degrée zéro de l'écriture* (Paris: Seuil, 1953)

Bhabha, Homi K., 'The Commitment to Theory', in *The Location of Culture* (New York: Routledge, 1994)

—. *Nation and Narration* (New York: Routledge, 1990)

Bissel, Elizabeth Beaumont, *The Question of Literature. The Place of the Literary in Contemporary Theory* (Manchester: Manchester University Press, 2002)

Bloom, Allan, *The Closing of the American Mind: How Higher Education Has Failed Democracy and Impoverished the Soul of Today's Students* (New York: Simon& Schuster Inc., 1987)

Bourdieu, Pierre, *La distinction: Critique sociale du jugement* (Paris: Minuit, 1979)

Bromwich, David, 'Canon Bashing', *Dissent*, 35 (1988), 479-81

Calvino, Italo, *Perché leggere i classici?* trans. by Martin McLaughlin (Milan: Mondadori, 1991)

Cancik, Hubert,'Kanon, Ritus, Ritual — Religionsgeschichtliche Anmerkungen zu einem literaturwissenschaftlichen Diskurs', in *Kanon und Theorie*

Eagleton, Terry, *Literary Theory: An Introduction* (Minneapolis: University of Minnesota Press, 1983)

Gates, Henry Louis, Jr., 'Talking Black', in *Loose Canons: Notes on the Culture Wars* (New York: Oxford University Press, 1992)

Girard, René, *La violence et le sacré* (Paris: Grasset, 1972)

Gorak, Jan, ed., *Canon vs. Culture: Reflections on the Current Debate* (New York: Garland, 2001)

Graff, Gerald, 'Taking Cover in Coverage', in *Critical Reasoning in Contemporary Culture*, ed. by Richard A. Talaska (Albany: SUNY Press, 1992)

Guillory, John, *Cultural Capital: The Problem of Literary Canon Formation* (Chicago: University of Chicago Press, 1993)

Hirsch, E. D., *Cultural Literacy: What Every American Needs to Know* (Boston: Houghton Mifflin, 1987)

Hooks, Bell, 'Postmodern Blackness', in *Yearning, Race, Gender and Cultural Politics* (Boston: South End Press, 1990)

Kaiser, Gerhard R. and Stefan Matuschek, *Begründungen und Funcktionen des Kanons: Beiträge aus derLiteratur- und Kunstwissenschaft, Philosophie und Theologie* (Heidelberg: C. Winter, 2001)

Kolbas, E. Dean, *Critical Theory and the Literary Canon* (Boulder, Colorado: Westview Press, 2001)

Lauter, Paul, *Canons and Contexts* (Oxford: Oxford University Press, 1991)

Löffler, Sigrid, *Wer Sagt Uns, Was Wir Lesen Sollen? Bücherflut, Die Kritik und der literarische Kanon* (The 2002 Bithell Memorial Lecture. Institute of Germanic Studies. University of London School of Advanced Study, 2003)

Mitchell, W.J.T., ed., *Against Theory: Literary Studies and the New Pragmatism* (Chicago: University of Chicago Press, 1982)

Moog-Grünewald, Maria, ed., *Kanon und Theorie* (Heidelberg: C. Winter, 1997)

Ngugi wa Thiong'o, Taban Lo Liyong, Henry Owuor-Anymba, 'On the Abolition of the English Department', in *Homecoming: Essays on African and Caribbean Literature, Culture, Politics* (London: Heinemann, 1972)

Ohmann, Richard, 'The Shaping of a Canon: U.S. Fiction, 1960-75', in *Politics of Letters* (Middletown, Conn.: Wesleyan University Press, 1987)

Patai, Daphne and Wilfrido Corral, eds., *Theory's Empire: An Anthology of Dissent* (New York: Columbia University Press, 2005)

Roche, Mark William, *Why Literature Matters in the 21st Century* (New Haven: Yale University Press, 2004)

Robinson, Lillian, *In the Canon's Mouth: Dispatches from the Culture Wars* (Bloomington: Indiana University Press, 1997)

Saussure, Ferdinand de, *Cours de linguistique générale* (Paris: Payot, 1955)

Smith, Barbara Hernstein, *Contingencies of Value: Alternative Perspectives for Critical Theory* (Cambridge: Harvard University Press, 1988)

South Atlantic Quarterly 98/1 (1990)

Wellek, René, *The Attack on Literature and Other Essays* (Chapel Hill: University of North Carolina Press, 1982)

West, Cornel, *Race Matters* (Boston: Beacon Press, 1993)

Caius Dobrescu

European Literary Canon-Building as Federalist Phenomenology

The paper explores the possibilities of hermeneutics and phenomenology, especially of the so-called 'identificationist' critical school, to explore cosmopolitanism not as an abstract political or philosophical doctrine, but as a process of profound value internalization, as a form of inner experience and inner commitment. This perspective could offer the key to a deeper understanding of the idea of 'European literary canon', in direct connection to the present debates over the federalist vs. confederational level of integration.

1. European Consciousness: The 'Homelandization' of Ideas

The search for a rationale to support the idea of a European supranational literary canon implicitly calls for a solution to the dominant philosophical concern of post World War II Western Europe, a dilemma that also confronted the dissenting intellectuals of Eastern Europe and that was powerfully reasserted in the context of the EU spectacular Blitz-enlargement of the post-Communist era: how can one promote supranational context-free 'cold' values and at the same time preserve the 'warmth' of a context-bound communal memory. The manner in which this challenge was approached was by replacing the alleged imperialism of Enlightenment Rationalism with an enthusiasm for everything that is diverse, pied, patched, interlaced, osmotic, fading, dissolved, nuanced, spectrum-like, disseminated, fasciculated, and rizomatic. A mental pattern (or quasi-pattern), that tries to avoid the alleged violence done to the world of experience by conceptual abstraction and generalization, while simultaneously asserting the fact that diversity is not clearly distributed, discreet, morphologically delineated but, for the most, transgressive and random. Cultural diversity should, as a consequence, be represented as a complicate interrelated tissue.

This celebration of diversity may be imaginative and stimulating but, from the point of view of the present survey, it carries with it a major shortcoming. The resulting cultural charts are much too complex to be filtered down to a manageable European literary canon. This particular attempt of construing a supranational and trans-ethnic sense of 'experience' might lead some to intense spiritual gratifications, but it is much too ispersed in order to be meaningful, let away instrumental, in the wider context of a potential European canon-building. The logical consequence of the apology for the intricate/inextricable diversity is that the very notion of 'canon', of a hierarchical selection oriented by rules and by a consistent value system, loses its entire *raison d'être*.

If we look for a stronger theoretical foundation to support the above-mentioned supranational literary canon, one that would help articulate, in intellectual and symbolic terms, a cohesive European identity, we might try to radically reconsider the traditional application of the phenomenological method to this subject matter. This is a mental experiment that would attribute to the *intellectual* discourse, to *ideas* and social *projects*, to the *cogito* at large the phenomenological quality of 'warmth', in direct defiance of the society vs. community tradition that roughly labels abstract thought as 'cold'. Meaning: unable to dispense the emotional benefits of authentic inwardness. In other words, a supranational literary canon could become part of a more daring and self-assured European cultural integration policy if centered on a phenomenological understanding of 'European-ness' as a genuine and innerly-cohesive event of consciousness.

A criterion for the inclusion in a tentative European literary canon could be whether a work captures the process, if not the very emergence, of a distinctly supranational (self)consciousness. This concern could, among other things, help one make a clear delineation between a literary European canon of felt/lived values and the current recommendations/regulations of political correctness ideologies. The difference of approach should not lie in the values themselves. There is not much to add or to subtract, conceptually, when speaking of political, intellectual and creative freedom, equal opportunities and equal treatment by the law and the public institutions, caring for the weak and the impaired, opposing overt or covert forms of discrimination, safeguarding the equal dignity of the human persons irrespective of their somatic, social or cultural determinations, on the one hand, and the equal respect for such patterns of circumstantiation, on the other, as long as they function not as fatalistic or correctional inhibitors, but as support structures for a sense of individual/communitarian fulfillment. But the value-as-experience orientation of the canon building strategy outlined in the present paper implies a type of advocacy for the above-mentioned list of moral and political guidelines quite removed from the pedagogical strategies currently associated with 'political correctness'.[1]

With standard literary 'PC' approaches, norms, rules, and their subjacent philosophical justifications are both definite and finite. They are construed as either self-evident (as immediately speaking to our natural reason), or as resulting from an already concluded debate that has distillated contentious

---

[1]   Paul Berman, ed., *Debating P.C.: The Controversy Over Political Correctness on College Campuses* (New York: Dell Publishing, 1992); William Casement, *The Great Canon Controversy: The Battle of the Books in Higher Education* (New Brunswick, N.J.: Transaction Publishers, 1996); John Guillory, *Cultural Capital: The Problem of Literary Canon Formation* (Chicago and London: The University of Chicago Press, 1993).

ideas and emotions into an unshivering sense of moral clarity. So that the pedagogical mission consists simply of conveying already crystallized notional contents. On the contrary, a phenomenological value-as-experience perspective should profit from the fact that literature is a medium that has the rather rare quality of conserving not only the rounded-up conclusions of mental processes, but also something of their condition of perpetual (or 'suspended') works in progress.

Literature – European literature, in our particular case – is, however, not simply a repository of firm persuasions, but a cultural archive able to document, in its very specific way, the innermost blooming in an individual consciousness of what is to become a moral persuasion. Which means that a European literary canon centered on the phenomenological principle of the *authenticity* (consistency/intensity/texture) of experience should be able to seize the values and moral commitments identifiable as European as open consciousness processes. It is, of course, as possible to imagine undisputable examples of literary merit unassociated with any supranational ethics or philosophy, as it is to conceive of works that lean massively on European themes, but rather in the manner of lip service than in the mood of artistic candor. But a literary canon-building inspired by a phenomenology of the transethnic/supranational personal experience should try to detect precisely those historical instances in which artistic power and Euro-relevant conceptual intensity spontaneously intermingle.

That is to say that we should search not for the literary embodiment of an unlikely European catechism, but for works that confront their readers with those forms of hesitation, doubt, inner tension, (or, on the other hand, passion, motivation, enthusiasm) that accompany the process of spiritual miscegenation through which a consciousness raises itself above the intricacies of ethno-cultural affiliations and loyalties and embraces a wider and far more encompassing condition.

It is reasonable to assume that the emergence in the individual consciousness of a European arch-identity is not something that could be easily pinpointed. Therefore, the selection of the most powerful and relevant literary instantiations of this process presupposes a broader map of the poetic exercises and techniques of making the world of concepts and principles hospitable to the human senses – if not to the human body in its entirety. This is not the same as to speak about imaginary 'communities' or 'homelands'[2], even less to poetically exalt ideal or idealized homelands. What is distinctively European is a creative process that might occasionally interfere with different walks of modern nation building, but that in its essence is

---

[2]   Benedict Anderson, *Imagined Communities: Reflections on the Origin and Spread of Nationalism* (London: Verso, 1983); Salman Rushdie, *Imaginary Homelands: Essays and criticism, 1981-1991* (London: Granta Books; New York: Viking, 1991).

clearly distinct form any ethnocentric approach: the elaboration of a form of
sensitivity that would transform the ideas themselves in the precise
equivalent of a 'homeland'. Contrary to the immensely popular habit of
sharply distinguishing between the "warm" and hospitable culture and the
abstractly 'cold' civilization, contrary to the ethnic pride and the hostility to
the impersonal and supranational 'Reason' ostentatiously displayed by
prominent authors in different countries and epochs, a major and distinctive
tendency of interrelated European literatures was to perceptually explore the
world of intellectual abstractions.

To better circumscribe this historical experience we might consider an
equivalent of the Heideggerean concept of dwelling (*wohnen*). For
Heidegger, 'dwelling' presupposes an intimate, indiscernible relationship
with the Being, the World and the Language, mixed together into a kind of
ethereal promiscuity.[3] But the understanding of 'dwelling' that would suit the
present approach is one that captures (or 'brackets', to use a specifically
phenomenological concept) the very joy of *thinking*, the intimate, essentially
emotional intercourse with virtual entities generally called 'ideas'. Europe
being essentially an abstraction, the authors that would count as its literary
agents should be those able and willing to make ideas and values (the values
that we currently identify as European: personality, individuality, equality,
skeptical reasonability, etc.) their very existential environment, their
voluntary homeland. In the view of the present approach, it is impossible to
seriously consider the idea of a European literary canon otherwise than in
close connection with reconstructing the history of literature as educated
intellectual sensitivity. The configuration of a canon relevant for what we
may call 'non-ethnic European consciousness' should go hand in hand with a
historical exploration of literary enterprises aimed at asserting a sensitive and
often sensuous content to intensely felt and deeply assumed abstractions.

2. Mapping the Literary Manifestations of Supranational European-ness

Revisiting the 14th century Italian *fedelli d'amore*, and especially Dante
Aligheri's seminal contribution to the intellectualization of poetical emotions
(and to the appropriation of projects and ideas as initiatory experiences
internal to and determining for one's self/sense of selfhood), could, for
instance, constitute one possible testing ground for the phenomenological

---

[3]   Martin Heidegger, 'Bauen Wohnen Denken' in *Vorträge und Aufsätze* (Frankfurt am Main:
        Vittorio Klostermann, 2000); George Steiner, *Martin Heidegger* (Chicago, Ill.: University of
        Chicago Press, 1991).

approximations of supranational/trans-cultural, potentially European structures of individual consciousness and experience.[4]

The same could be said about the rich, decidedly pan-European experience of re-interpreting, (as in re-discovering'), the classical, Greco-Roman mythology and history. A process that, no matter if it emerged in the Western Renaissance, in the efforts of Byzantine intellectual elites to perpetuate their legacy after the fall of Constantinople, in baroque, neo-classical, Enlightenment, or Romantic times, as part of the successive waves of Westernization that swiped through Central and Eastern Europe, interspersed within *fin-de-siècle* aestheticism or constructivistic modernism, it has implied not the simple adoption of an allegorical conceptual language, but, in many instances, the explorative overcoming of inherited representations on cultural identity and selfhood.

Another promising field of investigation is the one configured by the interference between literature and different paths of utopian thinking. Philosophical utopianism represents, in a massive proportion, a pan-European intellectual heritage, as documented by all credible scholarly surveys dedicated to the subject.[5] Moreover, it is arguable that, under a variety of forms, utopianism was inbred in almost all attempts of giving substance to the notion of European identity as experienced by a sentient self. A literary canonization-oriented survey of this complex field should, nevertheless, distinguish between intellectual endeavors that take fiction as a pretext or as a disposable vehicle, and those works where the utopian projection is closely retrievable to what the Canadian philosopher Charles Taylor called the 'sources of the self'.[6] Obviously, not all detectable forms of 'felt' utopianism are compatible with values that would generally count as European (at least not in our contemporary understanding). There is, for instance, a world of difference between authoritarian and anarchist walks of utopianism. On the other hand, the ambivalence of literary imagination between an enthusiastic absorption of radical fantasies of unlimited emancipation and a sarcastic distancing that turns the latter into terrifying negative utopias is also to be considered with the utmost care. The relevance of these distinctions for a canonical selection process should be further examined in full fledged

---

[4] Virgil Podoabă, *Fenomenologia punctului de plecare* (*A Phenomenology of the Starting Point*) (Braşov: Transsylvania University Press, 2008).

[5] Frank E. Manuel and Fritzie P. Manuel, *Utopian Thought in the Western World* (Cambridge, Mass.: Belknap Press, 1979); James H.Billington, *Fire in the Minds of Men. Origins of the Revolutionary Faith* (New York: Basic Books, 1980).

[6] Charles Taylor, *Sources of the Self. The Making of the Modern Identity* (Cambridge, Massachussets: Harvard University Press, 1989).

research projects, but the essence of the above observations is that the utopian tradition is intimately connected to literature, that it is a decidedly pan-European modern phenomenon, and that it is preferentially associated with manners of 'dwelling' in the virtual, of turning intensely personalized abstract commitments into one's own existential identity.

Carefully applied means of phenomenological reduction could establish at least two different pan-European literary traditions, that, even if they both nurture Moebius continuum-like abstraction-sensation dynamics, still remain very different in point of existential attitude and worldview. On the one hand, we could consider a sense of upwards initiation, preserved in both Enlightenment and counter-Enlightenment traditions, which associates raising above the 'ground' of empirical data towards the 'sky' of concepts and categories to a death-and-rebirth remotely Gnostic passage rite.[7] On the other hand, the European literary heritage preserves a totally different manner of 'bracketing' the experience of lived ideas (of 'touching' the quality of ideality itself), a skeptical and ironical expressive praxis that intentionally 'descends' or 'scatters' abstractions among different modes of empirical sensitivity.[8] For the phenomenological approach of the literary canon that we are trying to imagine here, both these walks of artistic-intellectual endeavor are equally relevant as 'recruitment pools' for literary works expressive of an *emerging* European (supranational/supra- or trans-cultural) state of consciousness.

Another natural target for a phenomenological investigation of the emergence of supranational creative identities would be the geographical and historical areas that have witnessed, over a significant period of time, a vivid multicultural diversity confined within a more or less coherent system of supranational government. The classical example for this, one that has been attentively explored in recent times, starting, it is true, not from an inner European, but from an American intellectual impulse[9], is the Habsburg Empire, since 1867 officially known as Austria-Hungary. It is common knowledge that this cultural space resuscitated, until the wake of the 20th century and among the elites of all the national cultures represented within the empire, diverse and powerful literary expressions of a candid yearning towards a 'cosmopolitan self'.[10] But other equally promising historical

---

[7]   Ioan P. Couliano, *The Tree of Gnosis. Gnostic mythology from early Christianity to modern nihilism* (San Francisco: HarperCollins, 1992).

[8]   Mikhail Bakhtin, *Rabelais and His World.* Translated by Hélène Iswolsky (Bloomington: Indiana University Press, 1984).

[9]   Carl E. Schorske, *Fin-de-siècle Vienna. Politics and Culture* (New York: Alfred A. Knopf, 1961).

[10]   Guy Scarpetta, *Éloge du cosmopolitisme* (Paris: B. Grasset, 1981).

grounds of multicultural and multiconfessional interplay are far less investigated, a convincing example being the Oriental part of the continent comprised of what until the 1870s used to be known as the European possessions of the Ottoman Empire. The attention given to the succesive waves of ethnic revival that shook and still shake this geographical area shouldn't obscure its historical exposure to supranational and cosmopolitan ideals rained in from Western Europe mainly by a powerful network of Greek-speaking post-Byzantine elites.[11] The supranational influences of Enlightenment on the one hand and the historical experience of communicating and negotiating in a climate of thick ethnic diversity gave way to literary experiments that, more than once, convincingly expose devoted intimations of a supranational identity.

2. European Holistics

One of the most basic and therefore relevant mental events that count as consciousness experiences is that of perceiving wholes/entities/integralities. To some phenomenologists, the treatment reserved for this constitutive ability of human consciousness draws the line between the 'hermeneutics of suspicion' and the 'hermeneutics of trust'.[12] The hermeneutics of suspicion starts form the assumption that the highest peak of lucidity (which should translate as a blissful state of 'pure' consciousness) is reached in the exercise of critical analytical 'unmasking' faculties. On the contrary, the hermeneutics of trust hypothesizes that the root- or test-state of human consciousness is given by the experience of wholeness and plenitude.

This is not the right place to discuss these two perspectives in terms of hard, true-or-false options. It suffices to say that, for the purpose of exploring a phenomenological rationale for a pan-European supranational literary canon, the 'hermeneutics of trust' seems a more practical option. It is intuitive that the emergence of a literary-sensitive European consciousness is directly connected if not undistinguishable form a powerful perception of 'Europe' as unity and wholeness. At this level, we could reformulate our task as the hermeneutics of literary works susceptible of documenting a personal vision of Europe as a whole that is more than and irreducible to its constitutive parts. This means to enlarge the scope of our investigation from

---

[11] Paul Cornea, *Originile romantismului românesc. Spiritul public, mişcarea ideilor şi literatura între 1780-1840* (*The Origins of Romanian Romanticism. Public Spirit, Intellectual Trends, and Literature, 1780-1840*) (Bucharest: Minerva, 1972); Dionysios A. Zakythnos, *The Making of Modern Greece. From Byzantium to Independence* (Oxford: Basil Blackwell, 1976).

[12] Paul Ricoeur, *From Text to Action. Essays in Hermeneutics*, trans. by Kathleen Blamey and John B. Thompson (Evanston, Ill.: Northwestern University Press, 1991).

the search for literary works that express, in the form of lived experience, a free commitment to *European ideas*, to works that embody in a 'spontaneous' and 'authentic' (i.e. phenomenologically consistent) manner the very *idea of Europe* (i.e. 'Europe' as notional whole and emotional wholeness).

This perspective calls for an orientation towards forms of consciousness that are not commonly associated with mainstream literary canon-building. One of the existential situations logically expected to stimulate the emergence of the above-mentioned kind of experiences are travels. The consciousness processes of expatriated Europeans are plausible nesting beds for the revelation of 'European-ness'. A delicate but essential question with such an approach is the ability to finely dissociate between genuine European-ness as such and the configuration of Britishness/Englishness, Frenchness, Dutchness, Spanishness or other historically-consolidated (or - dissoluted) global nationalisms. The colonial experience of the dominant European powers has occasioned the birth of powerful literary works that inevitably verge on the topic of coming to terms or to grips with one's own inherited cultural identity. But to what extent such models of personal crisis are consistent with a sense of an overall European identity is a matter that has to be left to a future systematic scrutiny (that will, presumably, encounter many instances of unsurpassable indetermination, and have accordingly to resort rather to educated negotiations than to objective criteria).

Our mapping of the necessary areas of investigation should, then, address the particular historical situation of the European Jews. Even if the historical moment of the civic integration of Jewish communities in the European societies highly varies from one part of the continent to another, Jewish intellectuals and artists have significantly contributed to the modernization processes of all European nations. In so doing, they encountered the difficult dilemma of assimilation (total cultural immersion in a mainstream European ethnicity), versus conservation (preserving their own distinct cultural heritage). This tension generated a dramatic but highly creative gradient of identity-building solutions, which has been attentively studied especially in the case of *fin-de-siècle* Vienna,[13] but whose emergence and significance was certainly pan-European. Some of these solutions (often expressed in innovative literary terms), started from the intense perception of a supranational European spirit. It is beyond doubt that among the works of modern European Jewish writers one could find the most intensely felt, artistically accomplished, and visionary commitment to what we came to call today the 'spiritualization of Europe's inner borders'. The moral candor and generosity of these experiments in consciousness expansion are dramatically

---

[13]   Jacques Le Rider, *Modernité viennoise et crises de l'identité* (Paris: Presses universitaires de France, 1990).

underlined by the dreadful discrimination and later on extermination policies to which the European Jewish communities (including cosmopolitan intellectuals and artists such as those we have just mentioned) were brutally and systematically subjected until the end of World War II. A supranational literary canon built around the idea of *Europe as experience* should necessarily celebrate the contribution of the European Jewish fiction writers who in so many ways are the direct forerunners of our contemporary sense of 'European-ness'.

Another category of authors who would logically be able to spontaneously perceive Europe as a whole, as a homogenous cultural milieu, as an atmosphere or an intensely felt experience is the one of the Euro-enthusiastic non-Europeans. The major implication of this remark being that a canon-oriented phenomenological exploration of the literary bracketing of 'Europe' should necessarily include powerful non-European authors. Their view from without, their supposedly 'alien' gaze is one of the most powerful forces able to produce a unifying emotional substantiation of the concept of Europe. The self-inflicted exile of the American *lost generation* is indicative of the intensity and candidness of the European allegiance of the authors that have been placed under this banner.[14] But, even if in less manifest ways, there are also South American writers and literary works that offer an equally convincing blueprint of European-ness.[15] And the investigation should be extended to expats coming from other areas, such as the Near, Middle, or Far East. It is probable that the European literary canon, as defined in this paper, could profit from considering Turkish, Iranian, Egyptian, Lebanese, Japanese, Korean writers with an important European exposure.

It should also be said that the insider-outsider dialectics that defines European identity has clearly shifted over the time. It might be argued that some of the most charismatic experiences of European 'wholeness' came from cultural areas marginal to or excluded from the core process of European modernization originally associated with Great Britain and France. Germany in the 18th or Spain at the turn of the 19th century offer remarkable examples of how painful complexes of cultural marginality could fuel up artistic-intellectual experiences of daring cosmopolitan self-invention. The same is true for South-East Europe and Russia, where, precisely because of the radical economic marginality and the profound differences in cultural background, the perception of a consistent European Otherness has been the

---

[14]   Noel Riley Fitch, *Sylvia Beach and the Lost Generation: a history of literary Paris in the twenties and thirties* (New York: Norton, 1983).

[15]   Axel Gasquet, *L'intelligentsia du bout du monde: les écrivains argentins à Paris: Mario Goloboff, Luisa Futoransky, Arnaldo Calveyra, Juan José Saer, Silvia Baron Supervielle, Héctor Bianciotti* (Paris: Kimé, 2002).

driving force behind both compensatory ethnic revivalisms and (what is primarily relevant to the present context) militant Westernizing trends.

This provisional listing of phenomenological research opportunities could not be concluded without mentioning the cohesive and simultaneously sublimated perception of 'Europe' developed in different forms by intellectual and artistic counter-elites of Eastern European countries, in their direct or diffuse opposition to the totalitarian Communist state. The alternative culture of Soviet controlled Eastern Europe was, among other things, a literary laboratory that has occasionally distillated highly provocative and passionate representation of a European supranational identity.

3. Federalism, Nation-Building, and the Literary Canon

It is a general assumption that trust is an essential psychic ingredient of all successful social development processes, and that its absence can dramatically boost what economic scientists call the 'transaction costs'. The European Union has reached a turning point where the tacit consensus on matters of values and supranational cultural identity doesn't hold anymore. The enlargement has created a drastic decrease in trust, at the level of bi- or multilateral interactions, but also as far as the future of Europe as a meaningful intellectual project is concerned. Recreating trust is not a goal that could be approached with purely cultural instruments, but cultural policies can play an effective part in this undertaking.

This is the background against which we began to test the possibilities of constructing, from a phenomenological perspective, a supranational, implicitly trans-cultural literary canon. A literary canon, (that is to say an oriented, reflexive selection of a body of powerful and accomplished literary works with a potential to instill values and shape attitudes), deserves the attribute of "European" to the extent that it stands up to the difficulties of the ongoing phase of the integration process. Which means that it cannot simply summarize the existing local consensuses on what is ethnically relevant and representative, it cannot simply confederate historical-national literary establishments already in place. European identity can be but the fruit of a much more daring cultural federalism. This dynamics of risk and opportunity escapes a comfortable addition of finitudes, a regular geometry of ethno-national canonical crystallizations. A transnational European literary canon should therefore be able to manifest the basic cohesive identity that it logically presumes not as a structure, but as a process.

In order to represent something distinct and new, and not a simple transfer of didactic-taxonomic principles from a 'national' to a 'supranational' level, the project of such a canon should not only reflect the alleged emergence of a wider identity, but to reflect *on* it, on its very stakes and its very conditions of possibility. More than that, building a supranational literary canon means to meditate, in the provocative company of literary masterpieces, on the very possibility of the emergence of a European political nation.

WORKS CITED

Anderson, Benedict, *Imagined Communities: Reflections on the Origin and Spread of Nationalism* (London: Verso, 1983)

Bakhtin, Mikhail, *Rabelais and His World.* Translated by Hélène Iswolsky (Bloomington: Indiana University Press, 1984)

Berman, Paul, ed., *Debating P.C.: The Controversy Over Political Correctness on College Campuses* (New York: Dell Publishing, 1992)

Billington, James H., *Fire in the Minds of Men. Origins of the Revolutionary Faith* (New York: Basic Books, 1980)

Buber, Martin, *I and Thou*, trans. by Walter Kaufmann (New York: Touchstone, 1996)

Casement, William, *The Great Canon Controversy: The Battle of the Books in Higher Education* (New Brunswick, N.J.: Transaction Publishers, 1996)

Cornea, Paul, *Originile romantismului românesc. Spiritul public, mişcarea ideilor şi literatura între 1780-1840 (The Origins of Romanian Romanticism. Public spirit, intellectual trends, and literature, 1780-1840)* (Bucharest: Minerva, 1972)

Couliano, Ioan P., *The Tree of Gnosis. Gnostic mythology from early Christianity to modern nihilism* (San Francisco: HarperCollins, 1992)

Fitch, Noel Riley, *Sylvia Beach and the Lost Generation: a history of literary Paris in the twenties and thirties* (New York: Norton, 1983)

Gadamer, Hans-Georg, *Truth and Method*, transl. by J. Weinsheimer and D.G. Marshall (New York: Crossroad, 1989)

Gasquet, Axel, *L'intelligentsia du bout du monde: les écrivains argentins à Paris: Mario Goloboff, Luisa Futoransky, Arnaldo Calveyra, Juan José Saer, Silvia Baron Supervielle, Héctor Bianciotti* (Paris: Kimé, 2002)

Guillory, John, *Cultural Capital: The Problem of Literary Canon Formation* (Chicago and London: The University of Chicago Press, 1993)

Heidegger, Martin, 'Bauen Wohnen Denken' in *Vorträge und Aufsätze* (Frankfurt am Main: Vittorio Klostermann, 2000)

Lévinas, Emmanuel, *Humanisme de l'autre homme* (Montpellier, France: Fata Morgana, 1972)

Manuel, Frank E. and Fritzie P. Manuel, *Utopian Thought in the Western World* (Cambridge, Mass.: Belknap Press, 1979)

Martels, Zweder von, ed., *Travel Fact and Travel Fiction: studies on fiction, literary tradition, scholarly discovery, and observation in travel writing* (Leiden; New York: E.J. Brill, 1994)

Podoabă, Virgil, *Fenomenologia punctului de plecare* (*A Phenomenology of the Starting Point*) (Braşov: Transsylvania University Press, 2008)

Ricoeur, Paul, *From Text to Action. Essays in Hermeneutics*, transl. by Kathleen Blamey and John B. Thompson (Evanston, Ill.: Northwestern University Press, 1991)

Rider, Jacques Le, *Modernité viennoise et crises de l'identité* (Paris: Presses universitaires de France, 1990)

Rushdie, Salman, *Imaginary Homelands: Essays and criticism, 1981-1991* (London: Granta Books; New York: Viking, 1991)

Scarpetta, Guy, *Éloge du cosmopolitisme* (Paris: B. Grasset, 1981)

Schorske, Carl E., *Fin-de-siècle Vienna. Politics and Culture* (New York: Alfred A. Knopf, 1961)

Steiner, George, *Martin Heidegger* (Chicago, Ill.: University of Chicago Press, 1991)

Taylor, Charles, *Sources of the Self. The Making of the Modern Identity* (Cambridge, Massachussets: Harvard University Press, 1989)

Zakythnos, Dionysios A., *The Making of Modern Greece. From Byzantium to Independence* (Oxford: Basil Blackwell, 1976)

Note

I would like to make a special mention of the support I received in the elaboration of this paper from Professor Virgil Podoabă, my esteemed colleague from the Comparative Literature Department of the Transsylvania University in Braşov, Romania. His experience with applying the ever-evolving phenomenological methods to the study of literature, an intellectual commitment he has now been constantly observing for over three decades, is an inestimable source of information and inspiration.

Delia Ungureanu

What to Do about Constructing the Literary Canon: Canonicity and Canonical Criteria

Is it necessary to have a literary canon nowadays? After all deconstructions of modern(ist) constructs in a multicultural and postcolonial age, the literary canon is dismissed as one of the many ideological structures of power which tend to impose a certain view on (literary) history. Defenders of the Modern(ist) and / or Romantic canon will take the word on the aesthetic criterion's behalf and decide to stand against the mainstream. If for them the issue is not the necessity of a literary canon, the criteria which decide the elected and / or the chosen must take the lead, as well as the theory behind it. While Harold Bloom's stand is on the defenders' side, fighting what he coins as 'The School of Resentment' and reloading the Romantic's Western canon with Shakespeare at the centre, Frank Kermode, Robert Alter, Geoffrey Hartman, and John Guillory discuss the problems of the literary canon from both sides of literary and cultural studies, with less nostalgia than Harold Bloom and without his elegiac tone. This analysis looks into the theory and criteria which stand behind the literary canon in the West by comparing Bloom's proposal of a Western Canon with its implicit canon theory to the theoretical approach of the above-cited literary critics and theorists.

Ever since it emerged in the 18th century as a shaking of hands of two rival approaches to literature – aesthetical criticism and historicist criticism –, the literary canon has been nothing but trouble, both for writers and critics and, mainly after the 1990s, for literary theorists, too. The present context of occurrence for the renewed discussion about the canon is the possibility or, for some, like Frank Kermode, even risk, that literary studies might be swallowed up by cultural studies. Danger, risk, or simply a change in the way we perceive cultural products, this conflict between literary studies and cultural studies made the object of Professor Frank Kermode's Tanner Lecture on Human Values, which afterwards was published in the volume *Pleasure and Change: The Aesthetics of the Canon*. Kermode's two lectures on *Pleasure* and *Change* are followed by commentaries by Geoffrey Hartman, John Guillory and Carey Perloff, and a final rejoinder by Kermode.[1] The lecture dating from November 2001, which was published in 2004, came as a response from a theoretical perspective on the ardent

---

[1] Frank Kermode, *Pleasure and Change: The Aesthetics of Canon* (New York: Oxford University Press, 2004).

problem of the literary canon, which took over the intellectual field of discussion in the West after 1990, due to the powerful attack come from the cultural studies, from Feminism, Marxism, Postcolonialism, which dismissed the literary canon as a coercive structure of ideological power, in the good old Foucauldian tradition.

Departing from the idea that the canon is a structure of power, Frank Kermode reinforces and defends the literary canon by going back to the canonicity criteria, which are aesthetically-centered. His theoretical stand dating from 2001 reminds us of Harold Bloom's practical stand from 1994, *The Western Canon*. To Bloom's main typological and canonical criteria – the canonical battle and the canonical strangeness – Frank Kermode responds with the old and indeterminate concept of 'pleasure', i.e. aesthetic reception.

Both Bloom and Kermode share a modern perspective on the canon, while Hartman and Guillory share a post-modern one, as they do not accept (aesthetic) pleasure as the main criterion for canonicity, because it draws too much on Wallace Stevens' 'abysmal instrument' and because it is historically late respectively. Moreover, Guillory, stronger than Hartman in his advocating for dropping out the idea of literary canon altogether, rejects the criterion of 'higher' pleasure to distinguish between the canonical and the non-canonical works. What he dismisses as antidemocratic is the idea of hierarchy, which stands at the canon's very core. To the author of *Cultural Capital: The Problem of Literary Canon Formation*, pleasure is not higher or lower, but simply different.

The canonic criteria are difficult to determine because they involve a definition, more or less restrictive, of literature. Having a set of coherent criteria involves the necessity of a theory for the canon, which, in its turn, is connected to the possibility of finding an answer to the question 'What is literature?' All canon discussions involve three theoretical conceptions of literature: what is literature, what is the theory underlying the historical sense of literature, and what is the history of literary theories.

Kermode, Robert Alter, Hartman and Guillory's theoretical stands raise a series of major literary canon problems, which can be grouped into seven categories: 1. the main canonical criterion: 'Pleasure' (for Kermode); 2. the source of pleasure: object vs. subject, i.e. text vs. reader; 3. the kind of (canonical) pleasure: canonical vs. non-canonical texts, i.e. higher vs. lower pleasure; 4. who canonizes: writer vs. critic; 5. the narrative of canon formation and change: Pleasure – Change – Chance (for Kermode); 6. defining canonicity: *Jouissance* (Pleasure & Dismay), Rewriting, Attention, and Conversation (for Kermode); 7. the theory of canon and change: aesthetic criticism ('unique' standard in judging all texts; reinforces continuity of the literary field; transgression of time) vs. historicist criticism (different standards for past vs. present; reinforces discontinuity of the literary field; fatality of time).

Preceding Kermode's point of view, Bloom's anti-multiculturalist view asserts an aesthetic value-centered canon, a canon that *emerges naturally* and in which the critic is only the observer of an external reality. Bloom's canon involves an order based on an ever different relating of the 'strange', which turns the canon into an integration of the exception. The canon means 're-reading', i.e. revisiting both the predecessors' works in the light of the new writers and the new writers as well. Bloom understands the canon as a relationship between the reader as individual and the writer with everything ever written and not as a list of compulsory books.

In a less acid tone than Bloom's, Kermode dismisses the new methods of literary studies as non-specific for the literary phenomenon: they are borrowed from linguistics, politics, anthropology, psychoanalysis. To this, we can cite Eagleton with a counterargument: literary theory has always borrowed its methods of analysis from other domains, it is not an acquisition of the poststrucuralist paradigm of thought (structuralism borrowed its method from linguistics, phenomenology and reception theory from philosophy, poststructuralism from psychoanalysis or anthropology).

For Kermode, two are the debates risen by the issue of canon: 1. canon as dislodgement and insertion (modern paradigm) and 2. canon as an 'abuse of power' (postmodern paradigm) (Kermode, p. 16). To justify the former, Kermode proposes a narrative of canon formation and change, relying on Wallace Stevens's essays: 'Pleasure', the main criterion for testing a canonical work, 'Changes' from an age to another, sometimes due to a simple, hazardous 'Chance' in what the social, economical, political, and cultural context is concerned. This triad is, for Kermode, the intertwining of the three canonicity criteria.

In Bloom's narrative of the canon, the criteria follow a writer's course towards canonization, from his relation with the tradition until the final acknowledgement: 1. the canonical anxiety and its context of occurrence: the saturation of the literary creativity valences; 2. fighting the predecessors – the *agon*; 3. the canonical strangeness or finding an inimitable, but emulating formula, standing for interiorizing the tradition; 4. the emulation or 'bringing to life' dignified followers, not epigones. This equation is the theory that underlies the canon. For Bloom, the use is refined and more specific, meaning 'overcome anxiety', the only test for canonicity, according to the Yale theorist. Bloom's concept for naming the Romantics' 'originality' is the 'canonical strangeness', a result of the overcome anxiety, where 'anxiety' stands for 'misreading' the grand masters.

Bloom looks into the process that leads from the creative interaction to the achievement of the canonical strangeness. The reader enters a dialogue with Tradition and, feeling the burden of an overwhelming inheritance, he achieves an anxiety of influence, which can transform him into a writer if he enters a battle (influence i.e. interpretation). He can win if he overcomes the burden of the past.

In Harold Bloom's case, the four criteria of canonicity display a theory of the canonizing process itself. They are in a relation of succession and consecutive determination. Although the canonical value is a subjective variable, difficult to capture and describe rationally, Bloom tries to define it as clearly as possible, reducing the arbitrary down to a minimum. Re-reading is implicit with the 1st and 4th criterion. Canonical anxiety appears when the literary creativity valences are saturated. Emulation, the 4th criterion, is a double re-reading: 1. from the past towards the present, the overcome anxiety coinciding with the achievement of a personal *écriture*; 2. from the present towards the future, the strangeness giving birth to new re-readings, both of one's own text and of the grand masters, who are selected once again in the horizon of the literary work. The re-reading i.e. misreading, organizes Bloom's entire equation, giving it a circular, dialectic character. It brings together the 1st and 4th criterion (circular), but also opens a double temporal relation.

When Bloom uses the concepts of 'originality' and 'aesthetical values', he redefines them according to his view of the canon, while Kermode's 'pleasure' remains too undetermined a notion, as Geoffrey Hartman argued. Bloom understands the aesthetical value as 'an interaction between artists' and thus invests it with a process-like component. Bloom escapes the static character of the subjective evaluation – the unquantifiable taste judgment – in order to underline the typological behaviour of the canon: 'the battle' as relating the past and present and vice versa, because not only the new writers choose their predecessors, but mainly it is the predecessors who 'elect' their followers.

Unlike Blooms' 'self-canonization' and 'election' of the canonical works, Kermode turns to the concept of 'chance' to explain the changes occurring in intellectual history: 'My point is that chance, aided by individual formation and the vagaries of personal interest and the interests of interpretive communities, may cause diversions that, in the long run, ensure the total neglect of the road not taken — and this is true of the history of modern literary criticism' (Kermode, p. 18). Chance leads to and explains change, which follows it, it is not simultaneous.

In his glossing the main canonical criterion, pleasure i.e. aesthetic response, Kermode cites Mukařovský: the artifact can be objectively analyzed, but it is only through the contact with a reader that pleasure arises, and together with it, its value. Its pleasure and value lies in the power of the object to transcend and depart from 'the accepted ways of such artifacts'. Bloom's stand is similar: the canon turns into an integration of the exception and the exceptional. What matters is that both Mukařovský and Kermode imagine a mutable pleasure and value. For the former, pleasure lies in the reader and his set of cultural references. For Bloom, pleasure is static and timeless, no matter the social and historical, political, cultural context. Therefore, both Mukařovský and Kermode believe in a mutable pleasure which 'changes' together with the reader. In Bloom, the reader doesn't have this dynamic role, for value is intrinsic to the literary work. Moreover, the doctrine of the elect theorized by Bloom excludes the reader completely from the canon formation. For Mukařovský and Kermode, the value may disappear, while for Bloom, it rests with the object (an essentialist Kantian perspective).

But pleasure glossed as 'aesthetical response' is not enough for Kermode, who takes a step forward and brings Barthes' *jouissance* in discussion (pp. 21-2) when it comes to distinguish between canonical and non-canonical texts. The text which causes *jouissance* to the reader has a plus pain in relation to the text which gives only pleasure. *Jouissance* is therefore connected to the sublime of the German Romantics and is superior to the mere pleasure derived from recognizing the familiar. While the text of pleasure requires some sort of 'social participation', the text producing *jouissance* forbids this, as it is an individual identity experience, manifested as dismay and cannot be talked of without plagiarizing the writer and repeating mimetically his discourse (Kermode, p. 22). '[B]y a peculiar grace, pleasure and loss are coactive in the creation of joy.' '[P]leasure is [...] one key to canonicity' (p. 30). What Kermode names 'loss' in this pleasure appears in Bloom's *Western Canon* as a determiner of his concept of pleasure: the 'difficult' pleasure, of Nietzschean and Burkian origin, arises from the confrontation with the titans and with a painful pleasure, for it dwells on human condition and existential experiences. It is difficult because it creates frustration and it defamiliarizes us with our cultural referential universe.

Like Bloom's canonical strangeness, Kermode's pleasure functions as a universal standard for texts, as Hume's common sense used to do in the 18th century (*Of the Standard of Taste*, 1757, states an *a posteriori* rule to level up the different aesthetical experiences. Hume is very prudent and says that even though beauty is not inherent in the object, the forms and qualities that enable this perception to emerge are).[2] But if there is a standard of taste, then how is change possible?

In terms of the way things change in the canon, Kermode departs from Bloom in that he agrees there is some part of 'chance' involved in canonicity. This matter of chance is totally unacceptable to Bloom, who believes in 'the doctrine of the elect' when it comes to explaining his list of selected writers. For Kermode, chance is usually the basis for the elimination or the

---

[2]   Jonathan Brody Kramnick, *Making the English Canon: Print-Capitalism and the Cultural Past, 1700-1770* (Cambridge: Cambridge University Press, 2004), p. 72.

acceptance of a book in the canon. The chance is for that book to be found, to gain a public's attention, not necessarily a cultivated one, and to become the subject for 'conversation', another concept introduced by Kermode as part of his theory of canon formation. So, in Kermode's theory, the initial starting point is something circumstantial, irrational, and totally hazardous: 'chance'. This idea is not new, as John Gilbert Cooper suggested before, in 1755, in his *Letters Concerning Taste*: what 'Cooper wants to suggest is that taste is an irreducible quality and the aesthetic primary experience that both take precedence over rational cogitation and practical utility' (Kramnick, p. 66).

The 'attention' we pay to a work of art and which includes it into the canon is a consequence of a 'change' in our understanding and taste. Works of art become canonical through an act of 'historical understanding'. Unlike Bloom's essentialist and object-focused canon theory, which reinforces the intrinsic, timeless qualities of the artistic object, Kermode's imagines a contextual shaped artistic value, not object-centered, but rather subject-centered (i.e. the reader). 'Changes in the canon obviously reflect changes in ourselves and our culture' (p. 36). Kermode's statement would definitely be rejected by Bloom, who attributes Shakespeare's artistic value to the intrinsic qualities of his plays and not to the perceiving eye. For Kermode, changes in the canon are actually 'a register of how our historical self-understandings are formed and modified' (p. 36).

Another way of 'changing the canon' is giving a different interpretation, which varies in relation to the reader's context (time, place, cultural referential background, taste, education). In terms of interpretation, Kermode cites Gadamer, who no longer believes, like Schleiermacher, that hermeneutics is about philology and the *intentio auctoris*, but that the reader must accept his own prejudices as well as the fact that his understanding of a text is guided by *intentio lectoris* and the reader's dispositions and habits of interpretation. It is the reader's job to make a text new once again. Unlike Bloom's theory, Kermode's draws a lot on Barthes from *The Pleasure of Text* and on reception theory, mainly Gadamer. While Bloom's theory is textual and object-focused, Kermode's is *con*textual and subject-focused. The text 'must be made to answer to our prejudices, and they are necessarily related to the prejudices of our community, even if in reaction to them' (Kermode, p. 38).

Kermode's modern and somehow reluctant stand runs counter to a deconstructivist's stand like Geoffrey Hartman's. To him, Kermode's criticism is a creative one, thinking that the old can be 'renewed by new forms of attentions' (in Kermode, p. 55). Kermode's discourse is modernist-centered, as his education is. That's why he likes Eliot's theory about going back to the classics in order to modernize them and to bring them back in the present. However, Hartman notes that Kermode is a little ironic when he emphasizes the modernist credo, which is also his: that the new must and will be replaced by new. Kermode's sense of canonical change is called by Hartman 'conservative revolution' (in Kermode, p. 55). Hartman justly remarks that this conservative revolution accounts for the changes in the canon, in Kermode's vision, where the canon is no longer monumental and static, but able to change considering its context of occurrence.

For Kermode, the 'idea of pleasure' is always associated with a 'changing canonicity', in that what actually changes is the reader's habits of reading and perception of the beautiful. Therefore, canonicity changes because the reader's taste in literature changes. So, pleasure is something that can be taught, just like the 18th century thought about taste (Kramnick, p. 65). In this respect, Kermode goes back to German hermeneutics and, more precisely, to Jauss' reception theory. In Hartman's vision, the canon changes due to two different causes: 1. 'the need to refresh perception' (the formalists, the adepts of the eternal 'make it new', even Mukařovský saw art as the transcendence of everyday life, clichés and bourgeois values); 2. time, which imposes sometimes hazardously the necessity to change the way we look at the world and the interpretation of texts (in Kermode, pp. 55-6).

However, Hartman is quite sceptical about Kermode's concept of pleasure as a standard for canonicity, because it 'glides over the abyss': 'Pleasure is a strange word to bear such a strong emphasis: it is surely on the side of Chaucerian "solas" rather than "sentence". Can it really become as sententious as Kermode wishes it to be?' (Hartman in Kermode, p. 57). Hartman is afraid of terms which escape a rational logical definition, and 'pleasure' is more connected to the senses than to reason, ever since the 18th century aesthetic criticism, starting with Shaftesbury's *Characteristicks of Men, Manners, Opinions and Times*, drew on Lockean psychology, with its emphasis on senses and imagination rather than on understanding (Kramnick, pp. 55-6). Hartman is rather reserved in accepting the concept of 'pleasure' and he tends to deconstruct it: pleasure becomes theory only if we think of poetics as theory. What Hartman fears is the laxity of this concept, which, when expanding so generously its limits, turns into what Wallace Stevens calls 'an abysmal instrument'.

Three are the reasons for which Hartman rejects the concept of 'pleasure' as 'changing canonicity': 1. its onomatopoeic pallor – this is a poet's argument, not a critic's (lack of expressivity); 2. its inability to transmit all its historical associations – few concepts can do that. The historical associations are brought by the reader's cultural background, not by a concept; 3. it glides over the abyss – this is actually the true reason for Hartman's mistrust of Kermode's concept (in Kermode, p. 58). For a rational and very Apollonian figure like Hartman, pleasure sounds too Dionysian. Pleasure is too non-descriptive and too vague for it to turn into a technical concept, while the Barthesian association with *jouissance* moves it to the even more dangerous field of sexual experience. The sexual connotation is another reason to be

Delia Ungureanu

cautious about this concept. Mainly due to its Freudian implications: if it produces some kind of sexual pleasure, than it is the product of some repression, and the work of art is anything but disinterested. Secondly, because Barthes' *jouissance* endangers any kind of identity construct.

If Hartman expresses doubt and fear over Kermode's pleasure-centered theory, it is Guillory's turn now to bring the discussion to the field of cultural studies, which he strongly defends as a natural expanding of literary studies. In today's literary criticism, the literary object has come to be thought of in social, historical and political terms, which leaves out the old pleasure effect as something to be embarrassed about. It is a correlative to the movement away from the representation of the literary object as aesthetic value-centered.

The political turn in literary criticism is not new; it has been going on since the 16th century, when humanists, who were mainly philologists, became interested in the social, ethics and politics (Guillory in Kermode, p. 67). What Guillory emphasizes is the continuity in literary history and on this point he departs from Kermode, who thinks that this political turn is a consequence of poststructuralist thought. This is because, although very balanced in his discourse, Kermode has a sense of the 'ending' of literature, which is expressed also by Bloom with his chaotic age. But pessimism is not that pessimistic. Even the nostalgic and elegiac Bloom waits for a new theocratic age to come.

Unlike Hartman, Guillory accepts the concept of pleasure as a standard for canonical works, but he departs from Kermode when stating that the aesthetical pleasure is not 'higher' in degree than other kinds of more immediate pleasure. This is because Guillory does not claim for cultural criticism the authority it had a century ago over economy and politics and social criticism. This authoritarianism of culture culminated with Matthew Arnold and I.A. Richards' privileging poetry over all literary products (a late Romantic reminiscence). In fact, Guillory's position invites not to classify literary products in the hierarchical terms of the very best, but to a rather relaxed way of simply 'comparing' these products in terms of what the 'difference' between them is, not which is best.

Therefore, cultural criticism has developed another strategy nowadays, retreating from poetry in order to claim authority over mass culture (Guillory in Kermode, p. 69). And it is from this point that all the problems about the canon emerged, according to Guillory. To Guillory, cultural studies are a continuation of Carlyle, Arnold, Eliot, and Richards' work in that they propose a criticism of society. Guillory cites Jean-Marie Schaeffer with his *Art of the Modern Age*, where the critic attributes the failing of the aesthetic value to the overburdening with monumentality of the high arts: poetry, painting, sculpture, music. 'It was as a result of this philosophical overburdening of high art that aesthetic pleasure became so vulnerable to moralistic or political neutralization' (in Kermode, p. 69). Jonathan Brody Kramnick argues that the principle of art was endowed, in the 18th century, with a theoretical and philosophical importance (p. 54).

Monumentalizing the work of art kills aesthetic pleasure. A monument of art doesn't ask for pleasure in the receiver, but for admiration. Guillory's suggestion is hence to remove the status of 'high' pleasure from the work of art so that aesthetical pleasure can be experienced again. Guillory reinforces the rhetoric of tolerance, of the I and the Other, simply different, but willing to enter a democratic dialogue. To say today that a work of art has either 'salvational effects' or 'philosophical profundity' is out of fashion, 'too late historically' (Guillory in Kermode, p. 70).

Instead, the aesthetical pleasure, i.e. 'beauty' for Guillory, has been extended to large cultural and civilization manifestations. Therefore, for Guillory, unlike for Hartman, there is no problem in enlarging the referential domain for the concept of aesthetical pleasure. For Kermode, aesthetic pleasure is a distinguished type of pleasure from other pleasure experiences, as a mixture of pleasure and dismay. This 'higher' pleasure would thus be reserved for canonical texts only.

Kermode used Wallace Stevens' concepts of 'change' and 'pleasure' from *Notes toward a Supreme Fiction*, leaving out a third concept, to which Guillory now appeals: 'abstraction'. Any canonical work of art should answer these three criteria. To Guillory, abstraction is another symptom of the project of poetry's supremacy, and a means of rendering philosophical profundity.

To Kermode's citing Eliot and his touchstones with their mixture of sexual and aesthetical pleasure, which are actually one and the same, Guillory responds with a citation from Empson, who dismisses Eliot's touchstones as individual, idiosyncratic canons. Guillory thus points out the great jeopardy rising from building a literary canon widely accepted: the jeopardy to generalize idiosyncratic literary experiences. Even more ironic and acid, Guillory considers Eliot's touchstones 'the expression of an individual pathology' (in Kermode, p. 74). In conclusion, the aesthetic experience cannot function as the one and only criterion for 'evaluation or canonicity', as Kermode would like it to.

'My response to this uncertainty would be to retreat from attempting to make the connection between the quality of pleasure and the judgment of canonicity, and further to withdraw the claim that aesthetic pleasures are in any defensible sense "higher pleasures"' (Guillory in Kermode, p. 74). This makes all canonical selection suspicious and one should take them all with a grain of salt.

Guillory's conclusion to his comment is highly astonishing: after arguing slightly polemically on behalf of the democratization of (aesthetic) pleasure and after avoiding very elegantly the issue of canon, which was actually

Kermode's prime interest in the two lectures, he breaks it off very bluntly. 'Canonicity' is thus a high 'risk' which literary texts, capable of becoming monumental, run. Canonicity is no longer something to be desired and cherished, but something to be avoided as a grand peril for genuine aesthetical pleasure. So, in Guillory's theory, canonicity destroys rather than distinguishes a text, because being distinguished is no longer a quality, but a fault. His plea for generosity, for difference and no hierarchy is actually a plea for leaving behind what we used to call 'literary canon', because it discriminates against other types of pleasure, such as the pleasure for the mass culture, for travelling or eating or making love.

Hence, 'Works of art will escape the annulment of their pleasures, the effect of monumentalization that is always the risk of their elevation to the status of canonicity' (Guillory in Kermode 2004: 75). If we were to sustain Guillory's argument, one could quote Jonathan Culler's relaxed and optimistic vision of today's open canon expressed in *Literary Theory: A Very Short Introduction*. What has changed is the field covered by the study of literature, which is reflected in the opening of the canon: 'What has changed is an interest in choosing works to represent a range of cultural experiences as well as a range of literary forms'.[3] Similarly to Guillory's argument, Culler does not prevent us from canonizing works of art lest we should monumentalize them.

After Hartman dismissed Kermode's notion of pleasure as too 'abyssal' to function and after Guillory attacked the very core of a literary canon, i.e. hierarchy, Robert Alter defends Kermode's theory because he defines the literary canon in a very similar way: 'A canon, after all, constitutes itself as a trans-historical community of texts, and it lives its cultural life through a constant dynamic interplay between each new text and an unpredictable number of antecedent texts and formal norms and conventions' (Robert Alter in Kermode 2004: 7).

Robert Alter argues that the idea of dismay or loss detaches literary pleasure from physical pleasure and it draws on the philosophical contents of literature, which reflects on human existence. With Bloom, however, the dismay refers rather to the authors who feel frustrated when reading canonical writers than to the reader himself and it is associated to the experience of '*la chair est triste, hélas, et j'ai lu tous les livres*', an exhaustion of the creative literary valences, which leaves none for the reader who wants to turn into a writer.

For Hartman, this intertwining of happiness and dismay in canonical works covers the same semantic and cultural area as the concept of the sublime (Romantic paradigm of representation), by no means different from

---

[3]   Jonathan Culler, *Literary Theory: A Very Short Introduction* (New York: Oxford University Press, 2000), p. 49.

Barthes' *jouissance*. Robert Alter, in his turn, warns us that not all canonical texts respond to the concept of the sublime. The two exceptions are the literature of daily life (satiric poetry, novels, drama) and comedy. They involve an 'adult sort of pleasure' (Robert Alter in Kermode, p. 9), which does not mean 'higher', like Kermode would want it. These works do not express loss or dismay, yet they afford pleasure.

From these exceptions, we gather that there are different kinds of 'literary' pleasure (not different kinds of mere pleasure, like for Guillory) because there are different sources of literary pleasure. In this, Robert Alter departs from Bloom, who uses the same concept of canonical strangeness to refer to both tragedies like *King Lear* and to Molière's comedies. Bloom doesn't go beyond this canonical strangeness to make it explicit and define it, because he does not differentiate between various forms of sources which produce this canonical strangeness. Robert Alter distinguishes between the 'seriousness' involved in the sublime (happiness & dismay) and the 'playfulness': play with language, forms of speech which other canonical texts display (in Kermode, p. 100). In Bloom, there are four criteria to which all his 26 elected writers seem to respond. The canonical strangeness is understood as a sum of: 1. a strong sense of innovative and figurative language; 2. originality; 3. cognitive power; 4. knowledge and exuberance in style.[4] However, not all his elected writers display all these components: Tolstoy responds to 3, but not to 1. Jane Austen responds to 1 and 4, but not so much to 2.

According to Robert Alter, in Bloom's theory, playfulness has no role whatsoever and neither in Kermode, Guillory and Hartman's sense of pleasure, as if pleasure couldn't be afforded by literature which aims at playfulness rather than at seriousness, although neither of them is Bloomian. To Kermode, literary studies have developed not an un-canonical reading, but rather a 'strange' view of the canon. He is not as polemic and acid as Bloom, but the conclusion he reaches stays the same.

Robert Alter proposes a more optimistic view of the canon and in this he is followed by Carey Perloff, Artistic Director of San Francisco's American Conservatory Theatre: 'Pleasure, then, does prove to be one reasonably serviceable criterion for the canonical' (Robert Alter in Kermode, p. 12).

The literary canon is not only useful nowadays, but also necessary. Not as a battle stand against cultural studies, because the only battle remains the 'canonical battle', but as a cultural memory able to stimulate a creative reception. Pleasure and dismay, and, yes, playfulness, as Robert Alter puts it, stay at the very heart of canonicity as a distinguished experience which orders and makes hierarchies among cultural products. Without a hierarchy,

---

[4]   Harold Bloom, *Canonul occidental* (*The Western Canon*), trans. by Delia Ungureanu (Bucharest: Art Publishing, 2007), p. 55.

as John Guillory's comment entails, there would be no competition among writers and, consequently, nothing to fight for, no arena where the challengers can meet the champions *en titre*.

WORKS CITED

Bloom, Harold, *Canonul occidental* (*The Western Canon: The Books and School of the Ages*) (Bucureşti: Art, 2007)

Culler, Jonathan, *Literary Theory: A Very Short Introduction* (New York: Oxford University Press, 2000)

Kermode, Frank, *Pleasure and Change: The Aesthetics of Canon* (New York: Oxford University Press, 2004)

Kramnick, Jonathan Brody, *Making the English Canon: Print-Capitalism and the Cultural Past, 1700-1770* (Cambridge: Cambridge University Press, 2004)

Adina Ciugureanu

From Art to Literature: Towards a Counter-Canonical Canon?

Any discussion of the canon should probably start from its initial use in the visual arts where it established itself as a grid of proportions which the artist should observe in order to represent, as realistically as possible, the surrounding world. Though the primary meaning of the 'canon' (Gr. Kanón) was literally a measuring rod or rule, hence the grid of measures that any artist knew, the later connotations of the canon included its applications to ecclesiastic law, the church, ethics, art, music and, obviously, literature. The purpose of this article is twofold: to foreground the connection between the canon in the visual arts and its use in literature and to argue that the shifts in the canon in both art and literature have caused the rise and growth of a counter-canon common to both, which, apparently, has replaced what is ordinarily called 'the traditional canon'.

.

Any discussion of the canon should, I think, start from its initial use in the visual arts where it established itself as a grid of proportions which the artist should observe in order to represent, as realistically as possible, the surrounding world. Though the primary meaning of the 'canon' (Gr. *Kanón*) was literally a measuring rod or rule, hence the grid of measures any artist knew, the later connotations of the canon included its applications to ecclesiastic law, the church, ethics, art, music and, obviously, literature. The purpose of this article is twofold: to foreground the connection between the canon in the visual arts and its use in literature and to argue that the shifts in the canon in both art and literature have produced the rise and growth of a counter-canon common to both, which, apparently, has replaced what we might call the traditional canon.

1. The canon and ancient visual art

Though etymologically, the word 'canon' is usually associated with Greek language and art, its origin does not lie in Greece, but in Egypt.[1] According to Erik Iversen, it was old Egyptian art that first advanced 'a proper theory of human proportions', which 'developed into an artistic canon determining the

---

[1]   Erik Iversen, 'The Canonical Tradition' in *The Legacy of Egypt*, ed. by J.R. Harris (Oxford: Clarendon Press, 1971), pp. 55-82.

ratios of the various parts of the body' (Iversen, p. 56), with a view to mirroring natural proportions. Thus, the basic unit in the Egyptian measurement system was the cubital armlength from the elbow to the tip of the thumb, known as 'the forearm', which was divided, according to natural proportions into 6 palms or handbreaths measured on the back of the hand across the knuckles. One handbreath represented four fingers, unless it was a full handbreath, which represented four fingers and the thumb. The full handbreath was also called the royal handbreath and was used as the basic unit of measurement in the visual representation of the body in art. To comply with the natural proportions, the Egyptians invented a grid divided into 18 squares, representing the geometrical projection of the canon, against which they drew (or carved) the body from foot to hairline (Fig. 1).

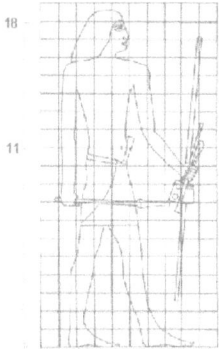

Fig. 1   Fig. 2

(Seated figure and the Saite canon)

The body was drawn on both sides of an axis, which divided it into two equal parts and went from the foot to the top of the head along 18 squares. Each square is the equivalent of one full handbreath, representing a clenched fist with thumb, the ideal body measuring 18 full handbreaths in height. Even when the figure was seated the artist followed the canonical representation, placing the squares 6 to 10 on a horizontal line. If the figure were straightened out along the axis, it would be 18 squares long. Irrespective of the size of the figures, they were drawn by observing the same rules (Fig. 2).

As Iversen points out, 'the same method was used to construct any other type of figure and to make every single gesture, movement, and position, however stylized or complex, conform with the system of proportions' so that the canon developed into an 'enormous code' which lay at the basis of Egyptian art for over two millennia (Iversen, p. 65). Yet, during the Twenty-sixth Dynasty, round about the sixth century BC, the divisions of the old canon change slightly by enlarging the basic unit of measurement which leads to the growth in length of the body representation from 18 to 21 squares. It is the new canon, known as Saite, (because the capital of Egypt was at Saite at that time) that was considered more relevant than the former in its more 'realistic' representation of the human body that seems to have impacted Greek art (Fig. 2).

The Egyptian influence was strongly felt in Crete and Greece where artists took over the canonical representations of the body, yet paying more attention to the harmonious proportion of its component parts than to the strict compliance with measurement. Although the idea of the immutability of the canon as well as of its stable regularity is still to be found with Plato, the concept of beauty in connection with symmetry and proportion is more and more voiced among the Greeks and the Romans, thus adding a strong aesthetic, besides the technical, dimension to art. The patterns were still preserved, but the focus in art was less on measurement and more on symmetry and eurhythmy which were considered as an intrinsic condition to expressing the 'real' nature of beauty. It also opened the way, as Iversen claims, for a new relation between the artist and the subject in space and time and to shifts of perspective which, in their turn, reduced the inflexibility of the canon to a more theoretical standard against which deviations could be measured (Iversen, p. 80). However, these 'deviations' or 'innovations' within the canon were meant to be more suggestive of spiritual values and to enhance a higher aesthetic dimension in the search of perfection both in the human body itself and in its artistic representation.

2. The canon and its 'deviations'

Under the influence of the Saite canon, the Greek sculptor Polycleitus (late fifth and early fourth century BC), did not change the proportions, but shifted to reveal greater anatomical accuracy (Iversen, p. 78). However, Polycleitus became really famous when he 'deviated' from the strict rules of body representation and 'invented' the *counterpoise* (Fig. 3), which shows the human figure standing with its weight on one foot, ready for action, or on the contrary, suggesting relaxation.

Adina Ciugureanu

Fig. 3

Polycleitus: A marble copy of the *Doryphoros*, an early
example of classical *counterpoise*.

The Saite canon was also revised and changed by the
Roman architect and engineer Vitruvius (end of the first
century BC) who inserted the human body with extended
arms and legs in a circle, then in a square, counting 21
smaller squares both on the vertical and on the horizontal
lines (Fig. 4). Vitruvius's point was to demonstrate the
perfection of architecture through the perfection of the
human body: whether placed in a square or in a circle, the diagonals will
always cross the very middle of the body that is the navel. Against the
obvious influence of the Saite canon (21 squares), Vitruvius brings in a new
interpretation: the human body is built in such a way to fit the two
geometrical forms that render architecture perfect – the circle and the square.
It thus becomes the symbol of beauty and perfection.

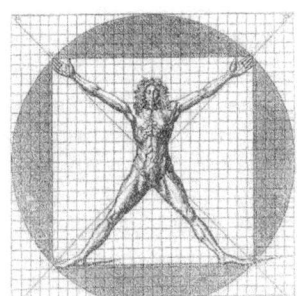

Fig. 4

Leonardo da Vinci's *Homo Vitruvianus*, 1521

Both the canon of Polycleitus and that of
Vitruvius, echoing the Egyptian tradition, were revived by the artists of the
Renaissance and became a distinct feature in Western art, mainly with
Leonardo and Michelangelo. Before reproducing *Homo Vitruvianus* in the
Italian edition of 1521 (Fig. 4), Leonardo played with it thirty years earlier,
by superimposing the circle on the square to suggest the possibility of motion
from one position to another (Fig. 5). Also, Leonardo did not insert the whole
square in the circle, as Vitruvius did, but left its corners outside, which added
to the impression of movement and dynamism, like a cartoon drawing.

Fig. 5

Leonardo da Vinci: *the Vitruvian Man*, 1490, also known as 'The canon of proportions'

Moreover, Leonardo deviates from Vitruvius's representation by depicting, in their proper historical ratio and drawn to scale, nine historical units of measurement known at the time in Europe (the Yard, the Span, the Cubit, the Flemish Ell, the English Ell, the French Ell, the Fathom, the Hand, the Foot as represented in Fig. 6). In his depiction, Leonardo also uses the Egyptian handbreadth which brings us back to the classical Egyptian canon of pre-Saite times. Yet, the novelty of the drawing lies both in its focusing on dynamic movement and in demonstrating that, whatever units of measurement one may use, the final composition of the body is the same, therefore it is perfect and central to our understanding of the universe. By joining, in a single picture, all the possible units of measurement known at his time, Leonardo seems to argue that our whole understanding of the world is made through the lenses of proportions. Yet the classical proportions could be changed if the artist's intention is to draw the viewer's attention on inner motion or feelings that cannot be expressed through measurement.

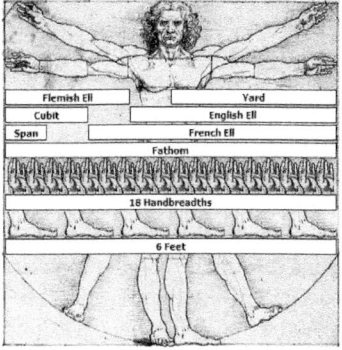

Fig. 6

A similar attitude, with a somewhat different effect, can be detected in Michelangelo's *David* (1504) (Fig. 7). *David*'s posture owes a lot to Polycleitus in the perfect use of the *counterpoise*. Michelangelo did not visualize the Biblical hero in the relaxed and triumphant pose after defeating the giant, as was customary at the time, but immortalized him in the tense moment before the launching of the stone, which could not last, in real time, more than a second. Moreover, Michelangelo deviates from the canon of proportions by turning David into a giant (5.17 m high) and by making his head and hands too big and out of proportion compared to the other parts of the body. This 'innovation' is meant to focus the viewer's attention on what the head and hands symbolize (Thought and Action) rather than on the canonical representation of a young male body.

Fig. 7   *Fig. 8*

Michelangelo: *David*, 1504   Diego Velásquez: *Las Meninas*, 1656

Deviations from the norm, be it 'the canon of proportions' in Leonardo's vision or the technique of reproducing it (color, perspective), are not only recurrent in visual arts throughout centuries, but also the background against which new canons have been established. The fresher and more striking the deviation is, the more famous the work of art seems to become. A relevant example to this point is Velasquez's *Las Meninas* (1656) (Fig. 8), a 'canonical' work which breaks the rules of canonical theme and perspective – the depiction of the King and Queen of Spain (to be seen in the mirror), by shifting the focus from what should have been central to the painting to the sudden intruders and unexpected viewers of the work: the dwarfs, the Infanta, the ladies-in-waiting, the servants, Velasquez's relative in the door, the painter himself facing the double viewers: the King and Queen, reflected in the mirror, and, virtually, ourselves. Described as the 'theology of painting' by a fellow Italian painter in the 17th century and as the 'philosophy of art' in 18th century England, Velasquez's *Las Meninas* challenges the baroque canon with a number of innovations which will ignite Picasso's imagination to play with them in his own representation of *Las Meninas* (1957) (Fig. 9), and Michel Foucault's to devote a whole chapter to the painting in his *Order of Things* (1966).

Fig. 9

Pablo Picasso: *Las Meninas*, 1957

For Foucault, *Las Meninas* contains the first signs of a new episteme or way of thinking, in European art. It represents a mid-point between what he sees as the two 'great discontinuities' in art history, namely the classical and the modern. As he himself points out with reference to the painting, there may exist, in this painting by Velázquez, 'the representation as it were of Classical representation, and the definition of the space it opens up to us'.[2] This leads the viewer to a fresh understanding of representation which, Foucault says, 'freed finally from the relation that was impeding it, can offer itself as representation in its pure form' (p. 18).

It is this new definition of representation and the opening up of space that Picasso exploits in his series of paintings inspired from *Las Meninas*. Though the deviations from the canonical representation of the human body are more than obvious, Picasso still preserves the seven layers (or zones) of composition on the canvas which caused the debate on the relation between space and representation in Velásquez's painting with Foucault.[3]

A number of conclusions can be drawn so far as regards the canon and visual arts: (1) that there cannot be one canon, but several, therefore canon

---

[2]   Michel Foucault, *The Order of Things* (London and New York: Routledge, 2004), p. 17.

[3]   The painting seems to be divided into seven layers or zones, like a stage set for performance: the first represents the figures of the large dog and male dwarf on the right. The second zone contains the figures of the Infanta and her maids and dwarf. The third zone is occupied by the artist himself with the chaperone and guard set slightly behind him; the fourth zone is defined by the rear wall with its rows of paintings. The fifth zone is represented by the figure in the open door. The sixth zone is located in the depth of the mirror on the rear wall, which, like all mirror images seems to project the painting itself outward into the space of the viewer, thus creating a seventh zone in which both the viewer and the king and queen stand.

should be referred to in the plural; (2) that the European canons, set up by various deviations from the original canon, are tributary to ancient Egypt; (3) that the deviations were established by a change in perspective and proportion as well as in attitude rather than by mere changes in measurement; that the turn to the 20th century (Cezanne, Picasso, Braques, Brancusi) has established a counter-canonical (or anti-canonical) canon, which, like the counter-poise revived by Michelangelo, shifts the focus on the dynamic dimension of art through the use of color, proportion and perspective.

3. The (counter-)canon and the written arts

However strange this may seem, representation in visual arts can be used as analogy or as metaphor for representation in written arts, whether by this we mean, generically, literature or cultural discourse. In his *Order of Things,* Foucault dwells on the theory that there was a radical similitude between language and the things expressed by it in the pre-Babel language. This was lost in post-Babel languages, yet was preserved in Hebrew, the only language in which things and names still bear an 'immediate resemblance' (Foucault, p. 41). Initially, written language was ideographic or ideogrammic, which created a much stronger connection between image, word, thing, and meaning. An example to this effect is the love poem inscribed on the Nacht-Sobek papyrus, the second millennium BC, whose deciphering and translation may not have caused so many problems of interpretation then compared to present day translations of the poem facing both language and cultural misappropriation and misunderstanding. David Damrosch's ample analysis of the possible versions and translation problems of old Egyptian literary texts is a revealing example to this effect.[4]

On the other hand, in his discussion of the relation between words and their representational capacity to name things, Foucault finds fault with the shift that occurred at the end of the 17th century in the system of signs in the Western world from ternary to binary. The former was used from antiquity to the end of the Renaissance, the latter, according to him, from the 17th century to our postmodern world. In the ternary system of the classical age, the signifier and the signified are connected by 'conjuncture', which articulates language to the 'things' represented by it; in the binary system of the modern age, language becomes autonomous, severed from 'conjuncture', and therefore less representational. The effect of modern thought expressed through language lies in the necessity of the analysis of meaning and signification. As Foucault states, with modern thought 'the profound kinship

---

4   David Damrosch, *What is World Literature?* (Princeton and Oxford: Princeton University Press, 2003), pp. 147-69.

of language with the world was thus dissolved' (Foucault, p. 47). Hence, the translation problems one may encounter with ancient and medieval texts.

If in the visual arts the canon was usually connected to measurement and proportion, in the literary field, according to Harold Bloom, the canon (the Western one) originally meant the choice of books in teaching institutions, with the Christian Bible held in the highest esteem in all ages with, maybe, the exception of the modern and postmodern ones.[5] Bloom describes four 'ages' in the literature of the world which, more or less, correspond with the major 'ages' in visual arts, and, generally, in culture, in the sense that an 'invention' or 'innovation' in technique or in perspective or the re-visitation of older techniques and perspectives triggered schools, periods, movements. Though Bloom confesses to have been influenced by Vico's division of civilization into ages in organizing his study,[6] he is equally tributary to Eliot's view on tradition. Bloom's concept of 'canonical memory', which he develops in Chapter 10 of *The Western Canon* strongly recalls "the historical sense' in Eliot's *Tradition and the Individual Talent*. Bloom's naming Petrarch and Wordsworth as the two great figures to have 'invented' Renaissance poetry (the former) and modern poetry (the latter), which 'has been a continuum for two full centuries now' (Bloom, p. 239) reminds one of Eliot's description of 'the historical sense', a perception which compels man to write 'with a feeling that the whole of the literature of Europe from Homer and within it the whole of the literature of his own country has a simultaneous existence and composes a simultaneous order'.[7]

Moreover, Bloom's use of the word 'invent' regarding two major breakthroughs in lyrical poetry (Petrarch and Wordsworth), which resulted in the rise of two different ages: the Aristocratic and the Democratic, may be paralleled by 'inventions' or 'deviations' in visual art, crucial for the establishing of Renaissance art (Leonardo, Michelangelo) and modern art (Velásquez). Yet, the fourth age that Bloom describes as 'chaotic' is, to my mind, more problematic as it encompasses a large number of twentieth century writers and texts which have long become canonical, having been included in anthologies, textbooks, literature curricula, referred to by critics or turned into film scripts and made popular to large audiences (Joyce, Woolf, Beckett, Hardy, Wells, Galsworthy, Lawrence, Foster, Orwell, Dreiser, Fitzgerald, Hemingway, to mention only mainstream Anglo-American writers, and the list can go on and on). Bloom does not seem to be

---

[5]   Harold Bloom, *The Western Canon* (London: Macmillan, 1995), p. 15.

[6]   Giambattista Vico divided civilization into three ages: the divine, the heroic, and the human.

[7]   T.S. Eliot, 'Tradition and the Individual Talent' in *Selected Prose of T.S. Eliot*, ed. by Frank Kermode (London and Boston: Faber and Faber, 1975), p. 38.

interested in finding criteria to classify twentieth-century writers, besides his prophecy of 'periods' and 'multiculturalism'. Nor does he show too much interest in 20th century literature compared to the traditional, canonical authors of the previous ages: Shakespeare, Dante, Cervantes, Milton, Whitman, Dickenson, Dickens, George Eliot, Tolstoy, Ibsen, besides Petrarch and Wordsworth. His Chaotic Age seems to have collected works in an anti-canon, or a counter-canon in which texts by Joyce, Proust, Beckett, Woolf and Pessoa are mainly regarded as tributary to previous canonical texts, as if still struggling with the 'anxiety of influence'.

Returning to Foucault and his theory of representation in language, one cannot resist correlating it to Jacques Derrida's undermining any graphic mode of representation (word or image) of a pre-existent reality in his *Of Grammatology*, published in 1967, one year after Foucault's *Order of Things*. Moreover, like Foucault, Derrida questions the assumption that word / image and world coincide and that word / image and deed are one. Yet, Derrida goes further and, by analyzing the basic binary oppositions which structure our world and our understanding of it, he introduces the term "supplement," which he applies to the second term of the opposition in an attempt to reveal an existing tense relation in the pair. The second term of the opposition (e.g. 'chaos' in order-chaos) is not only secondary because it is artificial and incomplete, but it also reveals an almost irreconcilable relation to the former term ('order'). Bloom's lists of authors and texts reflect, arguably, the order-chaos dichotomy of Derrida's theory if we considered the first three ages (Theocratic, Aristocratic and Democratic) as canonical and the Chaotic one as counter-canonical. Thus, the texts thrown into the large pool of the chaotic, read as forming the counter-canon, could be easily described as a supplement to the canon. Yet, unlike most major binary pairs (order-chaos, good-evil, nature-culture), which also imply an opposition between positive and negative values, the canon/counter-canon opposition reveals a more fluid relation between the terms, even, to a large extent, free of ethical judgments.

While Harold Bloom struggles with ways of reconciling order and chaos in the Western Canon, David Damrosch seems to solve the problem of the canon(s) by establishing the concept of 'world literature' by which he reconciles, or at least he attempts to do so, the Anglo-American canon, written in English, with 'national literatures' whose contribution to world literature and, therefore to the establishing of canons, depends on translation. The concept of 'world literature', grounded on three factors (the world, the text, and the reader), is, according to Damrosch, 'an elliptical refraction of national literatures' and 'writing that gains in translation'. Yet, it 'is not a set of texts, but a mode of reading, a form of detached engagement with worlds beyond our own place and time' (Damrosch, p. 281). By focusing on reception, be it critical or popular, and by encouraging the dissemination and circulation of national literatures through translation, Damrosch enlarges the meaning of 'world literature' through the acceptance of any text that is relevant, in a way or another, to the understanding of a certain period in history or in culture. The meaning he gives to 'world literature' could be comparable to Derrida's famous 'arche-writing'. Like Derrida's term that encompasses 'speaking' and 'writing', thus solving the tension between them, 'world literature' is a sort of *arche*-canon that covers both the canonical and the non-canonical.

The constant 'deferring' of the canon *in stricto senso* has as a result a shift of balance from the canonical to the counter-canonical, by which we should not understand the giving up on the canon, but its continuous revaluation, the featuring of its dynamism at the expense of its fixity (as in the poise-counterpoise move invented by Polycleitus). In this sense, and only in this sense, we are struggling, as we have been for the past decades, both as academics and common readers, with a counter-canonical canon.

WORKS CITED

Bloom, Harold, *The Western Canon* (London: Macmillan, 1995)

Damrosch, David, *What is World Literature?* (Princeton and Oxford: Princeton University Press, 2003)

Foucault, Michel, *The Order of Things* (London and New York: Routledge, 2004)

Harris, J.R., ed., *The Legacy of Egypt* (Oxford: Clarendon Press, 1971), 55-82

Kermode, Frank, ed., *Selected Prose of T.S. Eliot* (London and Boston: Faber and Faber, 1975)

Note

Research for Adina Ciugureanu's article *From Art to Literature: Towards a Counter-Canonical Canon?* has been partially supported by UEFISCSU grant no. 820/2009 [code 1223] for a research project titled *The Cultural Institution of Literature from Early to Late Modernity in British Culture.*

Simona Drăgan

Episteme and Literary Canon.
A Parallel between Michel Foucault and Harold Bloom

My paper proposes a theoretical analysis and parallel between the two widespread concepts of *episteme* and (literary) canon, which are mostly related to the theories of two scholars, Michel Foucault and Harold Bloom, and particularly to their books *Les mots et les choses* (*The Order of Things*, 1966) and, respectively, *The Western Canon: The Books and School of the Ages* (1994). Both the aforementioned theorists divided these theoretical constructs into periods, and a parallel between the two concepts should not ignore the approximate intrinsic order, as well as periodicity of both *epistemes* and literary canons, which is much more striking as not only Bloom, but also Foucault refers, more or less overtly, to four *epistemes*/ literary canons and expresses the same doubts with respect to the last. My paper focuses on the interplay of similarities and dissimilarities between their theories and findings, on the complementariness proven by their central points and targets, and notes that, in the end, there is a point when the different, even antagonistic stands of Michel Foucault and Harold Bloom finally seem to come to an agreement.

Over the last decades the concepts of *episteme* and, respectively, (literary) *canon* have been mostly related to the theories of two scholars, Michel Foucault (b. 1926- d. 1984) and Harold Bloom (b. 1930), and particularly connected to their books *Les mots et les choses* (*The Order of Things,* 1966) and, respectively, *The Western Canon: The Books and School of the Ages* (1994). A theoretical parallel between *episteme* and canon could be grounded firstly on the approximate constitutive order of both epistemes and literary canons, and secondly, on the tendency that the two theorists manifested toward dividing these theoretical constructs into periods. No need to mention that the interplay of similarities and dissimilarities between them, and the complementarity proven by their central points and targets, make these famous theoretical concepts very rewarding in a comparative approach, while, on the other hand, the different, even antagonistic stands of Michel Foucault and Harold Bloom finally seem to come to an agreement.

It is interesting to note from the very beginning that *episteme* is a concept applied to 'science', while canon refers to 'literature' (even when it includes philosophers or very old religious and historical works, it is exclusively interested in their aesthetic values). And yet, despite this striking difference, it is quite intriguing to note that both aforementioned theorists set out four epistemes and, respectively, four canonical ages, which cannot help us wonder if they are somehow related or not, insofar as they reflect the two

sides of mankind's spirituality (its scientific evolution and its artistic life).
Let us make it clear that these concepts are neither total nor global, since they
only refer to particular sciences and, respectively, to literature of all arts
(excluding, for instance, visual arts or other artistic forms of human
manifestation) and, last but not least, they mostly account for Europe, which
makes them fallible and open to criticism. This fact has already been proven
by all the big questions raised around them, but no serious scholar has yet
denied their applicability and exportability, or at least their improvable
character to a better use or purpose. It is nice to see that even people who
disregard these concepts, considering them outdated or irrelevant or just too
pretentious, sometimes appeal to them in their commentaries about present
cultural phenomena.

                                        *

To start from a definition, it is obvious, as I anticipated, that epistemes and
canons belong with very different fields of spirituality. 'Episteme', on the
one hand, is a scientific term, seen as a virtual system which opens a
possibility for knowledge in a particular historical age. This concept was
theorized in the first part of Foucault's activity, which is closely connected to
his interest for structuralism. In *Les mots et les choses*, 1966 (*The Order of
Things. An Archaeology of the Human Sciences*), Foucault defines three
epistemes, namely three virtual fields of knowledge, which anticipate the
proper emergence of historical ideas. In outlining the Renaissance, Classical,
and Modern episteme, the concept of episteme refers to a homogeneous
dissemination of certain discursive laws in a few scientific fields, organized
according to the same principles. For instance, Foucault thinks that the
Renaissance overrates Resemblance against any other forms of knowledge,
while the Classical episteme, to give another example, makes Representation
its ultimate principle (in linguistics, literature, natural history, etc.).

Yet despite his 'epistemological' interests, Foucault, like artists, deems
language the load-bearing structure of all changes. Starting his demonstration
with the Renaissance, he finds that this age perceived human language as a
hidden natural entity, a 'writing of things',[1] while the knowledge of the time
was a mixture of erudition and magic, which attempted to restore this
primary language concealed in the very heart of the world. With the 'Port-
Royal Logic' (1662), a binary system of the linguistic sign was set, which
anticipated Saussure's linguistic theories; the language entered the era of
representation and was established as 'discourse', defined by Foucault

---

[1]   Michel Foucault, *The Order of Things. An Archaeology of the Human Sciences* (London and
      New York: Routledge Classics, 2001), p. 38.

through order and abilities to represent rational thought with high precision. Only at the end of the 18th century and the beginning of the 19th, did the picture reorganize pursuant to a mysterious break. Words parted with things and philology, biology and economy were now set as 'positive' sciences, in the train of general grammar, natural history and analysis of wealth, their previous pre-scientific avatars. The opening time of the Modern 'episteme' was marked by Kant, who undertook a critique of representation, just like Bacon or Descartes, on the edge between the first two epistemes, had performed a critique of resemblance. Kant was also the first philosopher to lay stress on the human subject, while Life, Labour and Language (written with capitals) now became invisible functions by which man's finitude was revealed.

A new philosophy was now born, materialized in a search of the lost unity, through the formalization of disciplines, but also a counter-philosophy, namely an intuitive reflection on the human being, as the other side of the philosophical subject. The modern world thus divided into formal and empirical fields, into *a priori* and *a posteriori* sciences, into structuralism and phenomenology.[2] With the birth of the human sciences (in Foucault's analysis: modern history, psychoanalysis and ethnology), sciences to explore the individual and social subconscious, mankind passed to a *fourth episteme* which Foucault had only an insight into, but failed to name or describe it, as he felt still involved in the opening of the former horizon. This last emergent episteme was subsequently called by the critics 'contemporary' or even 'postmodern', as an extension of a time yet to come during Foucault's early years.

The Western literary canon, on the other side, is the guideline highly esteemed by Harold Bloom in *The Western Canon: The Books and School of the Ages* (1994), which is not so much a theory of the concept as it is a defence of the 'great books' before the assault of the multiculturalists. The concept has been usually defined as 'a list of books for required study';[3] but also, in Bloom's volume, as an anthology of texts fighting for survival or 'the literary Art of Memory' (see the above note). The canon could be therefore seen as a list of 'survivors', namely of writers who struggled for 'eternal life' by literary means. In theorising this term, Bloom resorted to its older 'anxiety of influence' concept, formerly defined as the writers' anguish in front of great dead poets, which is nothing, according to the new terms, but their anguish toward mortality and, consequently, a longing for everlasting life. In literary terms, this can be possible only by entering the canon, the only way to perpetuate yourself in your countless heirs.

---

[2]   See the main influences in the France of Foucault's early career.

[3]   Harold Bloom, *Canonul occidental. Cărţile şi şcoala epocilor* (*The Western Canon: The Books and School of the Ages*), trans. by Diana Stanciu (Bucureşti: Univers, 1998), p. 17.

*

Speaking of survival, let us note that, if not a single-use concept, 'episteme' is yet a very refutable one, often criticised for being an intellectual construction early abandoned by its author itself (who, nevertheless, pleaded in his last years for an integrated understanding of his 'archaeologies' and 'genealogies'). On the contrary, the 'literary canon' is a very useful and general concept, supported by educational institutions (most especially by the University, which uses it as a mean of identification). The canon has been assigned since always the very difficult and delicate mission of educating people and creating the so-called 'taste' for beauty and aesthetic values.

On the other hand, a methodological difference between epistemes and canons will refer to their original area of applicability. Episteme was applied only to Europe, particularly to France, whose mentalities make the central point of Foucault's books. Foucault was even denied as a learned scholar and defined as a respectable author of the (post)-Enlightenment France exclusively.[4] Apparently this is not the case with Harold Bloom, who includes in the Western canon (made mainly of authors from Europe and the USA) also books from the Ancient Far East and India, the Koran as well, and opens also to Russia and East Europe. However, despite his visible open-mindedness, Bloom was still accused of being too exclusive, but in the end, we can say that one central point in defining the canon will be right its exclusivity, while in the episteme will be the recurrence of some principles and laws.

As a result, there is no arguing why the canon is made up of individuals (and even individual books), while the episteme deals with rules and principles, disregarding individuals. Foucault was explicitly proven to do that, as pointed by his interpreters (and even admitted by himself): 'Individuals play almost no role in his work. He is not concerned with the discoveries of "great men"',[5] said Pamela Major-Poetzl, who also noticed, quite frequently, several abstract words such as 'classicism' or 'the 19th century' in the syntactical function of subjects. Contrariwise, Bloom is highly concerned with individuals, so that the traditional author plays a crucial part in his theories. Last but not least, he explicitly objected to the 'death of the author' post-structuralist myth, which, according to him, is pure nonsense.

---

[4]   See Camille Paglia, 'Why I hate Foucault', http://www.mail-archive.com/pen l@galaxy.csuchico.edu/msg34512.html. 'It is simply untrue that Foucault was learned: He was at a loss with any period or culture outside of post-Enlightenment France (his later writing on ancient sexuality is a garbled mishmash).'

[5]   Pamela Major-Poetzl, *Michel Foucault's Archaeology of Western Culture. Toward a New Science of History* (Chapel Hill: University of North Carolina, 1983), p. 166.

*

In spite of all the differences set between the two concepts, what suggests a strange similarity between them is this curious, coincidental four-age division of both. Foucault's most passionate readers might object to this allegation, saying that Foucault does not speak of four epistemes in his 1966 philosophical best-seller. I shall base my assertion on a 1983 study on Foucault's archaeologies, where the American interpreter Pamela Major-Poetzl makes clear points in considering a fourth episteme, which she calls 'Contemporary'. It is true that Foucault named and described only three epistemes (Renaissance, Classical and Modern), but in the last chapters of his book, and most particularly in the one about the human sciences, he repeatedly referred to the end of the modern episteme and the emergence of new times, about which he was not very comfortable or clarified yet. As an intellectual of modern times, he practically remained stuck in his last modern episteme, foreseeing its end but not actually picturing the future (let's say, the post-modernity whose forerunner he seems to be). However, his insights into the signs of this forthcoming future were deep enough, so that the cited American theorist could use accurate Foucauldian words when she sketched the last unprocessed (and actually still operational and ongoing) episteme.

Quite a similar thing happened with Harold Bloom's last canonical age, so-called Chaotic, about which the critic expressed serious doubts. Bloom suggested four canonical ages (Theocratic, Aristocratic, Democratic, and Chaotic), inspired by Giambattista Vico's three cyclic ages, and the fourth one, which is originally Bloomian, refers to the 20th century, just like Foucault's contemporary episteme. This last canonical age has the same degree of uncertainty and incompletion as Foucault's last episteme, Bloom overtly declaring that this final list is not ultimate, and that he is not so sure about the choices made for it (according to him, critics should need two generations after the contemporary success of an author so as to testify for its indisputable value).

Here I shall proceed to a visual representation of the division that the two theorists proposed for their epistemes and, respectively, canons, considering the approximate centuries (and even the particular years indicated by themselves, in some cases), together with the transition points in-between:

EPISTEME (M. Foucault, 1966)	CANON (H. Bloom, 1994)

	THEOCRATIC AGE Antiquity, Hellenistic Greece, (Latin and Arab) Middle Age
	Dante (end of Middle Age, emergent Renaissance) – d. 1321
RENAISSANCE (1500-1660)	**ARISTOCRATIC AGE** (starts with Dante; lasts about 500 years)
Cervantes ('Don Quixote')	
CLASSICAL (1660 – 1800)	
Sade, Marquis de - d. 1814	*Goethe* (end of literary Classicism) – d. 1832
MODERN (1800 – 1950)	**DEMOCRATIC AGE** (19th century)
Nietzsche - d. 1900	
CONTEMPORARY	**CHAOTIC AGE** (approx. 1900 to the present)

As one can see, there are striking correspondences, but also differences, as the two types of historical distributions are not perfectly analogous. The last two ages are practically synonymous, while the first two do not actually match. The first two ages are to a certain extent dissimilar: Foucault does not consider any scientific episteme in parallel to Bloom's theocratic age (which is easily understandable why, considering the late birth of positive sciences), while the Aristocratic age of the latter covers 500 years and is much longer by far than the corresponding Renaissance episteme (it is actually 'covered' by two Foucauldian scientific epistemes, the Renaissance and the Classical one).

Foucault was criticised for imposing a uniformity of thought upon much too longer time periods (150 years), and we can see from this table that he operates almost mathematically, which is not actually realistic. At the same time, he does not operate with accurate cultural typologies: Renaissance actually started in the 15th century, in Italy, and, according to some specialists, even longer before, in the 14th century (Bloom is accurate in this respect). On the other hand, the year 1660 is quite an abusive delayed limit to mark its end, considering that even Shakespeare, which is late Renaissance, dies in 1616. In turn, Bloom also seems to disregard cultural typologies, as he prefers Vico's marginal and somehow philosophical typology over serious cultural distinctions, which might have been more operational. For instance, his Aristocratic age is largely indistinct: it lasts for 500 years and includes the cultural Renaissance, the Classicism and the Baroque, ending with emergent Romanticism (see Goethe, who is still 'Aristocratic'). However, to his defence, this Aristocratic age ends approximately the same time with the French Revolution, which makes sense as an end of the 'Ancien Régime', whose power relied mainly on the monarchy and the aristocracy.

Yet, it is good to see that both Bloom and Foucault choose the same time reference to start their Modern, respectively Democratic ages: marquis de Sade and Goethe died approximately the same time. To Foucault, the marginal Sade bears the same importance as Goethe to Bloom. Georges Canguilhem used to say that the authors selected and discussed by Foucault were like 'major philosophical events'[6] in his books. He meant that Foucault, who apparently disregarded individuals (and pleaded, let us remember, for the free circulation of texts) always make them strikingly important in any change of episteme. It is always a writer or a philosopher who gives powerful expression to the break of all epistemic laws in an exhausted episteme.[7] For instance, Nietzsche is placed approximately in the same intervals by both theorists: he is a modern (namely 'democratic') writer with Bloom and a pioneer of the contemporary episteme with Foucault. With the latter, Nietzsche marks rather a turning point: he actually puts an end to the modern episteme, just as Cervantes (by his character, Don Quixote) put an end to the Renaissance episteme. Great writers are therefore 'signs of crisis' to Foucault, which is approximately the same idea expressed, from other logical premises and stands, by Harold Bloom.

---

[6] Georges Canguilhem, 'The death of man, or exhaustion of the cogito?' in *The Cambridge Companion to Foucault* (Cambridge University Press, 1994), p. 71.

[7] See, for instance, the importance of Cervantes or Sade as turning points at the transition time between two epistemes (*The Order of Things*).

Finally, a similar point made by the two theorists is that they both praised (directly or indirectly) the disruptive force of literature and of the authors of (what Bloom called) 'imaginative literature'. Bloom defined the great writer, among other features, through his/her aesthetic power, originality, creative use of solitude, or strangeness, which is quite similar to the qualities also accounted for by Foucault when selecting the 'great deviant artists'[8] that played so important parts in his theoretical fictions. Defined as 'a particular source of expression',[9] Foucault made an important distinction between the great writers (in Bloom's words) and the 'founders of discursivity' or 'transdiscursive' authors, such as Marx or Freud. The transdiscursive authors are not inimitable stylistic hallmarks, but on the contrary, they 'have established an endless possibility of discourse' (p. 154), creating not only their works, but also 'the possibilities and the rules for the formation of other texts' (see the above note).[10] The difference is that the first party (the great writers) will always make an irreducible difference, while the second one (the transdiscursive) has led to the emergence of particular 'discursive practices', which Foucault has advocated as a theorist.

Nevertheless, despite his being assimilated by Harold Bloom with the 'School of Resentment', Foucault always showed high esteem to great artists like Hölderlin, Nerval, Nietzsche, Sade, Mallarmé, Artaud, and Bataille (usually modern artists) who, according to him, had the power of shock and consciousness-raising upon people. To Foucault, it is precisely their inimitability and non-'discursivity' which makes them so unique and valuable in a history of ideas and truth. Even to the author of epistemes, we can conclude, the literary canon proves to be a truth bearer more reliable than any 'episteme'.

---

[8]   Gary Gutting, 'Introduction. Michel Foucault: A user's manual', in *The Cambridge Companion to Foucault*, p. 21 (Speaking of Foucault's myths, the critic reminds 'the dazzling transgressions of mad artists such as Nietzsche, van Gogh, and Artaud' as reactions to 'the grand bogeyman of French intellectuals since Flaubert: bourgeois society' – *ibidem*).

[9]   Michel Foucault, 'What's an Author', in *Textual Strategies. Perspectives in Post-Structuralist Criticism*, ed. by Josuē V. Harari (New York: Cornell University Press, 1979), p. 151.

[10]   'They have created a possibility for something other than their discourse, yet something belonging to what they founded.' Freud, for instance, laid the basis of the psychoanalytical discourse, which made possible, subsequent to it, the differences toward Freud himself.

WORKS CITED

Bloom, Harold, *Canonul occidental. Cărţile şi şcoala epocilor*, trans. by Diana Stanciu (Bucureşti: Univers, 1998)

Foucault, Michel, *The Order of Things. An Archaeology of the Human Sciences* (London and New York: Routledge Classics, 2001)

Gutting, Gary, ed., *The Cambridge Companion to Foucault* (Cambridge: Cambridge University Press, 1994)

Harari, Josuē V., ed., *Textual Strategies. Perspectives in Post-Structuralist Criticism* (New York: Cornell University Press, 1979)

Major-Poetzl, Pamela, *Michel Foucault's Archaeology of Western Culture. Toward a New Science of History* (Chapel Hill: University of North Carolina, 1983)

Paglia, Camille, 'Why I hate Foucault', http://www.mail-archive.com/pen l@galaxy.csuchico.edu/msg34512.html

Zakaria Fatih

The Literary Canon and its Religious Precursor

Notwithstanding studies that have been published on the nexus of literature and religion, the literary canon's indebtedness to religion has not yet received all the attention it deserves. The goal of the present article is to shed light on the commonalities that the literary canon shares with the religious canon, showing how the formation and the conception of the literary canon owe a great deal to the religious canon and to the way it has been debated for centuries. The ultimate purpose of the article is to contribute to the debate on religion and literature in a context marked by transformations affecting literary criticism and theory.

The love affair between religion and literature has taken center stage again in the aftermath of 9/11. Recent publications, such as John Updike's *Terrorist* and Don DeLilllo's *Falling Man*, affirm that the recondite relationship of religion and literature only needed an event to come back to life. Throughout history, interest for this relationship swayed between moments of obsession to periods of indifference. Given the response to recent events, André Malraux's prediction that our century would be a religious century may not have been a wild guess after all. With the fall of communist ideology and the rise of dormant rivalries, such as the supposed clash of civilizations, memories of zealotry and religious fanaticism are conjured. Believing in Malraux's prediction, however, would be the same thing as thinking that religion vanished from view when, in fact, it is post-enlightenment propensity to secularism that has downgraded religion and minimized its role in shaping and defining the literary canon.

This fact does not mean that the relationship has not drawn the attention of literary critics; on the contrary, Northrop Frye's *The Great Code* is one of several exemplary works on the importance of this relationship to twentieth century literary criticism; critical theory, on the other hand, has shown an unparalleled interest in religion since mid-twentieth century. Frye himself writes that: 'Many issues in critical theory today had their origin in the hermeneutic study of the Bible; many contemporary approaches to criticism are obscurely motivated by a God-is-dead syndrome that also developed out of Biblical criticism; many formulations of critical theory seem to me more defensible when applied to the Bible than they are when applied elsewhere'.[1] Frye's assertions about the kinship of religion and literature and the role that religion has played in fashioning literary rhetoric and in forming the literary imaginary, reaffirm in theory what in practice has already been established,

---

[1] Northrop Frye, *The Great Code: The Bible and Literature* (San Diego: A Harvest Book, 1982), p. xix.

mainly the omnipresence of the religious in human consciousness and artifacts.

Notwithstanding, the relationship suffers from fatigue and exhaustion, not because all issues have been tackled, but more because the combination of religion and literature does not sound as appealing and contemporary as the relationship, say, of literature and culture. No one wants to sound religious when dealing with literature, an apprehension that conceals the continuous influence that religion has had on literature. With the extent of this influence still shrouded in mystery, the relationship of religion and literature remains ambiguous and in need of rehabilitation. One of the areas where this influence can be acutely visible lies in the discussion around the literary canon. This fact does not mean that the influence has been explored to the degree that such a relationship merits. On the contrary, there is so much out there about this influence that needs to be unraveled, especially when we know how much of religion is embedded in discussions of the literary canon. Whether in their perception or in their definitions of the canon, critics have relied, consciously or otherwise, on tools that have been used to define the religious canon; they also considered the corpus of literary classics as limited and sacred as if it were a body of Scriptures. It is thus my intention in this essay to examine a number of essays by critics who, in trying to define the classic, rely heavily on religious imaginary and on conceptions and jargon that conform to religion's definition of the canon.

Historically speaking, literature and religion have always had a relationship one way or another and were, from the outset, at the heart of canon formation. As simple as it sounds, this fact may not always be obvious, given that the origins of the religious canon had been a mystery until interest in the issue picked up pace. Outside of religion, scholars have investigated the relationship of the Bible, mainly the Jewish Bible, to pre-biblical and Mesopotamian literatures and cultures, partly exploring the overlap between stories in the Bible and those in the literature of the time, and partly examining the influence that biblical imagery has had on literary modernity. In *Narrative Covenant*, David Damrosch explores the overlap, arguing for the double canonization of the Scriptures and the presence of a substantial nexus between biblical narratives and Mesopotamian literature. More recently, Robert Alter also takes up the same issue in *Canon and Creativity*, focusing on the secular side of the Bible, i.e. on stories that subvert the moral injunctions of the holy book and that continue to pervade the works of modern writers, such as Joyce, Bialik, and Kafka.

While the examples of Damrosch and Alter attest to the growing interest in the relationship of literature and religion, they represent a sample of many other interests too broad and numerous to list here. The fact that the scope of interest in this relationship has expanded, for example to theory, shows the popularity and relevance of religion and literature to contemporary issues, a reversal, in Frye's opinion, from the setback the relationship suffered in the beginning of the twentieth century: 'There was a misguided vogue fifty years ago for attacking the Romantics on this point, asserting that they confused literature and religion; but critical theory is coming back into focus, and many contemporary critics are well aware of the relevance of biblical criticism to secular literature' (p. xix). Again, Frye could not have been more accurate in his assertions, given how religion has become almost the focal point for many critics and theorists, from Derrida and Girard to Cixous and Gadamer. In itself, Frye's contribution to the fields of religion and literature remains one of the highlights in twentieth century literary criticism and, judging by the two volumes that were recently devoted to his work, his contribution to religion and literature is the one that led to the renewed interest in his work.[2]

One of the issues that come to mind and to which Frye did not contribute directly is that of canon formation. This fact means that notwithstanding his broad interests, Frye's contributions are naturally not representative of all the issues and certainly not of those that specifically treat the influence of religious canonicity on literary canonicity; neither does this deficiency mean that his ideas cannot be made to bear on the canon debate. In a review article titled 'The Persistence of Vision: Northrop Frye in the Context of Religion',[3] David Gay argues in favor of Frye's implication in social and cultural issues of the eighties and nineties.[4]

There are for the present work some lessons to learn in Eagleton's attack on Frye. At least until the publication of *The Great Code* in 1982, Frye did not consider it necessary to engage politically in the defense of his view of

---

[2]   The books to which I am referring are Glen Robert, *Northrop Frye and the Phenomenology of Myth* (Toronto: University of Toronto Press, 2006), and Mark A. Hamilton, *Categorizing Twentieth-Century Film Using Northrop Frye's* Anatomy of Criticism*: Relating Literature and Film* (Lewiston: The Edwin Mellen Press, 2006). Both of these books have been reviewed by David Gay in *Christianity and Literature*, Winter (2008), a review from which I will be quoting later on.

[3]   Gay writes that Terry Eagleton describes Frye 'as a clergyman-turned critic' (p. 1), a label that not only put an end to Frye's reputation in the seventies but followed him wherever he goes until his death in 1991.

[4]   David Gay's review article gives an indication of the direction Frye's legacy has taken after his death and the renewed interest in his work. On the relevance of Frye's ideas to contemporary issues, Gay writes: 'If we shift our perspective from the past influence of *The Anatomy of Criticism* and instead look more broadly at his lifelong exploration of the relations between literature and religion, we find Frye participating in some of the central social concerns of recent theorists from his reading of the Bible and his sense of the relationship between the secular and sacred writing. In short, the language of "concern" that links these two spheres of writing encourages social as well as critical vision' (p. 1). By implication, Frye could also be seen to contribute to the canon debate and the culture wars.

literature or to push for the celebration of the great classics from which he predominantly quotes. As a matter of fact, at the time Frye published his book, one would have expected from Cultural Studies to stand, following the example of critical theory, in favor of religion as a component of culture that is also highly relevant to literary studies. Instead, religion was cast aside, presumably for its supposed association with traditional aesthetics at a time when, paradoxically, religious imaginary and symbolism continue to appeal to literary and cultural sensibilities of all sorts. Today, it seems as though an amendment was finally taking place slowly but surely in the background, a move that only confirms, a little too late for Frye, his assertions about the relevance of religion to secular literature. This shift, however, could not have come at a better time, especially when recent developments in theology and literary studies entail, by implication, an overhaul of a string of issues closely related to the canon.

With the publication of *The Canon Debate* in 2002, a large volume dedicated to the religious canon, the contributors debated a number of questions that had been left unanswered for centuries. The volume's editors, Lee Martin McDonald and James A. Sanders, raise the profile of certain theological questions that have been acutely pressing and that, because of archeological finds and developments in the fields of theology and history, necessitate a new outlook and a reformulation of old assumptions about them and the religious canon in general. One such question is that of the nature and the definition of the canon about which the contributors say that 'there is no universally accepted position'.[5] In turn, the contributor to this particular question, Eugene Ulrich, does not dispute this claim, stating in his article 'The Notion and Definition of Canon' the usual confusion surrounding the term and permeating discussions about it. Against this state of affairs, Ulrich sheds light on the nature of the 'canon' by exploring its etymology and discussing a number of definitions from different traditions.

Of the nine definitions that he lists from sources in English as well as in other languages, eight assert that the list of canonical works 'is closed or delimited'. Later on in his essay, Ulrich joins this view when he defines the canon as '[...] the definitive list of inspired, authoritative books which constitute the recognized and accepted body of sacred scripture of a major religious group [...]' (in McDonald, p. 29). The high frequency of 'closed or delimited' reveals the general perception that scholars have of the religious canon as a closed body of works with no possibility of change or additions. In considering religion as the realm of the divine and the sacred, it is expected from scholars to highlight 'closure' and 'authority' as bulwarks

---

5   Martin Lee McDonald and James A. Sanders, eds, *The Canon Debate* (Massachusetts: Hendrickson Publishers, 2002), p. 4.

against attacks on the canon, thereby shielding its sanctity from heresy and the works of Man.

No one knows with certainty when the canon as a religious term made its way to the humanities. The Oxford Literary Dictionary lists the term, assigning it various entries; the closest to the literary canon appears under '2 *gen*.B, referring to a logical, grammatical, or metrical canon; canons of criticism, taste, art, etc.' Under this heading, the two quotations that are listed appeared in nineteenth century roughly around the same time: '1874 Sayce Compar. Philol. i 58 The canon of taste and polite literature. 1879 Farrar St. Paul I. 613 We may assume it as a canon of ordinary criticism that a writer intends to be understood'. Although quotations from Shakespeare and Milton are also listed under the same entry, they do not convey the meaning of 'a body of literary and artistic works' nor do the two quotations just listed. This means that until the end of nineteenth century, a term close in meaning to the idea of a literary canon was nonexistent in literature.

The absence of such a meaning, however, does not imply a lack of awareness about what constitutes a great book. The awareness is perceived in aesthetic judgments, a critical practice that is as old as literature itself. Although they are a necessary accompaniment to works of art, aesthetic judgments are usually formulated in accord with commonsense; that's to say, they contribute to widely-held assumptions about appreciation. Artists depend on this early yet critical stage for recognition and success; the more accolades, the better attention they will receive. Most works of art benefit from these kinds of judgments upon being released, but only a few captivate critics' attention *ad infinitum* and become eligible for canonicity. Thus the fact that the 'canon' as a term has made its way to literature only recently does not preclude the presence of discussions on great works of art and judgments about them. By examining the historical evolution of the canon debate, it appears that although critics never used the term 'canon', they engaged in discussions around the classic, a topic that is not much different in breadth and scope from the current debate on the canon. To speak of the classic is to evoke an important stage in the canonization process that is comparable to the process by which Scriptures were canonized. We speak of a body of texts that may become an authority in literary studies over the years. The analogy is most visible in the conception and the definitions assigned to the literary classic.

Before it turned political, the discussion of the literary canon started as an investigation on two fronts: the first concerns the role of culture in education (Mathew Arnold) and, the second, the nature and the definition of the classic (Sainte-Beuve, Eliot, Kermode etc). From the outset, some of those involved in the discussion of the classic did everything they could to dodge political implications.[6] Not surprisingly, the repudiation of the political conveys a view of art antagonistic to social dynamics and inimical to any supposition that attaches a historical mission to artifacts. As a matter of fact, the classic, for Sainte-Beuve as well as for Eliot, is always fixated on the past, although their definition of it may state otherwise. In a number of writings about this issue, Eliot highlights, in *Tradition and the Individual Talent*, the aesthetic importance that past works have in judging contemporary works of art. The standards of modernity are thus not fit enough for this task:

> In a peculiar sense he [a poet] will be aware also that he must inevitably be judged by the standards of the past. I say judged, not amputated, by them; not judged to be as, or worse or better than, the dead; and certainly not judged by the canons of dead critics. (p. 2208)

In judging it by the normative standards of the past, the work of art should be situated somewhere between originality and conformity.

This double quality that the work of art should have is important only to the extent that it builds awareness about the past. It is merely a repositioning of the work vis-à-vis the past tradition and a reinterpretation of its legacy. In other words, the new should be at the service of the old in order to expand its horizon of possibilities: 'What is to be insisted upon is that the poet must develop or procure the consciousness of the past and that he should continue to develop this consciousness throughout his career' (p. 2209). No wonder that the part allocated to the new, if not restricted, is surely less important than past masterpieces against which the quality of the new is to be judged. Without really discarding the possibility of change altogether, Eliot insists that the new should contribute to the legacy of European consciousness, 'the mind of Europe', as an entity inevitable to dismiss or set aside: '[...] and that this change is a development which abandons nothing en route, which does not superannuate either Shakespeare, or Homer, or the rock drawing of the Magdalenian draftsmen' (p. 2208). The selection not to be superannuated, which he supplements elsewhere with Virgil,[7] is exactly that of the masterpieces of European literature. It is a list that has acquired a status of something almost as untouchable and sacred as the scriptures of the religious canon.

---

[6]   T.S. Eliot writes in his article, 'What is a Classic?' the following about the terms 'romantic' and 'classic': 'And, finally, I think that the account of the classic which I propose to give here should remove it from the area of the antithesis between "classic" and "romantic" — a pair of terms belonging to literary politics, and arousing passions which I should wish, on this occasion, Aeolus to contain in the bag' – *What is a Classic? An Address Delivered Before the Virgil Society on the 16th of October 1944* (London: Faber and Faber Ltd., 1944), p. 9.

[7]   'What is a classic' (London: Faber and Faber Ltd., 1944).

In his famous essay, 'What is a Classic?' Eliot explores the idea of the ideal European past which he identifies in Greco-Roman times. Examining Latin and Greek texts seems to be highly important to his thesis, for the simple reason that the two languages, Latin and old Greek, are dead: 'It is necessary to go to the two dead languages: it is important that they are dead, because through their death we have come into our inheritance — the fact that they are dead would in itself give them no value, apart from the fact that all the peoples of Europe are their beneficiaries' (p. 28). The death presupposes some sort of historical legitimacy that is not acquired through their rich heritage, but instead through their finitude as languages no longer in use for social communication. It is their status as dead and closed languages that bestows value to them and attaches merit to their time and works. Exactly like the religious canon as a body of 'closed and delimited' writings with eternal values for the community of believers, the classic, the literary masterpiece from a distant past, written in a dead language, can attain the highest possible degree of legitimacy only through historical maturity and linguistic exclusivity.

Eventually, it is Latin, and not Greek, that still preserves the European spirit, as incarnated in Virgil the poet: 'No modern language can hope to produce a classic, in the sense in which I have called Virgil a classic. Our classic, the classic of all Europe, is Virgil' (p. 31). In the way that he is venerated and lifted above all poets, '[...] in a position which no other poet can share or usurp' (p. 29), Virgil becomes a prophet, much closer to God by the qualities of perfection that Eliot assigns to him than he is to the imperfect world of humans.

Although he does not credit Sainte-Beuve with discovering Virgil much less acknowledge the debt he owes to him — except in passing – for writing 'What is a Classic?', Eliot seems to reiterate some of the views that Sainte-Beuve had expressed about Virgil in his *Etude sur Virgile* (*Study on Virgil*). One of the characteristics that they both share lies in what Eliot calls 'comprehensiveness', or that which reveals all the genius of a people, an idea that seems to echo Sainte-Beuve's assertion about Virgil as 'le poète de la Latinité tout entière' (the poet of the entire Latin world).[8] The judgment that Virgil alone is the classic poet *par excellence* is motivated as much by the poet's personal temperament and aesthetic qualities as it is by a desire on the part of Sainte-Beuve and Eliot to confer this status to only one person. It is as if by this choice they wanted to insist, in terms somewhat reminiscent of Christianity's call for unity, on the unity of the European spirit.[9] Sainte-Beuve propounds Virgil's reconciliatory qualities as a poet, lauding his

---

[8]   C.A. Sainte-Beuve, Etude sur Virgile (Paris: Garnier Frères, 1857), p. 1.
[9]   David Said: 'Behold, how good and how pleasant it is, for brethren to dwell together in unity!'

amnesty and pity;[10] he sees in him the hope that can make amends and restore peace to the soul and to the nascent Roman Empire. Virgil has an aversion to wars, dissensions and violent struggles and through Aeneas, his protagonist in the *Aeneid*, he gives an image of Emperor Augustus on whom are projected the poet's hopes for a peaceful Rome.

Sainte-Beuve's eulogy of Virgil draws on religion and religious history. Virgil symbolizes the moral guide whose words, like those of the Lord, carry the promise of a better tomorrow. With his golden chain, writes Sainte-Beuve, Virgil links the past to the present and speaks of virtues long lost to the Romans. His main protagonist, Aeneas, in Sainte-Beuve's eyes, is an early incarnation of Saint-Louis, aka Louis IX, whose rule has no peer in the history of the French monarchy. Politically, he stabilized France but, more importantly, he is considered the ideal Christian ruler, the one that fought tirelessly against the Saracens in the Middle East and North Africa where he eventually died: 'Son Enée est le Saint Louis de l'antiquité' (His Aeneas is the Antiquity's Saint Louis) (p. 78). The eulogy reaches a zenith with the implicit claim that Virgil is somewhat the precursor of Christ.[11] Sainte-Beuve's semantic lends itself to two meanings. It can imply the moral rectitude and Aeneas' unflinching integrity that Virgil assigns to him and that, in some way, paves the scene for Jesus Christ's message of salvation, or refers to Virgil's *Eclogue four* in which he predicts the coming of Jesus, which is more likely the case:

> Our is the crowning era foretold in prophecy:
> Born of Time, a great new cycle of centuries
> Begins. Justice returns to earth, the Golden Age
> Returns, and its first-born comes down from heaven above (p. 23).

In both cases, the semantic meets a religious quality that Virgil seems either to have or evoke. If Sainte-Beuve is not as explicit as he is in his essay 'Qu'est-ce qu'un classique?' (What is a classic?) about who the master of European literature is, he makes it clear in *Etude sur Virgile,* not just because he devotes a whole book to Virgil, but more by the terminology he uses to eulogize him, most of which attach great importance to questions of religious ethics and literary aesthetics.

---

[10]   In his *Discours d'ouverture* at the Collège de France, he writes that: 'Virgile, en un mot, poète de l'amnistie et de la pitié, des réconciliations et des miséricordes [...]' (To put it shortly, Virgil [is] a poet of amnesty and piety, of reconciliation and misericordia) (p. 24).

[11]   Sainte-Beuve writes that: 'La venue même du Christ n'a rien qui étonne quand on a lu Virgile' (Christ's birth itself isn't surprising at all when we've read Virgil) (p. 78).

Unlike Sainte-Beuve and T.S. Eliot, Kermode's view of the classic appears to be much broader and flexible to be reduced to one author. Kermode seems to be in a privileged position, since he was present at the waging of culture wars, a historical juncture which enabled him to formulate carefully his thoughts about the classic and the canon. By the time *Forms of Attention* was published, the canon as a term had already been circulating in literary circles and its use had acquired a meaning quite distinct from the religious canon. This distinction, however, has not prevented critics from thinking of the literary canon in religious terms and defending it using religious jargon: 'To be inside the canon is to be protected from wear and tear, to be credited with indefinitely large numbers of possible internal relations and secrets, to be treated as a heterocosm, a miniature Torah'.[12] Kermode maintained this attitude at least until the publication of *Forms of Attention* where he champions 'permanent modernity' as a criterion for immortalizing canonical works. 'Permanent modernity' is supposed to mean the seductive power that the work possesses and that, accordingly, attracts the critics to the work and makes them interested in it.

However, there are limitations to this criterion, mainly because works that draw attention to themselves are works that have already enjoyed attention throughout history, works that have already been canonical. 'Permanent modernity' implies a preexisting status as a result of the constant 'forms of attention' that the work attracted over the centuries; it also means a hermeneutics far less receptive to newness or capable of inventing the canon. Even in more recent works, such as in *Pleasure and Change*, Kermode brandishes 'pre-understandings', a notion that he claims is closer to Gadamer's concept of the 'prejudice':

> Of course it isn't easy to be aware of one's own bias, but the reward promised is great: newness. Again, the fact is that it is our job to create that newness. Our way of doing so may be described as 'appropriative', meaning only that we have to do something drastic to a canonical text to make it ours, to make it modern. It must be made to answer to our prejudices, and they are necessarily related to the prejudices of our community, even if in reaction to them. [13]

In drawing on Gadamer's 'hermeneutics', Kermode is looking for a term deeply rooted in tradition and, upon research in Gadamer's works, it appears that the term has initially been used in religious circles. According to Gadamer, Heidegger developed it by relying on Wilhelm Dilthey who, in

---

[12]   Frank Kermode, *The Classic: Literary Images of Permanence and Change* (New York: The Viking Press, 1975), p. 90.

[13]   Frank Kermode, *Pleasure and Change: The Aesthetics of Canon*, ed. by Robert Alter (Oxford: Oxford University Press, 2004), p. 38.

Zakaria Fatih

turn, had transmitted it from Protestant theology.[14] It is also in religious terms
that Schleiermacher seems to have used the term: 'Schleiermacher's
hermeneutics shows him to be a leading voice of historical romanticism. But
at the same time, he kept the concern of the Christian theologian clearly in
mind, intending his hermeneutics, as a general doctrine of the art of
understanding, to be of value in the special work of interpreting Scripture'.[15]
While hermeneutics may no longer carry religious associations, at least not
directly, explanations that both Schleiermacher and Gadamer assign to it bear
on the religious. Gadamer calls 'hermeneutical' the practice of restoring 'to
its rightful place a positive concept of prejudice that was driven out of our
linguistic usage by the French and the English Enlightenment' (p. 9). What
has perhaps been removed from post-enlightenment use of 'prejudice' resides
in the absence of authority which, according to Gadamer, needs to be
rehabilitated: 'the concept of prejudice is closely connected to the concept of
authority, and the above image makes it clear that it is in need of
hermeneutical rehabilitation' (p. 9). One can only surmise that the loss is to
be redeemed by reviving pre-enlightenment hermeneutical practice that
unmistakably referred to a reading of the Scriptures.

    In trying to define the literary classic, the early scholarship, as
demonstrated by the examples of Sainte-Beuve, Eliot, and Kermode, has used
critical practice that was not much different from the course theology took in
order to define and judge the Scriptures. To the idea of eternal God and
everlasting scriptures, early literary scholarship on the classic intended to
maintain the text and its author in a constant state of relevance and permanent
modernity. They deployed techniques and literary devices designed to make
the classic respond to contemporary concerns. Judging by Robert Alter's
Canon and Creativity, religious symbolism and imaginary continue to appear
in modern literary works: 'The Bible in part seizes the imagination of the
modern writer because of his acute consciousness of it as a body of founding
texts, marking out one of the primary possibilities of representing the human
condition and the nature of the historical experience for all the eras of
Western culture that have followed antiquity'.[16]

    In my judgment, this practice calls attention to the function and the scope
of literary criticism. For centuries, critics focused on the internal operations
of the text, on aesthetics, rhetoric, and language; the classic was no

---

[14]   For a discussion of hermeneutics, see Hans-Georg Gadamer's *Philosophical Hermeneutics*
        (Berkeley: University of California Press, 1976).

[15]   Hans-Georg Gadamer, *Philosophical Hermeneutics*, trans. & ed. by David Linge (Berkeley:
        University of California Press, 1977), p. 7.

[16]   Robert Alter, *Canon and Creativity: Modern Writing and the Authority of Scripture* (New
        Haven: Yale University Press, 2000), pp. 17-8.

exception. It was discussed by the tools that were available to criticism and some of those tools were made available by theology, as one of the earliest forms of analyzing the Scriptures as well as the most favorite means to attaining truth. Although the literary climate has changed dramatically today, with the belated inception of the social, that is the cultural and the subversive trends calling for approaches receptive to multiculturalism and diversity, religious imaginary and symbolism seem to be deeply ingrained in our literary forms and culture. Religious presence in modernity is not only the result of irascible acts or the supposed clash of civilizations that keep reminding us of the centrality of religion in our time; it is also there because of the formative function that religion has played in shaping human consciousness since time immemorial. Developments in the fields of literary and cultural criticism can hardly deny this fact.

WORKS CITED

Abrams, M. H., ed., *The Norton Anthology of English Literature* (New York: Norton & Company, 1986)

Alter, Robert, *Canon and Creativity: Modern Writing and the Authority of Scripture* (New Haven: Yale University Press, 2000)

Arnold, Matthew, *Culture and Anarchy: An Essay in Political and Social Criticism* (London: Smith, Elder and Co., 1869)

Damrosch, David, *Narrative Covenant: Transformations of Genre in the Growth of Biblical Literature* (San Francisco: Harper and Row, 1987)

DeLillo, Don, *Falling Man* (New York: Scribner, 2007)

—. *What is a Classic? An Address Delivered Before the Virgil Society on the 16th of October 1944* (London: Faber and Faber Ltd., 1944)

Frye, Northrop, *The Great Code: The Bible and Literature* (San Diego: A Harvest Book, 1982)

Gadamer, Hans-Georg, *Philosophical Hermeneutics*, trans. & ed. by David Linge (Berkeley: University of California Press, 1977)

Kermode, Frank, *Forms of Attention* (Chicago: University of Chicago Press, 1985)

—. *The Classic: Literary Images of Permanence and Change* (New York: The Viking Press, 1975)

—. *Pleasure and Change: The Aesthetics of Canon*, ed. by Robert Alter (Oxford: Oxford University Press, 2004)

McDonald, Martin Lee and James A. Sanders, eds, *The Canon Debate* (Massachusetts: Hendrickson Publishers, 2002)

Sainte-Beuve, C.A. *Etude sur Virgile* (Paris: Garnier Frères, 1857)

Updike, John, *Terrorist* (New York: Knopf, 2006)

Virgil, *Aeneid*, trans. by Edward McCrorie (Ann Arbor: The University of Michigan Press, 1995)

—. *The Eclogues of Virgil*, trans. by C. Day Lewis (London: Jonathan Cape, 1963)

Frédéric Canovas

Against the Canon:
Jean Cocteau or the Rise of the Gay Cultural Icon

A very limited number of scholars who specialize in French art and/or literature and gay studies, have underlined the role played by Cocteau's work in the concept and articulation of homosexual identity. There is no doubt that Gide and Proust remain the central figures when it comes to studies dealing with homosexuality in modern literature, even if most scholars agree on the fact that their conceptualization of homosexual identity is outdated today. Thus any attempt to understand Cocteau's definition and representation of homosexuality without looking at his position toward Gide and Proust would be incomplete and inaccurate. In light of Cocteau's tumultuous relationship with Gide and Proust, this essay will attempt to retrace the emergence of Cocteau's written and visual discourse on homosexuality as well as his original role as a homosexual role model.

2009 marks the tenth anniversary of Jean Marais' death. A few weeks after his passing, the French gay magazine *Têtu* published the results of a national poll. Gay readers had been asked to select their favorite gay icons. Surprisingly Jean Cocteau (ranked number 1), who had died more than forty years ago, and Jean Marais (number 2) came ahead of contemporary pop stars like George Michael (ranked number 7) and Elton John (number 9), and French fashion's *enfant terrible* Jean-Paul Gaultier (number 8). Perhaps Cocteau's prediction was finally becoming a reality. After years of being considered too much of a frivolous[1] and shallow artist, Cocteau was finally granted what he had longed for during his entire life? In his diary, Cocteau wrote in 1943: 'Gide says that I am "incapable of being serious". I, Cocteau, accuse Gide, Valéry and Claudel of being diabolically frivolous...' It is normal that this fake seriousness bear its fruit in 1943, and that our own hidden seriousness be revealed only after the year 2000.[2]

---

[1]   The title of this essay was inspired by the title of Cocteau's second book *Le Prince frivole* published at the age of twenty one.

[2]   Jean Cocteau, *Journal 1942-1945* (Paris: Gallimard, 1989), p. 413. All translations are mine with the exception of quotations taken from Arthur King Peters' book, *Jean Cocteau and André Gide: An Abrasive Friendship*, New Brunswick: Rutgers University Press, 1973. Interestingly enough a poll on 'the best French writers of today' conducted in 1943 by the newspaper *Combat* placed Gide number one (with 423 votes), followed by Camus, Sartre and Malraux. Cocteau is number 17 (with only 93 votes) behind Montherlant, Claudel,

If it is indeed understandable, if not 'normal', for the young generation of the forties to identify with the works of Gide, Valéry and Claudel, was Cocteau actually right when he hinted at the fact that his own work would eventually be better understood and appreciated in the future unlike that of his rivals of 1943? It would be non-sense to claim today that the works of Gide, Valéry and Claudel have lost their meaning and purpose. Quite the contrary, these authors still enjoy much popularity in 2004, both in the academic world, in the French collective mind and among gay readers (in fact, Gide is ranked number 6 in the *Têtu* poll). As for Cocteau's wish to be, in the year 2000, where his rivals stood in 1943, things are not as clear-cut as he would have wished them to be. In spite of the public's undeniable fascination for Cocteau's character and creations, one is forced to admit that few of his works have received more – or even as much – attention than those of Gide for instance. Scholars generally tend to focus on a very limited number of books, films and plays. If Cocteau's murals and erotic drawings for instance have been the object of recent publications, his paintings, for example, still remain to be discovered.[3] For better or worse, Cocteau 2004 is as much of an ambiguous and contradictory figure as the Cocteau of the Forties. The 1943 prediction has not quite fully materialized yet. Gallimard's prestigious *Pléiade* collection has recently released two volumes devoted to Cocteau's poetry and drama.[4] However Cocteau had to wait for almost forty years to achieve what Gide, Julien Green and Marguerite Yourcenar, or even lesser known writers such as Julien Gracq and Nathalie Sarraute, had reached in their lifetime. In the field of what is called 'gay studies' or 'queer studies' in the American academic world, Cocteau's place seems rather discrete. A very limited number of scholars, who specialize in French art and/or literature and gay studies, have underlined the role played by Cocteau's work in the concept and articulation of homosexual identity.[5] For instance there is no doubt that Gide remains one of the central figures and the focus of all the attention when it comes to studies dealing with homosexuality in modern

---

Mauriac, Martin du Gard, Colette and Breton, among other writers [in Paul Léautaud, *Journal littéraire*, vol VII (Paris: Mercure de France, p. 291)].

3   See Suzanne Helde, *Les Murs de Jean Cocteau* (Paris: Herme, 1998), and Annie Guédras, *Ils: dessins érotiques de Jean Cocteau* (Paris: Le Pré aux Clercs, 1998). The completion of this essay coincides with the exhibition devoted to Cocteau by the Centre Georges Pompidou, the first major retrospective show of Cocteau's works in many years.

4   *Œuvres poétiques complètes* (Paris: Gallimard, 1999), and *Théâtre complet* (Paris: Gallimard, 2003), under the direction of Michel Décaudin.

5   See essentially Christopher Robinson's *Scandal in the Ink* (London: Cassel, 1985), and Pamela Genova's entry on Cocteau in *The Reader's Guide to Lesbian and Gay Studies* (Chicago: Fitzroy Dearborn, 2000).

western literature, even if most scholars agree on the fact that Gide's conceptualization of homosexual identity is outdated today and represents a turning point, if not a new point of departure, in the history of homosexuality, from which or against which later generations of homosexual artists, including Cocteau, would position themselves.[6] Thus any attempt to understand Cocteau's definition and representation of homosexuality without looking at his position toward Gide would be incomplete and inaccurate. In light of Cocteau's tumultuous relationship with Gide, this essay will attempt to retrace the emergence of Cocteau's written and visual discourse on homosexuality as well as his original role as a homosexual role model and perhaps the first global figure of what was going to become a new literary canon: the gay canon.

If *Têtu*'s gay readers of 1999 are in favor of Cocteau and his almost mythical lover Jean Marais, it may very well be because both men embody, in their own way, a more contemporary and positive homosexual identity, which today's gay men feel comfortable with. This shows how contradictory Cocteau's figure remains. Although his written work is not as widely read as Gide's, nor does it receive the kind of attention Gide's work does, particularly in the academia, Cocteau's popularity as a cultural icon is stronger than Gide's, especially among the younger general public. Cocteau's ideas and style can be understood as a pure product of his times. Much like Christian Bérard, Raymond Radiguet, Robert Mallet-Stevens, and Jean-Michel Frank for instance, to name a few, Cocteau embodies for us in 2004 the nostalgic charm and the brilliant creativity of the Twenties and Thirties, a world that would eventually vanish with the outbreak of World War II and the revelation of its atrocities. Thus the fascination of *Têtu*'s modern gay readers with the legendary couple Cocteau-Marais can be construed as a semi-conscious nostalgia and desire for a glamorous and carefree life in a world where economic hardship and AIDS have become normal components of daily life. For Cocteau, postwar celebrity had a bitter-sweet taste. On one hand he was finally awarded official recognition: in 1946, he received the Louis-Delluc prize for *La Belle et la Bête*, the same year Marguerat began the publication of his complete works; in 1949, he was made chevalier de la Légion d'honneur; in 1950, he received the 'Prix international de la critique' at the Venice film festival for *Orphée*; in 1952, a large number of his paintings was exhibited in Munich; in 1955, he succeeded Colette at the Belgian *Académie royale de langue et de littérature françaises* and was elected at the Académie française; the following year, he was made doctor *honoris causa* at Oxford and, in 1957, an honorary member of the American

---

[6]   As an example, in Florence Tamagne's recent *Histoire de l'homosexualité en Europe* (Paris: Seuil, 2000), there are more than forty references to Gide versus only ten references to Cocteau.

National Institute of Arts and Letters, and so forth until his death in October 1963. On the other hand, it seems as if the official consecration of Cocteau's work by the highest international authorities did not entirely fulfill his dreams as a person and as an artist. Cocteau suddenly feared that he was losing some of his main characteristics, mainly the capability for his work to remain original, ahead of its time, and against the establishment. Curiously enough, Cocteau soon found himself in a contradictory situation where his work had finally been blessed officially, something he had always hoped for, while the artist felt further and further removed from his roots and the kind of audience which he once had wished to conquer. His relationship with Jean Genet, for instance, a writer Cocteau truly admired, reveals Cocteau's difficulty to reconcile wide public recognition with his artistic aspirations and personal needs. Cocteau wrote in his *Journal* in 1952 about his correspondence with the author of *Notre-Dame-des-Fleurs*: '[Genet's] letter underlines a loneliness which comes from the fact that, while I do not drive my boat correctly and believe that it is fair for me to do so, I ended up wrecking my boat on a desert island from which my signals cannot be seen any longer'.[7] In other words, Cocteau felt that he had trapped himself. If his need to be officially recognized is at least as strong as his desire to appear original and modern, at the same time he realizes that it is difficult – if at all possible – for an artist to constantly remain inventive and unsurpassed while his artistic values slowly become part of the canon, and are fully accepted by all social groups, even the most conservative ones. Cocteau may have simply underestimated his own capacity to gain public recognition, or the audience's willingness to quickly assimilate new ideas (including homosexuality) and original forms.

If Cocteau's prediction of 1943 is not entirely inaccurate today, in 2004, it is not quite right either. The contradiction at the core of Cocteau's figure is most probably the product of his own method of working or artistic conception. In a 1921 letter to Gide, who was questioning his sincerity (as an artist) as well as his work ethic, Cocteau replied: 'Our entire misunderstanding stems from your not wanting to understand that precisely what sets me apart from the *masters* is that I, having taken the *back*stairs on the way up, wish someday to go back down by the grand staircase'.[8] How could Cocteau hope to reach the level of Gide's reputation as a writer (or of any other 'master' of that time including Valéry and Claudel) while deliberately working against the grain? By refusing to become a 'master' in the old sense of the word, that is according to the humanist tradition, in which

[7]   *Le Passé défini 1951-1952* (Paris: Gallimard, 1983), p. 303.

[8]   Qtd in Arthur King Peters, *Jean Cocteau and André Gide: An Abrasive friendship* (New Brunswick: Rutgers University Press, 1973), p. 243, Cocteau's emphasis.

the teachings brought by the master to his disciples follow a rational and analytical process requiring efforts and self-discipline on behalf of both parts, Cocteau – like the surrealists – offered an alternative to those who could not or did not want to accept the social norms of that time when it comes to the educational values of art and literature. Cocteau's genius may have consisted in anticipating the fact that future generations would eventually disregard literature and reading in favor of the realm of visual arts: drawing, painting, sculpture, dance, theater, film, television, and, although Cocteau died too early to witness it, computer art and the internet. Like many of *Têtu*'s gay readers, Cocteau enjoyed a relatively easy and prosperous life as a child and teenager. Circus and theater probably played early in his life a similar role to that of television and the internet in children's life today. He obviously did not care much about school, but was fortunate enough to receive private lessons after dropping out of high school. A bright young man, who did not have to work to support himself, but lived a mundane life instead, Cocteau foretells a gay lifestyle, in which entertainment and free time carry as much – if not more – weight than work, and a society which privileges originality and talent over the values of hard work and discipline. Cocteau was indeed a very talented and original writer and artist. Both his writing and his visual work could be conceived as a rejection of the classical – and essentially heterosexual – models of creation, which required a series of efforts and logical steps towards better understanding. Instead, Cocteau's art short-circuits the traditional process, which somewhat painfully leads to knowledge, to provide his audience with a ready-made response to their interrogations. Certainly, for Cocteau, a formula in a book or in a play and a few pen strokes in a drawing can save the time and the effort which the teachings of the 'masters' require from us. Gide was probably one of the first writers to realize that the dominant traditional models of education were being threatened, that his own authority as a role model would inevitably be overshadowed by the new models and eventually replaced. To a certain extent Gide's relationship with the young Marc Allégret followed a more traditional pattern, closer to Plato's Greek love,[9] although Gide's moral standards were quite different from those of the early Twenties especially when it comes to sexuality. Gide was already notorious for his apology of desire in *Les Nourritures terrestres* (1897), *L'Immoraliste* (1902) and *Saül* (1903), which demonstrated in their own time a high sense of freedom and liberation from moral and social constraints. Nonetheless, one can understand why Marc Allégret, a young man drawn to the power of images, who was later going to become an important film maker, soon became disinterested with Gide's philosophical *morale* and *esprit critique*, while fascinated with

---

[9]   Although Gide's Socratic dialogue on homosexuality *Corydon* was first issued publicly in 1924, it was already completed by 1911.

Cocteau's brilliant visual aesthetic and contagious enthusiasm for new artistic forms. In a letter to Allégret dated 1919, Gide warns his disciple of the dangers such a false artistic enterprise may cause:

> ... that determination to expose only the extreme points of his [Cocteau's] feelings or his thoughts, compressing the sentence, that is to say his route from one point to another and at the same time the gait that would remain exclusively his own – makes his poetic style the easiest thing in the world to imitate, which he himself already imitates without meaning to or being aware that he does it, and which doesn't permit one to glimpse any nuance by which such a sequence of words (I dare not say, such verses) by Cocteau would be distinguishable from another such sequence by one of his disciples (take care not to become one) or by some awful Futurist predecessor (I am thinking of Marinetti) (see note 2 above, pp. 240-1).

Quoting this sentence in its entirety, with its many clauses and parentheses, is probably one of the most concrete ways to illustrate how much Gide's teachings and method differ from Cocteau's. Even when he attempts to be brief and concise for his disciple, Gide remains incapable to simplify his ideas and to reduce the many nuances of his thought. Gide concludes: 'In short, that stuff [Cocteau's poetic art] is not hard to do, and the qualities that I find in his work in spite of everything, those gifts for analogy wherein his delicate sensitivity is revealed, have nothing to do, or only very little, with that novel typographical layout that he would like to feel he invented...' (see note 2 above, p. 241).

Cocteau's criticism of Gide reached its peak during the last years of Gide's life and after his death, which seems rather odd considering that both men had finally reconciled after a few years of avoiding each other. Cocteau's attitude towards Gide in the Forties and Fifties reflects his contradicting personality. In public, Cocteau demonstrated not only respect but also affection for Gide, while in his diary his comments are often extremely violent and somewhat unfair. Here is an example dated 12 February 1945 (Gide is 76 years old): 'Letter from Gide to Jean Denoël. Look at him [= Gide] turning and tossing! He wants to write, to answer, and to publish articles. "Because, he says, lies always end up being right." He can be assured that he will be right' (see note 2 above, p. 623). Less than two weeks later, Cocteau writes to Gide, calling him '[m]y dear André': 'I think of you with all my heart and cannot stop myself from writing to you... Each day your face fills my small room at the Palais-Royal'. He ends his letter after 'hugging [him] faithfully'.[10] How can one reconcile the cruel sentences in Cocteau's diary with the tender ones in his letter to Gide? What did Cocteau mean by 'faithfully'? Which part of himself was he being faithful to? To the one who never ceased to admire and cherish the author of

---

[10]   *Lettres à André Gide* (Paris: La Table Ronde, 1970), pp. 185-6.

L'Immoraliste or to the one who secretly nourished all his life a feeling of envy towards the respected and honored writer he himself wanted to become? Cocteau probably didn't quite know himself. In his homage to Gide for the *Nouvelle Revue française* commemorative issue published after Gide's death, Cocteau began by saying that '[o]ne cannot allow himself to judge André Gide in a straight-forward fashion.'[11] Cocteau seems to acknowledge his ambiguous feelings towards the late writer, but his wording also betrays his feeling of guilt in having allowed himself to judge Gide in an inappropriate way from time to time. Indeed a few weeks prior to his contribution to the *N.R.F.* issue, Cocteau had written about Gide at length in his diary (Gide had died six months earlier). Among other things, he ridiculed the 'monstrous stupidity of Gide's *Journal*' calling it a 'bunch of lies and hypocrisies', 'the most boring *herbier*, the most insignificant collection of dry leaves'. And Cocteau concluded his entry by writing: 'His immoralist's moral is a stupidity. His Nobel prize is a joke' (see note 7 above, pp. 29-30). How could an intelligent, sensitive reader and writer such as Cocteau allow himself to write such virulent comments if not by mere jealously? During his meetings with Cocteau in preparation for his 1945 study of the writer, Claude Mauriac had already felt that 'well hidden beneath the friendship that [Cocteau] claims to feel for Gide, and disguised too by joking in a good-natured manner' lied 'a definite unfriendliness, the reasons for which do not seem unselfish to me. I had a presentiment of jealousy – and my heart tightened a moment, the discomfort was so strong – and of some unutterable anguish'.[12] As I shall demonstrate, other reasons than purely aesthetic ones may have pushed Cocteau to disagree with Gide's *morale* and style. In the rest of this essay I shall attempt to 'utter' Cocteau's anguish when it comes to Gide in order to understand what seems to be a refusal to take Gide seriously, to recognize his canonical place in modern French literature, and a rejection of constructive criticism for the benefit of formulas ('Gide's *Nourritures terrestres* is a Zarathustra for campers' – see note 7 above, p. 193) and lines of attack ('Gide had no genius in no way' – see note 7 above, p. 156), those same formulas for which Gide blamed Cocteau, as seen earlier in his letter to Allégret.

While preparing a short text for a photographic essay on Gide in 1952, Cocteau acknowledged that he could 'only find unfriendly sentences' to write (see note 7 above, p. 176). Was Cocteau expressing his true feeling for Gide, or did he himself find his words to be 'unfriendly', and thus unfair, toward the late writer? Judging from these remarks and the amount of gossip on the

---

[11]   'On ne peut se permettre', *La Nouvelle Revue française* (November 1951), p. 90.

[12]   Claude Mauriac, *Jean Cocteau ou la vérité du mensonge* (Paris: Odette Lieutier, 1945), quoted in King Peters, p. 256.

'Tout Paris' included in his diary, one is forced to admit that Cocteau's
Journal is far inferior to Gide's when it comes to style and depth. Any good-
faith reader will agree that Cocteau's *Journal* is more a personal record of
events, phrases and reactions with very little – if at all – literary value other
than an anecdotic one. Cocteau's 'unfriendly sentences' on Gide are so
'abrasive', to use Arthur King Peters' word, that they are difficult not to
interpret like mood swings or fits of jealousy, that is to say subjective
feelings, thus reinforcing the interpretation according to which Cocteau kept
a diary as a kind of therapeutic exercise. This would also explain why
Cocteau could not enjoy or even see the originality and quality of Gide's
enterprise in his *Journal*, which Gide conceived as a work of art equal to his
fictions and the rest of his autobiographical work. For Cocteau, this genre had
little or no literary value at all, but rather a practical one. However, far from
being limited to Gide's *Journal*, as time went by, Cocteau's negative
perception of Gide in the Forties and the Fifties seemed to encompass Gide's
entire literary work. This is suggested by Cocteau's generalizing comments
in his own *Journal*. When comparing Gide's work to those of Péguy and
Barrès, Cocteau finds it 'incredible that Gide wins over such masterpieces,
which the stupid youth refuses to read' (see note 2 above, p. 32). Of course
very few people would agree with this opinion today. How many readers
have read Barrès' *Colette Baudoche* or *Le Voyage de Sparte* since 1942,
when Cocteau was already blaming the younger generations for embracing
Gide and ignoring Barrès? Even Barrès's most acclaimed novel *Les
Déracinés* seems very foreign to modern readers. Of course Péguy's and
Barrès' works could always regain popularity in the future, however there are
reasons to believe that they will probably become more and more obscure for
future generations, and only accessible to a very small number of highly
specialized scholars. Cocteau's rejection of canonical writers (Gide, Valéry,
Claudel) and his comments in favor of secondary figures (Barrès, Péguy) can
be interpreted as the result of his own desire to portray himself in his diary as
an original and highly discriminating mind, able to foresee the future of
literature (the 'real' canon), as well as a precursor, whose ideas and style are
too advanced for his contemporaries. It is also possible that his negative
feelings for Gide forced him to exaggerate the qualities of Gide's
contemporaries such as Barrès in an attempt to overshadow the exceptional
longevity, strength and popularity which Gide still enjoyed among young
readers in 1942. Always in favor of Rousseau against the Encyclopedists,
convinced that Rousseau was not paranoid but truly persecuted by his peers,
Cocteau sometimes sounds much like the author of *Confessions* in his diary
while Gide is often compared to one of the Encyclopedists: 'It will be proven
one day (probably after my death) that I took the narrow path, and that those,
like Gide, who thought they did, and who accuse me to have taken the wide
path, mistook the narrow path with a certain poverty of their soul and a total

lack of heroism in the use of their activity' (see note 2 above, p. 393). Was Cocteau right in making these comments?

In a fragment of his *Journal* about Cocteau, Gide wrote in 1918: 'Nothing is more foreign to me than this concern for modernism which one feels influencing every thoughts and decision of Cocteau... I do not seek to be of my epoch; I seek to overflow my epoch'.[13] Although some of Gide's positions may sound outdated today in light of queer theory for instance, the fact that his works almost always contain their own self-criticism, presented as possible alternatives to the main argument, allowed Gide's works to remain highly valuable over time and to captivate new generations of readers who could identify one way or another with the characters, their behaviors and their ideas. By not limiting the work of art to one point of view (in particular to what may have seemed to be an original one, or a modern one at the time of writing), but rather by multiplying the number of points of view, Gide succeeded in representing the thought process common to any human being (man or woman, black or white, straight or gay, etc.), and thus allowing each reader to play an active role in the reading of his works. For Cocteau, such a method 'consist[ed] of faking to say everything in order to hide everything'.[14] Cocteau's criticism calls for two remarks: judging from the explicitness of Gide's writings (both public and private) when it comes to sexuality, one can say that Gide has left very few things unsaid, and thus cannot be accused to have faked anything more than any other writer. Moreover it can be said that faking is, to some extent, at the core of literary creation. Cocteau's own mythology and imagery do not seem more real than Gide's. It is therefore difficult to understand what Cocteau could possibly mean when he wrote that Gide was guilty of 'hiding everything': is it an allusion to Gide's hesitation to differentiate between homosexuality (a highly controversial form of sexuality) and pederasty (an illegal practice punishable by law)? I shall return, in the conclusion of this essay, to this particular issue, which Cocteau may have had in mind at the time he accused Gide of 'hiding everything': as we shall see, Cocteau's conception of homosexuality was very different from Gide's. It is because Cocteau was always more concerned with the result of an idea and the effect it would have on the audience (and the way it would shape the audience's understanding of the author) than with the thought process itself (and its rational and logical properties) that he may have found himself in the position of someone who had lost full control over his audience; an audience who, according to Cocteau's own words, could not see any longer the 'signals' he was sending from the 'desert island' where he had 'wrecked [his] boat'. In his attempt to force the audience to see his works

---

[13]   André Gide, *Journal 1884-1925* (Paris: Gallimard, 1997), p. 1063.

[14]   *Le Passé défini 1953* (Paris: Gallimard, 1985), p. 48.

as a series of self-portraits, always different (the portrait of the multi-talented and original mind which he truly was), it is possible that Cocteau neglected to provide his audience with enough self-initiative or freedom in their interaction with his works. For Gide, who very early in his career wrote about the book as a sort of even 'collaboration' between the author and the readers (i.e. the foreword of *Paludes* in 1895), Cocteau's conscious effort to control his audience's emotions, by focusing all his energy and talent on the effect that words and/or images were supposed to produce on them, seems ultimately vain. Cocteau's 'art degenerates in artifice' concluded Gide (see note 13 above, p. 1216). Although he was sensitive to the 'extreme genius of [Cocteau's] images' (p. 1216) and his 'delightful, stunning pages' (Cocteau's descriptions of a circus are 'a wonder', Gide wrote[15]), Gide also blamed Cocteau for what he perceived as a series of efforts to embrace modernism for the sake of modernism, and for his insistence on 'feeding' his readers words and images with an 'ultra-modern sauce' (see note 13 above, p. 1205). Gide's criticism of Cocteau's work is not entirely free of ambiguous feelings, and may very well have been conditioned by his own personal animosity toward Cocteau. In fact, Gide seems to confuse Cocteau's artistic work with Cocteau's personal voice. Interestingly enough, the traits which he despises in Cocteau the person – '[Cocteau's] protests, his curses, the play of his sword-cane, his entreaties, his oaths on the head of his parents' (qtd in King Peters, see note 8 above, p. 77) – are also the ones he blames in Cocteau the writer: 'What empty agitation in the tales he relates!' Gide wrote of *Le Livre blanc* in 1929, 'what affectation in his style! what a play to the gallery in the poses he strikes!... what artifice!...'[16]

Although Gide may have emphasized Cocteau's 'huge poetic exaggeration' for personal reasons, he is not the only one to have mocked Cocteau's melodramatic attitude (see note 13 above, p. 884). In a letter to Reynaldo Hahn dated March 1911, Marcel Proust wrote of Cocteau: 'Cocto [sic] wrote me... a letter next to which the one you are referring to could have been signed by Alceste, Obermann, Hamlet, Werther and Jacques the fatalist, and next to which again the beginning of *Carmen*'s opening scene is reserved, septentrional and slow'.[17] Like Gide, but in a more dubious fashion, Proust had alerted Cocteau to the dangers of such a behavior in a letter he wrote him in December 1910, soon after they met. But Proust's most efficient commentary on Cocteau's overstated attitude remains of course the satirical

---

[15]   Letter to Cocteau quoted in King Peters, p. 253.

[16]   *Journal 1926-1950* (Paris: Gallimard, 1997), p. 151, qtd by King Peters, see note 8 above, p. 252.

[17]   Marcel Proust, *Correspondance*, vol. X (Paris: Plon, 1983), p. 248.

portrait of Octave (almost an anagram of 'Cocteau') in *Albertine disparue*.[18] Indeed Cocteau's first works *La Lampe d'Aladin* (1909), *Le Prince frivole* (1910) and *La Danse de Sophocle* (1912) are a strange pot pourri of various themes (the ballet, the Orient, Ancient Greece) mixed together in a mundane, frivolous and melodramatic style. Cocteau, who did not feel comfortable with the effeminate aspects of his early work as well as his own personality, was to disavow these three texts as early as 1918, and destroy whatever copies he would lay his hands upon. For Angelo Rinaldi, Cocteau could not 'stand any longer to see again, even in a literary portrait, the person he had been before the crisis, the death of his lovers, his addiction to opium, and his embracing of modern art: a young man excessively effeminate in the process of becoming some kind of a Anna de Noailles in Sodoma'.[19] Indeed, the poems included in Cocteau's first three collections of poetry are reminiscent of those written by his close friend Anna de Noailles, whose influence he had not yet freed himself from. Likewise, Cocteau's drawings of this period are close to the pastels of Marie Laurencin, another intimate female friend. Certainly Cocteau's alleged effeminate behavior made Gide uncomfortable. In a letter to Gide dated 1912, Cocteau wrote that he was going through 'a phase', and admitted that *La Danse de Sophocle*, a copy of which he had recently sent to Gide along with a warm inscription, bore 'childish influences' (see note 10 above, p. 31). Cocteau probably meant 'female influences': those of Anna de Noailles – Cocteau called her '*une rose crétoise*' in his letter to Gide (de Noailles's mother was Greek, see note 10 above) – and Marie Laurencin, who was to illustrate the cover of Cocteau's *La Rose de François* in 1923. For Cocteau, drawing is a form of writing: '*le dessin est une écriture*'.[20] At the crossroads between writing and drawing, and between text and image, Cocteau's handwriting truly embodies the person he was before he attempted to free himself from his early models. Cocteau recalls in *Opium*:

> In the stupidity of extreme youth I had manufactured a handwriting for myself. This false writing, revealing to a graphologist, made me false to the very soul. I looped a little loop to the big loop of my capital J's. One day as he was leaving my house, Gide, in the doorway, said to me, overcoming his constraints: 'I advise you to simplify your J's'. I was beginning to understand what a sorry glory was built on youth and brio. The surgery on that loop saved me. I forced myself to go back to my real handwriting and, with the help of the handwriting, I recovered the naturalness I had lost (qtd in King Peters, see note 8 above, p. 212).

---

[18] Interestingly enough, both Proust's depiction of Octave (alias Cocteau) in *Albertine disparue* and Gide's ironic portrait of Passavent (inspired by Cocteau) in *Les Faux-Monnayeurs* came out in November 1925.

[19] 'Cocteau l'encyclopédiste', *Service de presse* (Paris: Plon, 1999), p. 217.

[20] *Journal d'un inconnu* (Paris: Grasset, 1953), p. 115.

Although anecdotic, this episode is particularly relevant because it demonstrates how much Cocteau's writing and drawing are tightly connected with one another, and how they always evolved together at the same pace and in the same direction. Cocteau's early drawings, much like his writing, focused on rather frivolous and mundane subjects (his early drawings published in *Le Mot* resemble the art of popular cartoonists Sem and Cappiello). This 'lack of seriousness', according to Gide's words, is obvious in Cocteau's choice of topics and in the way he portrayed them in his writings and drawings. Cocteau's letters, including the ones he sent to Gide, illustrate (so to speak) Cocteau's original and frivolous style. These letters mix writing and drawing with no respect for any type of formality, and instead of following a straight line, Cocteau's handwriting circles and loops around in an untidy fashion. Similarly, by the late Twenties and early Thirties, Cocteau's depictions of male characters were still rather 'childish', to use Cocteau's own word, and effeminate. In the series of drawings of naked males he drew for the first illustrated edition of *Le Livre blanc* in 1930, curved and serpentine lines outnumber straight ones, and match the book's flowery and melodramatic tone. Cocteau would eventually try to diffuse the pathos of his book in 1949 by replacing the effeminate figures of 1930 by a series of stronger, more masculine and positive ones.

A series of events could have influenced Cocteau from 1930 to 1949 in what seems to be, at first glance, a sudden and unexpected change in his perception of himself and his depictions of homosexuals. The two decades spanning from 1930 until 1949 seem to have been rich in learned lessons. Of course the rise of nationalism in Europe as well as the experience of the war had to play a role in the way Cocteau now envisioned himself and the people around him. Frivolity and the *insouciante joie de vivre* soon became a thing of the past. Hitler's rise to power in 1933, which coincided with the death of Anna de Noailles, could help us pin down the beginning of Cocteau's metamorphosis. If the political events in Germany seemed to have had very little influence on Cocteau's work besides the fact that he was certainly able to witness a sudden change in the state of mind of French intellectuals and artists, Anna de Noailles' death probably marked the end of one of Cocteau's earliest and strongest influences during the first twenty-five years of his career. The death of Cocteau's long-time friend Christian Bérard in 1949 would play the same role as de Noailles' death sixteen years earlier, and could be used as the milestone marking the end of Cocteau's metamorphosis. With Bérard's death, not only was Cocteau losing a close friend, but also one of his most admired models and pre-war influences. Finally the death of Cocteau's mother in 1943, in the midst of the war years, certainly had a strong impact on Cocteau's lifestyle, his sudden ability to change his personal life and to publicly express his most hidden secret. Let us not forget that it was for fear of embarrassing his mother that, according to his own words,

Cocteau had published *Le Livre blanc* anonymously in 1928, and again in 1930.

Cocteau's losses in the Thirties and Forties were compensated by some important personal and artistic discoveries. 1933 is the year Picasso, a close friend of Cocteau, started working extensively on the Vollard Suite. There is no doubt that Picasso's depictions of the Minotaur, a highly masculine if not animalistic erotic figure, impressed Cocteau and soon influenced him in his own portrayal of male figures. Picasso's Minotaur also reminded Cocteau of the art of Michelangelo, one of the artists to whom Cocteau refers the most in his diary during these years. Incidentally, Michelangelo's name is associated twice with that of Arno Breker. In his homage to Breker, Cocteau wrote of the German sculptor: 'the large hand of Michelangelo's *David* has shown you the way' (see note 2 above, p. 133). Cocteau was particularly fascinated by Breker's recent sculpture of a naked wounded man: 'One guesses that everything in him comes from Michelangelo's *David*' (p. 126). After Picasso's hyperbolic representations of the Minotaur and Michelangelo's powerful figures, Breker's ideally perfect and virile sculptures of German naked warriors could not have left Cocteau the artist and the homosexual indifferent. It is still with Michelangelo in mind that Cocteau talked about another one of his discoveries during the war years. In March 1943, at the home of a wealthy art collector and bibliophile, Cocteau saw for the very first time the original and non-expurgated version of El Greco's *Martyrdom of Saint Mauritius* refused by El Escorial.[21] That night, Cocteau jotted down enthusiastically in his diary: 'Treasures. The most beautiful pieces of furniture in the world. All the first editions of Pascal, Descartes, Racine, etc. But the object which fascinates is the El Greco (see note 2 above, p. 290). What part of El Greco's painting was Cocteau fascinated with? 'His painting tied from top to bottom is an arrangement of hard penises. This is why he [El Greco] resembles Michelangelo. Ah! their biceps, their stomachs, their calves, their knees!' (p. 291). El Greco's powerful and explicit canvas could be seen as a revelation as important for Cocteau as that of Michelangelo's *David* in his youth. There is no doubt that El Greco's uncensored painting also reminded Cocteau of the male figures which Michelangelo had painted for the Sistine Chapel. It also made him more eager to find out what was hidden under the added pieces of fabrics painted on the bodies of the numerous male figures.[22] A few days prior to writing his description of El Greco's *Martyrdom of Saint Mauritius*, Cocteau wrote the following entry in his diary: 'Perhaps true greatness consists in doing like Michelangelo? To

---

[21]   The original of the painting is in the collection of El Escorial outside Madrid.

[22]   Several erotic drawings of male figures included in Annie Guédras' book on Cocteau's male erotic drawings are based on Michelangelo's compositions.

deceive the pope, and to deceive God. To fill up the churches ceilings and the public squares with one's secrets' (p. 272). Although it may not have been Michelangelo's primary motivation in adorning the Vatican and the city of Florence with depictions of male figures, it seems that this type of motivation influenced more and more Cocteau's own attitude in his life and his art after the war. Cocteau's attraction to strong, masculine, and positive male figures in art, whose muscles and sexual organs seem free from any attempt to be hidden or constricted, coincides with his urging need to come out and to present himself in a completely different fashion.[23] His love affairs with Marcel Kihl (met in 1933), the actor Jean Marais (met in 1937), the African-American boxer Al Brown (met in 1937), and finally Edouard Dermit (met in 1947) are the concretization of his new sense of identity. Masculinity and physical strength are without any doubt the main features one can think of in front of these four men. Their strong and almost God-like physiques, and the drawings they inspired Cocteau, are also in complete opposition with the long string of frivolous and effeminate homosexual characters Cocteau had described in *Le Livre blanc*, and the figures he had drawn for the 1930 illustrated edition. The 1949 drawings, inspired by the bodies of Kihl and Brown, are closer to the ones Cocteau had drawn two years before for the illustrated edition of Genet's *Querelle de Brest*. Interestingly enough Cocteau mentions El Greco's *Martyrdom of Saint Mauritius* in conjunction with the work of Jean Genet and the lattter's explicit and untamed depictions of hyper masculine homosexuals in his then unpublished novel *Notre-Dame-des-Fleurs* which Cocteau had just read for the first time. In short, the loss of his mother and some intimate friends and influencing artists (de Noailles, Bérard) and the rejection of the frivolity, which had once characterized his life, combined with the discovery of new artists (Breker, El Greco) and writers (Genet), contributed to slowly metamorphosing the artist and the homosexual. Long gone were the days when Cocteau could find role models in Proust's sad and pathetic depictions of homosexuals. Cocteau now judged his past effeminate and frivolous behavior as a 'brilliant stupidity of that time' (see note 7 above, p. 299) and a 'series of serious mistakes' (see note 20 above 22). Finally it is also because Cocteau's metamorphosis was so radical over a period of twenty years that he may have found himself in the position of someone who had lost full control over his audience; an audience who, according to Cocteau's own words, could not see any longer the 'signals' he was sending from the 'desert island' where he thought had 'wrecked [his] boat'.

Before attacking Gide in the Forties and Fifties, when it was clear that Gide's 'immoralism', or 'homosexual moralism' to use Patrick Pollard's

---

[23]   It is particularly obvious in Cocteau's erotic drawings of young sailors, cooks and other lower-class characters.

words, would remain intact even after his death,[24] Cocteau had expressed to Gide his feeling of thankfulness for the kind of constructive criticism Gide had given him early in his career: '[I] owe you so many things, Cocteau wrote in 1929, without your intervention, my life was at loss', and again in 1931: 'scold me. I listen to you. I suppose that you are right and I will watch myself' (see note 10 above, pp. 158, 165-6). One of the few issues on which Cocteau seemed to agree with Gide was Proust's representation of homosexuality in *La Recherche du temps perdu*. Cocteau's comments in his *Journal* upon rereading Proust in the early Fifties echo those Gide had made in his own *Journal* when *Sodome et Gomorrhe* first appeared in 1921. More than thirty years after Gide, Cocteau continued to blame Proust for 'hiding himself behind the *other*' (see note 7 above, p. 281, Cocteau's emphasis) – Gide had called it a 'camouflage' and an 'offense to the truth' (see note 13 above, p. 1143) – and the 'comical vulgarity' of his depiction of homosexuals (see note 7 above, 269) (Gide had referred to it as 'grotesque' and 'abject' – see note 13 above, p. 1127). While rereading Proust's *Recherche du temps perdu*, Cocteau felt the same annoyance – which Gide had once felt for him – towards what he called 'Proust's sick snobbism', his 'unbearable' and 'never-ending snobbism' (see note 7 above, p. 294, p. 300). By resuscitating the ghost of his old self, the new reading of Proust could only reinforce Cocteau's new identity and his rejection of the kind of person he once had been. It also allowed him to measure the importance of his metamorphosis. From that point until his death in 1963, Cocteau's repetitive and almost obsessive visual representation of aroused hyper masculine figures can be seen as a series of continuous attempts to permanently erase his old frivolous self, his previous effeminate representations of homosexuals and his former conception of homosexuality, in order to replace them with his new sense of identity and a stronger, more positive and attractive image.

In spite of the indignation they both felt and expressed in their diaries about Proust's (mis)treatment of homosexuality in *La Recherche*, Cocteau and Gide were far from sharing the same ideas when it came to homosexuality. If the figure of David plays an important role in both their personal mythologies, the biblical character bears a different face – and above all a different body – for Cocteau and for Gide. Gide's ideal companion is Donatello's *David* with his 'small delicate body' and his 'oriental grace' or, at most, Verocchio's 'admirable' but surprisingly youthful *David* (see note 13 above, p. 207). For Cocteau, on the contrary, only one David ever existed: Michelangelo's muscular and manly giant, precisely the kind of figure he had eventually chosen as a model for himself after Proust

---

[24]   Gide received the Nobel prize for literature in 1947 approximately at the time the Vatican included his works in the *Index librorum prohibitorum*. There is no doubt that Cocteau would have prided himself on receiving both distinctions.

and Gide had revealed what he thought was an unbearably effeminate and melodramatic individual. Cocteau also disagreed with Gide's Socratic conception of homosexuality: '[Gide's] instincts seemed to push him toward extremely youthful behavior and toward Greek forms of love, wrote Cocteau. Now, what matters in this area is when strength pairs with strength' (qtd by King Peters, see note 8 above, p. 269). Nothing and no one, even the young biblical hero, would ever reconcile Cocteau and Gide, whose most constant feature – in their lives as in their works – had been their love and admiration of persons of their own sex.

Glancing at the pages of *Têtu* today, as well as other gay magazines around the world, one is forced to admit that Cocteau's representations of homosexuals – if not his whole conception of homosexuality – often coincide with that of younger generations of gay people who have a hard time identifying with Gide's characters and his own conception of homosexuality. Although it remains difficult to measure the impact that Cocteau's visual representations of the gay male body had on later artists in Europe and in the United States, it seems that his influence can be found in the works of artists such as Jean Boullet and Gordon Harris, in the Fifties, and in those of Andy Warhol and Tom of Finland in the Sixties and Seventies. Short of being considered as canonical a writer as Gide, Valéry and Claudel, there is no doubt that Cocteau can still be seen today, forty years after his death, as one of France's finest contributors to pop culture and gay subculture.

WORKS CITED

Primary Sources

Cocteau, Jean, *Journal 1942-1945* (Paris: Gallimard, 1989)

—. *Le Passé défini 1953* (Paris: Gallimard, 1985)

—. *Le Passé défini 1951-1952* (Paris : Gallimard, 1983)

—. *Lettres à André Gide* (Paris: La Table Ronde, 1970)

—. *Journal d'un inconnu* (Paris: Grasset, 1953)

Gide, André, *Journal 1884-1925* (Paris: Gallimard, 1997)

Proust, Marcel, *Correspondance* (Paris: Plon, 1983)

Secondary Sources

King Peters, Arthur, *Jean Cocteau and André Gide: An Abrasive friendship* (New Brunswick: Rutgers University Press, 1973)

Pollard, Patrick, *André Gide Homosexual Moralist* (New Haven: Yale University Press, 1992)

Magda Răduță

The Day Before, the Day After.
Canonic and Self-Legitimation Changes in the Romanian Literature Before and After the Fall of the Communist Regime

After the fall of the Romanian communist regime, the socio-cultural background changed dramatically. Literature, understood either as a protest discourse or as cheering the Ceaușescu regime, was replaced by an opening to the public space. Romanian literary life closely followed these changes: one can now see new roles emerging in the literary space and fights for a better position that modify the literary field. The purpose of this article is to analyze the strategies used in the literary struggle for power as well as the way one can assume a literary position in the last of the communist years and in the first post-communist years. It aims at a better understanding of both the Romanian writer's change in identity and the revival brought by the first days of a free society.

The questions I am trying to answer are the following: 1. the way the Romanian writers see their identity in the new context of the free public spirit and frontier openness; 2. the vision of the literary practice in a post-totalitarian era shocked by a limitless freedom and, last but not least, 3. what to do with *les plumes indignes*, i. e. Ceaușescu's regime collaborators.

In terms of the theoretical background I am going to rely on two sociological directions that are quite well-known in French sociology: that of Natalie Heinich (2000) and that of Bernard Lahire (2006), that take into account the social dimension of the writer as an actor, on the one hand,[1] and the polemics on the writer's responsibility as a guideline of his identity, on the other.[2]

---

[1]   Nathalie Heinich, *Être écrivain* (Paris: La Découverte, 2000) and Bernard Lahire, *La Condition littéraire. La double vie des écrivains* (Paris : La Découverte, 2006).

[2]   For the relation between ethical responsibility and the writer's self legitimation, see Anna Boschetti's chapter (in *Sartre et 'Les Temps modernes'* [Paris, Minuit, 1985] on Sartre's well-known sentences, published in the first issue of *Temps modernes*: 'L'écrivain est en situation dans son époque: chaque parole a des retentissements. Chaque silence aussi. Je tiens Flaubert et Goncourt pour responsables de la répression qui suivit la Commune parce qu'ils n'ont pas écrit une ligne pour l'empêcher. Ce n'était pas leur affaire, dira-t-on. Mais le procès de Calas, était-ce l'affaire de Voltaire? La condamnation de Dreyfus, était-ce l'affaire

The paper takes a quick glance at two significant situations concerning the literary changes occuring in the first post-communist year: the struggle to choose between civic activism and a 'pure' writer career, the latter still considered almost the only – the strongest, in any case – identity at hand for a Romanian writer, and the canonical confrontations arising from the trials of adjusting the position of ethics in the interior of the literary canon.

As an example for our theory, I chose a generation of Romanian writers that strongly imposed itself in the last communist decade and also managed to hold a strong position of power after 1989, in the new Romanian literary climate: the '80s Generation.[3] It is not possible, within the limits of this paper, to follow all the strategies used by the '80s Generation, a generation of grouped voices, to become a generation of individualities, more or less adapted to the movements in the literary field, to the free market of artistic goods and to the hardships of a writer's life without a secondary profession. This paper looks into the literary magazines of the so-called 'the day after', of the first post-communist year. All quotations are selected from *România Literară* magazine (*Literary Romania*), the flag journal of the autonomous pole that, in the communist period, sees aestheticism as the only possible way to autonomy and, consequently, as the only way to survive the regime pressures; a second magazine used for reference is *Contrapunct* (*Counterpoint*), a literary journal founded in the first day of freedom by the active core of the '80s Generation.

---

de Zola? L'administration du Congo, était-ce l'affaire de Gide? Chacun de ces auteurs, en une circonstance particulière de sa vie, a mesuré sa responsabilité d'écrivain'. Recent studies on this topic can be found in Gisèle Sapiro, 'La responsabilité de l'écrivain: de Paul Bourget à Jean-Paul Sartre', in Joseph Jurt (dir.), *Le Texte et le contexte. Analyses du champ littéraire français XIXe-XXe* (Berlin verlag Arno Spitz, 2001), pp. 219-240, and 'Le principe de sincérité et l'éthique de responsabilité de l'écrivain', in Eveline Pinto (dir.), *L'Ecrivain, le savant et le philosophe. La littérature, entre philosophie et sciences socials* (Paris: Publications de la Sorbonne, 2004), pp. 183-202.

[3] The '*80s Generation* is the name of the literary group of poets, novelists and literary critics that made their debut at the end of the '70s; they became notorious by sharing the same characteristics in writing: ludic texts, intertextuality, refusal of the social and philosophical novel and of excessive metaphors in poetry. The group's cohesion manifested mostly in literary circles of Romanian universities and in faculty literary magazines. In the second half of the 80s, some young writers (Mircea Cărtărescu, Gh. Crăciun, I. B. Lefter etc.) became known for theorizing the literary contribution of their group as postmodernist.

1. The New Wave – A Short Presentation of a Won Battle

In the late '70s, a new literary movement began to force its way into the Romanian literary life. The new group displays all the characteristics of an avant-garde movement: all its members are young, and have recently finished their philological studies; they have a strong literary conscience and don't hesitate to declare their rupture from the past generations. These last characteristics, being naturally included in the logic of literary fields, can be differently understood when perceived in a particular context that modifies, mixes and seldom completely transforms the rules of the field: the context of a communist society. Imposing itself as a movement of philologists, the '80s Generation makes itself conspicuous through a common literary program, situated in the autonomous proximity of the literary field. 'The new wave' rapidly becomes a group which defends autonomy and aestheticism through literary works that state the author's and the text's supremacy, using a meta-discourse as well as the theoretical position which defends art for art's sake. Their legitimating strategies also include a clever use of the conditions offered by the literary field: the editorial practice of collective debut, used by publishers to obey the ideological commandments (and to manage to publish in a time of paper shortage) is once again cleverly used by the new generation of writers to transform the collective volume in a true means of collective debut as an already formed group. At that time, their literature was thought of as a literature with double purpose: it chose to denounce, through realism, the true state of the society, but, at the same time, it didn't abandon the true power of fiction. The young literary group imposes itself rapidly and without opposition through strong means of literary socialization (literary circles, student reviews and collective volumes), but equally through other means: a continuous common work of self-legitimation, the direct verdicts of the most notorious critics of the time and of their opponents. The evolution of the '80s Generation includes a literary program that resembles the classic mechanism of all avant-garde movements: the rejection of their predecessors, finding affinities with other groups of rupture and promoting new ways of writing. The members of the '80s Generation display another novelty: they pass themselves for the initiators of a new literary paradigm, i. e. postmodernism, in order to state their individual position in the literary field.

Their positions are therefore similar to the critics who are contributors to *România Literară* magazine. They are the same critics that support the debut of the new generation. In the late '70s and early '80s, the distribution of positions in the Romanian literary field displays a change when compared to the 'classic' structure of Bourdieu's theory: the supreme instance of legitimation in the field (that is, in the Romanian case, historically placed under the sub-field of literary criticism) is concentrated around the autonomous pole (and in the chart of the most prestigious ones) and visibly supports the newcomers. These literary godfathers of the young writers form the group of critics who establish the literary hierarchy and are part of the juries that distribute the national prizes of literature: Ov. S. Crohmălniceanu (1921-2000), Nicolae Manolescu (b. 1939), Eugen Simion (b. 1933), Ion Pop (b. 1941), Marian Papahagi (1948-1999), Alexandru Călinescu (b. 1945), Livius Ciocîrlie (b. 1935). This group of literary parents displays three main fundamental characteristics that account for their position of power at the centre of the field. They are at the same time:

- literary columnists at central or province local journals, and to the same extent, literary historians who center their interests on specific 'autonomous' values (modern literature debuts, the history of Romanian literary criticism, Italian and French literature in the beginning of 20th century);

- professors at the Faculty of Letters in the most important universities in Romania (Bucharest, Cluj, Iaşi, Timişoara);

- members in the boards of other non-political structures of power of the Writers' Union[4].

The group of critics reached this position of power at the end of a startling course. Having managed to impose themselves in the late '50s, under the political conditions of the so called 'slight thaw' (the first attempt, partly successful, to escape socialist realism), they have the same starting point as the poets of the '60s. First of all, they use the same strategy: they try to recover the literary values specific to the inter-war period and reestablish the hierarchies of *l'art pur*, leaving out any trace of ideology, and thus trying to diminish the damages of such a long period of heteronymic literature supremacy. Throughout the '70s, one can witness a separation (though difficult to see, still there) between the groups of critics, on the one hand (that remain in the proximity of the autonomous pole to defend art for art's sake), and the poets and novelists who managed to be 'accepted' by the regime and who move towards the pole of the most important ones in the chart,[5] on the other.

---

[4]   To read more about the importance of the Writers Union in Romania see Lucia Dragomir, *L'Union des Écrivains. Une institution littéraire transnationale à L'Est: l'exemple roumain* (Paris: Belin, 2007).

[5]   Though seductive, a detailed explanation of this separation in the middle of the '60s generation cannot be discussed here. However, I would like to launch a hypothesis: criticism is, by its structure, less permeable to the political ideology, simply because it has its own

This movement jams again the field's lines at the moment of the new generation's debut. In the late '70s, the image of the field ('frozen in time' here to facilitate comprehension) is as follows:

A) the new generation is supported by the literary critics who possess the strongest symbolical power, establish the canonical list and are, at the same time, their mentors in literary circles and in literary magazines.

The young writers receive their credentials at the beginning of their career in Romanian literary life: in 1978-1979, one can read a series of articles full of praises for the *nouvel esprit* that manifests itself in the literary circles of Romania[6]; these articles are signed by the best-rated critics in the legitimating hierarchies. This is a situation that contradicts all the natural dynamics of an avant-garde movement: the struggle for a better position in the field bypasses the 'classical' course,[7] and the new group comes to the hybrid situation of being supported in its process of ascension by the critics of the time.

Henceforth, the process develops a double dimension: the enthusiastic praises of the critics are seconded by efforts of the young writers, as well as by their powerful legitimating activism. An important conclusion imposes itself: the two dimensions of the field are simultaneous. The literary touchstones of the generation are Nicolae Manolescu's creation (in 1978, in an interview by an active member of his literary circle) under the reserve of probability (rhetoric, in its turn) – 'you and your colleagues, born in this very

---

ideology to defend. When criticism ceases to defend specific values, there is no turning back, and it becomes partisan criticism. This is not the case with poetry and prose, which prove more permissive, probably because of a more clever use of mechanisms in the process of fiction.

[6]   See Mircea Martin, 'Group Portrait', *Echinox*, No. 10-11-12/ 1978, p. 3; Mircea Iorgulescu 'The Newcomers', *România Literară*, No. 21/24 May 1979, p. 3; Nicolae Manolescu, 'The Youngest Writers', *România Literară*, No. 47/22 November 1979, p. 10; Ştefan Augustin Doinaş, 'For a New Literary Generation', *România Literară*, No. 50/ December 13, 1979, p. 4. In these articles (and in many others published throughout this decade) one can witness a long series of legitimating discourses (prefaces, afterwords, quotations, etc.) signed by these critics.

[7]   In one of the most renowned studies dedicated to the historical avant-garde movement, Renato Poggiolly makes up a dialectical movement that consist of four stages: activism, antagonism, nihilism and agonism. Cf. *The Theory of the Avant-Garde,* translated from Italian by Gerald Fitzgerald (the original Italian edition, *Teoria dell'arte d'avant-guardia,* Società editrice Il Mulino, 1962), 3rd edn, (Cambridge, Massachusetts, London: The Belknap Press of Harvard University Press, 1982). In what concerns Romania's case during the '80s, I believe that only the first two moments are more prominent, with an emphasis on activism (namely, exactly the one that R. Poggioli refers to as being 'the least important or, in any case, the least characteristic', p. 27).

moment of our debut, you could be the first visitors from another galaxy we meet today, in the space of literary history'. His next interviews point out the evolution of the feed-back process of the young literature. Four years after the announcement of the great literary promise, these once young poets are now, the critic said, 'talented poets, appreciated authors and literary award winners'[8]. Finally, a year later, the mentor of the '80s Generation has already formed a complete image of their evolution, but is equally aware of the difficulties his young apprentices went through: 'In literature, the arrival of a generation doesn't cease to amaze us. [...] It's dazzling how the most frequent reaction resembles fear: no, it's not possible, this is not a generation, it's just a... literary group, nothing more! As if the linguistic taboo could chase away the danger, the devil!...'[9] For the other mentor of the literary circle, Ovid S. Crohmălniceanu, the moment to publish a new collective volume of his young students' short stories is also the moment when he confesses his paternity: 'But of course, they are all my children. I became father at 62 and now, better than I expected, I have numerous offspring I am very proud of'.[10]

B) Their position of new entries in the field is not menaced by other groups of young writers who could claim affiliation to the same autonomous pole;

1. The most notable writers – that include, among others, the poet Nichita Stănescu (1933-1983) and novelists of the de-Stalinization period as D. R. Popescu (b. 1935), A. Buzura (b. 1938) and Nicolae Breban (b. 1934) – don't act yet as their enemies. The writers of the '70s generation have, at first sight, an uncanny position in the late '70s: they possess the same amount of symbolical, cultural and economic capital. Being supported – by the same critics (once belonging to the same generation) – as the most important writers of the after-war period, living a comfortable life thanks to their writing, they never acted as legitimating instances. They continue writing politicized novels (at the will of the new leading class, a 'progressivist' one, the same that replaced the so-called

---

[8]   The title of the interview is almost as rich in significations as the direct declarations of the critic: 'The credo of all of us who are concerned about the new literature should be: "literary value above all"' – Nicolae Manolescu, Interview in *Amfiteatru*, No. 5 (149)/1978, p. 10.

[9]   The quotation that gives the title always consists of a sort of allusion for the reader of those times: 'Talent and principles are synonymous in every profession that needs moral conscience' – Nicolae Manolescu, Interview by Gh. Grigurcu, Familia, 5 series, No. 31 (120)/ March 1983, p. 9.

[10]   Ov. S. Crohmălniceanu, Interview in *Tribuna*, No. 14/5April, 1984, p. 5.

'apparatchiks') and metaphorical poems, which continue Mallarmé's experiences; they are included in literature textbooks and effortlessly join the politicized structures of the Writers' Union and, at the same time, the Central Committee of PCR (Romania's Communist Party);

C) The writers gathered around the ideological pole conduct an aggressive political attack against the 'autonomists'. The members of this group (writing for *Săptămâna / The Week* magazine) are deprived of symbolical capital due to their writing and complete subordination to the will of the party; they represent the most violent opposition against the young writers.[11]

This last action became more and more obvious after the moment when Eugen Barbu (1924-1993), editor in chief of the *Săptămâna* magazine, was denounced for plagiarism by *România Literară*.[12] The scandal is the most visible line that separates the fields in the Romanian literary life of the last communist decade. Looking at this threshold, we come across an interesting situation: to expose the literary theft of one of the closest members of the Party is, undoubtedly, one of the most daring political stands of the men of letters grouped around the magazine of the autonomous pole, but, according to the definition of the field's reflexion effect, the political stands become visible only by means of literary stands. The will to break up with the group of nationalist writers that paid their respects to Nicolae Ceaușescu undergoes a manifestation which was supposed to belong exclusively to the literary universe: the specific value of the writer's identity and originality. Eugen Barbu and his acolytes are not exposed as ideologized writers and totalitarian art disciples, but merely as charlatans, as impostors who violate the specific code of the literary game.

---

[11] The concepts of 'constrained' and 'approved' literature are to be found in Eugen Negrici's volume *Literatura română sub comunism* (Romanian Literature under the Communist Regime, vol. I) (Bucharest: Pro Publishing House, 2002). The latter concept defines the literary productions that were entirely written under the Party's constraints: massive editions glorifying the party and its leader.

[12] In an article published in *România Literară* (no. 2, January 1979), N. Manolescu unveils the multiple literary thefts of Eugen Barbu from the memoirs of K. G. Paustovski, *Temps de jadis*, from Ilya Ehrenburg (the IVth volume of *Les gens, les années, la vie*), from M. Koltsov's and from some fragments of A. Malraux and Hemingway's novels. The manner and the writer are publicly rejected by The Writers Union and Eugen Barbu loses his position in the Central Committee of PCR (Romanian Communist Party). For details, see Mircea Martin, 'Romanian Culture Between Communism and Nationalism', 22, No. 45 (661)/11 November 2002, p. 11.

It is this detour of the specific laws of literature that makes us witness the birth of the most aggressive opponent of the 'new wave'. For the ideologically-biased writers gathered around *Săptămâna* magazine, the new comers are guilty because they claim to come from the autonomous literature and because their mentors are the same aestheticist critics who denied the slightest literary recognition for the Party's followers.

2. To believe in the Power of Literature – the First Words of Liberty

When communism collapsed, the literary field modifications came from the strategies of the '80s Generation, willing to take over the positions of authority. This is what makes the moment interesting – and this deserves a closer look –, namely, the canonical appeal – long awaited, imagined, dreamt about over the years – didn't naturally follow with the new air of liberty; moreover, these stakes are intermediated by the eternal confrontation between fame and the defense of professional values, on the one hand, and ethical judgment, on the other.

3. The Concord, the Guilt and the Future

Surprisingly enough, a survey of the collection that contains the first 'free' issues of the two literary magazines displays a sort of concord: the entire intellectual world agrees that literature had the role of a quiet resistance, and that especially in literature – more than in other domains – ideological intrusions were forever stopped. The old question of intellectual responsibility appeared to be overlooked: on the first day after December 1989, the literature written under Ceauşescu's regime was seen by the 'men of letters' as 'nearly tidy' and clear. In the general enthusiasm, the word of order was that the *pan littéraire* has successfully supplemented (or replaced) the lack of truth. A Romanian literary critic, Gheorghe Grigurcu, states in his article, 'Morality and Opportunism' that: 'The majority of Romanian writers have refused to be compromised [...] Their forms of protest were many, from the significant silence in the view of triumphalism [...] to the expressions between the lines, and to innuendoes of the truth concerning everything about the presence of censorship and finally, more than once, to the attitude of refusal and firm rejection of imposture, the real representatives of Romanian literature have taken part in a long an tiring fight that had for purpose an equally artistic and moral ideal'.[13]

The concord concerning the status of literature goes hand in hand with the emphasis on further pursuing the pure aesthetic dimension, seen as the only choice available for a writer. Nicolae Manolescu, the most important autonomous critic of the period, the notorious leader of the aestheticist group and godfather of the '80s Generation, sees the difference between 'writing in solitude' and 'social implication' as a fundamental and specific dimension:

> We have to write about books, ideas and not about the immediate reality, alive as it may seem to us, especially in the last weeks [...] The document doesn't replace the novel. The adhesion or the protest do not entail the presence of a literary critic [...] Of course, we will not abandon reality, but we'll never count just on the cult of declarations and on the present moments; one cannot wait forever for a real work to be written, thinking that we are not morally purified enough. These processes are and will stay parallel for a long time, and if we really want to clear away the new opportunists and the old compromised, this is not going to happen by mere declarations or by pointing the finger, but by artistically valid works. Let us be mature, calm and lucid.[14]

Thus, the critic ends his plea for coming back to the writer's tools, the only possibility he conceives for 'a return to normality' (see note 14 above).

This image of a literature sheltered from ideological intrusion is part of a superposition (most characteristic for the last communist decade in Romania) between the non-participative and the resistance. Affirming the quasi-'cleanness' of literature in Ceauşescu's time, the old 'autonomists' take a big step forward in imposing themselves in the emergent field: they assume the position of resistance and of guardians of literary purity in difficult times. From here, they draw the lines of the new Romanian literary space, fixing the coordinates of the future *travail de mémoire*, the necessary recoveries and the way of the new literature in times of freedom. Thus, they occupy the decisive positions in the new literary politics, using the experience acquired in the structures of power of the old Writers' Union.

The model of the cultural future is synthesized in the first free issue of *România Literară*, in an interview with the new Minister of Culture, Andrei Pleşu. Philosopher and art historian, a former opponent of the communist regime, condemned in 1989, he proposes (in his first public speech after he was invested) the sacred model of cultural resurrection, bearing in mind the discourse of pure art, the privilege of the sacred ones:

---

[13] Gheorghe Grigurcu, 'Morality and Opportunism', *România Literară*, 6 January 1990, p. 8.

[14] Nicolae Manolescu, 'Return to normality', *România Literară*, 11 January 1990, p. 3. Two years later, Nicolae Manolescu became the president of a civic party, and in 1996 he ran (unsuccessfully) for Romania's presidency.

We have to have here, as in everything else, a sacred model. God has a left arm and a
right arm: the arm of rigor and the arm of love. They never work but together. [...]
There is only one single criterion in culture: value, the 'providential value', which
doesn't entail only competence. One has to make the distinction between value and
competence. Someone can be a hyper-competent economist, but 'culture doesn't need
this type of competence, it needs grace'. Grace cannot be administered; grace is not
equally distributed and cannot be thought of democratically. Grace is of super-
individual nature' (Pleşu 1990, emphasis mine).

For the new minister, the cultural renaissance of the country has a historical
model; the paradigm of resistance as non-participation must be reinforced by
another paradigm, the one of the return to the historical model of culture
active during the inter-war period: 'to be honest, I've never thought about
great solutions concerning public organization. Bearing in mind the risk of
being taken for a retrograde, I have to tell you that my ideal image for a
cultural Romania is, inevitably, the Romania of the inter-war period. It is
about a retrospective model, not about a project, it's nostalgia more than
utopia. If Romania in the inter-war period signifies that Romania that
produced Cioran, Eliade, Noica, Eugen Ionescu and Nae Ionescu, if such
values have been produced in the inter-war period by Romania, this means
that things were never better for intellectuals. We just hope to find the vigor
and the verve of that time...'[15]

The 'normal times' Nicolae Manolescu wrote about are brought to a new
dimension by this return to the 1930s: in search for models, Romanian
culture (traditionally centered on literature) chooses the spiritual international
figures and the singularities. What seems to be forgotten in the paradigm
proposed in the first days of freedom is the project of a *travail de la mémoire*
for the recent past. After the fervency of the moment when Ceauşescu was
sentenced to death, the general tone of the magazine (in the first issues of
January and February analyzed here) doesn't seem to bear any trace of a
vindictive or an incriminating tone. The effort to remember structured itself
around an axis of the victims' memory – writers killed in the communist
prisons, exiled people, and forbidden liberties – and around the need to save
their work. In what concerns the collaborators of the Ceauşescu regime, there
were just a few harsh voices even if their harshness comes from the
'punishment of silence'. In the first editorial (signed using the name of the
magazine), one could read: 'We are asking neither for the elimination of the
press, nor for the prosecution of the compromised writers; we are only asking
for a little common sense and a few moments of silence, a memento for the
Just Ones that were killed for freedom'.[16] The matter of canonical vs. ethical

---

[15]   Andrei Pleşu, 'Finally, All Illusions Are Allowed', Octavian Paler in dialogue with Andrei
        Pleşu, Minister of Culture, *România Literară*, 6 January 1990, p. 3.

[16]   'The *Magic eye* box', *România Literară*, 6 January 1990, p. 2.

changes is not yet discussed and the French model of Conseil National des Écrivains is excluded as noxious and as a communist remnant: 'This is not about being vindictive, just to avoid a troublesome and irrational situation, but "we cannot forget" (emphasis mine)' (Grigurcu, see note 13 above). In these first days, the list of the guilty ones is not populated with names of collaborationist writers, but with the ideologists of communist culture and with the aggressively ideologized ones (like those grouped around the *Săptămâna* magazine). Even when punishment is asked for, the discourse cannot abandon the 'purist' rhetoric, in which the writer's art is sacred. This is the case of the denunciation written by Ion Băieşu (1933-1992, a writer once close to the communist regime, but marginalized by Ceauşescu's machine of terror, and author of a novel under censorship in 1985) against the head of Romanian culture, Mihai Dulea. Vice-president of the Cultural and Educational Socialist Council, Mihai Dulea becomes the leader of the censorship boards of the Romanian cultural institutions. His name comes first on Băieşu's list; the old writer addresses a virtual prosecutor: 'Sir, do not forget Dulea! Accuse him of crimes against Romanian culture', but he continues his threats in an unique, incredible way: 'If you don't do it, I, the undersigned, Ion Băieşu, and other colleagues of mine, want to make an appeal to the International Court of Hague [...] And if this Court can't indict him, I warn you, Mr. Prosecutor, I will go on ink strike. I will write with an empty pen, as a violinist playing a stringless instrument. Beware!'[17] This little pathetic metaphor stands for one writer's sacred rhetoric about being exceptional and imagining art as a separate domain, with no connection whatsoever to 'human' justice. When he puts on paper the vision of abandoning the sacred tool as supreme 'reprisals', the writer draws, indirectly, the real hierarchies of values: to succeed in dragging the accused in front of the Court is a little too improbable, but the real threat is to give up his art, to abandon and to deny his vocation.

4. The New Wave and the Choice of Freedom

Not all the young writers in the new wave act and believe the same. Mircea Cărtărescu (b. 1956), a first rank poet of the generation, has become the most renowned and the most translated Romanian writer of the moment, and he is the one who, in 1990, gave the most firm consensual judgment:

> The real writers have always fought for the aesthetic sense of their art; the books published in the last decade, though many of them were mutilated, don't display a puzzled attitude, but a consensual one. There is a real literature that was written in the

---

[17] Ion Băieşu, 'Souvenirs from My Sleepless Nights. Dulea', *România Literară*, 6 January 1990.

last years, a literature of 'proper' books and values. [...] I believe that literature [...] has not kneeled to the same extent other cultural domains have. To say it plainly, there is no confusion of values in this domain, quite the contrary.[18]

Cărtărescu's stand becomes even more interesting if we take into account the fact that his presence among *Contrapunct*'s contributors is ephemeral (nearly two months). The team debated the guidelines in the first issues of the magazine and, at the moment its cultural line was decided – political and interdisciplinary activities, social and political studies, dictionaries of new 'parliamentarian' and 'democratic' terms – he quits the committee, faithful to his credo: 'I thus plead for a pure literary line of the new magazine and, generally, of the young writers' movement' (see note 18 above). Even now, Cărtărescu claims that he is indebted almost entirely to the literary field of his literary protectors, the partisans of autonomy. This is the first sign which announces that the generation will change its stand; activism remains their tough and militant task, a task which is accounted for, among others, by Ion Bogdan Lefter (b. 1957) and Florin Iaru (b. 1954), while the literary part, the only possible (and triumphant) occupation as the result of an individual's choice, becomes Cărtărescu's field, who thus turned into the ideal cosmopolitan writer.

'The day after' didn't bring any violent or declarative canonical change: it is obvious that this is imminent, but the first months of 1990, frozen in time, will not witness any sudden change. One of the possible explanations for these changes is the specific aspect of the literary field after 1989, based on a boundless belief in the literature's power to renew and justify itself. For a very long time – almost two decades, if we consider 1971[19] as a starting point – critics and writers believed that aesthetics and ethics are one and the same (an understandable confusion in a totalitarian context; dictatorship deprived of humanity because of its rejection of moral values). By defending autonomous values, they glorified a non-participative, though benign, elitism.

---

[18]   Mircea Cărtărescu, 'What to do?', *Contrapunct*, 12 January, 1990, pp. 1-2.

[19]   The moment of the July 1971 thesis stands for the beginning of a *sui-generis* cultural revolution of Ceaușescu's regime: after claiming to have found many 'deficiencies and insufficiencies in the political, ideological and cultural-educational work', the document (read by Ceaușescu himself and unanimously approved) proposes 'to emphasize the Party's leading role in all the domains of political-educative activity; therefore, measures for a better orientation of the publishing programs must be taken, so that their editorial production would better respond to the communist educational demands'. Therefore, 'we must sustain a more careful control to prevent works that don't correspond to the demands of the political and educative activity of the Party from being published and also avoid the apparition of books which expose noxious ideas and conceptions to the interests of socialism in progress' – N. Ceaușescu, *Measures for Improving the Political and Ideological Activity, for Party Members and the Education of the Workers in the Spirit of Marxist-Leninist Ideas*, Speech at the PCR Meeting for the Ideological and Political Activity Field (Bucharest: Politica Publishing, 1971).

5. The Young Writers and Their Past. The Prodigal Son Becomes Master of Arts

For the new wave, another pretext for challenge is the use they make of the past, turning it into a reason to be offended. It is, nevertheless, a past transformed and reread by themselves, drawn to light by a sustained effort of self-legitimation. Their argumentative weapon is the background for their former marginal, quasi-exiled position, which blocked the slightest ideological tentative to compromise them by receiving the advantages offered by the regime. In their first public address in a free world, the young writers assumed the role of direct victims of the ideological battle:

> The young writers' literature – automatically considered subversive, undisciplined and dangerous by the authorities – has been systematically marginalized through methods that wanted to shock [...] if a young writer wanted to publish a second or third volume, the difficulties he ran into were impossible to surpass: rejections, perpetual delays, mutilating acts of censorship [...] Forced to find other methods of literary survival, the young '80s Generation finds refuge in underground literary circles [...] that become 'real' cultural and pedagogical institutions. This vigilance of the censorship has been executed not only under its blind fury or obstinacy. The literary police of the past decade effectively construed in the poetry, prose and literary essays of the young writers a certain kind of subversive writing. They could sense it, but they were never capable of understanding it.[20]

The young writers belonging to the generation's militant core seem to understand the political transformations of the post-communist space as the ideal occasion for assuming, once and for all, the militant role for civic values, the public messenger's position they were deprived of for so many years. For the '80s Generation, the absence of this position was a source of frustration as great as the one felt by the members of the literary group of the 60's, but the latter allowed themselves to be moulded by the interdiction, as a form of defense. For an important novelist of the young generation, Mircea Nedelciu (1950-1999), assuming the experience of the marginal past was synonymous to becoming teachers of freedom for the first post-communist generation:

> Thus, our experience is more complex than the one of most veterans. Today, it is a debt of honor for us to shelter the youth from all the traps of politics. We want to be regarded as a battalion of engineers (in the military sense of the word). Our youth was stolen from us, so there is no use crying over spilt milk. You, young people who now step into life or into the Romanian literature, please, let us be your engineer soldiers![21]

---

[20]   I. B. Lefter, 'A certain *sound*', *Contrapunct*, 9 January, 1990, pp. 1-3.

[21]   Mircea Nedelciu, 'Is the Writer Afraid of Politics?', *Contrapunct*, 12 January, 1990, pp. 1-2.

This approach offers a better understanding of the profile of a generation in full development: the efforts of the young wave gave birth to a new school of literature and, at the same time, taught them to think according to their model. The young writers have entered the university field, became the protectors for new generations of writers, moving from the position of an extravagant child to that of founding father. Everything is a field mechanism that becomes work in progress, and the most seductive dimension of this analysis is that the struggle for power in the field between academics and the new arrivals in the 80's are far from being done away with. This is how I see the current position of those who once were the extravagant children: they stick to their position of avant-garde artists and, at the same time, they never stop envisaging the new assault generation.

Around the leaders of this generation, a new school that has been following very closely the theories and literary struggles of its masters started to develop. These former students that had as compulsory bibliography for their literature exams the poetry and prose of the collective volumes published between 1980 and 1983 had the same kind of literary debut: collective volumes, literary circles led by an older member of the group, virulent attacks against the compromised writers of the old '60s generation. The 'nouvelle nouvelle vague''s masters are the former members of the avant-garde now part of the mainstream.

To have a clear image of this field hypothesis remains the most difficult issue, but at the same time, it is the most exciting part of this investigation. The field confrontations and declarations, the public declarations and fractures, the dissidence and crisis situations are part of the image of this generation which I tried to represent at the moment of its establishment.

WORKS CITED

Primary Sources

Băieşu, Ion, 'Souvenirs from My Sleepless Nights. Dulea', *România Literară*, No.1/6 January 1990

Cărtărescu, Mircea, 'What to do?',*Contrapunct*, No. 2 / 12 January 1990, pp. 1-2

Crohmălniceanu, Ov. S., Interview in *Tribuna*, No. 14/ 5 April 1984, p. 5

Doinaş, Ştefan Augustin, 'For a New Literary Generation', *România Literară*, No. 50/ 13 December 1979, p. 4

Grigurcu, Gheorghe, 'Morality and Opportunism', *România Literară,* No. 1/ 6 January 1990, p. 8

Iorgulescu, Mircea, 'The Newcomers', *România Literară,* No. 21/ 24 May 1979, p. 3

Lefter, I. B., 'A certain *sound*', *Contrapunct,* No. 1 / 9 January 1990, pp. 1-3

Manolescu, Nicolae, Interview in *Amfiteatru,* No. 5 (149)/ 1978, p. 10

—. Interview in *Ateneu,* No. 7/ October 1982, pp. 2-3

—. Interview by Gh. Grigurcu, *Familia,* 5 series, No. 31 (120)/ March 1983, p. 9

—. 'The Youngest Writers', *România Literară,* No. 47/ 22 November 1979, p. 10

—. 'Return to normality', *România Literară,* No. 2/ 11 January 1990, p. 3

Martin, Mircea, 'Group Portrait', *Echinox,* No. 10-11-12/1978, p. 3

—. 'Romanian Culture Between Communism and Nationalism', in *22,* No. 45 (661)/ 11 November 2002, p. 11

Nedelciu, Mircea, 'Is the Writer Afraid of Politics?', *Contrapunct,* No. 2 / 12 January, 1990, pp. 1-2

Negrici, Eugen, *Literatura română sub comunism* (*Romanian Literature under the Communist Regime*), vol. 1 (Bucharest: Pro Publishing House, 2002)

Pleşu, Andrei, 'Finally, All Illusions Are Allowed', Octavian Paler in dialogue with Andrei Pleşu, Minister of culture, *România Literară,* No.1 / 6 January, 1990, p. 3

*** *RL.* 'The *Magic eye* box', *România Literară,* No.1/ 6 January 1990, p. 2

Magda Răduță

Secondary Sources

Bourdieu, Pierre, *Les Règles de l'art. Genèse et structure du champ littéraire* (Paris : Seuil, 1992)

Heinich, Nathalie, *Être écrivain* (Paris: La Découverte, 2000)

Jurt, Joseph, ed., *Le Texte et le contexte. Analyses du champ littéraire français XIXe-XXe* (Berlin: Verlag Arno Spitz, 2001)

Lahire, Bernard, *La Condition littéraire. La double vie des écrivains* (Paris: La Découverte, 2006)

Pogiolli, Renato, *The Theory of the Avant-Garde,* trans. from Italian by Gerald Fitzgerald (the original Italian edition, *Teoria dell'arte d'avant-guardia,* Società editrice Il Mulino, 1962) (Cambridge, Massachusetts, London: The Belknap Press of Harvard University Press, 1982)

II. RESHAPING LITERARY STUDIES

David Damrosch

Comparative World Literature

World literature is often regarded today as a global phenomenon, sometimes even seen as a cultural expression of an emerging 'world system'. More expansively still, world literature can be considered to be the sum total of the world's literatures from every period since the invention of writing. Yet any view of the world is a view from somewhere, and in practical terms, world literature is experienced very differently in different places. This essay explores the shaping of world literature in different national cultural and institutional environments, looking at the United States, India, and China as examples.

We encounter world literature as the body of material that is actually available to us: works that are assigned in schools, sold in bookstores, reviewed in our morning paper, and analyzed in our country's scholarly journals. In this essay, I would like to explore the shaping of world literature in different national cultural and institutional environments, looking at the United States, India, and China as examples. I will argue that the American and Asian cases show reciprocal possibilities and limitations, located at opposite ends of a spectrum of inclusion or exclusion of their own national literature within their study of comparative and world literature. An understanding of this divergence should be helpful not only to scholars in these countries but to comparatists elsewhere, who may consider – and perhaps decide to rethink – their own personal and national place along this spectrum.[1]

I will begin with my own country. Though we have become increasingly attuned to the limitations of the traditional Eurocentrism of Comparative Literature, American-based comparatists have yet to think through the impact of our cultural and institutional location, both as a limiting factor and as an arena of possibility. The question of our standpoint becomes particularly important as we seek to develop a global literary vision on American campuses. What national and cultural predispositions define the parameters of world literature in America today, as it is taught on our campuses, discussed at conferences of the American Comparative Literature

---

[1] An earlier version of this essay, addressed to American comparatists, was previously published in the journal of the Southern Comparative Literature Association, *The Comparatist* 39 (2009), under the title 'How American Is World Literature?'

David Damrosch

Association, and analyzed in American journals and anthologies? Just how American, in short, is our view of world literature? How American should it be? My argument here will be that shadowing the debates over Eurocentrism is a largely unacknowledged Americentrism, a factor that is at once repressed and pervasive in American comparatism, even as American literature itself is largely neglected in American comparative studies.

The relative invisibility of our American standpoint is itself a characteristically American trait. A peculiarly American feature of literary study in many institutions in the United States has long been the subordination of American literature. It rarely enjoys the independence and visibility of its own department, but has been located at most schools within the English department. There, American literature has been relegated to second-class status, with British literature garnering far more appointments, even though Americanists typically enjoy (or are overwhelmed by) far higher enrollments. The unusualness of this situation regularly strikes visitors from abroad. It would be as though the French universities had no departments of French but only departments of Romance Languages and Literatures, with the specialists in French substantially outnumbered by those in Italian and Spanish – reasonably enough at an American university, perhaps, but unthinkable in the mother country itself.

Within English departments, Americanists have long lobbied for stronger representation, and over the course of the twentieth century they gradually developed a range of institutional alternatives in American Studies, often finding more visibility in association with historians and sociologists than with professors of British literature. Yet Comparative Literature departments have rarely been involved in these efforts. Many of our programs took shape in the 1950s at the hands of European émigrés, and these displaced Europeans were pleased and relieved to find themselves in universities that did not give pride of place to a dominant national literature and its cultural agenda. A good example of this is the perspective of René Wellek, founder of Yale's department of Comparative Literature, and a dominant figure in the disciplinary debates of the 1950s and 1960s. In a 1960 essay called 'The Crisis of Comparative Literature', Wellek clearly views the United States as a location to look *from* rather than a culture to look *at*, a space of separation in which comparatists could rise free of national entanglements elsewhere. In his essay, he mounts a strong critique of the nationalistic bent of much European comparatism, all too often culminating in scholarship showing the greatness of France – in particular – as radiating influence abroad or creatively transforming foreign influences. Such crypto-nationalism has had a long, inglorious history in comparative literature. A vivid expression of this can be seen in an early lecture by one of the founders of Comparative Literature in France, Philarete Euphémon Chasles, when he introduced his new course in 'The Comparison of Foreign Literature' in Paris in January of

1835. Opening his lecture with the figures of Cervantes and Shakespeare, unappreciated in their lifetime by their own countrymen, Chasles announces that his course will study the influence of great minds beyond their own borders – and above all, in France. This focus, he tells his students, simply reflects the fact that 'France is the most sensitive of all countries', receptive to the passionate advances of all nations. Contemplating his homeland's charms, Chasles falls into an extended erotic reverie:

> She is a sleepless and restless country that vibrates with all impressions and that palpitates and grows enthusiastic for the maddest and the noblest ones; a country which loves to seduce and be seduced, to receive and communicate sensation, to be excited by what charms it, and to propagate the emotion it receives. [...] She is the center, but the center of sensitivity; she directs civilization, less perhaps by opening up the route to the people who border her than by going forward herself with a giddy and contagious passion. What Europe is to the rest of the world, France is to Europe; everything reverberates toward her, everything ends with her.[2]

And so on. Infinitely receptive as Chasles's France is, she carefully controls her own borders: she will go out for a mad fling when and where she pleases, but for her foreign lovers, a Green Card is not in the cards. Scholars today are perhaps a little less bold in their claims for the beauties of their national tradition, but Chasles has a more sophisticated descendant in Pascale Casanova, whose 1999 book *La République mondiale des lettres* programmatically asserts that Paris has for centuries been the sole center of international literary circulation, *the* capital of 'the world republic of letters' from the Renaissance until World War II.

René Wellek wanted none of that sort of higher nationalism. In his essay on 'The Crisis of Comparative Literature' he asserts that

> We still can remain good patriots and even nationalists, but the debit and credit system will have ceased to matter. Illusions about cultural expansion may disappear as may also illusions about world reconciliation by literary scholarship. Here, in America, looking from the other shore at Europe as a whole we may easily achieve a certain detachment, though we may have to pay the price of uprootedness and spiritual exile.[3]

In this essay, Wellek does make a passing reference to Washington Irving as a possible source for a Pushkin story, but other than that, his only mention of any American authors is negative: he criticizes a nationalist history of American literature that 'blithely claims Dostoevsky as a follower of Poe and

---

[2]   Chasles qtd. in *Comparative Literature: The Early Years*, ed. by Hans-Joachim Schulz and Philip H. Rhein (Chapel Hill: University of North Carolina Press, 1973), pp. 21-22.

[3]   René Wellek, 'The Crisis of Comparative Literature' (1960). Reprinted in *Concepts of Criticism*, ed. by Stephen G. Nichols, Jr. (New Haven: Yale University Press, 1963), pp. 295.

even of Hawthorne'. Fortunately, Wellek remarks, such cultural jingoism has been relatively rare in the United States, 'which, on the whole, has been immune to it partly because it had less to boast of' (Wellek, p. 289). In the body of his essay, Wellek's attention is focused squarely on the literatures of France, Germany, Italy, and the British Isles, whose authors he mentions by name thirty times, along with references to three Russians and two classical Greeks.

The politics of comparative study were the subject of an essay by Werner Friedrich from the same year of 1960, based on a conference on the teaching of world literature held at the University of Wisconsin. A Swiss émigré, founder of the *Yearbook of Comparative and General Literature*, Friederich criticized American world literature courses for their heavy emphasis on the literatures of a few European great powers:

> Apart from the fact that such a presumptuous term makes for shallowness and partisanship which should not be tolerated in a good university, it is simply bad public relations to use this term and to offend more than half of humanity. . . . Sometimes, in flippant moments, I think we should call our programs NATO Literatures – yet even that would be extravagant, for we do not usually deal with more than one fourth of the 15 NATO-Nations.[4]

The limited focus of the era's comparative study was all the more apparent to scholars in Asia. A few years later, writing in Friederich's *Yearbook of Comparative and General Literature*, the Japanese comparatist Sukehiro Hirakawa used a still more pointed military-political analogy to advance a parallel critique:

> It is true that great scholars such as Curtius, Auerbach and Wellek wrote their monumental scholarly works in order to overcome nationalism. But to outsiders like me, Western Comparative Literature scholarship seemed to be an expression of a new form of nationalism – the Western nationalism, if I may use such an expression. It seemed to us an exclusive club of Europeans and Americans. It was a sort of Greater West European Co-Prosperity Sphere.[5]

In his critique of the emphasis on Western European literary 'great powers', Werner Friederich emphasized the need to move outward to study of non-Western literatures; at the same time, his essay rather closely resembles Wellek's in a virtual silence concerning American literature itself.

There are signs in recent scholarship of a change in the longstanding occlusion of America in American presentations of world literature, as we

---

[4]   Werner Friedrich, 'On the Integrity of Our Planning', in *The Teaching of World Literature*, ed. by Haskell Block (Chapel Hill: University of North Carolina Press, 1960), pp. 14-15.

[5]   Sukehiro Hirakawa, 'Japanese Culture: Accommodation to Modern Times', *Yearbook of Comparative and General Literature* 28 (1979), 46-50 (p. 47).

can see in Gayatri Spivak's recent book *Death of a Discipline* – which, appropriately, began life as the 2000 Wellek Library Lectures at the University of California at Irvine. In her book, Gayatri Spivak includes discussions of Toni Morrison, Gertrude Stein, and W.E.B. Du Bois along with her (admittedly, more extensive) analyses of works by Joseph Conrad, Virginia Woolf, Mahasweta Devi, and Tayyib Salih. She prefaces her book, moreover, with a sardonic glance at the development of new American collections of world literature:

> Between the presentation of the lectures in May 2000 and the final revision in May 2002, the discipline of comparative literature in the United States underwent a sea change. Publishing conglomerates have recognized a market for anthologies of world literature in translation. Academics with large advances are busy putting these together. Typically, the entire literature of China, say, is represented by a couple of chapters of *The Dream of the Red Chamber* and a few pages of poetry. Notes and introduction are provided by a scholar from the area commissioned for the purpose by the general editor, located in the United States. The market is international. Students in Taiwan or Nigeria will learn about the literatures of the world through English translations organized by the United States. Thus institutionalized, this global education market will need teachers. Presumably, the graduate discipline of comparative literature will train those teachers.
>
> The book you are about to read is therefore out of joint with the times in a more serious way than the Wellek Library Lectures of May 2000 were. I have changed nothing of the urgency of my call for 'a new comparative literature'. I hope the book will be read as the last gasp of a dying discipline.[6]

On this view, world literature is fast becoming a creature of American conglomerate capitalism, an export trade in English translation purveying a superficial view of the world's literary cultures. For Spivak, the whole project ultimately become little more than exercises in American-style multiculturalism – the 'multi-culti' trendiness that she criticizes throughout her book.

The situation is probably less dire than Spivak here suggests, if only because the American anthologies are not in fact, so far as I know, marketed in either Taiwan or Nigeria. This is not because the American publishers shrink from selling their wares anywhere they can, but because world rights for translations are prohibitively expensive, and so the publishers only acquire North American rights for these anthologies. But it is certainly true that for their American audiences, the American anthologies provide a distinctively American-based view of world literature. They are created largely by editors based in America and their contents are tailored for use in classrooms in the United States and Canada, so that the selections offered are

---

[6]   Gayatri Chakravorti Spivak, *Death of a Discipline* (New York: Columbia University Press, 2003), p. xii.

fundamentally shaped by the wishes of potential adopters in these two countries.

However deathly our discipline may be, it is important to bear in mind that Spivak is talking only about comparative literature in America, at least at the start of the passage just quoted; by the end of the passage, as elsewhere in the book, a quiet slippage or expansion has occurred and she seems to be referring to the discipline as a whole. Yet Comparative Literature has never been practiced exclusively in the United States; there are dozens of Comparative Literature associations around the globe, and there are sixty comparative literature programs in China alone. In a review essay on *Death of a Discipline*, the French comparatist Didier Coste expressed his bemusement that even as she champions 'planetarity', Spivak should be so resolutely American-centered in her disciplinary discussions. In his essay, Coste comments on Spivak's fidelity 'au milieu universitaire étasunien', arguing that:

> Dès les premiers paragraphes du livre nous apprenons que les choses changent à toute vitesse dans la Littérature Comparée aux États-Unis, par exemple entre 2000 et 2002 (le 11 septembre étant, cela va de soi, la cause de ces bouleversements). Dans une perspective moins myope et moins anhistorique, il serait tout aussi frappant de constater que presque rien n'a changé dans la conception de la discipline en France depuis des dizaines d'années. Ce qui est construit en événement capital par l'idéologie américaine et qui est toujours récent (chute de l'Empire soviétique, attaques terroristes à New York et à Washington) déplace le moins récent, et occulte les logiques de long terme dans le passé comme dans l'avenir. (From the very first lines of the book, we find out that things change in full speed in the U.S. Comparative Literature, for instance between 2000 and 2002 (9/11 being obviously the cause of this upheaval). In a less short-sighted and ahistorical perspective, it would be just as striking to observe that almost nothing changed in the conception of the discipline in France in years. What is turned into a capital event by the American ideology and is always very recent (the fall of the Soviet Empire, terrorist attacks in New York and Washington) replaces the less recent and hides away the long term logic in the past as well as in the future.)[7]

It appears that American-based comparatists remain in something of a double bind: Americentric in disciplinary terms, and yet in literary terms often Amerifugal – fleeing America, ignoring the situation at home.

Taking seriously the idea that we must begin from where we stand, the solution to this double bind can best be found by a double movement, both inward and outward. We need to do more to connect our comparative work to the literary culture in which we live, and at the same time we need to enlarge our disciplinary horizons to take far fuller account of the varieties of comparatist practice around the world. Far from being incompatible, these

---

[7]   Didier Coste, 'Votum Mortis'. Published in the online journal *Fabula* at www.fabula.org/revue/cr/449.php.

two movements rapidly start to come together if we do look at comparatism abroad.

Here I will take examples from the study of world of literature in Asia, where comparative literature has developed within institutional contexts that have privileged their national literary traditions far more than has been the case in the United States. To begin with India, the leading Indian universities typically have several departments devoted to Indian languages and literatures, including one for Sanskrit, one for Hindi, and whichever other language or languages are dominant in the particular university's region. Comparative Literature has evolved in India in symbiosis with these national literature departments, even as they have reached out to European, American, and East Asian literature and theory.

The nature of this symbiosis can be seen in the tables of contents of the *JadavpurJournal of Comparative Literature*, published by India's premier comparative literature department. Issue 28, for instance, from 1989-90, consists of eight articles on the theme of 'Cultural Relativism and Literary Value'. Five of the eight essays are explicitly concerned with one or more Indian literatures, only sometimes in relation to non-Indian works. Typical titles are Jasbir Jain's 'Cultural Relativism and Perspective: Naipaul Chaudhuri and Forster', C. T. Indra's 'Cultural Relativism and Tamil Fiction', and Gurbhagat Singh's 'Search for a Common Denominator: Western Structuralism and Indian Dhvani'. The issue's focus is not exclusively Indo-centric; it includes an essay by the Nigerian writer Gabriel Okara, 'Towards the Evolution of an African Language for African Literature', and there are more general essays on Orientalism and on cultural otherness.

Fifteen years later, issue 41 (2003-04) shows a comparable Indian emphasis. There are two exceptions: a comparative study of Hemingway and Walcott, and an article by Didier Coste on American global comparatism. The issue's ten other essays all have a clear (and often exclusive) Indian basis, starting with an article by Amiya Dev, "Between the One and the Many: Rethinking Indian Literature," and continuing with articles centered on Gujarati, Kannada, Bengali, Oriyan, and Assamese works among others. In the issue's closing article, 'Multiculturalism: Forced and Natural', Swapan Majumdar discusses the rise of cultural studies abroad and makes a plea for a continued literary emphasis in India. Interestingly, Majumdar takes as a given that 'the rise of Comparative Literature in France, Germany, Italy, the East European Slavic countries and the US [...] was most certainly dictated by the compelling natural necessities of their literature'.[8] It is a little surprising to see the United States in this list, since it is surely a range of institutional and

---

[8]   Swapan Majumdar, 'Multiculturalism: Forced and Natural, A Comparative Literary Overview', *Jadavpur Journal of Comparative Literature* 41 (2003), 139-144 (p. 140).

cultural-political factors, rather than compelling literary necessities that led to the frequent 'neglect' of American literature in American comparatism. But broadly speaking, it has usually been the case that comparative literature has developed in most countries in direct dialogue with the national literary traditions.

A comparable situation can be seen in China as well, as shown in a wide-ranging article by Zhou Xiaoyi and Q. S. Tong, 'Comparative Literature in China', published in the Canadian-based electronic journal *Comparative Literature and Culture* in 2000. In that article, Professors Zhou and Tong argue that comparative literature in China has always been closely bound up with national needs and preoccupations, throughout the twentieth century, starting with the early comparative work of Hu Shih and particularly from the field's establishment as an academic discipline at Tsinghua in the 1920s. They note that

> in the early decades of the twentieth century, comparative literature in China was preoccupied with literary and cultural encounters between China and three major cultural sites: India, Russia, and Europe [...] In Chinese comparative literature concerning Indian and Chinese literature and Russian and Chinese literature, it is noticeable that much of the scholarly attention is focused on how Chinese literature and Chinese culture have been influenced by inspirations drawn from India and Russia, respectively, and comparatively. In contrast, critical inquires into the encounters between Chinese literature and European literature have been largely centered on China's influence on Europe, in particular on English-language literature.[9]

Zhou and Tong go on to show that in more recent years, great attention has been paid to comparative poetics and to the application of Western literary theory to Chinese works. They conclude that 'Chinese comparative literature as a critical practice may thus be considered a product of China's pursuit of modernity in the twentieth century'.

A good expression of this nationally-oriented comparative study is found in the journal *Comparative Literature in China* (*Zhong Guo Bi Jiao Wen Xue*). A typical issue (2008, number 3) begins with an essay on current developments in American Comparative Literature and then proceeds to articles on translations into and out of Chinese, with articles on the translation practice of Qian Zhongshu, English translations of *Guan Zhui Bian*, and Chinese translations of Doris Lessing. Then comes a section devoted to 'Overseas Chinese Literary Study', including Chinese literature in South-East Asia, analyses of Zhang Ailing and of Ah Qi, and the reception of Rainer Maria Rilke in China. One article discusses British Romantic poetry,

---

[9]   From the electronic journal *Comparative Literature and Culture* 2:4 (2000); http://clcwebjournal.lib.purdue.edu/clcweb00-4/zhou&tong00.html. Repr. in *Comparative Literature and Comparative Cultural Studies*, ed. by Steven Tötösy de Zepetnek (West Lafayette: Purdue U.P., 2003), pp. 268-83.

but the other articles all concern Chinese literature abroad or foreign literature in China.

Both the *Jadavpur Journal of Comparativce Literature* and *Comparative Literature in China*, then, display almost an inverse proportion to what is typically found in American journals such as *Comparative Literature* and *World Literature Today* – originally founded in 1927 under the title *Books Abroad*; a typical recent issue includes poems, articles, and interviews involving exciting new writers from Algeria, Catalonia, Israel, Portugal, and Lebanon, but no discussion of any American writers either at home or abroad.

This brief survey suggests that it would be well worthwhile to undertake a comparative study of world literature as it is construed in differing locations around the world. It could help scholars everywhere to think directly about the relations between their national traditions and their presentation of the wider field of world literature, whether these relations are symbiotic or hegemonic, whether they are unusually close or unusually disjointed. A fuller sense of the range of possibility might keep scholars from falling unwittingly into nationalistic patterns in the construal of global literary relations. Perhaps in time only a third of the essays in the *Jadavpur Journal of Comparative Literature* and of *Comparative Literature in China*, instead of most of them, would center on a single Indian or Chinese author abroad, or a foreign author's reception in India or China.

American comparatists, on the other hand, seem clearly to be at the far end of the range of continuity/discontinuity. For too long, we have accepted a degree of uprootedness and internal exile that had a certain logic for the émigrés who taught us or our teachers; this makes less and less sense for our field today, even for foreign-born scholars. There are encouraging signs of a budding rapprochement between American and comparative literary studies, seen for instance in a valuable recent collection edited by Wai Chee Dimock and Lawrence Buell, *Shades of the Planet: American Literature as World Literature* (Princeton, 2007). It is symptomatic, though, that both editors are based in English and American studies departments rather than comparative literature. They and their contributors are seeing the benefits that can accrue to American studies by taking a fully comparative and global perspective. More departments of Comparative Literature, in turn, need to accept the converse realization, that a vital comparatism can best thrive in creative symbiosis with its home traditions as well as those of the wider world.

A comparative study of different national approaches to world literature should also help us all to do a better job of construing the world's literary traditions, whether to move beyond an overemphasis on a few literary great powers, or to avoid either overemphasizing or undercutting our own national tradition. The study of world literature in many parts of the world will gain if we attend more closely to the varied ways in which world literature is construed in different countries and regions, bringing a global perspective to our scholarship as well as to the literature we study.

WORKS CITED

Block, Haskell, ed., *The Teaching of World Literature* (Chapel Hill: University of North Carolina Press, 1960)

Hirakawa, Sukehiro, 'Japanese Culture: Accommodation to Modern Times', *Yearbook of Comparative and General Literature* 28 (1979), 46-50

Majumdar, Swapan, 'Multiculturalism: Forced and Natural, A Comparative Literary Overview', *Jadavpur Journal of Comparative Literature* 41 (2003), 139-144

Schulz, Hans-Joachim, Philip H. Rhein (eds.). *Comparative Literature: The Early Years* (Chapel Hill: University of North Carolina Press, 1973)

Spivak, Gayatri Chakravorti, *Death of a Discipline* (New York: Columbia University Press, 2003)

Wellek, René, 'The Crisis of Comparative Literature' (1960). Reprinted in *Concepts of Criticism*, ed. Stephen G. Nichols, Jr. (New Haven: Yale University Press, 1963)

Dumitru Radu Popa

Globalization and Comparative Literature Revisited – An Analytical Survey

In his paper D.R. Popa starts by noticing the variety of conflicting ways to define globalization. This new reality put an end to what we used to call territorialism, and as a result our social geography is not exclusively territorial anymore. The move from national to transnational brings serious challenges in the literary field. Goethe's *Weltliteratur* was based on national literatures; and Comparative literature, as a discipline, has been based on Goethe's paradigm. However, Goethe himself opened the door to trans-nationalism with his holistic vision. As Claudio Guillen stated, the local-universal dialog was inherent in the Goethe's paradigm. Under the current conditions, Comparative literature is supposed to relocate its relational terms of comparison. D.R. Popa endorses David Damrosch's vision and the twin foci of the discipline. World literature means therefore not a canon of texts but a mode of circulating and reading. Between Spivak's pessimistic view in *Death of a Discipline* and Haun Saussy's cheerful *Report*, it is fair to assume that Comparative literature is neither in decline nor in rise, but simply changing and adjusting to new circumstances and contexts.

Globalization has lately become a buzzword, a conversation-stopping word, and those using the term often have contrasting, if not completely opposite, understandings of what it means. No wonder, much of the talk about globalization is utterly confused and confusing. Yet the concept of globalization itself has long been a contested turf described in conflicting normative dialogues that provide the concept with positive, negative, or ambivalent connotations.

The darkest reality of it, according to Eva Kushner, stands in 'the uniformisation and loss of control to economic forces defying not only the will of individuals but the rule of entire states'.[1]

The impact on literature, literary studies, and humanities at large has been tremendous. Thinkers such as Kushner and many others witnessed the fact that the *universal/particular* dichotomy stated by Montaigne when writing that 'chaque homme porte en soi la forme entière de l'humaine condition' – which, by the way, worked for so many centuries! – collapsed in the age of globalization, when the pattern microcosm expressing the macrocosm does not work anymore.[2] Moreover, the protective walls and borders of the nation-state (national security, national product and economics, national ethos, national culture, national literature, etc.) are themselves, not only

---

[1]   Eva Kushner, '"Globalization" and "Individuation" in Comparative Literature Studies', *Neohelicon*, 28 (2001), 31-4 (p. 31).

[2]   Michel de Montaigne, *Essais* (Paris: Les beaux lettres, 1967), II, p. 530.

symbolically, but really supposed to collapse under the mighty hammer of all those 'trans-whatever' concepts. In cultural, arts, and literary terms the phenomenon points up the individual's unavoidable mediation with the totalitarian regime of commoditization and consumption (be it even MacDonaldization!) that 'either universalizes desires or particularizes traditions'.[3] Anticipating, this tension leads, in George Ritzer's words, to the troika: 'globalization-glocalisation-grobalization'.[4]

In Anthony Giddens' opinion about globalization, it is 'the intensification of worldwide social relations which link distant localities in such a way that local happenings are shaped by events occurring miles away and vice versa'.[5] And David Harvey goes even further, towards a kind of Sci-Fi scenario regarding globalization as 'a time-space compression' that eventually could be labelled as an 'extraordinary speed-up of social life on a global scale together with the shrinkage of physical space through technology and the reduction of time to a perpetual and schizophrenic present'.[6]

With all these in mind, let's look at the uncommon diversity of definitions for the same fundamental phenomenon.

---

[3]   David Lewei Li, 'Globalization and the Humanities', *Comparative Literature* (Fall 2001), 275-282 (p. 275).

[4]   George Ritzer, 'Rethinking Globalization: Glocalization/Grobalization and Something / Nothing', *Sociological Theory* 21 (2003), 193-209. In short, what George Ritzer brings as a new aspect in the tension global-local is the concept of 'grobalization' to complement the idea of the 'glocalization'. Globalization is not a singular process with uniform results, but a term that encompasses a number of transnational processes. He distinguishes between two broad sub-processes under the larger heading of globalization – 'glocalization' (the integration of the global and the local) and 'grobalization' (the imposition of the global on the local). He also explores the distinction between 'nothing' (forms that are centrally conceived and controlled and largely lacking in distinctive content) and 'something' (forms that are indigenously conceived and controlled and comparatively rich in distinctive content). Ritzer emphasizes on two pairings that result from relating these sets of concepts: the grobalization of nothing and the glocalization of something. In the realm of culture in general and consumption in particular, the conflict between these two processes is a central issue in the world today. The triumph of the grobalization of nothing promises cultural homogeneity, while the glocalization of something offers at least some hope for cultural heterogeneity in a world in which the truly local has almost entirely disappeared.

[5]   Anthony Giddens, *The Consequences of Modernity* (Stanford: Stanford University Press, 1990), p. 64.

[6]   David Harvey, *The Condition of Postmodernity: An Enquiry into the Origins of Social Change* (Cambridge: Blackwell Publishers, 1990), p. 240.

1. The definition puzzle

> Globalization refers in general to the worldwide integration of humanity and the compression of both the temporal and spatial dimensions of planet wide human interaction.[7]

> The increasing world-wide integration of markets for goods, services and capital that began to attract special attention in the late 1990s.[8]

> A term used to describe growing interdependence of people around the world with regard to societal influence, economies, and cultural exchanges.[9]

> A process that encompasses the causes, course, and consequences of transnational and transcultural integration of human and non/human activities.[10]

> The effort to standardize consumer habits, values, and ways of thinking that contributes to the development of global markets, greater efficiencies and profits.[11]

> Globalization in its literal sense is the process of globalizing, transformation of some things or phenomena into global ones. It can be described as a process by which the people of the world are unified into a single society and functioning together.[12]

> Globalization could be defined as the pervasive translocation of the local unto a diffuse plane where the location of culture, literary or

---

[7]   Richard L. Harris, 'The Global Context of Contemporary Latin American Affairs', in *Capital, Power, and Inequality in Latin America*, ed. by Sandor Halebsky and Richard L. Harris (Boulder, Westview Press, 1995), pp. 279-80.

[8]   *Deardorff's Glossary of International Economics*, IASB, 2001.

[9]   www.csa.com/discoveryguides/afraid/gloss.php.

[10]   Nayef Al-Rodhan, *Pilars of Globalization* (Genève: Slatkin Publishers, 2006), p. 4.

[11]   www.centerforecojusticeeducation.org/index.php.

[12]   http://en.wikipedia.org/wiki/Globalization.

> otherwise, is simultaneously rendered as emphatically incomparable isolate and as subsumed, homologated site.[13]

> Globalization has replaced the Cold War as the defining international system. [...] Globalization is the inexorable integration of markets, nation-states and technologies to a degree never witnessed before – in a way that is enabling individuals, corporations and nation-states to reach around the world farther, faster, deeper and cheaper than ever before.[14]

Whenever the same object happens to be defined in so many and contrasting ways I generally tend to think that it is somehow like with *pornography*: I don't know how to define it, but I certainly recognize it when I see it!

Attempts to define the G-word offer such an intriguing variety and ambiguity, Fredric Jameson argued, partly because people tend to focus the discussions not on the process itself, but rather on its effects, good or bad.[15]

2. National Literature, Comparative Literature, and Globalization

Globalization is, as paradoxically as it may sound, a polarizing term. Even if we accept Thomas Friedman's sentence about the 'inexorability' of the move from national to trans-national, and from isolation to integration, we still face important challenges such as the role of the culture in this globalization movement. Will it divide or unite? And of more immediate concern to us, can literature propose or even help shape a different model of global society than the one being already advanced by the trans-national, supra-national, and multinational entities, mostly based on business and trade?

Considering national literature in light of the theory of inter-literary systems may deepen our understanding of its limits and the criteria which define them (Naftali Bassel)[16]. Accordingly, any national literature has an organic, natural connection to the historical destiny of its ethnic group, and a national language as the basic medium of its existence. Its roots are in the folklore and the mythology of its ethnic group. A national literature shows

---

[13]   Djelal Kadir, 'Comparative Literature, the Transnational, and the Global', *Neohelicon*, XXVIII/1 (2001), 25-9 (p. 25).

[14]   Thomas Friedman, *The Lexus and the Olive Tree* (New York: Farrar, Strauss & Giroux, 1999), p. 4.

[15]   Fredric Jameson, 'Globalization and Political Strategy', *New Left Review*, 4 (July-August 2000), at http://newleftreview.org./A2255.

[16]   Naftali Basel, *Poetics Today* 12:4 (Winter 1991) (p.773).

stability and dynamism as an aesthetic system, for there is an important indigenous, self-aware artistic tradition interacting naturally with other national art forms (there is, therefore a social and aesthetic heterogeneity). A national literature's development and growth take place under the influence, or in correlation, with other national literatures, and the world literary process at large, belonging to various inter-literary systems, such as regional, zonal, and ethno-linguistic. In the end, I have to agree with Naftali Bassel that every national literature is characterized by a specific combination of these attributes, which distinctly define *a national, literary, and aesthetic system.*

As Gonzalo Navajas emphasizes, for Ernest Renan, Menendez y Pelayo, Ortega y Gasset, and Thomas Mann, among others, the nation was the absolute fundamental source of individual and collective identity.[17] Its overarching structure surpasses any other concepts, be they freedom and justice, as the primordial principle of social and political organization.

Goethe introduced the term 'World Literature' (*Weltliteratur*) in 1827. It was in an issue of the journal *Uber Kunst und Altertum.* The circumstances are all well known. After translating into German a passage from a favorable review of the French edition of his drama *Torquato Tasso* in the *Paris Globe,* he points out that the relatively long quotation provided there is not in fact intended to emphasize attention on his own literary creation. The most important features of this historical statement are the *holistic vision* (his remark that he had in mind something higher than his own work, and that progress for world and human race should be envisioned as a whole); the proclamation of the world literature (*eine algemeine Weltliteratur*); and the fact that this world literature is based on national literatures (when he says that, within world literature, the German literature is meant to play an important role).

However, one could argue that Goethe somehow anticipates or opens the door to 'trans-nationalism'. And even if, at the time, he clearly associated World literature with European literature, he did not exclude other entities, given the intensity and ever increasing rapidity of trans-national interchanges. To be clear, his claim for a World Literature was not dismissing the discrete national literatures that were conceived as the basis of the inter-national or trans-national concept.

Comparative literature, as a discipline and field of scholarship, enthusiastically embraced Goethe's paradigm of *Weltliteratur* as quintessential for the field.[18] Ulrich Weisstein, in *Comparative Literature and*

---

[17] Gonzalo Navajas, *Transnational Literature and Film between Borders* (http://lehman/edu/faculty/guinazu/cyberletras/v14/navajas.htm).

[18] John Pizer, 'Goethe's "World literature" Paradigm and Contemporary Cultural Globalization', *Comparative literature,* 52 (Summer 2000), 213-227.

Literary Theory finds the notion extremely useful 'because of its stress on international contact and fruitful literary interrelationships'.[19] François Jost comes quite close to his point in stating that comparative literature is nothing but 'an organic Weltliteratur' that provides the basic material to be organized by the discipline from historical and critical view point.[20] Thus, for Jost Goethe's concept is a 'prerequisite' for comparative literature. Claudio Guillen, expressing a very comprehensive view, after noticing the historical importance of Goethe's *Weltliteratur* for the emergence of the comparative literature as a discipline, discusses the 'local-universal dialogue'[21] inherent in the paradigm. And that paradigm as Goethe conceptualized it 'has continued to breathe life into the best comparative studies' (Pizer). Guillen's position is a momentous one, as it captures the potentiality of the transnational, global dialogue.

For comparative literature does not, and can not, represent nowadays only the collective reservoir of all texts and from all places and all times, or, more narrowly, canonical works 'that putatively represents the highest achievements of the Western tradition' (Pizer, p. 220). Under the current conditions, Comparative Literature is supposed, in its praxis and intellectual approach as a discipline, to relocate its relational terms of comparison. Moreover, as Kadir puts it:

> At the threshold of the twenty-first century, Comparative Literature can no longer just contend with neatly definable hemispheres. Comparative Literature must now countenance the flux and reflux of spherical entanglements, global and globalizing formations, polyglossic aesthetics and heteroglossic constructs, radically enmeshed textualities and historical contexts, in relations to all of which the comparative itself can no longer remain disengaged as *tertium quid* or *tertium comparationis*. Everything is enmeshed and interrelated, including the comparative function and Comparative Literature as a discursive field, as cultural institution, and as historical formation (p. 28).

It may be productive to place today's fate and the future of Comparative Literature between Spivak's pessimistic views in *Death of a Discipline*[22] and Saussy's vision in his *Report*[23] – and the essays assembled there –, arguing

---

[19]   Ulrich Weisstein, *Comparative Literature and Literary Theory: Survey and Introduction* (Bloomington: Indiana University Press, 1973), p. 20.

[20]   François Jost, *Introduction to Comparative Literature* (Indianapolis: Pegasus, 1974), p. 21.

[21]   Claudio Guillen, *The Challenge of Comparative Literature* (Cambridge: Harvard University Press, 1993), p. 40.

[22]   Gayatri Chakravorty Spivak, *Death of a Discipline* (New York: Columbia University Press, 2003).

[23]   Haun Saussy, *Comparative Literature in an Age of Globalization* (Baltimore: The John Hopkins University Press, 2006).

that it might be fair to say that Comparative Literature is neither in decline nor on the rise but simply changing and adapting to new circumstances and contexts, institutional, communicational, theoretical, methodological, disciplinary, and literary.

For a complex approach of the new challenges of Comparative Literature an excellent reference is the Spring-Summer 2000 issue of *Literary Research/Recherche Littéraire*, where major scholars in the field where enjoined by the Editor, Prof. Călin Mihăilescu, to identify *The Natural Enemies of Comparative Literature*.

In her remarkable study, *Ghosts in the Disciplinary Machine: The Uncanny Life of World Literature,* Vilashini Cooppan notices that 'the global confronts comparative literature and other disciplines now in a different way than it has in the past, as a distinct kind of epistemological object'.[24] Whoever reanimates Goethe as a global theorist *avant la lettre*, has therefore to distinguish between *history*, 'which binds disciplinary futures to the past' and historical method, 'which tells a different story [...] of changing practices, emergent paradigms, new methodologies (p. 16). And she continues forcefully: 'Our task is thus to read the past for its differences from, as well as its similarities to the present; to locate our ghostly forefathers within their own historical and ideological moment, and to discern in them the skeleton of a method that might visit us again in the uncanny form of something at once old and new, familiar and strange' (p. 16).

A compact and meaningful 'critical genealogy' of this understanding of Comparative Literature would have to mention Ernest Robert Curtius, Leo Spitzer, and – last but not least – Auerbach, whom she calls 'the other patron saint of the discipline' (p. 16), especially for the opening towards inter-nationalism he brought. Auerbach's philological *citizen of the earth*[25] – in a utopian way or not so much – discounts the ongoing force of nations and national identifications, somehow opening the way for Fredric Jameson's 1986 essay, *Third-World Literature in the Era of Multinational Capitalism,* famous for his claim, quite original at the time, that all the Third-world texts should be included in the contemporary *Weltliteratur*, as being nothing but national allegories:

> Today, he says, the reinvention of cultural studies in the United States demands the reinvention, in a new situation, of what Goethe long ago theorized as 'world literature'.

---

[24]   Vilashini Cooppan, 'Ghosts in the Disciplinary Machine: The Uncanny Life of World Literature', *Comparative Literature Studies*, 41 (2004), 10-36 (p. 15).

[25]   Erich Auerbach, *Mimesis: The Representation of Reality in World Literature* (Princeton: Princeton University Press, 1953), and 'Philology and Weltliteratur', *The Centennial Review*, 13 (1969), 1-17.

In our more immediate context, then, any conception of world literature necessarily
demands some specific engagement with the question of third-world literature.[26]

Jameson therefore sticks to the idea of nation and national expression, while
scholars such as Anthony D. King, from the perspective of relational
thinking, identifies two fundamental trends: on one hand the traditional
(obsolete for some) national entities as the actors in the field, on the other
hand 'the rejection of the nationally constituted society as the appropriate
object of discourse and the tendency to conceptualizing "the world as a
whole"' (e.g. the network, the global, the glocal).[27] While Jameson is
confined by a national, as opposed to global, set of concerns, Franco Moretti,
for example goes as far as to prove the limitations of national boundaries,
borrowing patterns from the globalized world of capital trade and economics.
Moretti talks, in his *Modern Epic: The World-System from Goethe to Garcia
Marquez,* about 'world-texts', those that bring 'a geographical frame of
reference' that is definitely 'no longer the nation-state, but a broader entity –
a continent, or the world system as a whole'.[28]

Personally, as a fiction writer and literary critic, I have problems with
books written from a so called 'global perspective': to be clear, I very much
doubt about the existence of such a perspective. I know there are scholars
producing titles such as Rushdie's *Satanic Verses,* or Kenyan writer's Ngugi
wa Thiong'o' novel *Devil on the Cross* as cases in point. However, to
identify a global perspective in such writings only because they reflect a
pattern of displacement or a spirit of – allow me to create the term – trans-
bounderity (transbounderness?) is not enough to homologate a quite new
reality, an original, unique *Weltanschauung.* I would rather agree with the
position Damrosch adopts when, in order to better understand contemporary
phenomena, he goes back in time to works elaborated before the coagulation
of national states.[29] He points out that works that precede the birth of the
modern nation 'were produced in local or ethnic configurations that have
been subsumed into the national traditions within which they are now
preserved and transmitted' (p. 3) (works such as Homer's epics or Dante's
writings, for example). What is the most exciting about his vision stands in

---

[26]   Fredric Jameson, 'Third World Literature in the Era of Multinational Capitalism', *Social
Text,* 14/15 (1986), 65-88 (p. 68).

[27]   Anthony D. King, ed., *Culture, Globalization, and the World-System* (Binghamton, 1991), p.
ix.

[28]   Franco Moretti, *Modern Epic: The World System from Goethe to Garcia Marquez* (New
York: Verso, 1996), p. 50.

[29]   David Damrosch, *What is World Literature? (Translation/Transnation)* (New York:
Princeton University Press, 2003).

the 'twin foci' of the discipline. As literature born of the nation but disseminated beyond its boundaries, world literature occupies for Damrosch an 'elliptical space' with two centers or foci: the source culture and the host culture. Essentially, world literature is for Damrosch 'a mode of circulation and of reading' (p. 5). Presenting world literature not as a canon of texts but as a mode of circulation and of reading, Damrosch argues that world literature is work that gains in translation. When it is effectively presented, a work of world literature moves into an elliptical space created between the source and receiving cultures, shaped by both but circumscribed by neither alone. Temporal and spatial move are not necessarily in one direction. Damrosch stipulates that the 'work of world literature exists in two planes at once: present in our world, it also brings us into a world very different from ours, and its particular power comes from our doubled experiences of both registers together' (p. 164).

I particularly like Damrosch's approach not only for its inclusiveness (both on the temporal and spatial plans), but also for the very creative comments that it inspired. One of my favourites is Laurence DeLooze's elaboration. [30] If we extend Damrosch's suggestion to mean '*at least* two foci, we can understand that Comparative literature is necessarily somewhat baroque in its construction – and as a result always a little off-balance as well: a bit unstable, even slightly out of "focus"' (p. 4). He explains this situation in relation to the fact that European culture has lost its clear sense of being the epicentre of civilization after the discoveries of the Americas. Together with this anxiety came the lost of a single focal point – Renaissance's art's characteristic – for an art of ovals, distorted shapes with al least *two foci*. The examples, DeLooze says, are many,

> though the most eloquent is perhaps Bernini's brilliantly propagandistic Piazza in front of St. Peter's in which the reach of the Catholic Church now embraced an *oval* space for humanity, just as it elliptically reached out to associate the New World with the Old. Should we be astonished that the oval insistently returns centuries later in Cubism, that other art born of a new reflection on relativity at the beginning of the 20th century? [...] The constant quest and the multiple foci of Comparative Literature deconstruct the constructions of singular or national identities both in terms of the objects of our attention and of our own affiliations. [...] Nevertheless, Comparative Literature, with its multiple foci, offers (like Bernini's Piazza) a huge embrace (p. 4)

What can I say: to me, it is beautiful and, therefore, true!

---

[30] Laurence DeLooze, *The Foci of Comparative Literature* (University of Western Ontario, 2008) (electronic version), pp. 1-5.

3. Conclusions

Nowadays, the world has become a huge and single unit which consists of regions constantly interacting with each other. In the economic field for example, the world is becoming more and more a single market. But one can argue that such a globalized and borderless world is, however, in a serious cultural confusion. Yes, we live today in the age of 'multiculturalism'. In the previous ages, globalization meant just a domination of the world by the strong western civilization. This older type of globalization was based on homogenization and assimilation. Historically speaking, it is obvious that the precedent major civilizations always had a tendency of homogenization. The ancient civilizations of Rome and China built empires by forcing the other peoples to accept their own value system.

However, today's globalization is fundamentally different from the homogenization by the western modernity or the so-called 'internationalization'. This is so because the hegemony of western modernity has lost its efficiency and impact. Various ideals, world views or historical perspectives made by the western modernity, which Jean-François Lyotard called 'Le Grand récit' (the Grand Narrative) of the modernity in his book *The Postmodern Condition*, have gradually faded. Contemporary globalization leads to multiculturalism. Of course, multi-ethnicity or multiculturalism itself is not a rare case in history. In his recent book *Bound Together: How Traders, Preachers, Adventurers, and Warriors Shaped Globalization*, Nayan Chanda makes the point that globalization is an expression of human desires, which dates back to the dawn of time, when the first humans left their African homeland and set out in search of a better life. 'Globalization, perceived by its critics as a radical break with the past, looks to Chanda like a very familiar phenomenon. The traders, preachers, adventurers and warriors who acted as agents of globalization in ages past, now wear different clothes and have access to new technologies. The Spanish missionaries of the 16th century find their modern counterparts in idealists spreading a secular gospel of social justice, like Amnesty International, or aid workers bringing relief to third-world countries.'[31] The recent multiculturalism seems to be still unique, compared with them only because it has an unprecedented scale, and a diversity of style in each region. Still, a matter *of intensity* won't make Globalization, to use Lyotard's formula *Le Grand récit*. Not even close! Jean Bessière[32] makes it very clear:

---

[31]   William Grimes, 'Book review: Bound Together', *The New York Times*, 1 June 2007 (http://www.nytimes.com/2007/06/01/arts/01iht-booktue.html?_r=1).

[32]   Jean Bessière, 'How to Reform Comparative Literature's Paradigms in the Age of Globalization', *Neohelicon* XXVIII/1 (2001) (p. 23).

Defining the prevailing current and communication policies and executions as global, and developing what one can name 'fable of globalization' do not imply that we consider this globalization as 'faisant époque'. Globalization does not commend us to think that it defines our world in an essentially original way not that history has come to a new and specific moment today.

There is no doubt that Globalization has introduced new assumption in the field of humanities, especially of the ways in which culture circulates and the processes through which it fulfill its goals. One of the major aspects of this new reality has been the need to understand culture in terms of sets of connections and networks, or through its way, channels of transmission, rather than through its relationship to concrete spaces and places. For the most part, however, globalization brings a collection of multifaceted challenges and queries for Comparative Literature rather than *any new theory*. In other words, this is just a natural ongoing historical reality, since Comparative literature as a discipline not grounded in the literary tradition of any single language or nation, has always took important advantage from periodical re-examination and adjustments of its basic principles and practice.

In the end, as Haun Saussy puts it: 'Responding to the frequent attacks against contemporary literary studies, the Comparative Literature in the age of Globalization proves the continuing vitality of the discipline and its rigorous intellectual engagement with the issues facing today's global society' (back cover).

WORKS CITED

Al-Rodhan, Nayef, *Pilars of Globalization* (Genève: Slatkin Publishers, 2006)

Auerbach, Erich, *Mimesis: The Representation of Reality in World Literature* (Princeton: Princeton University Press, 1953)

—. 'Philology and Weltliteratur', *The Centennial* Review, 13 (1969) 1-17

Basel, Naftali, *Poetics Today* 12 (Winter 1991) 773 *et seq.*

Bessière, Jean, 'How to Reform Comparative Literature's Paradigms in the Age of Globalization'. *Neohelicon*, XXVIII/1 (2001), 13-24

Dumitru Radu Popa

Chanda, Nayan, *Bound Together: How Traders, Preachers, Adventurers, and Warriors Shaped Globalization* (New Haven: Yale University Press, 2007)

Cooppan, Vilashini, 'Ghosts in the Disciplinary Machine: The Uncanny Life of World Literature', *Comparative Literature Studies*, 41 (2004), 10-36

Damrosch, David, *What is World Literature? (Translation/Transnation)* (New York: Princeton University Press, 2003)

DeLooze, Laurence, *The Foci of Comparative Literature* (University of Western Ontario, 2008 (electronic version), 1-5

Friedman, Thomas, *The Lexus and the Olive Tree* (New York: Farrar, Strauss & Giroux, 1999)

Giddens, Anthony, *The Consequences of Modernity* (Stanford: Stanford University Press, 1990)

Guillen, Claudio, *The Challenge of Comparative Literature* (Cambridge: Harvard University Press, 1993)

Harris, Richard L., and Sandor Halebsky, eds, *Capital, Power, and Inequality in Latin America* (Boulder: Westview Press, 1995)

Harvey, David, *The Condition of Postmodernity: An Enquiry into the Origins of Social Change* (Cambridge: Blackwell Publishers, 1990)

Jameson, Fredric, 'Globalization and Political Strategy', *New Left Review*, 4 (July-August 2000) (http://newleftreview.org/A2255)

Jameson, Fredric, 'Third World Literature in the Era of Multinational Capitalism', *Social Text*, 14/15 (1986), 65-88

Jost, François, *Introduction to Comparative Literature* (Indianapolis: Pegasus, 1974)

Kadir, Djelal, 'Comparative Literature, the Transnational, and the Global', *Neohelicon*, XXVIII/1 (2001), 25-9

King, Anthony D., ed., *Culture, Globalization, and the World-System* (Binghamton: Binghamton University Press, 1991)

Kushner, Eva, '"Globalization" and "Individuation" in Comparative Literature Studies', *Neohelicon* 28 (2001), 31-4

Li, David Lewei, 'Globalization and the Humanities', *Comparative Literature* 275 (No. 4. Fall 2001), 275-82

Lyotard, François, *The Postmodern Condition* (Manchester: Manchester University Press, 1984)

Montaigne, Michel de, *Essais*, II (Paris: Les beaux lettres, 1967)

Moretti, Franco, *Modern Epic: The World System from Goethe to Garcia Marquez* (New York: Verso, 1996)

Navajas, Gonzalo, *Transnational Literature and Film between Borders*

(http://lehman/edu/faculty/guinazu/cyberletras/v14/navajas.htm)

Pizer, John, 'Goethe's "World literature" Paradigm and Contemporary Cultural Globalization', *Comparative literature*, 52 (No. 3, Summer 2000), 213-27

Ritzer, George, 'Rethinking Globalization: Glocalization/Grobalization and

Something/Nothing', *Sociological Theory*, 21 (No. 3. September 2003), 193-209

Saussy, Haun, *Comparative Literature in an Age of Globalization* (Baltimore: The Johns Hopkins University Press, 2006)

Scholte, J. A., *Globalization. A Critical Introduction* (London: Palgrave, 2000)

Spivak, Gayatri Chakravorty, *Death of a Discipline* (New York: Columbia University Press, 2003)

Weisstein, Ulrich, *Comparative Literature and Literary Theory: Survey and Introduction* (Bloomington: Indiana University Press, 1973)

Reference Works

Deardorff's Glossary of International Economics. IASB, 2001

www.csa.com/discoveryguides/afraid/gloss.php

www.centerforecojusticeeducation.org/index.php

http://en.wikipedia.org/wiki/Globalization

Oana Fotache

'Global Literature' – In Search of a Definition

This paper investigates the current theories and meanings attached to the notion of global literature, trying to find provisional answers to questions such as: What does it mean for literature to 'go global'? How is negotiated the relationship between local grounding and global success? What academic disciplines are called for to analyze this new/not-so-new concept?

The term 'globalization' has acquired during the past two decades such an epistemic power that it could almost dispense with explanatory attempts. So diverse are its contexts of use that it is now much more than a concept. It is a framework in which theories are proposed and thinking takes place. The much discussed 'topographical turn'[1] in human sciences has been made possible by the emergence of a global space in which ideas and values interact and modify each other.

Yet despite the impressive amount of theoretical labor encompassing the globalizing of politics, societies, or disciplines, the implications of this new reality upon the fields of literary production and research have not been thoroughly accounted for. In this paper I will try to examine more closely a single issue pertaining to this complex causality and interaction: the current boundaries of a theoretical object – 'global literature' – as traced by recent studies in different cultural and academic fields.

My focus will not be on the phenomenon of globalization as such, or on the redefinition of comparative literature in this context (questions addressed by a few papers in this volume). I will discuss instead the theories of and meanings attached to the notion of 'global literature'. What does it mean for a work or a writer to 'go global'? (a simple answer would be: to be translated in more than 20 languages and accordingly to sell millions of copies.) Is this notion useful as a research category? Which literary disciplines are best equipped to accommodate such issues? I will look first at the contexts in

---

[1] See Michael C. Frank, 'Imaginative Geography as a Travelling Concept', *European Journal of English Studies*, 13/1 (2009), and Sigrid Weigel, 'On the "Topographical Turn": Concepts of Space in Cultural Studies and *Kulturwissenschaften*. A Cartographic Feud', *European Review*, 17 (2009), for comprehensive accounts on the origins and development of this process.

which 'global literature' is discussed and try to expose a few legitimating strategies (if not actual meanings) from them.

1. From literary globalization to global literature

Globalization was first employed to describe 'the development of an increasingly integrated global economy marked especially by free trade, free flow of capital, and the tapping of cheaper foreign labor markets' (www.merriam-webster.com). An economic process became associated with strong political and social effects and interests. The corresponding notion in the field of literary study was not 'literary globalization'[2] or 'global literature' but, interestingly enough, 'world' or 'comparative literature'. Globalization soon acquired the status of a Foucauldian episteme, a sort of synonym for 'postmodernity'[3], a frame of reference in which contemporary literature was easily situated. We deal here with a pattern of transfer from one field (defined by the advance of postindustrial capitalism, ICT development, and the like) to another (cultural/literary). The difficulties inherent to such a shift are emphasized by Jean Bessière. Bessière comments on a discontinuity that is difficult to surpass:

> any direct application of the notion or reality of globalization to other fields, and especially to literatures, may appear groundless, because, most often, literary works are not written from a global perspective, although they may reflect that global perspective.[4]

There is an inherent ambiguity with this term that has consequences: contemporary literature is/tends to some extent to be globalized, and at the same time globalization is a theme of reflection for this literature. Moreover this transfer presupposes a change of emphasis – from the process (global-

---

[2]   When the term is employed by a celebrated global writer as Nobel laureate Orhan Pamuk its meaning is somehow distorted as to sound optimistic: 'Instead, Pamuk talked of the "literary globalization of the world" and outlined the way the novelist's imagination – when employed to evoke "the other, the stranger, the enemy that resonates inside each of our heads" – can be a powerful, liberating force' (quoted by *The Washington Post*, 30 October, 2007).

[3]   See for instance Stuart Hall's category of the 'global post-modern' -- 'The Local and the Global: Globalization and Ethnicity', in *Culture, Globalization, and the World-System*, ed. by Anthony D. King (Binghamton, NY: Department of Art and Art History, State U of New York at Binghamton P, 1991).

[4]   'How to reform comparative literature's paradigms in the age of globalization', *Neohelicon*, 28 (2001), p. 14.

ization) to its result (becoming global). A similar discursive (and epistemological) dynamics was involved in the invention of 'the Orient' as investigated by Edward W. Said (*Orientalism,* 1978). The transfer as such is problematic since it reactivates the mechanism of domination[5] and places the source discourse in the position of an explanatory metanarrative (see Bessière, Lyotard).

Jean Bessière's approach starts from Bourdieu's sociological analysis of the cultural/artistic field as relatively autonomous from the field of power[6]; thus he does not push to the limit Said's relativistic premise (which could lead to a perception of globalization as one of the constructs of imaginative geography). If we were to reread Bourdieu in this context, the interaction might lead to the emergence of a different *forma mentis* and to what H. R. Jauss has earlier termed 'the social function of literature' ('Literaturgeschichte als Provokation der Literaturwissenschaft', 1969). In other words literary globalization would mean that a new audience is being formed, one prepared to read beyond national literary traditions and gradually rework its immediate or larger social context through its literary representation.

2. The global as *pharmakon*

Another, perhaps more adequate, proximate genus for 'global literature' is postcolonial theory. Seen as a departure from imperialism the global turn appears as a redemption, a cure for the ills of postcolonialism', as Peter Kalliney assesses[7]. And he furthermore adds: 'We need to evaluate, in other words, whether or not globalization theory represents the logical next phase of postcolonial literary scholarship' (p. 52). Nevertheless when Linda Hutcheon looks for a way out the rigid pattern of national literary histories, she only discovers the return of the teleological model employed by European literary historical narratives in the 19th century. Hutcheon stages a cultural drama with a meaning yet to decide: 'earlier European imperialism created a "web of global commitments"'[8] (drawing on Stuart Hall's work on

---

[5]   For a critical perspective on globalization as the 'age of empire', see Antonio Negri, 'Art and Culture in the Age of Empire and the Time of the Multitudes', *SubStance* #112, 36/1 (2007).

[6]   For instance, in *Les Règles de l'art: genèse et structure du champ littéraire* (Paris: Seuil, 1998).

[7]   'Globalization, Postcoloniality, and the Problem of Literary Studies in the *Satanic Verses*', *Modern Fiction Studies*, 48 (Spring 2002), p. 51.

[8]   Linda Hutcheon, 'Postcolonial Witnessing – and Beyond: Rethinking Literary History Today', *Neohelicon* 30 (2003), p. 25.

globalization and ethnicity); the only gain is that 'the nation is now no longer the single dominant defining power in supranational imperialisms' (p. 25). In other words globalization as a theoretical construct has a tendency towards self-undermining and deconstruction which functions by turning Westernization or Americanization against themselves.[9]

More confident about the heuristic value of 'global literature' is Vilashini Cooppan in 'World Literature and Global Theory: Comparative Literature for the New Millennium' (2001). The emergence of a 'transnational, transregional, global literature' as she calls it involves in the same measure a reworking of the past literary tradition(s). The same old corpus requires new readings to survive. In the vein of Homi Bhabha's paradigmatic narrative (*The Location of Culture*, 1994), Cooppan focuses on 'the colonized, the migrants, the refugees' and their literary productions/representations. Yet one cannot help wondering whether this transfer of present research methodologies to past literary traditions is more justified than the travels of contemporary theories from one discipline to another. She suggests that the most appropriate and effective impact of globalization in literary studies concerns the transformation of audiences and reading practices: '[…] we could all of us begin to read globally. Globalized reading meant giving up the certitudes of the center in favor of the difficulties of dissemination'.[10] One can see why this turn is most appealing to postcolonial thinking.

3. Exile or migrant writing?

A shift from the circuits of reception to those of production occurs when one considers the circumstances under which a global literature takes shape. To this respect an undoubtedly privileged category is that of exile/migrant writers. The composite field of *diaspora studies* thus became well situated for an analysis of globalization's effects on contemporary writing. 'Diasporization and globalization can thus be considered as coeval processes, with globalization having the most impact on the contemporary phase', states Michele Reis in 'Theorizing Diaspora: Perspectives on "Classical" and "Contemporary" Diaspora'.[11] Reis embraces Appadurai's account (1996) on

---

[9]   Arjun Appadurai, *Modernity at Large: Cultural Dimensions of Globalization* (Minneapolis: University of Minnesota Press, 1996); Paul Jay, 'Beyond Discipline? Globalization and the Future of English', *PMLA*, Special Topic: Globalizing Literary Studies, 116 (Jan. 2001), 32-47.

[10]   Vilashini Cooppan, 'World Literature and Global Theory: Comparative Literature for the New Millennium', *Symploke*, 9 (2001), 15-43 (p. 39).

[11]   Michele Reis, 'Theorizing Diaspora: Perspectives on "Classical" and "Contemporary" Diaspora', *International Migration*, 42 (2004), p. 47.

the leveling effect of globalization as concerns the public and private spheres, the social classes, the local and the national, a.s.o. Contemporary diasporas are much more connected to their home country that anytime in the past; their formation and existence have been de-dramatized. What does this imply when it comes to the literary production originating from these ('virtual' as well as 'imagined') 'communities'?

The advantages of an external position have been noticed by theorists such as Pascale Casanova and John Neubauer when writing about the possibility of a transnational, European literature.[12] At a larger scale, the experience of circulation between cultures and languages has proven to be ideal for the apparition of a different way of being in the world. Recently the concept of 'migrant writing' tends to replace (as better suited to the context) that of 'exile literature'.[13] Then is migrant literature to be read as global literature? Definitely not (always). Both concepts involve a hesitation between intention (as seen in the choice of theme, for instance) and effect (large circulation by means of translations, adaptations, etc.). The local, 'very Turkish' quality of many of Orhan Pamuk's novels does not prevent them from travelling globally. Moreover, a typology that involves the experience of the writer to such an extent in determining the nature of his/her writing displays a narrow deterministic vision on literary creation.

4. The Global Pop

One does not have to be a keen observer of the cultural market to notice that pop culture is much more globalized than high culture. Children's literature (Narnia or Harry Potter series, to point to the obvious), or comics, or science fiction have long been globally priced. In an insightful essay that addresses the changes – and challenges - brought about by globalization, Sieghild Bogumil draws the readers' attention towards the potential of the new media also. Since the understanding of textuality was radically transformed by the Internet, the hypertext, and more recently by the idea of an *open access* literary culture[14], Bogumil pleads in favour of a broad meaning of 'global literature':

---

[12]   See Pascale Casanova, *La République mondiale des lettres* (Paris: Seuil, 1999), and John Neubauer, 'Voices from Exile: A Literature for Europe?', *European Review,* 17 (2009).

[13]   See Rebecca L.Walkowitz, 'The Location of Literature: The Transnational Book and the Migrant Writer', *Contemporary Literature,* 47 (2006), 527-545. Carine M. Mardorossian, 'From Literature of Exile to Migrant Literature', *Modern Language Studies,* 32 (2002), 15-33.

[14]   See Simone Murray, '"Remix my Lit": Towards an Open Access *Literary* Culture', *Convergence,* 16 (2010), 23-38.

on the one hand it means the desire to open literature to the other cultural practices in such a manner that literature would figure as one among them, and, on the other hand, it means the claim to take account of all kind of texts in the generic as well as in the geographic sense. [...] That is why the notion of world literature, dealing even in the most overt sense with books and aesthetics, as mentioned above, does not fit and has to be replaced by the term global literature.[15] (p. 48)

In order to justify – if that would be the case – the use of this theoretical coinage, 'global literature' has to establish, on one hand, a network of references to other related concepts (world and comparative literature mostly, but also 'local'/national literature), and to be clearly distinguishable from any of them, on the other. What does 'global' mean when it comes to literature?

The temptation to interpret it as a synonym for 'world literature' is huge. I will not review here the impressive amount of scholarship[16] devoted during the past years to the theorizing of world literature, starting from Goethe's *Weltliteratur*, revaluing the contribution of the German school of stylistic criticism (mostly Erich Auerbach's), up to the incorporation of current disciplinary developments in comparative literature. It is more useful instead to show why 'global' does not mean 'world' here.

First and foremost, because 'global literature' gestures towards its general readership, whereas the delineation of 'world literature' is a matter of critical response and canon formation.[17] The fact that literary tradition also became global (through school and university curricula, educational migrancy, a.s.o.) does not make the two concepts interchangeable. The corpus of world literature might be moving towards the encounter with a global readership, as David Damrosch's remark on the expanding tendency of world literature might suggest.[18] Yet 'global' has a contemporary appeal, while 'world' in

---

[15]   Sieghild Bogumil, 'Comparative Literature, Globalization, and Heterotopia', *Neohelicon*, 28 (2001).

[16]   Most influential being David Damrosch's *What Is World Literature?* (Princeton: Princeton University Press, 2003).

[17]   In an influential study on 'World Literature and World Politics: In Search of a Research Agenda', published in *Global Society* (2003), Gerard Holden writes: 'today, the term [world literature] is more likely to be used to refer to the totality, or the best, of past and present global literary production" (p. 231). And few lines below: 'more frequently [...] used in English to denote the subject matter of comparative literature' (p. 231). There are of course several issues to be further explored here ('totality' as opposed to 'the best'; or 'past' and 'present' in connection with 'global'). Anyway the notion of world literature is value-centered in its narrow sense.

[18]   In 'World Literature Today: From the Old World to the Whole World', *Symploke*, 8 (2000), 7-19.

'world literature' embraces the past and by doing that, it triggers a series of issues of cultural dialogue and interpretation.

When John Pizer in exploring the relations between Goethe's original notion of *Weltliteratur* and its contemporary career employs the two terms as synonyms[19], he might be doing that as an argument for the continuity of the first concept that he endeavors to stress. Both terms' reference points toward a larger representation of 'the real' that is of course influenced by the general systems of perception of their time.

Very accurate in his theoretical proposal is Ian Baucom who distinguishes between two uses of global literary studies (as an emerging disciplinary framework for 'globalit'), as 'project' and as 'method':

> By *project* I intend the appeal to reconfigure literary study as the study of something called global literature. By *method* I mean the global spread of particular ways of studying something called literature.[20]

Definitely global literature represents an actual stage in a long history, a stage that is marked by an increased awareness of the interconnectedness of literary cultures.

I would suggest to view 'literature' and 'global literature' as sharing the extension involved in their broad meaning (the total of literary production...) while the narrower meanings are divergent (aesthetic value, canonical relevance, 'literariness', on the one hand; thematic and contextual aspects activated on the other hand). The two concepts interfere but cannot substitute one another.

The distinction between *global* and 'comparative literature' appears in a way to be more definite (object vs discipline). Comparative literature's approach has always been relational and transnational; only that now the density of contacts and networks involved is overwhelming.[21] It goes without saying that the traditional notion of literary influence and its implicit hierarchical constructions are overcome. As Sieghild Bogumil insists, global literature is not: an addition of all literatures of the world; a collection of the most important/influential literatures; or the ensemble of the functionally linked ones (p. 51).

---

[19]   'With the globalization of the world economy, a true world literature, which is to say a *global* literature, is being created.'; John Pizer, 'Goethe's "World Literature" Paradigm and Contemporary Cultural Globalization', *Comparative Literature,* 52 (2000), 213-227.

[20]   Ian Baucom, 'Globalit, Inc.; Or, the Cultural Logic of Global Literary Studies', *PMLA,* Special Topic: Globalizing Literary Studies, 116 (2001), 158-172 (162).

[21]   For a provocative and astute reading of the state of the discipline in global times see Haun Saussy, ed., *Comparative Literature in an Age of Globalization* (Baltimore: Johns Hopkins University Press, 2006).

In this respect – global literature as a reinterpretation of comparative literature's traditional scope –, Franco Moretti's use of the wave metaphor to account for 'the great unread' looks very appropriate for its ability to 'observ[e] uniformity engulfing an initial diversity'[22]. So the irony involved in the coincidence of the complit crisis and the advent of global literary studies[23] is only a matter of temporary concern, since comparative literature is able to readjust its tools to deal with this challenging object.

It will probably be helpful to view global literature as embracing two stages, similarly with comparative literature: a modern one that was characterized by direct cultural contact and influence (Moretti's tree pattern); and a more recent stage that involves less rereading and value construction, and more of a sense of rapid flows of circulation – a fast developing binary code structured on the logic of success and failure.

Finally, the complex dialectics of the *global* and 'the local' seems to have been resolved by its synthesis in the 'glocal'.[24] As handy as it may look, 'the global' is not just the extension or the translation of the local. Nor it is homogeneous and easy to grasp. Both 'global' and 'local' are loaded terms. Analyzing the intricate representations involved in their construction, Chun Allen writes ('On the Geopolitics of Identity', 2009):

> even more disturbingly, we seem to know a priori what is global and what is local, even before the phenomenon is invoked. There are even many global phenomena that have literally become universal, although they are rarely characterized as such. We do not call cars or phones global, much less western; they are just modern. [...] there are implicit value judgments associated with global and local, despite our best attempts to define them in neutral, analytical terms. Their relative positional status is one that inscribes or reflects a castle-like hierarchy.[25]

The same holds true for the relationship between national literatures and global literature. The latter is not a sum of national literatures but questions the very relevance of this concept and consequently provokes it to reinvent itself.

---

[22]   In 'Conjectures on World Literature', *New Left Review* 1 (2000), 54-69.

[23]   Noticed by Francesco Loriggio in his study on 'Disciplinary Memory as Cultural History: Comparative Literature, Globalization, and the Categories of Criticism', *Comparative Literature Studies*, 41 (2004), 49-79.

[24]   A sociologically informed analysis of 'the glocal' is undertaken by Robert Eric Livingston in 'Glocal Knowledges: Agency and Place in Literary Studies', *PMLA*, Special Topic: Globalizing Literary Studies, 116 (Jan. 2001), 145-157.

[25]   Chun Allen, 'On the Geopolitics of Identity', *Anthropological Theory*, 9 (2009), 331-349 (p. 345).

*

The conclusion of this survey cannot but be provisional and moderate. 'Global literature' is a concept whose resources and heuristic force are to be further tested. Presumably, 'it would be the result of a comparative method respecting literatures as heterotopias which at the same time form a whole' (Bogumil, p.52). The disciplines or interdisciplinary projects that are called to develop and frame it count, among others, literary and cultural studies, area studies,[26] even literary international relations (according to Holden[27]), cultural history, even ethnography (James Clifford, *The Predicament of Culture*, 1988). And last, but not least, *global literary studies,* which undergoes a similar process of development.

WORKS CITED

Allen, Chun, 'On the Geopolitics of Identity", *Anthropological Theory*, 9 (2009), 331-349

Appadurai, Arjun, *Modernity at Large: Cultural Dimensions of Globalization* (Minneapolis: University of Minnesota Press, 1996)

Baucom, Ian, 'Globalit, Inc.; Or, the Cultural Logic of Global Literary Studies', *PMLA*, 116 (2001), 158-17.

Bessière, Jean, 'How to Reform Comparative Literature's Paradigms in the Age of Globalization', *Neohelicon,* 28 (2001)

---

[26]   Whose reinvention Spivak advocates in *Death of a Discipline* (New York: Columbia University Press, 2003).

[27]   Gerard Holden, 'World Literature and World Politics: In Search of a Research Agenda', *Global Society,* 17 (2003), 229-252.

Bhabha, Homi, *The Location of Culture* (London and New York: Routledge, 1994)

Bogumil, Sieghild, 'Comparative Literature, Globalization, and Heterotopia', *Neohelicon,* 28 (2001)

Bourdieu, Pierre, *Les Règles de l'art: genèse et structure du champ littéraire* (Paris: Seuil, 1998)

Casanova, Pascale, *La République mondiale des lettres* (Paris: Seuil, 1999)

Clifford, James, *The Predicament of Culture: Twentieth-Century Ethnography, Literature, and Art* (Cambridge, Massachusetts: Harvard University Press, 1988)

Cooppan, Vilashini, 'World Literature and Global Theory: Comparative Literature for the New Millennium', *Symploke*, 9 (2001), 15-43

Damrosch, David, 'World Literature Today: From the Old World to the Whole World', *Symploke,* 8 (2000), 7-19

Damrosch, David, *What Is World Literature?* (Princeton: Princeton University Press, 2003)

Frank, Michael C, 'Imaginative Geography as a Travelling Concept', *European Journal of English Studies,* 13 (2009), 61-77

Hall, Stuart, 'The Local and the Global: Globalization and Ethnicity', *Culture, Globalization, and the World-System*, ed. by Anthony D. King. Binghamton (NY: Department of Art and Art History, State U of New York at Binghamton P, 1991), pp. 19-39

Holden, Gerard, 'World Literature and World Politics: In Search of a Research Agenda', *Global Society,* 17 (2003), 229-252

Hutcheon, Linda, 'Postcolonial Witnessing – and Beyond: Rethinking Literary History Today', *Neohelicon* 30 (2003)

Jay, Paul, 'Beyond Discipline? Globalization and the Future of English', *PMLA*, 116 (2001), 32-47

Kalliney, Peter, 'Globalization, Postcoloniality, and the Problem of Literary Studies in the *Satanic Verses*', *Modern Fiction Studies*, 48 (2002)

Livingston, Robert Eric, 'Glocal Knowledges: Agency and Place in Literary Studies', *PMLA,* Special Topic: Globalizing Literary Studies, 116 (2001), 145-157

Loriggio, Francesco, 'Disciplinary Memory as Cultural History: Comparative Literature, Globalization, and the Categories of Criticism', *Comparative Literature Studies*, 41 (2004), 49-79

Mardorossian, Carine M, 'From Literature of Exile to Migrant Literature', *Modern Language Studies,* 32 (2002), 15-33

Moretti, Franco, 'Conjectures on World Literature", *New Left Review* 1 (2000), 54-69

Murray, Simone, '"Remix my Lit": Towards an Open Access *Literary* Culture', *Convergence*, 16 (2010), 23-38

Negri, Antonio, 'Art and Culture in the Age of Empire and the Time of the Multitudes', *SubStance* #112, 36/1 (2007)

Neubauer, John, 'Voices from Exile: A Literature for Europe?', *European Review,* 17 (2009), 133-148

Pizer, John, 'Goethe's "World Literature" Paradigm and Contemporary Cultural Globalization', *Comparative Literature,* 52 (2000), 213-227

Reis, Michele, 'Theorizing Diaspora: Perspectives on 'Classical' and 'Contemporary' Diaspora', *International Migration,* 42 (2004)

Saussy, Haun, ed. by, *Comparative Literature in an Age of Globalization* (Baltimore: Johns Hopkins University Press, 2006)

Spivak, Gayatri Chakravorty, *Death of a Discipline* (New York: Columbia University Press, 2003)

Walkowitz, Rebecca L., 'The Location of Literature: The Transnational Book and the Migrant Writer', *Contemporary Literature,* 47 (2006), 527-545

Weigel, Sigrid, 'On the "Topographical Turn": Concepts of Space in Cultural
    Studies and *Kulturwissenschaften*. A Cartographic Feud', *European
    Review*, 17 (2009), 187–201

Mihaela Irimia

The Classic Modern Canon and the Disciplinary Separation

The cultural institution of literature is increasingly being looked into in terms of historical embeddedness, with such concepts emphasized as chronological pattern(ing), evolution and periodization, historical perspectivism, or downright alternative histories of literature. Literature shares with history the status of belated category of human knowledge and is born as 'belles lettres' as a result of the great disciplinary separation operated by 'classic modernity', aka the Enlightenment. From the modernity agenda perspective, the present article analyses this and other diachronic shifts now taken for granted: the emergence of the professional writer and of the national canon of authors, the assertion of literary criticism, and the establishment of taxonomies ordering what had accumulated as antiquarian material into modern classification.

Like any other cultural institution, literature has a history. So do literary history and the literary canon, equally part of the discourse of modernity. Likewise disciplinary separation, which has been long enough with us to simply pass as natural and be taken for granted. Yet, interdisciplinary studies, in abundance in recent years, testify to the contrary. Why then turn back to pre-disciplinary separation? The short answer could be: we have only been used to disciplines some two hundred odd years, long enough, that is, yet our long-term memory operates in an interdisciplinary manner. The long answer would follow the course of long developments, like the emergence, sedimentation and institutionalization of 'literature' and the accreditation of the 'classic modern canon' as constitutive of what I call 'the long modernity'. This paper will look at these interdependent phenomena as embedded in (cultural) history.

Modernity, I take it, is a set of forms of symbolic violence which have eventually made us feel at home in a God-forsaken world. While this brings in a Lukacsian note, it supplies a retort to the Wordsworthian 'we come from God, who is our home' and drives home the case I will be trying to make. Modernity is a *longue durée* originating in the first rebirth of the classic antiquity, AKA the Renaissance, traversing its second re-birth, Neo-Classicism, AKA the Enlightenment, and which I call 'classic modernity', and reaching out into the ostensibly irreversible departure from classic/neo-classic tenets and values, AKA Postmodernity, which we had better refer to as 'late modernity', to do justice to Vattimo. With such a negative agenda (modernity is some form or another of denied classicism), it may be fair to suggest that it confirms the 'nothing fails like success' story. Modernity, in my view, suffers from the 'collapse of the isomorphic model', a condition at once of ease and disease, like the famous Derridean φάρμακον. Richard Hurd's *Letters on Chivalry and Romance* of 1762 have been quoted to this end. Like Klee's Angel of History, our 'modern classic' is torn between the past and the present. Sitting on the horn of a dilemma, he singles out the sense of 'loss' inherited by a Europe benefiting from the immediate certainty of *modo, modo*, while he fosters the nostalgia for blurred mythical narratives in *illo tempore*: 'What we have gotten by this revolution […] is a great deal of good sense. What we have lost is a world of fine fabling'.I call the 'isomorphic model' the Platonic further implemented as the Christian *Weltanschauung*, which posits the perfect harmony of the world by rooting it in the good = truth = beauty equation, the classic *το καλοκαγαθόν*. Theorized by Tatarkiewicz (1981) as 'the Great Theory', its supreme value is 'the true'. We find it in Ficino's definition of God as coextensive with all three as one. Behind it lies the received idea of the ethical and mathematical implications of beauty as securer of the cosmic make and of its immanent canon. Human endeavours, in their turn, are regulated by eternal canons of beauty (κανόνες).

Nor should this surprise: 'early modernity' is not – leftwards on our imaginary axis – severed from premodernity. Nor is it – rightwards – distanced from 'classic modernity'. The latter, a time of Whiggish rationality, has bequeathed us the wardrobe with specialized drawers, shelves and hangers modelled as a piecemeal sartorial double of the human figure, in clever anticipation of structuralist Barthes's paradigmatic-syntagmatic choice of clothes, botanic classification reduplicating the vegetal reign with pigeonhole precision, the newspaper and periodical industry conferring upon the ephemeral the prestige of the written word, and other such taxonomic patterns meant to make of its own invented public sphere a place of societal syntax. It is a time of 'the correct' as supreme value, with the straight line (*recta*) promising progress in the world down here.

Classic modernity is replete with hypostases of symbolic violence: it allots itself an *a posteriori* name, what in McKeon's vocabulary is 'modernity's retrospective construction of the Enlightenment', by legitimating its educated classes via the institution of imitation, namely, of the ancient classics.[1] Past-geared emulation is the guarantee of present-directed prestige and future-pointing recognition in a melioristic world. It holds the ancients as the canonical authors (*auctores*) and procrastinates in promoting the study of the modern classics. When this does happen, it does on the periphery, with Edinburgh and Glasgow founding the first English

---

[1]   Michael McKeon, 'The Origins of Interdisciplinary Studies', *Eighteenth-Century Studies*, 28 (1994), 17-28 (p. 18).

chairs, way before Oxbridge. It cultivates the novel, yet it praises the epic and its rigorous discipline, it delights in the sparkling conversation piece, yet it has the ambition of learned debates, it has an eye for the lightness of life, yet it hypothesizes seriousness in ample treatises. Most of all, it delights in antiquarian profusion, while it is keen on finding a common denominator able to order the endless variety of the world. It eventually confects its metanarrative of history with Kantian turned Hegelian material, leaving behind the cumbersome accumulation of dates and data, 'dogmatic but historically rich' (the way of *quantis*) to put in place 'the rational but humanly impoverished' scheme (the way of *qualis*).[2] The visitor to the British Museum King's Rooms, in effect a huge cabinet of curiosities aimed at 'discovering the world', will instantly notice this typically modern mania for standardized precision. Consubstantial – from our vantage point – with high and late modernity, classic modernity is not indifferent to the call of the present, which its younger relatives have made as pleasurable and comfortable as possible. The supreme value of our recent modernity is 'the efficient'.

The one crucial gap in the inherited isomorphic model, the hiatus AKA the Scientific Revolution, ushers in modernity's historical and historic collapse. As revivals of the past – classicism reloaded –, early and classic modernity promote a mimetic and emulative model, torn from temporal immediacy and spatial contingency. They look for legitimacy in chronotopic difference, with the 'then' and the 'there' of their projections as morganatic landmarks. Their *deictic failure* is the basic prerequisite of all messianism. On the contrary, fully-fledged modernity lives in the *hic et nunc* of history, in 'deictic fulfillment', its messianism perpetually renewed: the media and the culture industry cooperate in commodifying life along the lines of an indefatigably guaranteed better future. This is the reign of the near future already alive and kicking in the immediate present, for the present itself is dying to be the future.

*

In its historico-cultural embeddedness, modernity has displayed correctness as attractive merchandise on its chronotopic counters in each of its confected stages. Here is its early one, the Renaissance 'public correctness' of the city or royal court and their appended institutions, from the theatre and printed books to the market place, all ready for salable carnivalized enjoyment; here is the 'professional correctness' of the Enlightenment with its campaign for

---

[2]   *History and the Disciplines: The Reclassification of Knowledge in Early Modern Europe*, ed. by Donald R. Kelley (Rochester, N.Y.: University of Rochester Press, 1997), p. 21.

correct prose, lexicographic regulation of language, complete works of the national authors, the 'disciplinary and epistemological division' still at work in universities today and responsible for a 'unified scheme of knowledge' (McKeon, see note 1), and the national literary canon. Violating the logic of logic, Romantic 'emotional correctness' building on the end of the Great Theory brings in the accidental, the unexpected, the irregular, the picturesque, the exuberant and the sentimental, validating beauty in terms of individual taste and imagination, discrediting the asserted and assertive norm, crediting a *sui generis* anti-canon. Realism promotes 'literal correctness' with photographic referential likeness at a time of mechanical reproducibility holding pride of place. 'Political correctness', our postmodern gender-class-race acceptability, observance of rules and acute awareness of otherness, feature as a new civility abiding by collective moral canons.

Along the lines of correctness, or rather, following the 'line' of correctness, classic modernity features the more prominently with its central value – 'the correct' – giving the epistemological measure of things. Such the classic modern canon itself patented in the passage from the first to the second re-birth of Classicism. The circumference of the classic ancient vision is supplanted by the vertical line which places the *artes liberales* underneath the *artes professionals*, ordered in homologous – canonical, that is – relation to the societal and the cosmic matrix. Enacting an epoch-making suspension in the inherited tradition, early modernity returns to the circle or cycle of learning as *encyclopaedias* and cultivates *humanae litterae*, an exercise still mobilizing the energy and passion of the Shandy brothers caught up between antiquarian quotes and modern military stratagems. This symbolic affront is not without canonical consequences. Petrarch reputedly promotes the classics of the Greco-Roman antiquity and their canons, in which he sees the light of knowledge, not homebred obscurity, yet prefers *il volgare* as linguistic vehicle. Here is the inception of modernity anchored in its antonym, while clothed in its updated garments.

When it resumes the modern line of progressive unfolding, Western thinking moves on to the institutionalization of the 'melioristic modern canon', basically an 18th-century invention, yet not before it orchestrates the worldly rearrangement of the onetime divinely sanctioned canon. 17th-century Eclecticism, an intellectual and epistemological endeavour in its own right, raises philosophy to the status of leading discipline on its proudly asserted interdisciplinary basis. This time of *crise de la conscience européenne* forms the substance of Paul Hazard's trailblazing study of 1935. Tellingly bound within *Livre de poche* covers featuring Blake's *Newton* on the sea bottom with a pair of compasses in his left hand, the 1994 French edition came out within one year of the postmodern statue of the same by Edoardo Paolozzi, a Scottish-bred British citizen of Italian descent. Eliot had seen the dissociation of sensibility as a 17th-century engendered phenomenon, while historians of ideas now emphasize the modern liberation of (individual) reason in the time's 'declarations of independence from magisterial authority [...] [as] "liberty of philosophizing"' (Kelley, p. 17).

The Scientific Revolution type of modern library as repository of all disciplines, with literature as whatever is written down in letters, a Renaissance conceptual legacy, stands at the head of more modern developments, such the Republic of Letters, the history of philosophy en route to Hegel's theory, philology stemming out of the Valla-Poliziano grammatical tradition intertwined with Biblical studies, or the secular natural and human law vs. scholastic universal eternities. Indeed, this 'collapse of the isomorphic model' dovetails with Cartesian dubitation, updated doxography verging on the history of opinions, burgeoning (cultural) relativism, theoretical and experimental rationalism, deism and the triumph of science.

And now to the second re-birth of Classicism, or else 'classic modernity'. It witnesses the separation of disciplines on which the Humboldtian university will be founded. It acknowledges the watershed between science and doubt, while placing opinion in the median position as a mental territory of (re)negotiations. It takes on board the literary tradition of the history of philosophy snowballing into the history of ideas, in the double acceptation of the word 'history', i.e. a teleological unfolding of events, and a teleological narrative of such an evolution – a modern view *par excellence*, if one with ancient roots in the classic ιστορία. To the former, it could be said, the century of enlightened knowledge adds a sense of rational pattern, history being credited with 'scientific' precision – the Kantian-Hegelian way capitalizing on Thucydidean material. To the latter, it appears, it confers the richness of chronotopic diversity – the Nietzschean way fed by the Herodotean vision.

The fruitful tension holding between the sciences and the humanities at the kernel of the binomial above is to be identified in the century's overall grappling with more and more information and its ambition to order, classify, categorize, and discipline it – at once an exercise in intelligence and in power. Analeptic views of the impressive amount collected in the course of history translate as proleptic displays governed by rigorous precepts. Classic modernity's 'intellectual Whiggery' has been regarded as 'an unavoidable condition not only of writing the history of particular modern constructs but also, as hermeneutics has made clear, of history in general' (Kelley, p. 25). Between the '–etic' of facts and the '–emic' of ideas of facts in history, or else what in the literature is also referred to in Windelband's terms, rises a fence on one side of which are '"nomothetic" [...] pursuits, which [attempt] to formulate laws', and on the other 'idiographic discourses, devoted to

unique events in all their specificity'.[3] This cultural(ist) fence was provided
with gates even in the Lovejovian narrative of ideas (sic).

In the mid-1700s the disciplines, like the literary canon come into being
as they are still with us, albeit undergoing sea changes like never before. As
imagined communities in their own fashion, they function within specified
territorial boundaries, according to specific laws and regulations, using
apposite vocabulary, practising their own protocols and rituals, addressing
their own audiences and bringing to the fore their own leaders of opinion,
populating the public sphere with might and right, at once disciplined and
disciplining. To the 17th century confection of *beaux arts* erected on Horatian
premises (the *utile dulci* norm) is added the institution of *belles letters*, both
undergoing historical rearrangements and eventually being regularized by the
Kantian *Critique of Judgement* sensitive to 'taste and the concept of
finality'.[4] The birth certificate of aesthetics proper is concomitant, as it were,
with the proclamation of the enlightened university teaching specialized
disciplines and a standard(ized) canon of authors and works.

This overtly modern development remains contemporaneous and
coextensive with its antonym, as Michael McKeon, one of the most brilliant
analysts of the novel today, has shown. His *Origins of the English Novel* is
underlain by the issue of a 'negative definition of interdisciplinary study –
that which overcomes and denies disciplinary division' (p. 17). His
evaluations have enlightened Enlightenment studies in yet insufficiently
acknowledged proportion. To think of 'the secularization of the relationship
between the divine and the human', 'the ambition to historicize knowledge',
'the empirical project that would separate the subjective act of knowledge
from its objects and discriminate modes and degrees of knowledge', 'the
effort to delimit a sphere of aesthetic judgment', 'the material and
institutional conditions [...] that have given the modern division of
knowledge a socio-political foundation' (pp. 17-8) amounts to assessing
'classic modernity' as the precursor of our late modernity and the offspring of
early modernity, i.e. walking in the track of the modern story of history, at
once disciplinary and interdisciplinary, canonical and anti-canonical,
internally and externally regulated. A story emerging in history, which it
narrates, while it is narrated by the latter's institutions.

---

[3]   Michael Holquist, 'The Last European: Erich Auerbach as Precursor in the History of
      Cultural Criticism', *Modern Languages Quarterly* 54 (September 1993), 371-91 (p. 376).

[4]   Władysław Tatarkiewicz, *Istoria celor șase noțiuni* (*The History of The Six Notions*), trans.
      by Rodica Ciocan-Ivănescu (Bucharest: Editura Meridiane, 1981), p. 113.

WORKS CITED

Cascardi, A.J., 'Totality and the Novel', *New Literary History*, History, Politics, and Culture, 23 (Summer, 1992), 607-627

Cohen, Ralph, 'Genre Theory, Literary History, and Historical Change', *Harvard English Studies*: Theoretical Issues in Literary History, 16 (1991), 85-113

—. 'History and Genre', *New Literary History*, Interpretation and Culture 17 (Winter, 1986), 203-218

Crawford, Robert, ed., *The Scottish Invention of English Literature* (Cambridge: Cambridge University Press, 1998)

Greenblatt, Stephen, 'What Is the History of Literature?' *Critical Inquiry*, Front Lines/Border Posts, 23 (Spring, 1997), 460-481

Greenblatt, Stephen & Giles Gunn, eds, *Redrawing Boundaries: The Transformation of English and American Literary Studies* (New York: The Modern Languages Association of America, 1992)

Hazard, Paul, *The European Mind: 1680-1715*, trans. by J. Lewis May (Harmondsworth. Middlesex: Penguin University Books Ltd, 1973)

Holquist, Michael, 'The Last European: Erich Auerbach as Precursor in the History of Cultural Criticism', *Modern Languages Quarterly*, 54 (September 1993), 371-91

Hutcheon, Linda & Mario J. Valdés, *Rethinking Literary History: A Dialogue on Theory* (Oxford: Oxford University Press, 2002)

Kelley, Donald R., ed., *History and the Disciplines: The Reclassification of Knowledge in Early Modern Europe* (Rochester, N.Y.: University of Rochester Press, 1997)

Kernan, Alvin B., 'The Idea of Literature', *New Literary History*, What Is Literature? 5 (Autumn 1973), 31-40

Korshin, Paul J., ed., *The Widening Circle: Essays on the Circulation of Literature in Eighteenth-Century Europe* (Philadelphia: University of Pennsylvania, 1976)

McKeon, Michael, 'The Origins of Interdisciplinary Studies', *Eighteenth-Century Studies*, 28 (1994), 17-28

Mattix, Micah, 'Periodization and Difference', *New Literary History*, 35 (2005), 685-697

Nisbet, H.B. & Claude Rawson, eds, *The Cambridge History of English Literature*, Volume 4: *The Eighteenth Century* (Cambridge: Cambridge University Press, 1997)

Orr, Linda, 'The Revenge of Literature: A History of History', *New Literary History*, Studies in Historical Change 18 (Autumn 1986), 1-22

Parrinder, Patrick, *Authors and Authority: English and American Criticism 1750-1990*   (London: Macmillan, 1991)

Passmore, John, 'History of Art and History of Literature: A Commentary', *New Literary History*, Literary and Art History, 3 (Spring 1972), 575-587

Praz, Mario, 'Literary History', *Comparative Literature*, 2 (Spring 1950), 97-106

Rehder, Robert, 'Periodization and the Theory of Literary History', *Colloquium Helveticum*, 22 (1995), 117-136

Rivers, Isabel, ed., *Books and Their Readers in Eighteenth-Century England* (Leicester: Leicester University Press & New York: St. Martin's Press, 1982)

Tatarkiewicz, Władysław, *Istoria celor şase noţiuni* (*The History of the Six Notions*), trans. by Rodica Ciocan Ivănescu (Bucharest: Editura Meridiane, 1981)

White, Hayden, 'Literary History: The Point of It All', *New Literary History*, A Symposium on Literary History, 2 (Autumn 1970), 173-185

White, Morton, *Foundations of Historical Knowledge* (New York & London: Parker & Row Publishers, 1965)

Note

Research for Mihaela Irimia's article *The Classic Modern Canon and the Disciplinary Separation* has been partially supported by UEFISCSU grant no. 871/2009 [code 1980] for a research project titled *The Cultural Institution of Literature from Early to Late Modernity in British Culture.*

Stefan H. Uhlig

Historiography or Rhetoric? A Road (Not) Taken in the Evolution of the Literary Field

It is a striking feature of the discipline of literary studies that a number of its basic values will resist debate without a fairly detailed understanding of their past. Indeed, its very focus on an object understood as literature presents a formative departure from the more expansive, classical traditions of both poetry and rhetoric. This essay reconstructs one aspect of this complex history by looking at the forking paths of rhetoric and literary historiography as they (either by contrast or directly) help initiate the subject's institutional career. Courses in rhetoric and belles lettres were exported from the Scottish universities and dissenting academies to enjoy a long career in the United States. In the same period, the first curricula of literary study featured in the University of London in the form of literary history. Soon, narrative synopses of the literary archive came to dominate the field. Yet there were other choices, not least those presented by Romanticism's reconception of the function of poetics. How the subject framed itself around 1800 is not least a basic question for debates about how literary studies might evolve.

In view of recent efforts to revise and reinvest in the idea of a world literature, this paper has a twofold aim. It seeks to speculate about the past prerequisites for such undertakings, and to historicize part of our focus on how literary studies are, or ought to be, configured now. What I would wish to stress is that there is an aspect of our explorations of 'world literature' that is traditional, by which I mean historically inherited. I aim specifically to sketch this aspect as a function of the fact that, roughly around 1800, we chose 'literature'—and not, say, 'poetry' or 'rhetoric'—as the key framing concept for what we accordingly inherit as the literary field. Consequently, the hypothesis I want to put forth, though much more briefly than would seem appropriate, is whether our investment in world literature would have differed in its shape and implications if we, on the threshold of the field's modernity, had made another set of choices in the basic categories for the discipline. Since I do not, indeed, regard the history of these choices as a trap, the question might be equally what our debates about the future of comparative, or even national, literary studies could now look like if we—at the present time—sought to conceptualize the field in different ways. Two points of method may be noted at the start. Some, though not all, of the conceptual developments I outline in what follows are historical in what I would refer to as a strong sense. That is to say, they do not simply have a history to the extent that they began or changed at certain times. Instead, they have remained historical in the specific and far more capacious aspect that we persistently require—or at least are greatly helped by—a knowledge of their past in order to understand how they work at present, what contribution they make now. I am—to make a second point about procedure—also working here on the assumption that conceptual developments can be tracked by specific terms; and that it therefore matters if, and when, we have historically referred to certain texts and practices as 'poetry', as 'rhetoric', or as 'literature'.

As readers may already know, the terms 'literature' and 'letters'—from their Latin origins until well into the seventeenth century—work as general, as all-inclusive terms for 'learning' as derived from texts, from letters or the written word; they denote knowledge-in-general, and not a set of texts that we could read, for as long as all knowledge is thought principally to derive from books. Starting from the ability to read and write (to handle letters), via some knowledge of grammar, of Latin, even Greek, then the vernacular these terms describe the various, more or less extensive levels of what we moderns would call book-learning—since for us the dominant models of learning have long been empirical, no longer textual. Accordingly as late as 1694, the dictionary of the Académie Française still defines 'letters' as 'any kind of science or doctrine', and 'literature' as simply 'erudition, doctrine'.[1]

Around 1750, the modern concept 'literature' enters its first formative stage in the context of philosophical aesthetics. For the first time, 'letters' are specifically connected with the beautiful. Following his better known *Les Beaux Arts réduits à un même principe*, Charles Batteux's 1747 *Cours de belles letters* – translated as *A Course of the Belles Lettres: or the Principles of literature* – complements Batteux's new canon of the 'fine arts' with a separate curriculum of poetry, oratory and history, which he defines as 'belles lettres'.[2] Batteux's aesthetic model for a basic education sets out to engage the students' individual taste before they move on to more abstract, intellectual sciences. The mind itself, Batteux writes, 'seizes first what is more perceptible by the senses, & then uses that to reach what is not'. In this way, the aesthetic version of 'belles lettres' aims to guide the student from beauty and goodness to truth. In contrast with conventional rhetoric, Batteux explains,

> Our aim is not to teach how to speak, but to teach how to read and to judge. Now, to learn how to judge, in matters of literature, we first need to practise on works where the beauties and faults, being more sensible, also offer more of a hold to taste and wit, where art shows itself without any mystery; & once this art has been fully recognised for what it is, and we are sure to have grasped its true principles, we will try to recognise it even in works where it usually hides itself (p. 3).

---

[1]   *Le Dictionnaire de l'Académie Françoise*, vol. 1 (Paris: Coignard, 1694), pp. 639-40.

[2]   See Charles Batteux, *Les Beaux Arts reduits à un même principe* (Paris: Durand, 1746, repr. Paris: Amateurs des livres, 1989); *Cours de belles lettres distribué par exercices*, 3 vols, (Paris: Desaint et Saillant, 1747-48); *Cours de belles-lettres, ou principes de la littérature*, 4 vols (Paris: Desaint et Saillant, 1753); and *A Course of the Belles Lettres: or the Principles of literature*, 4 vols (London: Law and others, 1761).

Alongside Batteux, the German philosophers Baumgarten and Meier recruit the 'fine sciences', or '*schöne Wissenschaften*', to commend their new project of '*Ästhetik*'. Their link between the beautiful and letters helps to integrate the sensate appeal of poetry and rhetoric with their broader ambition to create a beautiful 'science' or '*Wissenschaft*' of sensate cognition.[3] Aesthetics, as Meier has it, is ultimately a 'metaphysics of poetry and rhetoric'.[4]

For several decades, these aesthetic accounts of letters, or 'belles lettres' are discussed across Europe, by writers like Diderot, Gottsched or Mendelssohn as much as in Adam Smith and Hugh Blair's Scottish project of 'rhetoric and belles lettres'—to which I will return towards the end of these remarks. As a result, within eighteenth-century aesthetics, this specific association between 'letters' and the beautiful creates the first productive, intellectually expressive interest in a notion of 'literature'. However, in the long term and for us – that is, for the modernity in which we continue to think about and with the literary – this analytic promise or investment develops only up to a point, only until it is blocked, or frustrated, by the most influential account of aesthetic judgement that we have. Towards 1800, Kant's *Critique of Judgement* both secures aesthetics as a separate branch of philosophy, and categorically excludes the perspective of 'literature' from future debate about aesthetics—not just in theory, but overwhelmingly also in fact; that is to say in terms of what gets written in aesthetics after Kant.

In a direct attack on the recent proposals of 'beautiful letters' or 'fine sciences', Kant in effect trivializes this line of enquiry into literature's aesthetic core by driving a wedge between determinate conceptual cognition on the one hand, and reflective judgements of the beautiful, or the sublime, on the other. Irrespective of conceptual fixities, learning or knowledge, Kantian aesthetic judgement validates more fundamental, formal capabilities that precede any concrete knowledge of the world. 'An aesthetic judgement', in his paradigmatic terms, is thus

> of a unique kind, and affords absolutely no cognition (not even a confused one) of the object, which happens only in a logical judgment; while the former, by contrast, relates

---

[3] See Alexander Gottlieb Baumgarten, *Meditationes philosophicae de nonnullis ad poema pertinentibus* (Halle: Grunert, 1735); in Karl Aschenbrenner and William B. Holther, ed. and trans., *Reflections on Poetry. Alexander Gottlieb Baumgarten's 'Meditationes philosophicae de nonnulis ad poema pertinentibus'* (Berkeley: University of California Press, 1954); *Aesthetica*, 2 vols (Frankfurt an der Oder: Kleyb, 1750-58, repr. Hildesheim: Olms, 1986); and Hans Rudolf Schweizer, ed. and trans., *Theoretische Ästhetik. Die grundlegenden Abschnitte aus der 'Aesthetica' (1750/58)*, 2nd edn (Hamburg: Meiner, 1988).

[4] Georg Friedrich Meier, *Anfangsgründe aller schönen Wissenschaften*, vol. I. (Halle: Hemmerde, 1754, repr. Hildesheim: Olms, 1976), p. 5.

the presentation by which an object is given solely to the subject, and does not bring to our attention any property of the object, but only the purposive form in the determination of the powers of representation that are occupied with it. The judgment is also called aesthetic precisely because its determining ground is not a concept but the feeling (of inner sense) of that unison in the play of the powers of the mind. (*Critik der Urtheilskraft*)[5]

Kant insists that categories of learning or enquiry will be no use as we reflect on such experiences. Our critical responses must forgo the certainties of science in this view and—for us as for the creative artist—only the category of 'art' looks practical enough to escape the determinations of theory. Kant explains that however much critics may 'adduce' the more definite prescriptions of writers like '*Batteux* or *Lessing*',

There is neither a science of the beautiful [*Wissenschaft des Schönen*], only a critique, nor beautiful science [*schöne Wissenschaft*], only beautiful art. For if the former existed, then it would determine scientifically, i.e., by means of proofs, whether something should be held to be beautiful or not; thus the judgement about beauty, if it belonged to a science, would not be a judgment of taste.[6]

After the *Third Critique*, both new work and the textbooks on aesthetics turned away from 'literature' or 'letters', and returned to poetry or the fine arts as the appropriate aesthetic categories (thus Hegel, of course, uses 'poetry' to represent the verbal arts). Hence, modern 'literature' derives its most expressive analytic claim from the brief heyday of 'belles lettres'. Though this strand of enquiry had already dried up by the turn of the century, it provides whatever original focus the concept has: both the enduring sense that this in some way is a focused category, and the suggestion that aesthetic interests form its core. But once it had been sidelined from much of the future of aesthetic theory, this formative claim came to work as an unrealized, frustrated legacy, and serves, to my mind, to explain much of the concept's weakness as an analytic tool.

It follows from this version of events that, as part of a specifically aesthetic terminology, we would by now long have forgotten about 'literature'; and it is clear that, on the strength of its first formative debate, the category looks like an unlikely candidate for modern prominence. But at the same time as eighteenth-century writers on aesthetics discuss the sensory potential of 'belles lettres', the much more influential rise of literary

---

[5]   Immanuel Kant, *Critik der Urtheilskraft* (Berlin and Libau: Lagarde und Friederich, 1790); in Paul Guyer (ed.) *Critique of the Power of Judgment*, trans. by Paul Guyer and Eric Matthews (Cambridge: Cambridge University Press, 2000), p. 113.

[6]   Immanuel Kant, *Critique of Judgement*, in Wilhelm Weischedel (ed.) *Werkausgabe*, vol. 10 (Frankfurt am Main: Suhrkamp, 1974), p. 239.

historiography lends a pervasive, concrete presence to 'letters' as a retrospective focus for cultural self-understanding. This simultaneous stage of formation comes to define—or find for its purposes—an altogether new historical object. Here, 'literature' is for the first time understood as a substantial body of writing—waiting to be read, interpreted and studied.

As history becomes the object of historicism, it appears as its own source of explanations, that can rival those of synchronic analysis. And as a central, cultural part of that phenomenon, bodies of 'literature'—now in the sense of a semantic archive of evolving cultures—prove themselves the productive objects of a quest to understand culture as emphatically historical. John Pocock has suggested that 'the historicist revolution of the eighteenth and nineteenth centuries, which transformed our awareness of society and culture into an historical awareness of an unprecedented kind', is a revolution 'of the concepts used to organise and control the whole body of information about the past'. And 'literature' is a prime example of how, as Pocock writes, 'the history of historicism is that of the process by which these concepts became in the full sense historical'.[7]

In the growing number of narrative literary histories before and after 1800, 'literature' tracks an archive of writing that embodies qualitative changes over time. The modern literary histories by Friedrich Schlegel, Madame de Staël or Jean François de la Harpe agree that what are now called 'works' of literature look irreducibly diverse in different periods and languages, and that they thus provide condensed, indeed exemplary cultural documents. But Herder's 1767 fragments *On Recent German Literature* provide an especially powerful early instantiation of the literary archive as it settles into concrete fact. Herder envisions a periodical review of intellectual life that would contain

> more than letters, excerpts, and interpretations serving as diversions; a work that draws the outline of a complete and entire portrait of literature, in which no line is without importance for the whole, whether it be hidden in the shadow or standing out in the light.

To be able to grasp its object, Herder suggests,

> this universal and unique work would be necessarily based upon a *History of Literature*, from which it would draw support. Which stage has this nation attained? And which

---

7   J. G. A. Pocock, 'The Origins of Study of the Past: A Comparative Approach', *Comparative Studies in Society and History*, 4 (1961), 210, 246. On the development of an emphatically historical mode of explanation, see Reinhart Koselleck, 'Historia Magistra Vitae: The Dissolution of the Topos into the Perspective of a Modernized Historical Process', in *Futures Past: On the Semantics of Historical Time*, trans. by Keith Tribe (Cambridge, MA: MIT Press, 1985), pp. 21-38.

might and should it attain? What are its talents and what is its aesthetic sense? What is its extrinsic state in the sciences and in the arts?[8]

For Herder, 'language, *aesthetics*, history, and philosophy are the four provinces of literature, which reinforce each other mutually, and which are all but inseparable' (p. 95). However, language now serves not just as a 'tool' of intellectual culture (ibid. 101), but as its 'repository' or its 'quintessence', and therefore precipitates as a form which shapes the archive different cultures leave behind.[9] To varying degrees, Herder insists, all written sources will resist translation and conceived as 'literature', these traces of our multinational intellectual history must, in a fundamental sense, be read. The texts of 'literature' are objects found, indeed created by the newly dominant pursuit of literary history, and Herder symptomatically demands: 'Reader! Let history speak' (*Dritte Sammlung*, see the above note, p. 372).

We don't have time here to explore how these two separate contributions to the concept—on the one hand a defunct attempt to link the beautiful and 'letters', on the other a new, thriving literary historiography—begin to interact once 'literature' secures the literary field around the 1820s. But the basic pattern is, I think, familiar, or at least recognizable. On the plus-side, 'literature' in its historical capacity presents an archive of past writing whose interpretative promise, whose coherence and authority declare themselves as settled in advance. And since these built-in valuations are as circular as they are dependable, the category is hard to beat in academic contexts where stability is in demand. At the same time, the concept's formative yet never quite developed, and hence chronically weak, reference to the aesthetic would seem to suggest a focus for its work. Yet in its intimation of how texts and interests—as viewed through the concept—should be thought of 'literature' has not been a great help in working out the cogency of the discipline it helps to found.

Now to return to more straightforward history (in the weaker sense), if we look at the study of the literary field that's institutionalized, say, at London University in the new century, it's clear that 'literature' as relayed by its historiography has won the day (and already displays a version of the international claim that we're concerned with here). Yet at the same time there is a also a clear trace of an alternative, and this is where we're—in

---

[8]   Johann Gottfried Herder, 'On Recent German Literature: First Collection of Fragments', in *Selected Early Works 1764-1767: Addresses, Essays and Drafts; 'Fragments on Recent German Literature'*, ed. by Ernest A. Menze and Karl Menges, trans. by Ernest A. Menze with Michael Palma (University Park: Pennsylvania State University Press, 1992), p. 94.

[9]   Johann Gottfried Herder, 'Erste Sammlung. Zweite völlig umgearbeitete Ausgabe', in *Werke in zehn Bänden*, ed. by Martin Bollacher et al., vol. 1 (Frankfurt am Main: Deutscher Klassiker Verlag, 1985), p. 548.

conclusion—led back to the Scottish plans for 'rhetoric and belles lettres'. The 1831 prospectus for King's College London records that in

ENGLISH LITERATURE, &c.—The Lectures in this department…will embrace the several branches of English Literature, History, and Logic…

[The Professor of] FRENCH LANGUAGE AND LITERATURE will [offer a] Course of Eighteen Lectures on '*The History of French Literature*'…

[The Professor of] GERMAN LANGUAGE AND LITERATURE will [lecture on] '*The History and Development of German Literature*'…[10]

And ditto the Professor of Spanish. The 1827 statement by the Council of the University of London further spells out the expected benefits of learning languages through 'literature', and its historically recovered model-texts:

The comparison of various languages makes each of them better understood, and illustrates the affinity of nations… In the arts which employ language as their instrument, the contemplation of the original models, not only serves to form the taste…, but generally conduces to expand and elevate the human faculties.[11]

Yet this official statement equally holds on to a quite different view of how the language arts, and languages, might academically be taught, practiced and learnt:

Perhaps, also, Rhetoric may in time merit a separate Professorship,… to undeceive those rigid censurers and misguided admirers, who consider eloquence as a gaudy pageant; and to imbue the minds of youth with the wholesome assurance, that when guided by morality and subjected to logic, it is the art of rendering truth popular, and virtue delightful; of adding persuasion to conviction, and of engaging the whole man, the feelings as well as the understanding.[12]

Now what is interesting to me is that the kind of rhetoric here pointed to was in the early 1800s—in my view—the most important, serious competitor for 'literature' and literary history as the framework-category and -practice for the literary field. In fact while German and English Universities largely start to teach the subject 'literature' by way of, or indeed through, literary history, nineteenth-century American and Scottish Colleges work with rhetoric as a

---

[10] *Preliminary Statement of the Arrangements for Conducting the Various Departments of King's College, London* (London: Fellowes, 1831), pp. 12-15.

[11] *Statement by the Council of the University of London, Explanatory of the Nature and Objects of the Institution* (London: Longman, Rees, Orme, Brown, and others, 1827), p. 33.

[12] *Statement by the Council*, p. 35.

frame for cultural literacy (as do, in different ways, French universities).[13] As signalled by the London Council's disregard for 'eloquence' as 'gaudy pageant', the rhetoric that is being advocated here—that was competitive with 'literature'—is what is sometimes called the eighteenth century's new rhetoric.[14] So let me by way of conclusion clarify what was new, and possibly attractive, in the kind of rhetoric projected by Adam Smith and Hugh Blair's teaching of 'rhetoric and belles lettres'—whose recourse to a link between the beautiful and 'letters' was what led us to them earlier.

What the new rhetoric tries essentially to do is, firstly, to simplify style by demoting the classical toolkit of tropes and figures—now viewed as merely arbitrary, external ornament; secondly, to replace the conventional rhetorical techniques of invention and disposition with personal affect, with a genuine desire to communicate, or to express the self; and finally it draws on teaching by example rather than precept—hence its recourse to 'belles lettres', to models of poetic and prose style to teach the practical appreciation—i.e. the appreciation and practice—of a plain style that is affective in the sense of emotionally truthful. Thus Adam Smith describes the lectures he gives in Edinburgh and Glasgow from 1748 as 'a system of Rhetorick'; but he equally insists that they mark a departure, since the 'many systems of retorick both ancient and modern' are 'generally a very silly set of Books and not at all instructive'.[15] Smith's claim to originality revolves around his standard of a 'perspicuity of stile' (p. 3). His lecture, *Of what is called the tropes and figures of speech*, accordingly attacks conventional Ciceronian rhetoric for trying to base 'all the beauties of language' on rhetorical figures. Instead, Smith argues that an affective, and therefore genuinely communicative plain style already provides, before all ornaments, 'all that is noble, grand and sublime, all that is passionate, tender and moving':

---

[13]   See Gerald Graff's *Professing Literature: An Institutional History* (Chicago: University of Chicago Press, 1987), pp. 36-51; and Thomas P. Miller, *The Formation of College English: Rhetoric and Belles Lettres in the British Cultural Provinces* (Pittsburgh: University of Pittsburgh Press, 1997). On the French trajectory, see Françoise Douay-Soublin, 'La rhétorique en France au XIXe siècle, à travers ses pratiques et ses institutions: restauration, renaissance, remise en cause', and Antoine Compagnon, 'La rhétorique à la fin du XIXe siècle (1875-1900)', both in Marc Fumaroli, *Histoire de la rhétorique dans l'Europe moderne (1450-1950)* (Paris: Presses Universitaires de France, 1999), pp. 1071-1214, 1215-50.

[14]   See Wilbur Samuel Howell, *Logic and Rhetoric in England, 1500-1700* (Princeton, NJ: Princeton University Press, 1956).

[15]   Adam Smith, *Lectures on Rhetoric and Belles Lettres*, ed. by J. C. Bryce (Oxford: Clarendon Press, 1983), pp. 26-7.

> When the sentiment of the speaker is expressed in a neat, clear, plain and clever manner, and the passion or affection he is possessed of and intends, *by sympathy*, to communicate to his hearer, is plainly and cleverly hit off, then and then only the expression has all the force and beauty that language can give it. It matters not the least whether the figures of speech are introduced or not. (pp. 25-6)

Since figures have 'no intrinsick worth of their own' (p. 26), it becomes rhetorical 'common sense' and 'perfection of stile' (p. 55) simply to match, 'your meaning and what you would express, together with the Sentiment or affection this matter inspires you with' (p. 26).

Blair's Edinburgh lectures (which begin in 1759, are published in the 1780s and then endlessly re-circulated and translated deep into the nineteenth century) make it clear that this project is addressed to readers as much as to writers (of whatever clerical or more ambitious stripe) and, maybe less importantly, to public speakers:

> Some, by the profession to which they addict themselves, or in consequence of their prevailing inclination, may have the view of being employed in composition, or in public speaking. Others, without any prospect of this kind, may wish only to improve their taste with respect to writing and discourse, and to acquire principles which will enable them to judge for themselves in that part of literature called the Belles Lettres.

Which is to say with special reference to what Blair calls 'the most admired productions of genius, whether in poetry or prose'.

Now it would clearly not be easy to explain why this coherent project did not take (for all its pedagogical success right up to the most recent threshold of our disciplinary modernity). To trace why 'literature' and literary history became foundational where 'rhetoric and belles lettres' in the end recede involves us necessarily in trying to explain the end of rhetoric (or more plausibly its various endings). And I am certainly not going to attempt that here. Instead, I end by asking merely what conjectural questions these available scenarios—these choices around 1800—raise for our present discussion of globalization in the field of literary studies. Thus here are two suggestions of what may well be involved in 'literature' as a conceptual legacy in this respect. Firstly: unlike 'poetry' or 'rhetoric', 'literature' has at least in its inception—and it might be argued still, or analytically, to start with—no real stake in the activity of writing, of creative practice. 'Literature' works, constitutively, as an overwhelmingly descriptive, academic concept quite unlike, say, 'poetry' or 'rhetoric'. And secondly: the concept 'literature''s conjunction of a weak aesthetic claim with a strong historiographical perspective builds convenient bridges—perhaps all too convenient bridges—between textual archives that are not just individually, or nationally, heterogeneous but are all the more so globally diverse. Accordingly my speculative question is: what would a present-day discussion of 'world literature' analogous to ours (but obviously not characterized or organized like that) look like if the nineteenth-century literary field had not in our traditional sense come to be conceived as literary? Or—to try a different rationale for speculating in this vein—is our persistent sense of urgency about world literature a form of disciplinary retrenchment, a conservative response to change outside the discipline (say in the form of globalization)—a shoring up of legacies or canons—*or* does the debate in fact betray, possess potential as an effort to rethink the knowledge claim of literary studies—to revise what renders it coherent or what might, with certain changes, make it so?

WORKS CITED

Primary Sources

Batteux, Charles, *Cours de belles-lettres, ou principes de la littérature*, vol. 4. (Frankfurt am Main: Bassompiere and Vanden Berghen, 1755)

Baumgarten, Alexander Gottlieb, *Meditationes philosophicae de nonnullis ad poema pertinentibus* (Halle: Grunert, 1735) in *Reflections on Poetry. Alexander Gottlieb Baumgarten's 'Meditationes philosophicae de nonnulis ad poema pertinentibus'*, ed. and trans. by Karl Aschenbrenner and William B. Holther (Berkeley: University of California Press, 1954)

—. *Aesthetica*, 2 vols. (Frankfurt an der Oder: Kleyb, 1750-58, repr. Hildesheim: Olms, 1986), and *Theoretische Ästhetik. Die grundlegenden Abschnitte aus der 'Aesthetica' (1750/58)*, ed. and trans. by Hans Rudolf Schweizer, 2nd edn. (Hamburg: Meiner, 1988)

Herder, Johann Gottfried, 'On Recent German Literature: First Collection of Fragments', in *Selected Early Works 1764-1767: Addresses, Essays and Drafts; 'Fragments on Recent German Literature'*, ed. by Ernest A.

Menze and Karl Menges, trans. by Ernest A. Menze with Michael Palma (University Park: Pennsylvania State University Press, 1992)

—. 'Erste Sammlung. Zweite völlig umgearbeitete Ausgabe' in *Werke in zehn Bänden*, ed. by Martin Bollacher et al., vol. 1 (Frankfurt am Main: Deutscher Klassiker Verlag, 1985)

—. 'Dritte Sammlung' in *Werke in zehn Bänden*, ed. by Martin Bollacher et al., vol. 1 (Frankfurt am Main: Deutscher Klassiker Verlag, 1985)

Kant, Immanuel, *Critik der Urtheilskraft* (Berlin and Libau: Lagarde und Friederich, 1790); in *Critique of the Power of Judgment*, ed. by Paul Guyer, trans. by Paul Guyer and Eric Matthews (Cambridge: Cambridge University Press, 2000)

—. *Critique of Judgement*. in *Werkausgabe*, ed. by Wilhelm Weischedel, vol. 10 (Frankfurt am Main: Suhrkamp, 1974)

Meier, Georg Friedrich, *Anfangsgründe aller schönen Wissenschaften*, vol. I (Halle: Hemmerde, 1754, repr. Hildesheim: Olms, 1976)

Smith, Adam, *Lectures on Rhetoric and Belles Lettres*, ed. by J. C. Bryce (Oxford: Clarendon Press, 1983)

Secondary Sources

Fumaroli, Marc, *Histoire de la rhétorique dans l'Europe moderne (1450-1950)* (Paris: Presses Universitaires de France, 1999)

Graff, Gerald, *Professing Literature: An Institutional History* (Chicago: University of Chicago Press, 1987)

Miller, Thomas P., *The Formation of College English: Rhetoric and Belles Lettres in the British Cultural Provinces* (Pittsburgh: University of Pittsburgh Press, 1997)

Howell, Wilbur Samuel, *Logic and Rhetoric in England, 1500-1700* (Princeton, NJ: Princeton University Press, 1956)

Pocock, J. G. A., 'The Origins of Study of the Past: A Comparative Approach' in *Comparative Studies in Society and History*, 4 (1961)

III. TRANSGRESSING LITERARY AND CULTURAL BOUNDARIES

Elaine Martin

'Ceci tuera cela'? Literary Canons and the Challenge of Visual Imagery and Popular Culture

In his 1831 novel *Notre Dame de Paris* Victor Hugo undertook a comprehensive portrayal of medieval Paris. In a chapter entitled "This will kill that" (Ceci tuera cela), he argued that the printing press – the technical equivalent of the computer in our time – killed [the historical import of] architecture in 15th-century Europe. I suggest transposing this radical dethroning of one art by another to a current situation: the potential "death" of the book at the hands of both visual media and popular culture. Comparative literature could potentially help bridge the gap and help revitalize the role of literature in world culture because of its inherent interdisciplinarity, boundary-crossing orientation, and internationalism.

In his 1831 novel *Notre-Dame de Paris* Victor Hugo undertook a comprehensive portrayal of life in medieval Paris, including a chapter enigmatically entitled 'This will kill that' (*Ceci tuera cela*). The narrator alternatively interprets this phrase as 'the printing press will destroy the [Roman Catholic] Church', or that 'one art would dethrone another art. It meant: Printing will destroy architecture'.[1] In his exposé on the widespread and radical effect of the printing press, which in 15th-century Europe was the technical equivalent of the computer in our time, Hugo's narrator rages against the deleterious effects of the invention. 'The press', he says,

> that giant engine, incessantly gorging all the intellectual sap of society, incessantly vomits new material for its work. The entire human race is its scaffolding. Every mind is its mason. Even the humblest may block a hole or lay a stone [...] here too, there is a confusion of languages, untiring labor, incessant activity, a furious competition of all humanity, a promised refuge for the intelligence against another deluge, against another submersion by the barbarians (p. 188).

His critique is fourfold: of the staggering quantity of knowledge ('incessantly vomits new material'), of the machine's speed ('incessant activity'), of its ubiquity ('every mind'), and its universal engagement ('even the humblest may lay a stone'). This critique invites us to draw parallels with the role of the computer, and specifically the internet, in our culture. I suggest transposing this radical phenomenon of the dethronement-of-one-art-by-

---

[1]   Victor Hugo, *The Hunchback of Notre-Dame*, trans. by Walter J. Cobb (NY: The New American Library, 1965), p. 175.

another to a current situation: the potential demise of (serious) literature—
and with it the very concept of a canon—due to both the growing hegemony
of image media over text media and the overwhelming rise of popular culture
as a whole. While most of my examples will be drawn from American
culture, several studies suggest that the phenomena I am describing reflect
developments in other Western countries and perhaps even beyond.

Two simultaneous developments within the past 10 to 25 years have
radically transformed both the organization of society and individual lives as
lived on a daily basis. Popular culture has increasingly displaced higher
forms of culture as a common public medium. This, in turn, has led to two
separate developments: first, the gradual replacement of textual media by
images and second, a profound reconceptualization and realignment of the
relationship of the individual to society, including modes of communication.
How new are these developments? The computer pioneer Alan Kay once
said: 'Technology is anything that was invented after you were born'.[2] But
we can also use objective markers: widespread use of personal computers
dates to the mid-1980s, the internet rose to prominence in the early 1990s,
and electronic formats like blogging really gained popularity around 2003.
The twin ascendancies of the image and the individual ego, fueled by new
technologies, specifically the computer and the internet, have changed how
we work, communicate, socialize, and even think. Recent journal, magazine,
and newspaper titles also reflect this radical change; here a sampling: 'Future
Reading: Digitization and Its Discontents'; 'Twilight of the Books: What will
life be like if people stop reading?'; 'Is Google Making Us Stupid?; What the
Internet is doing to our brains'; 'Will Blogs kill Writing?'; 'The Future of
Reading; [Amazon's Jeff Bezos] believes he can improve on one of
humankind's most divine creations: the book itself'. Two of these essays
specifically address the future of reading in their titles and thus raise an
important issue. Who reads these days? And what do they read? If it is
literature, what kind? Several recent studies suggest some preliminary
answers to these questions. For example, a 2004 National Endowment for the
Arts study (*Reading at Risk: A Survey of Literary Reading in America*;
interviews conducted in 2002) revealed data on American rates of reading.
The percentage of people polled, who had read a book—of any kind—in the
immediately preceding year was 56.6%. When the question was refined to
specify having read a work of 'literature' in the preceding 12 months, the
percentage dropped ten points to 46.7%. Both of those numbers had declined
by about 4% from the previous surveys in 1982 and 1992. 'The report goes
on to examine many intriguing demographic differences', as Elaine Tuttle

---

[2]   Qtd. in Steven Levy, 'The Future of Reading: Amazon's Jeff Bezos already built a better
        bookstore. Now he believes he can improve upon one of humankind's most divine creations:
        the book itself', *Newsweek*, 26 November 2007, p. 57.

Hansen has noted: 'women read more literature than men, self-identified white people read more literature than self-identified Hispanics and African Americans, people with higher incomes read more literature than people with lower incomes, and the sharpest decline in literary reading rates has occurred among people between the ages of eighteen and thirty-four'.[3] This particular study has been challenged in some quarters, but its overall findings have been corroborated both by a 2007 follow-up study by the National Endowment for the Arts entitled *To Read or Not to Read: A Question of National Consequence*, which, in the words of NEA Chairman, Dana Gioia, 'contains vastly more data from numerous sources' and 'is the most complete and up-to-date report of the nation's reading trends'.[4] The findings of these two NEA studies are further supported by reading statistics compiled by the U.S. Department of Education using surveys conducted periodically, beginning in 1937. The NEA conclusions are threefold: 'Americans are spending less time reading. Reading comprehension skills are eroding. These declines have serious civic, social, cultural, and economic implications' (p. 5). The Department of Education studies emphasize the extent to which reading statistics also affect social interaction: 'In 1992, fifty-four per cent of twelfth graders told the Department of Education that they talked about their reading with friends at least once a week. By 2005, only thirty-seven per cent said they did'.[5] Trends in decreased reading have been found in other countries as well. Researchers in the Netherlands began asking people to keep time-budget diaries in 1955: 'During the next two decades, reading continued to fall and television watching to rise [...] By 1995, reading, which had occupied twenty-one per cent of people's spare time in 1955, accounted for just nine per cent. The most striking results were generational. In general, older Dutch people read more' (p. 135). In the United States, '[b]etween 1982 and 2002, the percentage of Americans who read literature declined not only in every age group but in every generation—even in those moving from youth into middle age, which is often considered the most fertile time of life for reading' (p. 135). Caleb Crain, in his essay 'Twilight of the Books' writes:

---

[3]   Elaine Tuttle Hansen, 'The Situation of the Humanities', *ADFL Bulletin*, 37 (winter-spring 2006), 2-3; 10-14 (p. 12).

[4]   *To Read or Not to Read: A Question of National Consequence*, Office of Research and Analysis, National Endowment for the Arts, Research Report #47, ExecutiveSummary (November 2007), p. 3. Available www.arts.gov.

[5]   Qtd. in Caleb Crain, 'Twilight of the Books', *The New Yorker*, 24 & 31 Dec. 2007, p. 135.

some sociologists speculate that reading books for pleasure will one day be the province of a special 'reading class', much as it was before the arrival of mass literacy, in the second half of the nineteenth century. They warn that it probably won't regain the prestige of exclusivity; it may just become 'an increasingly arcane hobby'. Such a shift would change the texture of society (p. 135).

He continues:

A reader learns about the world and imagines it differently from the way a viewer does; according to some experimental psychologists, a reader and a viewer even think differently. If the eclipse of reading continues, the alteration is likely to matter in ways that aren't foreseeable (p. 135).

While I agree with Cain's assessment that reading may become the pastime of a tiny elite, in essence of a mandarin few, I disagree that the changes this will occasion are unforeseeable. I think they are already occurring and they are very visible. If only 46.7% of people, that is, less than half the population, is reading literature on a regular basis, then is the concept of a canon still useful? John Ruskin observed: 'All books are divisible into two classes: the books of the hour, and the books of all time'.[6] But what if that distinction has been blurred or even erased? Or, what if the distinction still exists, but no one cares about it any longer? Might we need, at the very least, two canons, one for the non-serious-literature-reading half of the population and one for the other half? Would this then be a canon and an un-canon? Or might we need to expand the concept of the canon to more accurately reflect the reality of public practice, thus including not only traditional books, but other forms of communication such as graphic novels, or blogs, called by some 'electronic diaries'? Or what about moving images such as films and videos? We know that moving images and words have long stood in an antagonistic relationship to one another. 'The scholar Walter J. Ong once speculated that television and similar media are taking us into an era of "secondary orality", akin to the primary orality that existed before the emergence of text' (Crain, p. 137). Images, specifically moving images, tend to displace words, as reported by Caleb Crain: 'The antagonism between words and moving images seems to start early [...] In 2001, after analyzing data on more than a million students around the world, the researcher Micha Razel found "little room for doubt" that television worsened performance in reading, science, and math. The relationship wasn't a straight line but "an inverted check mark: a small amount of television seemed to benefit children; more hurt"' (Crain, p. 138). But what about the Internet? 'The Internet, happily', writes Crain, 'does not so far seem to be antagonistic to literacy [...] The study found that grades and

---

[6]   John Ruskin, *Sesame and Lilies*, ed. by Deborah Epstein Nord (New Haven and London: Yale University Press, 2001).

reading scores rose with the amount of time spent online. Even visits to pornography Web sites improved academic performance. Of course, such synergies may disappear if the Internet continues its YouTube-fuelled evolution away from print and toward television' (p. 139).

A decline in reading has ramifications for the continued vital role, and even the existence, of literature. In her review of a colloquium that took place at the University of Michigan in March 2008, Kate Jenckes writes the following about 'post-literature':

> [The colloquium] sought to explore the meanings and uses of the critically popular term *post-literature*, which appears to signify both the death of the institution of literature and an ongoing literary production that is substantially different from traditional conceptions of literature: post-literature designates forms of representation that perform a crisis and transformation in the practice, purpose, or possibilities of literary and artistic representation. The organizers resisted the strictly chronological sense of the prefix 'post,' preferring to understand the term not as a chronological category or as a literary period, but instead as the index of a limit or a caesura *within* literary and artistic history—one, however, that may be especially prevalent in contemporary works.[7]

By the time a phenomenon such as this is named, one can assume that it has largely permeated all levels of cultural production. Concerns for the disappearance of literature have been paralleled in cinematography by fears of the demise of the story. In response to this, a new Center for Future Storytelling has been created at the Massachusetts Institute of Technology Media Laboratory. Its mission, according to David Kirkpatrick, a founder of the undertaking, and as reported in a fall 2008 *New York Times* article, is the following: 'The idea, as we move forward with 21st-century storytelling, is to try to keep meaning alive'[8]. As Michael Cieply observes about the project, 'Mr. Kirkpatrick and company are not alone in their belief that Hollywood's ability to tell a meaningful story has been nibbled at by text messages, interrupted by cellphone calls and supplanted by everything from Twitter to Guitar Hero' (C7). The M.I.T. project will investigate 'how virtual actors and "morphable" projectors (which instantly change the appearance of physical scenes) might affect a storytelling process that has already been considerably democratized by digital delivery. A possible outcome [...] is that future stories might not stop in Hollywood [at] all' (C7). If reading, literature, and even stories all become passé, what will be left?

---

[7]   Kate Jenckes, 'Post-Literature in Latin America: A Colloquium to explore the meaning of "post-literature"', Department of Romance Languages and Literatures Newsletter, University of Michigan, Ann Arbor, MI (Fall 2008/Winter 2009), p. 3.

[8]   Michael Cieply, 'Saving the Story (The Film Version)', *The New York Times*, 18 November 2008, C1.

Let's take a closer look at the sources of images that are generally replacing texts in communication. In terms of current visual media one thinks immediately of feature-length films, videos, photo essays, computer games, 3-D simulations, and, interestingly and increasingly, graphic novels. Cinematic adaptations of literary works, usually novels, are as old as the filmmaking industry itself, dating to the late 19th century. Filmmakers raided literary texts to capitalize on known plots but also to legitimize the new art form. The relationship between literary works and their filmings has continued to evolve, but in a multidirectional sense. Novels have certainly provided a ready-made *Stoff* to cinéastes on numerous occasions, but films have also served to rekindle interest in long-forgotten (and often out-of-print) works. The symbiotic relationship goes so far as to feature film stars on the cover of the re-issued books—an anachronistic practice that nonetheless appears to sell books. The invention of videos, especially in the DVD format, has moved film viewing from the public venue of the local movie theater to the privacy of the home, so that watching a movie is no longer a group activity but an individual one. Films can even be delivered to one's mailbox, for example in the US via Netflix, obviating the necessity of leaving the refuge of the home altogether. Soon films may be available on demand on our television sets, computers, and electronic reading devices. Expanded DVDs offer behind-the-scenes access, interviews with the cast, and often the director's voiceover, narrating the making of the film, which deepens the experience of watching a film and offers a level of engagement with the metatext that no novel can rival.

Feature length films and computer/video games have, in some cases, developed a similar symbiosis, in which games are based on cinematic events and figures, the wildly popular *Indiana Jones* series being a case in point. The advantage of the video game is that the player can enter the world of the Hollywood film and become an active participant in that exotic and exciting world instead of merely a passive viewer. Virtual realities and imagined worlds, as they increase in sophistication, offer the participant an active role, usually as an avatar, thus replacing some of what literature traditionally has offered: the pursuit of a narrative, identification with one or more characters, and a free play of the imagination. Lest we doubt the socio-cultural importance of this phenomenon, a 2007 Pew Foundation survey (Pew Internet & American Life Project, Nov. 2007-Feb. 2008) found that ninety-seven percent of the 1,102 young respondents, aged 12-17, not only play video games but play them often: half of the respondents said they had played a video game the previous day.[9]

---

[9]   Martha Irvine, 'Most youngsters are gamers: Pew survey finds 97 percent play and many every day, *The Birmingham News* (The Associated Press), 17 September 2008, 4D.

One of the most obvious challenges to the written text has been the rise of the graphic novel. While the surge in the graphic novel, under that rubric, is quite recent, antecedents to the genre date to at least the Medieval Europe. What else was the *Biblia pauperum*, an illustrated manual used in the Middle Ages by the clergy to teach the Bible to illiterates, in which the illustrations took preponderance over the text? Some would argue that comic books for children, whose reading skills are not yet fully developed, have played a similar role. But the existence of *classic* comic books, which took as their themes great classics of world literature (i.e. the canon), began a process of blurring the Horatian distinction between entertainment and instruction. A similar, willful muddling of both artistic aim and target audience is characteristic of the graphic novel. Some works are created by professional cartoonists, who naturally turn to this medium to tell stories. Art Spiegelmann and his by now famous *Maus* books are a case in point. As a professional cartoonist, he logically chose graphics to represent his parents' stories of National Socialism and the Holocaust. But there is also a trend for the remaking of classical, canonic texts in graphic version; while there are numerous examples, a particularly interesting one is Kafka's *The Trial: A Graphic Novel*, translated into English and published in 2008. Across the bottom of the book's cover are printed, in the same sized typeface: Kafka – Montellier – Mairowitz, giving equal credit for authorship to the original writer, the translator/adapter, and the graphic artist who illustrated the text. The presence of a considerable amount of text and the black-and-white rendering suggest that the novel is intended for an adult audience. On the inside cover one reads: '*The Trial*, reinvented in this striking graphic novel, is the bleak tale of Joseph K.'. Thus the creators of this text claim to be 'reinventing' the original, not merely representing or translating it; it is not clear what all is entailed in this reinvention and precisely what the relationship between the Ur-text and the graphic rendition might ultimately be. In fact, what might it mean to 'reinvent' Kafka? Halfway between Spiegelmann's *Maus* and Kafka's *The Trial* there exists another phenomenon: original graphic novels written by non-professionals. One example of this is a work entitled *American Widow* (2008) written by Alissa Torres, whose husband died on 9/11. 'Seven years later, she has written a 210-page graphic memoir, or as she calls it, "an adult, literary comic book", about her marriage and first year as a widow and single mother'.[10] To create the book she worked with a professional illustrator (Sungyoon Choi) and commented on her choice of genres: '9/11 was such a graphic event. Just writing about it wasn't enough. I needed to take control of the images' (D2). She also told a friend: 'My life is like a comic book' (D2). Other comic

---

[10]   Bob Minzesheimer, '"Widow" pours out grief in images: 9/11 graphic memoir depicts raw first year', *USA Today*, 9 September 2008, D 1.

books that dealt with 9/11 include *The 9/11 Report: A Graphic Adaptation* by Sid Jacobson and Ernie Colón, that was a bestseller in 2006. This phenomenon of not only professionals but also amateurs representing serious topics via graphics, in some cases autobiographically, reflects a larger trend in which the place of the ordinary individual has been redefined in relationship to art, creativity, and cultural production.

If classical texts have not been declared off-limits for graphic treatments, neither have, apparently, sacred texts. Dag Söderberg, a Swedish advertising specialist, has created an illustrated Bible: *Bible Illuminated: The New Testament*, featuring 'big, glossy photos' and designed to 'entice [...] people who don't read the Bible'.[11] In a review of the publication, Jessica Bennet writes: 'The book opens with an Andy Warhol poster ("Repent—and Sin No More!") and often juxtaposes modern imagery with ancient scripture [...] [The scripture] Mark runs with photos of Gandhi, Nelson Mandela—OK so far—and Angelina Jolie' (p. 18). Philip Towner, of the American Bible Association, commented that 'the idea is to get the reader to move from the image to the text' (Bennett, p. 18), but the belief that the images will not, in fact, 'supplant' the text may be naive.

In the 1960s, one counterculture slogan maintained that 'the personal is political', but now we might say, rather, that 'the personal is public'. Reality shows, You-Tube videos, tell-all talk shows on television, blogging, and self-publishing would all suggest that this is true. What do the ideals of spontaneity, impermanency, and the performance of self mean for the future of the book? As the distinction between professional or expert and amateur or lay person has eroded or been devalued, so too has the potential opposition between writers and readers, producers and consumers. One can cite the increasingly proactive role taken by individuals in creating their own texts. Due to the internet and desk-top publishing, anyone can write and be published, and be read by others. One can also review books online, and one does not need to be Roger Ebert or David Densby to write film criticism. Sites like Amazon.com that invite such reviews, provide peer review of the reviews by posing the question of subsequent readers: 'Did you find this review useful?' The word 'useful' in this context points to a decidedly pragmatic approach to the evaluation of cultural artifacts and their enjoyment. Everyone can now create knowledge by writing encyclopedia entries for sites like Wikipedia. Tell-all talk shows on television, and reality shows in particular, have helped blur the distinction between reality and fiction. From shows like *American Idol* and *America has Talent* to *Survivor* and *Who wants to be a Millionaire*, the message is that ordinary people can be stars as well.

---

[11]   Jessica Bennett, 'Of God and Good Design', *Newsweek*, 27 October 2008, p. 18.

Not only can one write, publish, and review the work of others, one can also be a film director thanks to YouTube.

This kind of participatory role is integral also to the phenomenon of blogging, or web logging, the practice that Andrew Sullivan has called 'writing outloud'.[12] Sullivan, a professional journalist, admits that he was immediately hooked on blogging when he first tried it, and in a fall 2008 article in *The Atlantic*, he attempts to describe it and enumerate its advantages: 'instant and global self-publishing' (p. 106); 'spontaneous expression of instant thought—impermanent beyond even the ephemera of daily journalism' (p. 106); 'its borders are extremely porous and its truth inherently transitory' (p. 106); 'the historic form closest to blogs is the diary' and 'a blog, unlike a diary, is instantly public'(p. 108); [in comparison to] 'dead-tree publishing' [it is] 'intoxicatingly free' (p. 108); 'it's a broadcast, not a publication. If it stops moving, it dies' (p. 110); and 'the blogosphere, at its best, [is] a conversation, rather than a production' (p. 110). Sullivan emphasizes how important the readers are to a blog as contributors and, if you will, as co-creators of the blog. 'Some e-mailers', he notes, 'unsurprisingly, know more about a subject than the blogger does. They will send links, stories, and facts, challenging the blogger's view of the world, sometimes outright refuting it, but more frequently adding context and nuance and complexity to an idea' (p. 110). Who then, in this scenario, is the writer, who the reader? When Sullivan talks about writing 'for thousands and thousands of friends' (p. 112), it is clear that he has redefined the author/reader relationship in a way that clearly challenges the traditional dichotomy.

Active participation of the reader in creating the text is not necessarily new, but it has acquired new dimensions. Authors such as Charles Dickens, who published their novels serially, were famous for altering plots in response to readers' input. The ambiguity of much literature allows for reader engagement through the simple process of interpretation, but the activity can be more explicit, as in the case of multiple endings from which the reader must choose. Perhaps surprisingly, there have also been cinematic examples of this phenomenon such as the Japanese director Kurosawa's *Rashomon* (1950) in which conflicting variants of a story are offered or in German director Tom Tykwer's *Run Lola Run* (*Lola rennt*, 1998), which does the same thing. I learned of another interesting variation on reader participation several years ago from a colleague, who had a novel in which the paragraphs were printed one to a card. The 'reader' could then shuffle the cards/paragraphs and retell the story in a different sequence each time, thus maximizing the reader's role in creating and construing the text. Some

---

[12]   Andrew Sullivan, 'Why I Blog', *The Atlantic*, November 2008, 106-13 (p. 108).

authors have succeeded in replicating the speed, complexity, and density of the internet in their literary works. One such author is Jasper Fforde, famous for his series of novels about detective Thursday Next, and creator of *The Eyre Affair*, which has been dubbed a 'parallelquel' to Charlotte Brontë's gothic novel *Jane Eyre* (1847). Margarete Rubik has summarized the novel thus:

> In *The Eyre Affair*, characters from Brontë's novel interact with the 20th century protagonists: they appear in the actual text world set in 1985 and are involved in a spectacular criminal case; vice versa, the 20th century figures invade the universe of Brontë's masterpiece and interfere in its plot.[13]

According to Rubik, 'the sheer absurdity and unexpectedness of [the] new information on the *Jane Eyre* text world [...] forces readers to reconceptualise the model text in a radically irreverent way' (p. 167). These attempts to imitate internet experiences with dense information, layers of complexity, and reader engagement, have appeared similarly in other media as well. Ubiquitous television broadcasts with texts crawling along the bottom of the screen and pop-ups appearing in the corners at irregular intervals mimic the look of an online screen.

The bottom line is that there is no turning back. The differences both in reading habits and in habituation to computers, and technology more generally, are largely drawn along generational lines. The so-called millennials, or Generation Y (born 1977-1998), grew up with screens as an integral part of their daily lives, and they are used to a life that is 'faster, more spectacular, and noisier' than is customary for those addicted to reading books.[14] The millennials want to 'build portable knowledge' and they want to 'quickly acquire skills and competencies'; the emphasis for this generation is on access and speed.[15] As Anthony Grafton writes: 'Fast, reliable methods of search and retrieval are sometimes identified as the hallmark of our information age; "Search is everything" has become a proverb'.[16] There is no turning back because of the generational differences but also because— surprisingly, provocatively—the Internet has changed the way our brains work. Gary Small, a neuroscientist at UCLA (Univ. of California at Los

---

[13]   Margarete Rubik and Elke Mettinger-Schartmann, eds., *A Breath of Fresh Eyre: Intertextual and Intermedial Reworkings of* Jane Eyre (Amsterdam and NY: Rodopi, 2007), p. 167.

[14]   Carmen Martín Gaite, 'The Virtues of Reading', *PMLA*, 104 (May 1989), 348-53 (p. 348).

[15]   Jean M. McLean, 'Make room for Millenials: How Generation Y is changing the face of the workplace', *The Birmingham News*, 25 May 2008, I 1.

[16]   Anthony Grafton, 'Future Reading: digitization and its discontents', *The New Yorker*, 5 November 2007, 50-4 (p. 52).

Angeles), argues in his book *iBrain: Surviving the Technological Alteration of the Modern Mind*, that the brains of tech-savvy people, whom Small calls 'digital natives', are especially 'adept at filtering information and making snap decisions'.[17] In support of this theory, Nicholas Carr, writing about Google's effect on our brains, claims:

> My mind isn't going—so far as I can tell—but it's changing. I'm not thinking the way I used to think. I can feel it most strongly when I'm reading. Immersing myself in a book or a lengthy article used to be easy. My mind would get caught up in the narrative . . . Now my concentration often starts to drift after two or three pages. I get fidgety, lose the thread, begin looking for something else to do. [18]

Carr also reports on an academic friend who says his thinking has assumed 'a "staccato" quality'; the friend continues: 'I can't read *War and Peace* anymore [...] I've lost the ability to do that. Even a blog post of more than three or four paragraphs is too much to absorb. I skim it' (p. 58). Nicholas Carr has commented on the displacement force of the Internet in our quotidian lives: 'The Internet, an immeasurably powerful computing system, is subsuming most of our other intellectual technologies. It's becoming our map and our clock, our printing press and our typewriter, our calculator and our telephone, and our radio and TV' (p. 60). Certainly the phenomena described here constitute a major difference. But different is not necessarily bad; it may mean simply different.

In fact, not only is there no turning back at this point, we should not *want* to turn back, because new technologies have made it possible to improve in many ways on the book and on the reading experience. The American firms Google, Microsoft, and Amazon have separately been working on projects to make huge numbers of books available to readers worldwide and to develop new technologies for the delivery of those books. As Anthony Grafton has reported,

> Google has been at work on an ambitious project, Google Book Search. Google's self-described aim is to 'build a comprehensive index of all the books in the world', one that would enable readers to search the list of books it contains and to see full texts of those not covered by copyright [...] A second enterprise, the Google Library Project, is digitizing as many books as possible, in collaboration with great libraries in the U.S. and abroad (p. 50).

---

[17] Jeneen Interlandi, 'Your Brain Will Never Be the Same', Review of *iBRAIN: Surviving the Technological Alteration of the Modern Mind* by Gary Small, *Newsweek*, 20 October 2008, p. 16.

[18] Nicholas Carr, 'Is Google Making Us Stupid?', *The Atlantic*, July/August 2008, 56-63 (p. 57).

One of the potential barriers to the success of this and like-minded projects is the issue of copyright. According to Grafton, '[a] conservative reckoning of the number of books ever published is thirty two million; Google believes that there could be as many as a hundred million. It is estimate [...] twenty per cent [...] are out of copyright. The rest, perhaps seventy-five per cent of all books printed, are "orphans", possibly still covered by copyright protections but out of print and pretty much out of mind' (p. 53). Imagine the incredible wealth, opportunity, and future possibilities of having a hundred million books at one's fingertips—or even 32 million, for that matter! Kevin Kelly, of *Wired* magazine, expressed it vividly thus: 'all the books in the world' would 'become a single liquid fabric of interconnected words and ideas' (qtd. in Grafton, p. 50). Given the already impressive searchability of the internet, one gets a preview of what the future might hold. 'Google's famous search algorithm', writes Grafton, 'emulates the principle of scholarly citation—counting up and evaluating earlier links in order to steer users toward the sources that others have already found helpful. In a sense, the system resembles nothing more than trillions of old-fashioned footnotes' (p. 52). It would seem then, that, rather than jettisoning the strengths of earlier modes of interconnectedness, we have the potential for both retaining them and significantly improving upon them.

These projects for making masses of information available electronically are, without a question, awe-inspiring. But of nearly equal interest are projects to create electronic readers that simulate books. Following on the prototype of the earlier Sony Reader, Amazon has developed the Kindle, so 'named to evoke the crackling ignition of knowledge' (Levy, p. 57). Designed to 'project an aura of *bookishness* [...] [it] has the dimensions of a paperback, with a tapering of its width that emulates the bulge toward a book's binding. It weighs but 10.3 ounces' (p. 57). But most fascinating are the ways in which it is *not* a book, and that for the better: readers can change the font size; the device holds two hundred books, plus hundreds more on memory cards; readers can search a book for phrases or names; the Kindle has wireless connectivity; when a book is purchased, it is downloaded and shelved in the reader's library within one minute; the Kindle can turn to the web for searching and linking (Sony's Reader cannot); and readers can 'jot down a gloss on the page of the book' or 'capture passages with an electronic version of a highlight pen' (Levy, pp. 57-8). Critics of electronic readers fear that the all-important deep reading experience will be lost. Nicholas Carr summarizes these concerns:

> The kind of deep reading that a sequence of printed pages promotes is valuable not just for the knowledge we acquire from the author's words but for the intellectual vibrations those words set off within our own minds. In the quiet spaces opened up by the sustained, undistracted reading of a book, or by any other act of contemplation, for that matter, we make our own associations, draw our own inferences and analogies, foster

our own ideas [...] If we lose those quiet spaces, or fill them up with 'content,' we will sacrifice something important not only in our selves but in our culture' (p. 63).

Jeff Bezos, the CEO of Amazon, has weighed in on this topic as well, saying: 'The key feature of a book is that *it disappears*' (qtd. in Levy, p. 60). A good book, like a good film, should transport readers to a place where they lose consciousness of the medium. Despite initial skepticism, Kindle appears to have achieved this goal, although one might have to allow for differences in individual reader response. One thing is certain, Kindle's constant connectivity to the internet has given rise to a new era of 'connected books' or 'connected reading' (Levy, p. 61), in which author and reader may interact, as well as readers with each other.

What we have seen then in the past twenty-five years is the runaway development of popular culture and its absolute predominance over high culture; this phenomenon, which Andrew Sullivan has signaled as 'postmodern" (p. 113), has been driven by simultaneous and iconoclastic displacements: electronic media are overtaking print media; images are replacing words; amateurs are usurping the authority of professionals and experts; and ordinary people are being catapulted into (national) stardom. These radical changes have led to an overall 'popularizing' of culture and a democratization of participation in cultural production. As a result of the profound changes I have just described, a seemingly unbreachable divide has occurred between popular and high cultures. How might serious literature reach and engage the inhabitants of the popular-culture-world? Comparative literature could potentially help bridge the gap and help revitalize the role of literature in world culture because of its inherent interdisciplinarity, boundary-crossing orientation, and internationalism. 'On the scholarly front', Katherine Arens has written, 'comparative literature has in many ways led the charge because of its early attention to postcolonial studies, a classic setting for studies of meetings between dominant and nondominant cultures and for debates about the impact of national literature canons'.[19] By 'nondominant' she means, in this context, oppressed or marginalized cultures, but it could be expanded to include traditionally devalued popular culture as well. The underlying approach of comparing, contrasting, and contextualizing that is the modus operandi of comparative literature gives the basic enterprise of comparatists the feeling of universally connected or linked texts, similar to hyperlinked electronic texts.

Whatever the implications of living in a post-Gutenberg Age, as it has been called (Steven Levy: 'digital reading thrusts us into an exciting—and jarring—post-Gutenberg era', p. 58), it is clear that the changes are not

---

[19]   Catherine Arens, 'When Comparative Literature Becomes Cultural Studies: Teaching Cultures through Genre', *The Comparatist* 29 (2005), 123-47 (p. 123).

limited to the United States or even to Western countries. Rather, the changes are clearly global. The so-called butterfly theory speaks directly to this phenomenon: 'When a butterfly flutters its wings in one part of the world, it can eventually cause a hurricane in another' (*The Economist*).[20] We cannot but pay attention.

WORKS CITED

Arens, Catherine, 'When Comparative Literature Becomes Cultural Studies: Teaching Cultures through Genre', *The Comparatist* 29 (2005), 123-47

Bennett, Jessica, 'Of God and Good Design', *Newsweek*, 27 October 2008, 18

Carr, Nicholas, 'Is Google Making Us Stupid?', *The Atlantic* (July/August 2008), 56-63

Cieply, Michael, 'Saving the Story (The Film Version)', *The New York Times*, 18 November 2008: C1, C7

Crain, Caleb, 'Twilight of the Books', *The New Yorker*, 24 & 31 Dec. 2007, 134-39 *The Economist*, Advertisement for subscription to *The Economist*, 22 April 2002

Fforde, Jasper, *The Eyre Affair* (NY: Penguin, 2001)

Gaite, Carmen Martín, 'The Virtues of Reading', *PMLA*, 104 (May 1989), 348-53

---

[20]   *The Economist*, Advertisement for subscription to *The Economist*, 22 April 2002.

Grafton, Anthony, 'Future Reading: digitization and its discontents', *The New Yorker*, 5 November 2007, 50-4

Hansen, Elaine Tuttle, 'The Situation of the Humanities', *ADFL Bulletin* (winter-spring 2006), 2-3; 10-14

Hugo, Victor, *The Hunchback of Notre-Dame*, trans. by Walter J. Cobb (NY: The New American Library, 1965)

Interlandi, Jeneen, 'Your Brain Will Never Be the Same', Review of *iBRAIN: Surviving the Technological Alteration of the Modern Mind* by Gary Small, *Newsweek*, 20 October 2008, 16

Irvine, Martha, 'Most youngsters are gamers: Pew survey finds 97 percent play and many every day', *The Birmingham News* (The Associated Press), 17 September 2008 4D

Jacobson, Sid and Ernie Colón, *The 9/11 Report: A Graphic Adaptation* (NY: Hill and Wang (Farrar, Straus and Giroux)), 2006

Jenckes, Kate, 'Post-Literature in Latin America: A Colloquium to explore the meaning of "post-literature"', Department of Romance Languages and Literatures Newsletter, University of Michigan, Ann Arbor, MI (Fall 2008/Winter 2009), 3

Kafka, Franz, *The Trial: A Graphic Novel*, adapted and trans. by David Zane Mairowitz, illustrated by Chantal Montellier (NY and London: Sterling, 2008)

Levy, Steven, 'Can It Kindle the Imagination? We read the fine print on Amazon's new Gadget', *Newsweek*, 26 November 2007, 64

—. 'The Future of Reading: Amazon's Jeff Bezos already built a better bookstore. Now he believes he can improve upon one of humankind's most divine creations: the book itself', *Newsweek*, 26 November 2007, 57-64

McLean, Jean M., 'Make room for Millenials: How Generation Y is changing the face of the workplace', *The Birmingham News*, 25 May 2008, I 1

Minzesheimer, Bob, '"Widow" pours out grief in images: 9/11 graphic memoir depicts raw first year', *USA Today*, 9 September 2008, D 1, D 2

Reading at Risk: A Survey of Literary Reading in America (National Endowment for the Arts, 2004)

Rubik, Margarete and Elke Mettinger-Schartmann, eds., *A Breath of Fresh Eyre: Intertextual and Intermedial Reworkings of* Jane Eyre (Amsterdam and NY: Rodopi, 2007)

Ruskin, John, *Sesame and Lilies*, ed. by Deborah Epstein Nord (New Haven and London: Yale University Press, 2001)

Spiegelmann, Art, *Maus I: A Survivor's Tale: My Father Bleeds History* (NY: Pantheon Books, 1986)

—. *Maus II: A Survivor's Tale: And Here My Troubles Began* (NY: Pantheon Books, 1992)

Sullivan, Andrew, 'Why I Blog', *The Atlantic*, November 2008, 106-13

To Read or Not to Read: A Question of National Consequence, Office of Research and Analysis, National Endowment for the Arts. Research Report #47, Executive Summary. November 2007. Available www.arts.gov.

Torres, Alissa, *American Widow*, illustrated by Sungyoon Choi (NY: Villard, 2008)

Ion Manolescu

Popular Culture and the Romanian Postmodernist Canon. The Case of Comics' Authors

In the second half of the 20th century, the Western canon is being reshaped into an open field of literary choices and hierarchies. Several postmodern "canonic battles" rewrite a hybrid, flexible history of literature, defined by a productive merging between popular culture and academic culture. In terms of selection of its "great books" and "canonic authors", contemporary Romanian literature hardly follows this tendency to cultural openness and transparency. The case of Romanian comics' authors, who are never included in the main canonic instruments (dictionaries, anthologies, text books), is relevant to a present crisis of axiological criteria that this paper attempts to pinpoint and debate.

1. The Literary Canon. A Theoretical Approach

The present study focuses on the absence of comics from the Romanian postmodernist literary and cultural canon. Since Romanian critics and literary historians, as well as theorists of culture, almost never consider the work of comics authors as literarily valid, several questions may call for an explanation: are there any differences between Western canons and the Romanian canon? Can we agree on a basic list of criteria in shaping the canon? And, most of all, why is the Romanian canon opaque to popular culture/literature, in general, and to comics, in particular?

In the 20th century, theories of the Western literary canon are generally based on a binary logic of the 'either, or' type. They suggest either the existence of a 'unique, undividable canon' (the restrictive, unifying standpoint) or that of a 'multitude of canons' (the permissive, pluralist standpoint). No matter which perspective we chose to take into consideration, its arguments are being impaired by the weak dichotomy of criteria they rely on: beginning/end, acceptable/unacceptable, open/closed, negotiable/nonnegotiable, variable/fixed, and so on. If effective, such 'consensual' criteria would stand for a presumably undisputed structural stability of the canon. The literary canon would be as easily decidable as literary trends or cultural ages. It would also prove impossible to change.

However, several theoretical efforts in the eighties tried to challenge the assumption that the canon is, by definition, structurally stable. In 1979, Leslie Fiedler and Houston Baker Jr. inaugurated two university programs on English as the universal language for the institution of literature. Both brought to the public's attention axiological terms such as 'canonicity' and 'canon', which were regarded not only from an aesthetic point of view, but also from a sociological one. Later on, Fiedler and Baker Jr.'s programs led to vivid cultural polemics and a widespread academic debate called 'the canonical battle'.[1]

The term 'canon' preserved its singular form in 1981, as the very mark of yet an unchallenged cultural norm. Although, in *English Literature. Opening Up the Canon,* Fiedler and Baker Jr. criticized the hypocrisy, the duplicity and the theatrical masquerade of the English educational system, insisting on the captive force field of the curricula, they failed to deconstruct the monolithic literary canon. Their theoretical endeavor still relied on reductive, mutually-exclusive patterns (old/new, high/low, rigid/mobile) meant to enable the proclaiming of a prudent, almost peaceful declaration of war: 'We live at a time when literature, high and low, ceased to be an independent, self-perpetuating institution; yet, it is more institutionalized than ever'.[2]

Three years later, when Robert von Hallberg edited his famous anthology *Canons,* the plural form of the notion looked more like a figure of speech, than a legitimate operational concept. It was based on a comfortable logical assumption: should the canon of the educational system prove unsatisfactory, coercive, insufficient, and obsolete, it might be replaced by a 'multiplicity of canons',[3] possibly established after the cultural negotiation of certain 'ideal figures' (Altieri, see the above note, pp. 42-52). However, these 'ideal figures' in the 'multiplicity of canons' would have had the same cultural authority as the ones present in the initial canon. One rigid canon was being replaced by 'a multiplicity' of rigid canons.

A similar cultural perspective, depending on the 'either, or' logic, can be tracked down in the studies included in Virgil Nemoianu and Robert Royal's anthology, *The Hospitable Canon.*[4] Here, canonical structures, as well as the axiological criteria they are bound to follow, are formulated in dualist terms, such as: 'permission and oppression' (Altieri, see note 4 above, p. 20), 'good

[1]   The term 'canonicity' came to use in 1980, in the *Modern Language Association Bibliography,* while 'canon' was used one year later. See Jan Gorak, *The Making of the Modern Canon. Genesis and Crisis of a Literary Idea* (London & Atlantic Highlands, New Jersey: Athlone, 1991), pp. 222-3.

[2]   Leslie Fiedler and Baker A. Houston Jr., *English Literature. Opening Up the Canon* (Baltimore and London: The Johns Hopkins University Press, 1981), p. 73.

[3]   Robert von Hallberg, ed., *Canons* (Chicago & London: University of Chicago Press, 1984), pp. 1-2.

[4]   Virgil Nemoianu and Robert Royal, eds., *The Hospitable Canon. Essays on Literary Play, Scholarly Choice, and Popular Pressures* (Philadelphia/Amsterdam: John Benjamins Publishing Company, 1991).

and evil' (Furst, see note 4 above, p. 19), 'theme and code' (Clausen, see note 4 above, p. 199). However, Nemoianu's study, *Literary Canons and Social Value Options*, represents a significant theoretical breakthrough in the process of defining a split, chaotic canon, stretched according to various intensities; an elusive, volatile canon, never to be decided in a completely rational manner: 'The canon is invisible, undefined, flexible, with a continuous slow movement inside it: ultimately, an unknown realm, perceptible but not precisely measurable, or difficult to capture exactly' (see note 4 above, p. 222).

A chaotic, volatile postmodernist canon would no longer consider literature via a binary structured logic. It would cease to provide models of aesthetic validation based on opposed criteria, such as: past-present; high-low; academic-popular; able-unable to convey meaning, and so on. More tolerant than its theoretical predecessors, an 'open canon' would rely on the tensions within its body – meridians of flexible aesthetic, social, cultural or political practices and values. Such an open postmodernist canon would always make room for Shakespeare and Garfield, Dante and Superman, Dostoievski and Captain America. It actually seems to be the canon (or, should we say, 'canons') of the Western cultures and civilizations, made legitimate by normative instruments such as the Princeton, Columbia or Routledge encyclopedias or the Larousse dictionary. For instance, in the 1997 edition of *Le Petit Larousse Illustré*, comics' figures such as Uderzo's Astérix stand right next to Nobel Prize winner writers such as Miguel Ángel Asturias.[5] Moreover, both of them enjoy the benefit of illustration. At the same time, Hergé's comics' hero Tintin (p. 1714) is in close proximity to the famous Russian fiction writer Lev Tolstoy (p. 1716).[6]

2. Comics Outside the Canon. The Lack of Aesthetic and Sociological Criteria

Let us turn back to the main issue of this study: explaining the lack of accommodation of the Romanian literary canon with popular culture and, in particular, with comics' authors and their work. We already stated that, during the second half of the 20th century, the Western canon/canons is/are being reshaped into an open field of literary choices and hierarchies. Several

---

[5]   *Le Petit Larousse Illustré 1997. Dictionnaire Encyclopédique* (Paris: Larousse, 1997), pp. 1150-1.

[6]   In praise and recognition of his value as a universal cultural icon, Tintin is provided with generous space and illustration. His illustration in the *Larousse* is double in size, compared to Tolstoy's. It is also displayed at the center of the printed page, while Tolstoy's (smaller) portrait is placed near the inner right edge.

postmodernist 'canonical battles' rewrite a hybrid, flexible history of literature, defined by a productive negotiation of popular and academic options. Ultimately, this interactive process tends to eliminate the prejudicial distinction high brow-low brow culture and make such clear-cut typological and axiological definitions of literature both inoperative and irrelevant. However, in terms of selecting canonic figures, contemporary Romanian critics and historians of literature hardly follow this natural, democratic tendency to cultural openness and transparency.

The case of Romanian comics' authors, who miss the main instruments of canonic calibration (dictionaries, anthologies, encyclopedias, text books, etc.), is relevant to the present crisis of argumentative criteria in shaping the canon/canons of Romanian literature. A sociological investigation one may easily embark on would provide sufficient evidence for the assumption that Romanian critics and historians constantly reject the canonic importance of comics: the names of Sandu Florea, Mircea Arapu, Livia Rusz, Valentin Tănase, Viorel Pirligras, Marian Radu, Lucian Amarii, Alexandru Ciubotariu, Marian Mirescu, Victor Trifan, Roman Tolici, Călin Stoicănescu, Valentin Iordache or Traian Marinescu are almost never to be found in chronicles, monographic studies or books of history of literature.

Since many of these comics' authors are being published not only in Romania, but also in France, Italy, Hungary or the United States; since they receive constant praise from both critics and the general public, one may rightfully ask: why are they being ignored by Romanian critics and historians? This prejudicial cultural option seems the more surprising as it fails to embrace both the aesthetic and the sociological criterion. The same critics and historians write about recent books of fiction printed in less than 500 copies (by doing so, they violate the sociological criterion of relevance). Before vanishing from the cultural arena, while remaining on the shelves of the book stores, these books do not receive more than two or three chronicles, highly critical, in general (by doing so, critics and historians violate the aesthetic criterion of selection). Examples may be extracted from the Romanian literary market, by following the way in which critics select authors with low sociological visibility and poor aesthetic relevance: for instance, many of the authors included in Polirom's *Ego Proza* (Ego Fiction) collection or Humanitas' *Proza Debut* (Debut Fiction) collection. The use of a double critical standard, based either on the refusal to accept comics as part of literature, or on sheer cultural ignorance, may have personal motivations, but little cultural justification.

Romanian critics and historians of literature either do not possess any knowledge of comics, or they simply ignore it. In such appalling circumstances, it is no surprise to the reader that two of the presumably most influential present literary critics, Paul Cernat and Daniel Cristea-Enache, reject the axiological role popular culture and, particularly, comics would play within a 'respectable' culture.

Let us first hear Paul Cernat's verdict regarding the relation between 'high literature' and comics: 'Una e să reciclezi în maniera lui Pynchon cultura BD, alta e să intri pe terenul lui de la nivelul discursiv al comixurilor [*sic*!]' ('It is one thing to recycle the culture of comic books in the manner of Pynchon, it is yet another thing to do it from the discourse level of comix [sic!].').[7] (2008, on-line) In other words, although the recycling of comics' is allowed (albeit reluctantly) within the realm of 'great books' and their 'great authors', one is forbidden to do it by using the very object of his or her cultural interest (the comic books themselves). Cernat's judgment proves self-contradictory, therefore semantically unsustainable. On the other hand, the critic suggests that 'great authors' have intrinsic, unlimited aesthetic legitimacy: the way in which Thomas Pynchon writes (even about comics) is *a priori* 'good'/'right'/'relevant', while the way in which comics are being expressed in their own manner of style and discourse is *a priori* 'bad'/'wrong'/'irrelevant'. Cernat does not explain how he reaches such an authoritative implicit conclusion; nor does he provide any arguments for it.

Let us now move to Daniel Cristea-Enache and his criticism of popular culture and the 'unfortunate' success it relies on: 'Formele şi genurile artistice nu se acreditează prin tiraje de masă. Înflorirea sau epuizarea lor nu depind, matematic, de vînzarea produselor din aria respectivă. Dacă ar fi aşa, ar însemna că literatura comercială gen Dan Brown sau Paulo Coelho ar fi superioară prozei mari a lui Llosa şi Kundera. [...] Nici un critic serios n-ar putea susţine o asemenea enormitate' ('Artistic forms and genres are not validated via the number of copies sold. Be it so, commercial literature, such as Dan Brown and Paulo Coehlo's would be superior to the great fiction of Llosa and Kundera. [...] No serious critic would support such a stupidity.').[8] In Cristea-Enache's terms, popular literature, like the *Titanic*, has fatal internal flaws: it is intrinsic invalid from the aesthetic point of view, as it is intrinsic condemnable from the axiological point of view. 'Great fiction' belongs only to Llosa, Kundera and all the other authors who are immune to the malignant and culturally irrelevant process of 'copy-selling'. On the other hand, if we follow Cristea-Enache's logic to the end, whoever sells any 'number of copies' instantly becomes commercial, that is 'unserious' to critical judgment. Consequently, from its beginnings to present day times,

---

[7]   Paul Cernat, 'Din nou despre proza noastră tînără' ('Once Again on Our Young Writers' Fiction'), *Observator cultural*, 2 October 2008 (*on-line*).

[8]   Daniel Cristea-Enache, 'Cu cărţile pe masă' ('Laying the Cards on the Table'), *România literară*, 12 September 2008 (*on-line*).

literature and its canons (Llosa and Kundera included) solely deliver 'commercial', 'unserious' authors and works. At the other end of this questionable reasoning, if selling copies is by no means a canonic issue, since literary value is always 'great' in and by itself, it would suffice for one or several authors to write something down which is never going to be published/read by the public, in order to achieve the 'validation of a literary genre'. Let us imagine the canon/canons of Western fiction as a selection of thousands of invisible 'great' literary works: a collection of universal masterpieces never to see the light of day, perhaps even never to have been written. A potential canon, of paranoid proportions, in which each of us would find his or her undisputed place. As in Cernat's case, the contradiction in Cristea-Enache's argument is so obvious, that it immediately unfolds the logical fallacy of the critic.

Historians of literature also dismiss popular literature as culturally irrelevant and aesthetically unreliable. They ignore comics and their authors, as if the latter played no part whatsoever in the postmodernist circuit of values of pre- and post-1989 Romania. Laurenţiu Ulici, Dan C. Mihăilescu and Cornel Ungureanu are three of the most important examples of 'cultural blindness' to popular literature. None of them include any Romanian comics authors in their histories of literature: Ulici's *Literatura română contemporană* (*Romanian Contemporary Literature*) (1995), Mihăilescu's *Literatura română în post-ceauşism* (*Romanian Literature after Ceauşescu's Regime*) (3 volumes, 2004, 2006, 2007) and Ungureanu's *Istoria secretă a literaturii române* (*The Secret History of Romanian Literature*) (2007) are opaque to comics' authors such as Mircea Arapu, Sandu Florea, Viorel Pirligras, Marian Mirescu, Jup (Lucian Amarii) or Ciubi (Alexandru Ciubotariu).[9] The same phenomenon of 'cultural blindness' or aesthetic misconception with respect to popular literature is to be noticed in Alex. Ştefănescu's *Istoria literaturii române contemporane. 1941-2000* (*The History of Romanian Contemporary Literature: 1941-2000*).[10] The reader can find no trace of any comics author in this 1000-page history of present Romanian literature. Alex. Ştefănescu seems to make a strong statement: high literature is literature, while popular literature is not literature. Or perhaps the historian simply does not regard comics as part of literature.

A similar cultural prejudice seemingly governs Nicolae Manolescu's 1526-page *Istoria critică a literaturii române* (*The Critical History of*

---

[9]   Laurenţiu Ulici, *Literatura română contemporană* (Bucureşti: Eminescu, 1995). Dan C. Mihăilescu, *Literatura română în post-ceauşism*, 3 vols (Iaşi: Polirom, 2004; 2006; 2007). Cornel Ungureanu, *Istoria secretă a literaturii române* (Braşov: Aula, 2007).

[10]   Alex Ştefănescu, *Istoria literaturii române contemporane. 1941-2000* (Bucureşti: Maşina de scris, 2005).

Romanian Literature).[11] This 'critical' history of all-time Romanian literature acknowledges the existence of 'children books' and 'teenage literature' (see note 11 above, p. 1393) and even affirms they hold some canonic relevance in a chapter dedicated to 'children and youth literature' (*Literatura pentru copii și tineret*). However, although science fiction and detective novels are being treated (be it in a small, inconclusive paragraph) as a somehow relevant component of 'youth literature' (p. 1394), comics are utterly ignored in this respect.

To sum up, due to reasons of cultural reluctance/blindness, Romanian historians of literature generally exclude comics from the object of literature. Their rigid option rules out academic contributions such as Wolfgang Fuchs and Reinhold C. Reitberger's (1971), Will Eisner's (1990), Scott Mc Cloud's (1994) or Patrick Gaumer and Claude Moliterni's (1994), to quote just some of the most important Western historians and theorists of comics as an independent literary genre.[12] Should we choose to expel comics from literature on the grounds of their unsuitable 'graphic' condition, then the *Larousse* definition: 'La bande dessinée est d'abord la simple illustration d'un récit' ('Comics are, first of all, the illustration of a story') itself becomes useless.[13] If we accept that the 'story' is a part of literature, while its 'illustration' is not, comic books and albums such as Viorel Pirligras' *Caragiale. Dl. Goe. Amici. Telegrame* (2002) would belong to… 19th century Grand Classic fiction writer I.L. Caragiale, rather than to the 21st century postmodernist cartoonist.[14] Almost a century after Caragiale's death, Pirligras would be overwhelmed by the long-gone 'script writer' of his comic book, while the paternity of the graphic album would become undecidable.

In the same manner, Hugo Pratt's novel *Corto Maltese. Una ballata del mare salato*, published in Italian in 1995 and in French four years later (see Pratt, 1999), would be 'literature', while its source of inspiration, the homonymous comic album belonging to Pratt and published in 1967, would not.[15] Franz Kafka's modernist novel, *The Trial*, would also show

[11]   Nicolae Manolescu, *Istoria critică a literaturii române* (Pitești: Paralela 45, 2008).

[12]   Wolfgang Fuchs and Reinhold C. Reitberger, *Comics. Anatomie eines Massenmediums* (München: Heinz Moos Verlag, 1971). Will Eisner, *Comics & Sequential Art* (Poorhouse Press, Tamarac: Florida, 1990). Scott Mc Cloud, *Understanding Comics. The Invisible Art* (New York: Harper Paperbacks, 1994). Patrick Gaumer and Claude Moliterni, *Dictionnaire mondial de la bande dessinée* (Paris: Larousse, 1994).

[13]   *Le Petit Larousse Illustré 1997. Dictionnaire Encyclopédique* (Paris: Larousse, 1997), p. 123.

[14]   Viorel Pirligras, *Caragiale. Dl. Goe. Amici. Telegrame* (București: ALLFA, 2002).

[15]   Hugo Pratt, *Corto Maltese. La Ballade de la mer salée* (Paris: Denoël, 1999).

considerable resistance to genre, style and paternity credits. Its hybrid variant (comic book – graphic novel) printed by SelfMadeHero Press in 2008 is now called *The Trial: A Graphic Novel of Franz Kafka's Classic*, while its paternity is attributed to a fellowship of three authors: Franz Kafka, David Zane Mairowitz, Chantal Montellier.[16] As far as the comic book—graphic novel variant of *The Trial* is concerned, the hypothesis of the auctorial partnership with equal rights ('equal co-authorship') can not be ruled out: *The Trial* belongs as much to Kafka, as to Mairowitz and Montellier.[17]

At the same time, defining comics as 'the 9th art' also stands as a strong theoretical argument. Its acceptance may well and profitably question the comics' supposed 'literary' status. For instance, if comics are regarded as art, why should they be included in histories of literature, rather than in histories of art? And, if comics are being considered art (instead of literature), why should they ask for integration within a non-specific axiological system, such as the literary canon?

In the first case, the answer would be that, within the Romanian cultural field, comics do not belong to and are not present even in those histories which, according to the 'extra-literary' hypothesis, should best encompass their forms of expression (namely, the histories of art). Hence, comics search for a simultaneous integration in literature and art, while encountering the same aesthetic prejudices and axiological dismissal in both areas. In the second case, one may answer that, irrespective of the cultural area we decide to place them in (art or literature), comics should have the democratic right to be represented within the canon, in a manner similar or identical to other sub-genres of popular literature/culture: thriller, science fiction, horror, cyberpunk etc. If, for all of these sub-genres, critics and historians agreed on providing solid, stable criteria/units so as to determine their socio-aesthetic value and allow their participation to and within the canon, there should be no reason for refusing to apply the same criteria/units to comics, with identical effects.

One may also answer that, beyond the definitions of theorists who insist on the literary characteristics of the genre[18], comics are already included in significant instruments of canonic calibration, such as dictionaries and encyclopedias: Tintin, Astérix, Mickey Mouse, Pink Panther or Marsupilami

---

[16] See   more   at   http://www.amazon.co.uk/Trial-Graphic-Kafkas-Classic-Classics/dp/0955285690.

[17] The issue was debated by Professor Elaine Martin, from the University of Alabama, within the *Popular Culture* panel of the *National Literatures in the Age of Globalization* conference. The conference was held at the Faculty of Letters of Bucharest University, between October 31 and November 1, 2008.

[18] The literary characteristics of the genre are provided, among other things, by its format: comics are printed not only as graphic albums, but also as graphic novels.

are just some of the comics series and characters to have settled within the universal literary and cultural canon. Irrespective of the fact that comics are being defined as 'the illustration of a story' or as 'an art and a hybrid literary genre, which combines text and drawing on a page'[19], they are a familiar, customary presence of the Western cultures and civilizations. In the United States, France (where they are known as *bande dessinée*), Italy (*fumetti*) or Japan (*manga*), comics are always included in text books, anthologies or literary dictionaries.[20] In other terms, they gained a specific part and play a significant role within the cultural instruments which validate the canon and allow its circulation in space and time.

Moreover, the standard definition of literature ('an ensemble of written or oral works which reflect an aesthetic goal') and its determinations comprised in dictionaries of theory[21] regard consumerism as a valid, operative literary function and make way for the integration of comics within 'popular' literature: 'De o utilitate tehnică sînt diversele specificări şi determinări ale literaturii. Astfel, putem vorbi despre literatură scrisă şi orală, populară şi cultă, lirică, epică, dramatică, literatură de consum etc.' ('The different specifics and determinations of literature testify to a technical utility. As a result, one may consider written and oral literature, popular and academic literature, lyric, epic and dramatic literature, consumerist literature etc').[22] Should comics be a 'written (and graphic) work' with aesthetic (and not simply utilitarian) functions, then it is literature. Should comics be a part of 'popular' and/or "consumerist" literature, then, it has the same right to canonic representation as 'academic', 'lyric', 'epic' or 'dramatic' literature.

Last, but not least, one may also take into account the hybrid, indeterminate, relative, assimilative particularities of literature in the postmodernist age, as defined by Ihab Hassan's taxonomic and methodological catenae.[23] (1982: 184-85; 1990: 18-23). In a timeframe of the

---

[19] See, among others, Ion Manolescu, 'O călătorie în lumea benzii desenate' ('Travelling in the Comics' World'), *Dilemateca*, November – December 2006.

[20] Comics are even included in anthologies of the 'Ideal Library' type, which select works and authors of literature of the highest significance for the local or the universal canon. See, for instance, Boncenne's *La Bibliothèque idéale* (Paris: Albin Michel, 1988), in collaboration with the famous French TV literary critic, Bernard Pivot.

[21] See, for example, *Dicţionar de termeni literari* (*Dictionary of Literary Terms*), edited by Academiei Press, Romania's most prestigious scientific publishing house (Săndulescu, coord., 1976).

[22] Nicolae Balotă in Al. Săndulescu, (coord.), *Dicţionar de termeni literari* (*Dictionary of Literary Terms*) (Bucureşti: Academiei, 1976), p. 250.

[23] Ihab Hassan, *The Dismemberment of Orpheus: Toward a Postmodern Literature*, 2nd edition (Madison: University of Wisconsin Press, 1982), pp. 184-5. Ihab Hassan, 'Pluralism in

postindustrial civilization in which cultural forms and products tend to interact and merge, the border between a comic strip and a novella or a novel gets more and more blurred, while the 'story' and its 'illustration' become inseparable. Intermediary aesthetic formulas, such as the graphic novel (in Great Britain or the United States) or roman BD (in France) may no longer be included in a single category of genre, sub-genre, style or format. As a form of literature, art or literature-art, comics should benefit from the same canonic treatment as their 'popular' relatives. Unfortunately, such a process almost never occurs within the Romanian cultural space.

3. Comics Inside the Canon. The Exceptions

Still, comics authors Mircea Arapu, Sandu Florea are present in Dodo Niţă and Virgil Tomuleţ's *Dicţionarul benzii desenate din România* (*Dictionary of Romanian Comics*) (2005), as well as in Dodo Niţă and Mircea Arapu's *Dictionnaire de la bande dessinée roumaine* (2008, published in French), two fortunate exceptions to the rule of excluding comics from any canonic list.[24] In his 2008 dictionary, illustrated by Mircea Arapu, alongside the analysis of graphic works by Valentin Tănase, Livia Rusz or Viorel Pirligras, Dodo Niţă provides the reader with detailed bio-bibliographical information on Romanian-born authors Stan Lee, Marcel Gotlib, and Will Eisner.[25] Mircea Arapu (born 1955) is one of the most important authors of comics in France, works such as *Arthur le Fantôme* (after Jean Cezard), *Placid et Muzo* (after Nicolau) or *Pif* (after C. Arnal), as well as the participation in famous international comics reunions (such as *Le Salon BD* in Charleroi or *Le Festival de la Bande Dessinée* in Angoulême) needing no further comments. On the other hand, Sandu Florea's international reputation is even greater than Arapu's. Born 1946, Florea is one of the main comic authors from Marvel Comics and DC Comics in the United States. Comic strips such as *The Executioner*, *Conan the Barbarian*, *Buffy the Vampire Slayer* or *The X-Men* are just a few of his numerous masterpieces. Some of these strips sold worldwide over one million copies; they were highly praised by both critics and the general public. In order to understand the cultural significance of

Postmodern Perspective', in Matei Calinescu and Douwe W. Fokkema, eds., *Exploring Postmodernism*. (Amsterdam/Philadelphia: John Benjamins Publishing Company, 1990), pp. 18-23.

[24] Dodo Niţă and Virgil Tomuleţ, *Dicţionarul benzii desenate din România* (Craiova: MJM, 2005). Dodo Niţă and Mircea Arapu, *Dictionnaire de la bande dessinée roumaine* (Comics Factory: Constanţa, 2008).

[25] See the chapter *Les Auteurs de parents nés en Roumanie* (Dodo Niţă, 2008), pp. 41-5.

Sandu Florea's contribution to Romanian literature, let us keep in mind that Romania's only canonic postmodernist author, Mircea Cărtărescu, sold just about 100 000 copies of his glossy fiction book, *De ce iubim femeile* (*Why We Love Women*) (2004).[26] Cărtărescu is included in all the histories of post-1989 Romanian literature, while Sandu Florea is utterly ignored or excluded from these instruments. A flexible, open, democratic canon would provide space for the both of them.

Another exception to the rule of excluding popular literature authors from the canon may be considered Mihai Dan Pavelescu's *Dicţionar SF* (*Science Fiction Dictionary*) (1999). The book includes Sandu Florea, who is being described as: 'Cel mai prolific desenator român [...] In 1992, a debutat la cea mai mare editură americană, Marvel Comics. De atunci şi pînă în prezent, a publicat peste 50 de comic books la marile edituri americane' ('The most prolific Romanian comics' author [...] In 1992, he made his debut at the most famous comics' syndicate in the United States, Marvel Comics. Since then, Florea published over 50 comic books at America's greatest publishing houses').[27] On the other hand, the most influential dictionary of all-time Romanian literature, *Dicţionarul scriitorilor români* (*Dictionary of Romanian Writers*) (editors: Mircea Zaciu, Marian Papahagi, Aurel Sasu) ignores both Arapu (A-C, 1995) and Florea (D-L, 1998).[28] Nowadays, no Romanian comics' author gets even the smallest of places within this highly authoritative canonic instrument. The canon is not only singular, but also restrictive and prejudicial.

We may bring this study to a conclusion by observing the most influential cultural prejudices in shaping an exclusivist, rigid, inertial Romanian literary canon. First of all, the *elitist prejudice*, which asserts the superiority of mainstream literature over popular literature. The former means 'great literature', while the latter is the equivalent of 'subliterature' or 'poor literature' (strongly pejorative terms). Then, the 'prejudice of the closed canon', which defends the canon from any processes of cultural reassessments. It either prevents or forbids axiological access to authors and works belonging to the so-called 'low-brow' zone. Finally, the 'prejudice of the undisputed aesthetic authority of "high" or "great" genres'. It regards the novel or the novella as intrinsically superior to the comic strip or the comic book. Critics or historians whose works are based on such a triple prejudicial cultural perspective attempt to persuade the reader of how 'major' (or

---

[26] Mircea Cărtărescu, *De ce iubim femeile* (Bucureşti: Humanitas, 2004).

[27] Mihai Dan Pavelescu, *Dicţionar SF* (Bucureşti: Nemira, 1999), pp. 108-9.

[28] Mircea Zaciu, Marian Papahagi, and Aurel Sasu, eds., *Dicţionarul scriitorilor români*, vol. 1, A-C (Bucureşti: Albatros, 1995) and vol. 2, D-L (Bucureşti: Albatros, 1998).

'artistic', 'profound', 'high') genres are definitely related to writers/the writing process, while 'minor' genres have little to do with them. Since they do not possess an 'aesthetic quality' (as argued, mostly by means of omission, in Romanian dictionaries and encyclopedias), comics' authors should be kept both outside the canon, and outside literature itself.

Ultimately, only a fluid, alternative canon (or canons), depending on the interaction of its (or their) aesthetic and sociological variables may do justice to popular literature and, in particular, to Romanian comics' authors and their work. Such a flexible canon, close to Deleuze and Guattari's figure of the rhizome, would rely on permanent tensions and interactions of fields: a shattered, self-generating, anti-genealogic network of cultural tissues.[29] A canon with variable geometry (in terms of standards, criteria and selection) might just provide the space and value comics rightfully deserve within the dynamic evolution of Romanian literature.

---

[29]   See Deleuze & Guattari's contributions to rhizomatic morphogenesis: Gilles Deleuze and Félix Guattari, *Capitalisme et schizophrénie. L'Anti-Œdipe* (Paris: Minuit, 1995) (© 1972). Gilles Deleuze and Félix Guattari, *Capitalisme et schizophrénie. Milles plateaux* (Paris: Minuit, 1997) (© 1980).

WORKS CITED

Fiction & comics

Cărtărescu, Mircea, *De ce iubim femeile* (*Why We Love Women*) (Bucureşti: Humanitas, 2004)

Kafka, Franz, David Zane Mairowitz, and Montellier Chantal, *The Trial: A Graphic Novel of Franz Kafka's Classic* (London: SelfMadeHero, 2008)

Pirligras, Viorel, *Caragiale. Dl. Goe. Amici. Telegrame* (*Caragiale. Mr. Goe. Pals. Telegrams*) (Bucureşti: ALLFA, 2002)

Pratt, Hugo, *Corto Maltese. La Ballade de la mer salée* (Paris: Denoël, 1999).

Literary theory & history of literature

Boncenne, Pierre, *La Bibliothèque idéale* (Paris: Albin Michel, 1988)

Calinescu, Matei, and Douwe W. Fokkema, eds., *Exploring Postmodernism* (Amsterdam/Philadelphia: John Benjamins Publishing Company, 1990)

Cernat, Paul, 'Din nou despre proza noastră tînără' ('Once Again on Our Young Writers' Fiction'), *Observator cultural* (2 October 2008)

Cristea-Enache, Daniel, 'Cu cărţile pe masă' ('Laying the Cards on the Table'), *România literară* (12 September 2008)

Deleuze, Gilles, and Félix Guattari, *Capitalisme et schizophrénie. L'Anti-Œdipe* (Paris: Minuit, 1995)

—. *Capitalisme et schizophrénie*. *Milles plateaux* (Paris: Minuit, 1997)

Eisner, Will, *Comics & Sequential Art*, expanded edition (Poorhouse Press, Tamarac: Florida, 1990)

Fiedler, Leslie, and Baker A. Houston Jr., *English Literature. Opening Up the Canon* (Baltimore and London: The Johns Hopkins University Press, 1981)

Fuchs, Wolfgang, and Reinhold C. Reitberger, *Comics. Anatomie eines Massenmediums* (München: Heinz Moos Verlag, 1971)

Gaumer, Patrick, and Claude Moliterni, *Dictionnaire mondial de la bande dessinée* (Paris: Larousse, 1994)

Gorak, Jan, *The Making of the Modern Canon. Genesis and Crisis of a Literary Idea* (London & Atlantic Highlands, New Jersey: Athlone, 1991)

Hallberg, Robert von, ed., *Canons* (Chicago & London: University of Chicago Press, 1984)

Hassan, Ihab, *The Dismemberment of Orpheus: Toward a Postmodern Literature*, 2nd edition (Madison: University of Wisconsin Press, 1982)

Le Petit Larousse Illustré 1997. Dictionnaire Encyclopédique (Paris: Larousse, 1997)

Manolescu, Ion, 'O călătorie în lumea benzii desenate' ('Travelling in the Comics' World'), *Dilemateca* (November – December 2006)

Manolescu, Nicolae, *Istoria critică a literaturii române* (*The Critical History of Romanian Literature*) (Pitești: Paralela 45, 2008)

Mc Cloud, Scott, *Understanding Comics. The Invisible Art* (New York: Harper Paperbacks, 1994)

Mihăilescu, Dan C., (2007). *Literatura română în post-ceauşism (Romanian Literature after Ceauşescu's Regime)*, 3 vols (Iaşi: Polirom, 2004, 2006, 2007)

Nemoianu, Virgil, and Robert Royal, eds., *The Hospitable Canon. Essays on Literary Play, Scholarly Choice, and Popular Pressures* (Philadelphia/Amsterdam: John Benjamins Publishing Company, 1991)

Niţă, Dodo, and Virgil Tomuleţ, *Dicţionarul benzii desenate din România (Dictionary of Romanian Comics)* (Craiova: MJM, 2005)

Niţă, Dodo, and Mircea Arapu, *Dictionnaire de la bande dessinée roumaine* (Comics Factory: Constanţa, 2008)

Pavelescu, Mihai Dan, *Dicţionar SF (Science Fiction Dictionary)* Bucureşti: Nemira, 1999)

Săndulescu, Al., ed., *Dicţionar de termeni literari (Dictionary of Literary Terms)* (Bucureşti: Academiei, 1976)

Ştefănescu, Alex, *Istoria literaturii române contemporane. 1941-2000 (The History of Romanian Contemporary Literature: 1941-2000)* (Bucureşti: Maşina de scris, 2005)

Ulici, Laurenţiu, *Literatura română contemporană (Romanian Contemporary Literature)* (Bucureşti: Eminescu, 1995)

Ungureanu, Cornel, *Istoria secretă a literaturii române (The Secret History of Romanian Literature)* (Braşov: Aula, 2007)

Ion Manolescu

Zaciu, Mircea, Marian Papahagi, and Aurel Sasu, eds., *Dicţionarul scriitorilor români* (*Dictionary of Romanian Writers*) vol.1, A-C and vol. 2, D-L (Bucureşti: Albatros, 1995, 1998)

Alexandra Vrânceanu

National versus World Literature Seen as a Confrontation between Modernism and Balkanism

Starting from D. Damrosch's definition of world literature as "a double refraction, one that can be described through the figure of the ellipse, with the source and host cultures providing the two foci that generate the elliptical space within which a work lives as world literature, connected to both cultures, circumscribed by neither one" I would like to discuss the contrasting ways in which the works of two Romanian writers, Camil Petrescu and Panait Istrati, were interpreted in the twenties by the Romanian and French critics.

In *What is World Literature?* David Damrosch proposes a geometric analogy, the ellipse, for describing the way in which a literary work becomes part of world literature:

> World literature is thus always as much about the host's values and needs as it is about a work's source culture; hence it is a double refraction, one that can be described through the figure of the ellipse, with the source and host cultures providing the two foci that generate the elliptical space within which a work lives as world literature, connected to both cultures, circumscribed by neither one. [1]

Starting from this analogy I would like to discuss the contrasting ways in which the works of two Romanian writers, Camil Petrescu and Panait Istrati, were interpreted in the 1920-1930's by the Romanian and by the French critics. I will thus consider these two points of reference, the French and the Romanian culture, as the two foci of the ellipse because during that period the Romanian literary canon was mainly defined by the search for Modernism seen as the symbol of European culture. And, since France had been during the 19th century one of the most important cultural centres, and as Paris is at the beginning of the 20th century one of the main centres of Modernism, Romanian intellectuals saw French culture as a doorway to world literature.

Panait Istrati and Camil Petrescu are placed in opposite positions in relation to these two centres of the ellipse: Istrati was very much appreciated by the French readers and critics, whereas Camil Petrescu remained unknown to them, although he occupies a central position in the Romanian modernist canon. Instead, Istrati was despised by the Romanian critics who deplored his success in France with novels that didn't 'represent' Romanian culture and he

---

[1] David Damrosch, *What is World Literature* (Princeton: Princeton University Press, 2003), p. 283.

is still studied more in Europe than in Romania.[2] How can we explain such a contrast between the way French critics see Romanian writers and the way in which Romanian critics invent their literary canon?

1. Methodological *hors d'œuvre*

My research starts from an observation regarding the circulation of Romanian literary works during the first half of the 20th century. There is a contrast between the writers who were accepted into the Romanian literary canon and the writers whose works circulated in Europe. For example, Camil Petrescu or Liviu Rebreanu, considered as great novelists by the most important Romanian critics were completely unknown abroad, whereas Panait Istrati, who was published in Paris, was ignored by Romanian critics. This contrast between writers considered canonical by Romanian critics and writers considered important by the French or Europeans continues to this day and this is perhaps due to the fact that the most important Romanian literary history, written during the late forties by George Călinescu[3] is still the history that forms taste and opinions in Romanian school and university. A few years ago, when I was teaching Romanian literature in a French university I realized that the writers who had circulated in my students' culture and were known by them as being representative for the Romanian space, writers who had written in both languages, were not the writers considered by the Romanian critics, inventers of the canon, as important or characteristic. This is why I chose to discuss these two case studies, Panait Istrati and Camil Petrescu, and try to analyze this paradoxical contrast between two canons: the canon literary critics like E. Lovinescu or G. Călinescu forged for Romanian literary modernism and the image French critics constructed about Romania around literary figures they considered important or representative.

Circulation of literary works is essential for their integration to world literature. Let us start from the definition David Damrosch gives to world literature: 'I take world literature to encompass all literary works that circulate beyond their culture of origin, either in translation or in their original language' (p. 4). The concept of circulation is important because it

---

[2]   See some of the recent books about Istrati : David Seidmann, *L'existence juive dans l'œuvre de Panaït Istrati* (Paris: Éditions Nizet, 1984), Doina Popa-Lisseanu, *Panait Istrati: una escritura encendida (estudio de la obra de un escritor rumano de expresión francesa)* (Madrid: UNED,1988), E. Geblesco, *Panaït Istrati et la métaphore paternelle* (Paris: Anthropos, 1989), M. Jutrin-Klener, H. Lenz, D. Lérault, M. Popovici, E. Rossi, C. Rossi, J.-M. Santraud, *Les haïdoucs dans l'œuvre de Panaït Istrati: l'insoumission des vaincus* (Paris: L'Harmattan, 2002), Mircea Iorgulescu, *Panaït Istrati* (Paris: Oxus Éditions, 2004).

[3]   G. Călinescu's *Istoria literaturii române de la origini şi până în prezent* was first published in 1941.

helps us see how certain works transcend their national frame and are read and understood (or misunderstood) in different cultural spaces, becoming sometimes symbols of their culture of origin. This is for example the case of Panait Istrati's short stories, considered by many European readers to be the realistic description of life in the Balkans. Since Romanian literature didn't start to circulate until the first half of the 20th century, little was known about this space except for the descriptions of foreign travellers, who described it by using a lot of cultural stereotypes.[4]

During the first part of the 20th century Romanian writers were particularly attracted to Paris and to its cosmopolitan culture.[5] That is why, speaking about writers who published in the thirties, French culture can be considered a metonymy of world literature. There are more reasons than one to consider such a metonymy as functional: for the Romanians who wrote literature during the thirties, Paris was the centre of the cultural world and, not worrying too much about 'world literature', a concept irrelevant for them at the time, they were more interested in integrating French cultural values. Another reason to consider French literature as a metonymy for world literature, and as one of the centres of the ellipse is that having had success in France, Istrati was later translated into English, Spanish, German, and Italian, whereas Camil Petrescu, who was only famous in Romania, was translated very late, practically only during the last decades.[6]

Let us stipulate that European literature exists and let us also accept that we can speak about European literature because some literary works circulated in a certain geographical area and were accepted by each other's canon.[7] David Damrosch uses 'circulation' in order to define world literature along with two other concepts, 'reading' and 'canon':

---

[4] See Maria Todorova's studies on Balkanism, especially 'The Balkans: From Discovery to Invention', *Slavic Review*, 53 (Summer, 1994) and Katarina Gephardt, '"The Enchanted Garden" or "The Red Flag": Eastern Europe in Late Nineteenth-Century British Travel Writing', *Journal of Narrative Theory* 35 (Fall 2005).

[5] For the links between Modernism and globalization see Andreas Huyssen's 'Geographies of modernism in a globalized world', in *Geographies of Modernism. Literatures, cultures, spaces*, ed. by Peter Brooker and Andrew Thacker (London: Routledge, 2005), where he discusses the relationship between the Modernism from the metropolis with 'marginal', national Modernisms all over the globe.

[6] Only his second novel, *The Bed of Procrustes*, was translated in English by Ileana Alexandra Orlich (Ed. Fundaţia Camil Petrescu, 2008).

[7] This is, by the way, how E. R. Curtius defines European literature, by analyzing the *topoï* that constitute it and the influence of this method, we could call 'topology', can still be found in textbooks of European literature. Curtius too uses the metaphor of the ellipse in order to explain the relationship between two literary categories: one of the centres of his ellipse is Latin mediaeval literature and the other is European literature. Curtius makes this

> My claim is that world literature is not an infinite, ungraspable canon of works but rather a mode of circulation and of reading, a mode that is applicable to individual works as to body of material, available for reading established classics and new discoveries alike. [...] The variability of a work of world literature is one of its constitutive features – one of its greatest strengths when the work is well presented and read well, and its greatest vulnerability when it is mishandled or misappropriated by its newfound friends (p. 5).

In the context of my two case studies, Panait Istrati and Camil Petrescu, 'circulation' and 'reading' are the two coordinates that will explain why these two authors were placed in such contrasting positions by the two cultures.

2. The Importance of Being Modern

The emergence of the Romanian literary canon during the late twenties and thirties has a lot to do with the ideology of Modernism. The desire to belong to the European culture led some Romanian critics to give their appreciation to authors who were seen as compatible with French/European/world modernity and to exclude others, who seemed marginal, too traditional, or outdated. In an article entitled 'Literature as a World', Pascale Casanova analyses the importance of the concept of Modernism in Europe:

> I propose to call this the Greenwich Meridian of literature. [...] It is the place where the measurement of literary time—that is, the assessment of aesthetic modernity—is crystallized, contested, elaborated. To be decreed 'modern' is one of the most difficult forms of recognition for writers outside the centre, and the object of violent and bitter competition. [...] For example, once Joyce's *Ulysses* had been consecrated as a 'modern' work by Valéry Larbaud's 1929 French translation, winning the reviews and critical attention that had so far eluded it in English, it became—and remains, in certain regions of literary space — one of the measures of novelistic modernity.[8]

Some Romanian critics, as for example Eugen Lovinescu, were particularly receptive to the poetics of Modernism and this can be noticed in his theories, as well as in his activity as a literary critic[9]. He mainly encouraged those writers who could 'synchronize' Romanian culture to the European trends and during the thirties the formation of the national literary canon is conceived from such a perspective. Camil Petrescu was a member of the *Sburătorul* literary circle, led by Eugen Lovinescu, the most influential

---

analogy in the preface of his second edition of *Europäische Literatur und Lateinisches Mittelalter* in 1953.

[8]   Pascale Casanova, 'Literature as a World', *New Left Review*, 31 (Jan.-Feb 2005), pp. 75-6.

[9]   Eugen Lovinescu, 'Mutaţia valorilor estetice' in *Istoria literaturii române contemporane* (Bucureşti: Ed. Minerva, 1973) [1929], pp. 275-415.

Modernist critic. Modernism is, along with synchronism, a key concept in the theory and literary criticism promoted by Lovinescu at *Sburătorul*, and it is defined with an eye to the European culture. This affinity between Lovinescu and Camil Petrescu explains why the latter's novels played such an important part in the quest for Romanian Modernism. But Camil Petrescu was not only an important novelist, he also wrote dramas and a drama theory (his Ph.D. thesis), he was a philosopher, and later became the director of the Bucharest National Theatre.

The Romanian literary canon emerged mainly during the 19th century and it was built, like many others in the region, around a 'national' poet and around Romantic values.[10] But the essential moment for the forging of Romanian aesthetic values occured during the late '20s and the '30s. After the political unification of Transylvania with the Romanian kingdom in 1918, Romania with its many minorities and an insufficiently organized cultural system was confronted with an identity problem as it became a large country with a strong desire to belong to Europe. This explains why discussions about literature, national identity and European culture were at the centre of the public's attention.

Moreover, during the twenties and thirties Romanian critics began to pay attention to 'world literature', and they published literary histories in foreign languages in order to present Romanian literature and help it circulate in Europe.[11] Although it should be said that perhaps Romanian literary histories written in French had less impact than the circulation of some writers who published in foreign languages. The metaphor of the ellipse David Damrosch uses in order to describe the relationship between world literature and national literature is particularly interesting in this context, as some authors like Tristan Tzara or Panait Istrati got to be admitted into the French/European/world system by publishing their works in French and by circulating along with their work. These migrant writers blurred the margins of their nationality and tampered with one of the two foci of the ellipse – the national one. By writing in French, Eugen Ionescu or Emil Cioran's work circulated much better than if they had continued to publish in Romania. Sometimes writers reformulated their original work in the adopted language and, if we read carefully between the lines, we can see their new works are close to auto-translations. Ilinca Zarifopol, the translator of Cioran from

---

[10]   See Marcel Cornis-Pope, John Neubauer, 'Towards a History of the Literary Cultures in East-Central Europe: Theoretical Reflections', *ACLS Occasional Paper*, No. 52 (2002), pp.14-16.

[11]   Nicolae Iorga, *Histoire de la littérature roumaine contemporaine* (Bucharest: Editura Adevărului, 1934). Basil Munteanu, *Panorama de la littérature roumaine contemporaine* (Paris: Éditions du Sagittaire, 1938).

French to English, noticed such a process when she compared some of his Romanian works to those published in French.[12] In any case, as Ilinca Zarifopol suggests, the reason why she was asked to translate Cioran is not because he was an important Romanian writer, but because he had been adopted by the French culture. As David Damrosch argues, 'world literature is what gains in translation' (p. 281) and, obviously, by reformulating his ideas in French, Cioran gained a lot.

During the thirties both writers and critics were particularly open to ideas coming from Europe, and of course Modernism was at the centre of their attention, as it appeared to be the best way to circulate ideas and forms and thus integrate Romanian literature into world literature. Critics and writers started to realize that 'circulation' is fundamental and they began a dialogue with European culture that will only be ended with the Soviet occupation after the Second World War. Along with the acknowledgement of the importance of 'circulation' comes the understanding of the essential part played by 'reading'. What I am trying to show in this article is that this search for synchronism and cultural integration was oriented in such a way as to promote certain values and destroy others. In other words, Romanian critics tried to promote those writers that could be read/interpreted as 'Modernist', 'European' and thus associate to the Romanian culture values coming from the centre of the canon; at the same time, they tried to disassociate Romanian culture from 'Balkanism', 'Exoticism', 'Orientalism', which they perceived as values associated to the periphery, marginality and a non-European cultural universe.

3. Synchronising the Romanian novel with the European Modernist trends: Camil Petrescu and Proust

My first case study is Camil Petrescu, author of two novels considered to be among the best in Romanian literature. *Ultima noapte de dragoste, întâia noapte de război (The last night of love, the first night of war,* 1930) and *Patul lui Procust (The Bed of Procrustes,* 1933) were read as perfect symbols of modernist literature because of their author's admiration for Proust's narrative formula. Camil Petrescu praised Proust in a famous article entitled 'Noua structură şi opera lui Marcel Proust' (*The New Structure and Marcel*

---

[12] 'Soon I became aware that Cioran had actually rewritten major portions of his Romanian texts when he started publishing in French. In fact, it would not be far off the mark to say that his entire French oeuvre is a translation-*cum*-rewriting of his Romanian oeuvre.' Ilinca Zarifopol-Johnston, 'Found in Translation: The Two Lives of E. M. Cioran; or How Can One Be a Comparatist', *Comparative Literature Studies,* 44, No. 1–2 (2007), p. 23.

Proust's Work), where he explains his theory of the modernist novel.[13] In the theory he synthesizes in this article, originally a public conference, Camil Petrescu places Proust at the centre of the paradigm change that replaced the realistic novel. The Romanian novelist begins his argumentation from the idea that 'literature should be structurally synchronic to the philosophy and science of its time' and explains what he understands by 'the new structure' using examples from psychology, philosophy and biology. In this context he underlines and comments upon the relationship between Bergson and Husserl on the one hand and Proust's narrative formula on the other.

In *The last night of love, the first night of war* and *The Bed of Procrustes,* Camil Petrescu reinterprets Proust's technique, especially the games with narrative time and the subjective point of view of the narrator. The participants in the *Sburătorul* circle and especially Eugen Lovinescu welcomed the publication of these novels, which introduced in the Romanian novel, dominated by traditional themes and narrative devices, subjects related to the life of the city described from a new perspective. It is not a coincidence that Eugen Lovinescu's theory on synchronism comes close to Camil Petrescu's theory about the novel.

Although Camil Petrescu's novels weren't bestsellers, they quickly became a reference point in Romanian Modernism. In fact, perhaps one of the reasons why he occupies such a central place in the Romanian canon is the way in which he adapts modernist theories and comments upon modernist formulas. His writings and theories are well presented in the most canonical history of Romanian literature, written by G. Călinescu. After the war, Camil Petrescu is accepted into the Romanian Academy, along with G. Călinescu, and thus he remains one of the best known Romanian novelists. The battle around the canon after 1989 did not alter his place and so Camil Petrescu can be considered one of the most canonical Romanian writers, whose place has never been challenged.

But his work doesn't circulate. And this does not happen because his novels cannot be translated, because his themes are too 'national' to be understood elsewhere, or because his narrative formula is incomprehensible. The action of both his novels is placed in Bucharest in the late twenties and the plot is built around love affairs and social observation. Camil Petrescu's work has been translated into French, Spanish, and English. The main points revealed by the reviewers to these translations are: the interest for Romanian Modernism, the depiction of Bucharest society between the two world wars and Proust's influence. None of these reviews and very few studies consider his novels as part of world literature. Perhaps the reason for this is that 'his

---

[13] 'Noua structură şi opera lui Marcel Proust', *Revista Fundaţiilor Regale* (*The Royal Foundations Magazine*), 1935.

work doesn't gain in translation'[14] as David Damrosch thinks a text should in order to become 'world literature'.[15] Coming back to David Damrosch's principles that define world literature, we can argue that Camil Petrescu lacks one major point of the ellipse, that is, the opening to the European canon because he is seen more like an adapter of a French modernist formula[16] than as an original writer[17].

Judging from this example we may consider that not only 'world literature is an elliptical refraction of national literature', as David Damrosch puts it, but sometimes national literature is a refraction of world literature too. The fact that Camil Petrescu gets to be placed in the centre of the Romanian canon because he is a European Modernist shows how the history of national literatures can be determined by a globalized current and by the desire to belong to a cultural area.

4. Panait Istrati, the migrant writer

My second case study is Panait Istrati, a man who started his career by writing articles about communism, who did not have a proper education or a proper job, who circulated a lot in Europe and in the Orient, and who was found one morning, after having tried to commit suicide in a park in Marseille, with a letter addressed to Romain Rolland in his pocket. Struck by Istrati's literary talent and perhaps also by his life story, Romain Rolland helps Panait Istrati publish his first short story, *Kyra Kyralina,* in Paris in 1924. The story has a great success and for a few years Panait Istrati becomes quite famous in France.

The main story in *Kyra Kyralina* is told by Stavru, who explains his homosexuality to a friend, Adrian. Stavru is Kyra's brother and he begins by describing their adolescence in the Balkanic port of Brăila, a world full of picturesque details. Stavru and his sister, Kyra Kyralina, lived a life of

---

[14]   In France, *The Bed of Procrustes* was translated twice, the second time by Jean-Louis Courriol who also wrote a thesis on Romanian translations in French (*Madame T*, 1998). His first novel has been translated into French only recently (*Dernière nuit d'amour, première nuit de guerre*, 2006).

[15]   I do not define world literature as the sum of all literary works ever produced, but in the way D. Damrosch defines it.

[16]   In Larousse. he is defined as 'Romancier d'inspiration proustienne'.

[17]   Which is not necessarily true, as his novels are not so close to Proust's formula and they are quite interesting. My argumentation here doesn't take into consideration either the aesthetic value of the writers I am discussing, or the validity of the interpretations made by critics. I am simply interested to see how the values associated to 'world (read 'European') literature' determine the canon of 'national (Romanian) literature'.

oriental luxury with their mother, partially independent from their father. The two teenagers take part in their mother's luxurious parties but their destiny is sealed by a visit paid by their father, who beats their mother so badly that she is forced to leave them and find a hospital. They escape from the violent father only to fall victim to an old Turk who sells young and beautiful Kyra to a harem and keeps Stavru for his own pleasure. When he finally escapes the old man, Stavru, with no education or knowledge of the world, becomes the victim of different situations on the roads of Turkey, North Africa and Romania. Stavru, who had jealously protected Kyra from the men that admired her, is obsessed by her beauty, tries to find her, and all his voyages and adventures describe this neverending quest. Kyra Kyralina remains inconsistent, as she is more of an image in her brother's mind.

Istrati's success in France was perhaps influenced by the interpretation of a cultural stereotype. The story in *Kyra Kyralina* reinterprets the main topics (or even *clichés*) related to exoticism: a strange and seductive story, the voyages to a oriental world (the Turkish empire, oriental habits, and characters like harems, pashas etc.), picturesque details, sensuality and even sexual promiscuity, all of which are described in a first-person narrative made by a naive storyteller who explains his sexual preferences to a friend.[18]

Perhaps one of the reasons for Istrati's success in France comes from the fact that Stavru blurred the lines between the European civilized traveller/colonist and the exotic world he depicts. Like a *picaro*, Stavru ceaselessly travels and depicts this oriental world, without judging its characters and situations to be *exotic* in the European and etymological sense of the word, i.e. *foreign*. His national identity is vague and irrelevant, and although he obviously is not oriental, he does not look at this world with European eyes. The transnational links he creates through his friendships and love affairs place Stavru in-between the Romanian, Greek, Jewish, Turkish, and Arabic culture.

On the other hand, French readers of *Kyra Kyralina* were much influenced by Istrati's picturesque life and interpreted the story as biographical. This was due to Romain Rolland's preface to the first edition, which presented the story as inspired from its author's life. Much like his character, Istrati is *exotic* in the etymological sense, that is, a stranger everywhere he goes: born in Romania, he lives in Western Europe (France, Switzerland, Italy), in North Africa (Egypt, Syria), Turkey and the Balkans,

---

[18] The strong relationship between the autobiographical voyage and the exotic themes have been noted by Jean-Marc Moura, 'L'exotisme européen'. in Béatrice Didier, ed., *Precis de littérature Européenne* (Paris: PUF, 1998), p. 246. This probably explains the confusion made by Romain Rolland, who presents *Kyra Kyralina* as a story inspired from the life of its author because he is used to 19th century French literature, where these *topoi* go together.

and he feels at home everywhere.[19] And this 'internationalism', a concept he also theorizes in his political articles and in his essays, is quite a problem when we speak about the thirties and about national literary values.

Panait Istrati is described by Romain Rolland as a Balkanic Gorki and by most of his French reviewers as an oriental storyteller. He writes his stories directly in French, but he keeps some Romanian words, which add an exotic feature. All these facts assure Istrati's success in France and mark his identity as 'exotic, different, oriental' but become, in the eyes of Romanian critics, good reasons to exclude him from the Romanian canon.

This success is very badly perceived by the Romanian critics, who resent the fact that Panait Istrati is appreciated by the French readers for a short story with 'oriental' themes. Of course, in the '20s nobody had written clearly that the Western culture was inventing the Eastern one, and that Orientalism and Modernism are ways to oppose cultures, but Romanian critics had a bad feeling concerning this writer with an oriental touch. Critics like Nicolae Iorga or Octavian Goga (who were also politicians and poets) thought that French readers appreciated in Istrati's *Kyra Kyralina* only the exoticism.

This universe of moral decay, of pleasurable luxury is enhanced by the fact that the story is written in the first person. Homosexuality is a theme unknown to Romanian literature, and its novelty remains unappreciated by the Romanian critics. But the main attack is directed by Iorga and Goga against Istrati's art as a prose-writer. Whereas the French critics see in him a Balkanic Gorki, a great storyteller compared by some to Homer or Sheherezade, the Romanian ones see only vulgarity and inappropriateness in his short story.

Intellectuals and politicians like Nicolae Iorga or Octavian Goga, important spokesmen for the Romanian national spirit, harshly criticized *Kyra Kyralina*'s fictional universe for its immorality. They particularly disliked the fact that, because of Romain Rolland's introduction to the book, this story was presented to the French public as realistic and even biographical. Nicolae Iorga writes:

> A preface by Mr. Romain Rolland warmly recommends to the French public a short story written by a writer from Brăila, who has been living for a long time in France, Mr.

---

[19] He also had a strong connection to Russia, as Istrati had a deep sympathy for the communist party for almost all his life. His admiration changed to disillusion when he visited Russia and he expressed this disillusion in *Vers l'autre flamme*, a very powerful essay where he severely criticized the Russian communist regime; after that Istrati lost the sympathy of his French communist friends, he returned to Romania, where he was perhaps more marginal than in France. He died bitter and isolated shortly afterwards.

Panait Istrati. And the famous French writer doesn't forget to tell his readers that Mr. Istrati tells his own life in the pages that come after the preface.[20]

Iorga deplores the fact that this Balkanic and exotic universe might become in the eyes of the French public a realistic image representing Romania and he fears the confusion between reality and exotic clichés that a French reader might make. The review continues with a second statement, attacking the truthfulness of *Kyra Kyralina*.

> But the story that is told using the title of an old Romanian ballad cannot come from the memoirs of any man who has any respect for a human being. A murderer for a father, who badly beats and disfigures a mother whose occupation is to receive different guests every night, a sister who does the same and a homosexual for an uncle; fate simply cannot accumulate such horrors in the same group and nobody would go as far as to expose such a family story (see note 20 above).

The poet and politician Octavian Goga underlines Istrati's marginality in a polemic article which responds to an article where Istrati had criticized Mihai Eminescu, the 'national poet', for his nationalistic views. Goga describes Istrati and his literary work underlining the distance between a marginal writer like Istrati and a national figure, a centre of the Romanian canon, like Eminescu: 'The author of a *Kyra* from the suburbs of Brăila – who has seen the light of day in Paris – attacks the granite block'.[21] Istrati was a nephew of a Turk and the illegitimate son of a Greek, so we can easily understand that, even if he admires Eminescu as a poet, and he says, he does not approve of his Romantic views on ethnicity. But Goga sees Istrati's criticism as inadequate because it comes from an unknown, marginal writer, who dares to attack Eminescu, the national writer, symbolized by the granite.

5. Modernism versus Balkanism

Twenty years later, when he publishes his history of the Romanian literature, G. Călinescu canonizes Camil Petrescu and completely excludes Panait Istrati. It is also true that after 1947, Istrati could not have been published anyway in occupied Romania, because he had severely criticized the politics of the Soviet Union. But the contrast between the two writers continues to this day, when Camil Petrescu is to be found in all course books and literary histories, presented as one of the main inventors of Romanian modernist novel. Istrati instead is very little studied in Romania, although in France or

---

[20]   'Haiduci *à la française*', *Ramuri*, no. 14-15, 15 July-1 August 1924.

[21]   Octavian Goga, 'Pânze de paianjen', *Țara românească*, 5 October 1924.

Italy researchers organize conferences and publish critical studies and new editions of his works.[22]

The reason why Romanian critics never really appreciated Istrati's literary work has something to do with Balkanism. In his stories the main action takes place in a Balkanic Romania peopled by Turks, Greeks and other 'minorities', with the port of Brăila seen as a melting pot, where the inhabitants live an oriental way of life and this was not perceived as realistic. The fascination that French reader felt for this text filled with eroticism, voyages to oriental, colourful places, mysterious adventures is highly understandable since it corresponds to a literary pattern invented by the 19th century – or even the 18th, if we think of Voltaire –, but it does not correspond to the Romanian taste because exoticism had never been a common theme in our early Modern literature.

Maria Todorova's analysis has pointed out the nuances Balkanism takes in cultural studies.[23] She notices that although '"Balkanism" evolved independently from "Orientalism" and, in certain aspects, against or despite it, partially because southeastern Europe (or the Balkans) has been considered geopolitically distinct from the near or the Middle East' (p. 455), there are many links between them:

> Geographically inextricable from Europe, yet culturally constructed as 'the other', the Balkans became, in time, the object of a number of externalized political, ideological and cultural frustrations and have served as a repository of negative characteristics against which a positive and self-congratulatory image of the 'European' and 'the west' has been constructed (p. 455).

The main reason why Western Europeans saw the Balkans as oriental, especially during the 18th and 19th century, but then even during the first half of the 20th century, was its political association to the Ottoman Empire.[24] That is why countries like Bulgaria or even Romania, who is not

---

[22]   The last French edition is *Oeuvres* (Paris: Phebus, 2006). See also Gisèle Vanhèse's very recent *Deux migrants de l'écriture. Panait Istrati et Felicia Mihali* (Università della Calabria: Centro Editoriale e Librario, 2008).

[23]   Maria Todorova, 'The Balkans: From Discovery to Invention', *Slavic Review*, 53 (Summer, 1994), pp. 453-482. See also Marcel Cornis-Pope, 'Danubian Bridges and Divides: Balkan Multiculturality North and South of the Danube', in *Mythistory and Narratives of the Nation in the Balkans,* ed. by Tatjana Aleksić (Cambridge: Cambridge Scholars Publishing, 2007), and K. E. Fleming, 'Orientalism, the Balkans, and Balkan Historiography', *The American Historical Review*, 105 (Oct., 2000), pp. 1218-1233.

[24]   Pierre Loti, *Suprêmes visions d'Orient*, éd. Calman-Lévy, Victor Hugo, *Les orientales*, Paul Morand, *La nuit turque, Rien que la terre*, Grasset, 1926.

geographically in the Balkans, get to be described with the stereotypes associated with exotic spaces.[25]

There is a pejorative connotation associated to the Balkanic universe, imagined as a place where the oriental culture created a colourful universe where 'European' rules are out of place. Westerners perceive the theme of the voyage, the oriental tales, the *haidouks*, and characters like Kyra Kyralina or Stavru as exotic and thus, the Balkanic universe integrates oriental themes such as the voyage to the Far East. French intellectuals perceived Romanian authors as 'exotic', whereas Romanian writers hoped to be accepted as Europeans.

The difference between the ways in which these two writers were read by the Romanian critics is particularly interesting because it shows that everybody was well aware of the way in which literature generates a national image. Used during the 19th century in order to consolidate national identity, literature is seen at the beginning of 20th century as a way to integrate Western Europe by assimilating its culture. So, critics who appreciated the modernist qualities of Camil Petrescu's novels, like Lovinescu, considered him first of all a writer compatible with European literature. And Romanian literature had been looking at Western Europe, especially Austria, Germany and France, ever since the 19th-century Romantic Movement.

Belonging to European literature seems to be the deepest desire of two of the most influential Romanian critics who wrote between the '30s and the '40s and who practically made the Romanian canon, Călinescu and Lovinescu, – and Modernism is seen as a synonym to European.[26] The main point of my analysis has to do with the fact a central place in the canon is given to those writers that are considered to be compatible to the European canon. I do not mean to say that these critics pay attention only to the most fashionable forms in European literature or that they do not appreciate original writers. On the contrary, Călinescu, who is not particularly fond of Modernism, is very interested in original Romanian writers.

And what place has G. Călinescu reserved then for Camil Petrescu, our first case study? A central one, Camil Petrescu is considered, along with two other writers, Hortensia Papadat Bengescu and Liviu Rebreanu, the inventor of the Romanian Modernist Novel. And what place did Călinescu give Panait Istrati? None at all, he barely mentions his name pretending he does so

---

[25]   See Paul Morand's *Bucarest*.

[26]   See for example *Geographies of Modernism. Literatures, cultures, spaces*, ed. by Peter Brooker and Andrew Thacker (London and New York: Routledge, 2005), especially 'Geographies of modernism in a globalizing world' by Andreas Huyssen (geographical marginality and modernism) and Rebecca Beasley's 'Russia and the invention of the modernist intelligentsia' (how Russian literature was perceived by the English).

because Istrati wrote in French. The fact that Istrati's work circulated in Europe where he was considered an interesting writer had no relevance for Călinescu, who includes some Romanian writers who wrote in French.

No place then for the migrant writer who made such bad ideological choices: as Istrati had chosen during the thirties to be an internationalist when everybody was nationalist, a communist, when everybody preferred fascism, and then denounced the soviet model when everybody seemed to believe in this new utopia. In fact, every ideological choice he made, though understandable now, had very bad effects on his career and his place in the literary canon.

Ideology is always present in the making of a national history of literature. As David Perkins notices, 'narrative literary history is shaped by desires'[27], and 'Like all traditional narrative, it presents an entity – or hero – going through a transition' (p. 30). If we accept the fact that there is always a character in a literary history, then we should ask ourselves who the main character is in Călinescu's history. Călinescu's desire appears to be to write a history of literature that could show how Romanian literature is at the same time original *and* European. This is why his history is made from a comparatist point of view; and, if Lovinescu was mainly interested in the ideology of Modernism, Călinescu's choices are more canonical. He compares Camil Petrescu to Abbé Prevost's *Manon Lescaut*, to Stendhal's *La chartreuse de Parme* and, of course, to Proust. But Călinescu doesn't show any interest in the circulation of Romanian literature.

These two case studies are interesting because they show how the relationship between national literature and world literature is mediated by the confrontation between Modernism and Balkanism, seen as literary currents, set of *topoi* and styles, but also ideologies. In fact, we can consider that the great difference in the position these two authors occupy in the canon comes from the fact that they embody these two opposite literary worlds, Modernism and Balkanism. Their reception is so different because, on the one hand, there is no great interest for the French reader to see how a Romanian author, no matter how original or talented, adapted the Proustian narrative formula; instead, having the illusion that he travels in the oriental exotic Balkans and that he sees everything with the eyes of a homosexual teenager is much more appealing. On the other hand, an exotic story written in the Romantic style of the 19th century does not attract a critic who prefers instead a novel with an original and daring structure.

If we read G. Călinescu's *Romanian Literary History* with the eye of a comparatist we find many interesting aspects – not only has he a lengthy chapter on the 'discovery of Europe', but he also makes a lot of references to

---

[27]   David Perkins, *Is Literary History Possible?* (Baltimore: The Johns Hopkins University Press, 1992), p. 34.

European currents, writers and *topoï*. So he seems aware of the dialogue between world and national literature, but he only looks at what is coming in, and not at what is going out. Coming back to David Damrosch's definition quoted in my first lines, when speaking about world literature we should speak about 'a double refraction'. This double refraction is missing in our two case studies and this is what makes them interesting. My second conclusion is that sometimes the canon of a national literature is determined by world literature and this happened even before the recent globalization. Thus, when speaking about canon formation, we should already take into consideration the ellipse David Damrosch was talking about: in some cases the value of a national writer is negotiated in conformity with the international tendencies. But then again whether these international tendencies belong to 'world literature' rather than to 'global literature', it is another matter.

WORKS CITED

Primary Sources

Istrati, Panait, *Œuvres* (Paris: Phebus, 2006)

——. *Vers l'autre flamme* (Paris: Éditions Rieder, 1929)

Petrescu, Camil, *Ultima noapte de dragoste, întâia noapte de război* (1930), (trans. in French *Dernière nuit d'amour, première nuit de guerre*, 2006)

——. 'Noua structură şi opera lui Marcel Proust', *Revista Fundaţiilor Regale*, 1935

——. *Patul lui Procust* (1933) (in French M*adame T,* trans. by Jean-Louis Courriol, 1998; in English *The Bed of Procustes*, trans. by Ileana Alexandra Orlich, Fundaţia Camil Petrescu Publishing, 2008)

Morand, Paul, *Bucarest* (Paris: Editions Plon, 1934)

Secondary Sources

Aleksić, Tatjana, ed., *Mythistory and Narratives of the Nation in the Balkans* (Cambridge: Cambridge Scholars Publishing, 2007)

Brooker, Peter, and Andrew Thacker, eds., *Geographies of Modernism. Literatures, cultures, spaces* (London: Routledge, 2005)

Casanova, Pascale, 'Literature as a World', *New Left Review*, 31 Jan.-Feb. 2005

Călinescu, George, *Istoria literaturii române de la origini și până în prezent* (*The History of Romanian Literature from the Origins to the Present*) (București: Minerva, 1982)

Corniș-Pope, Marcel, and John Neubauer, 'Towards a History of the Literary Cultures in East-Central Europe: Theoretical Reflections', *ACLS Occasional Paper*, No. 52 (2002), 14-16

Curtius, Ernst Robert, *European Literature and the Latin Middle* Ages, trans. by Willard R. Trask (New York: Harper Row Publishers, 1953)

Damrosch, David, *What is World Literature* (Princeton: Princeton University Press, 2003)

Didier, Béatrice, ed., *Precis de littérature Européenne* (Paris: PUF, 1998)

Fleming, K. E., 'Orientalism, the Balkans, and Balkan Historiography', *The American Historical Review*, 105 (Oct., 2000), 1218-33

Gephardt, Katarina, '"The Enchanted Garden" or "The Red Flag": Eastern Europe in Late Nineteenth-Century British Travel Writing', *Journal of Narrative Theory* 35.3 (Fall 2005)

Geblesco, E., *Panaït Istrati et la métaphore paternelle* (Paris : Anthropos, 1989)

Goga, Octavian, 'Pânze de paianjen', *Ţara românească*, 5 October 1924

Iorga, Nicolae, *Histoire de la littérature roumaine contemporaine* (Bucarest: Editura Adevărului, 1934)

—. 'Haiduci *à la française*', *Ramuri*, no. 14-15, 15 July-1 August, 1924

Iorgulescu, Mircea, *Panaït Istrati* (Paris: Oxus Éditions, 2004)

Jutrin-Klener, M., H. Lenz, D. Lérault, M. Popovici, E. Rossi, C. Rossi, J.-M. Santraud, *Les haïdoucs dans l'œuvre de Panaït Istrati: l'insoumission des vaincus* (Paris: L'Harmattan, 2002)

Lovinescu, Eugen, *Istoria literaturii române contemporane* (*The History of Romanian Contemporary Literature*) (Bucureşti: Minerva, 1973)

Mougin, Pascal, and Karen Haddad Wotling, eds., *Dictionnaire mondial des littératures* (Paris: Larousse, 2002)

Munteanu, Basil, *Panorama de la littérature roumaine contemporaine* (Paris: Éditions du Sagittaire, 1938)

Perkins, David, *Is Literary History Possible?* (Baltimore: The Johns Hopkins University Press, 1992)

Popa-Lisseanu, Doina, *Panait Istrati: una escritura encendida: estudio de la obra de un escritor rumano de expresión francesa* (Madrid: UNED, 1988)

Seidmann, David, *L'existence juive dans l'œuvre de Panaït Istrati* (Paris: Éditions Nizet, 1984)

Todorova, Maria, 'The Balkans: From Discovery to Invention', *Slavic Review*, 53 (Summer, 1994)

Vanhèse, Gisèle, ed., *Deux migrants de l'écriture. Panait Istrati et Felicia Mihali* (Università della Calabria: Centro Editoriale e Librario, 2008)

Zarifopol-Johnston, Ilinca, 'Found in Translation: The Two Lives of E. M. Cioran; or How Can One Be a Comparatist', *Comparative Literature Studies*, 44 (2007)

Ileana Orlich

Modernism and the Male World:
The Crisis of Masculinity in *The Bed of Procrustes*

And still they come and go: and this is all I know –
That from the gloom I watch an endless picture-show.
Siegfried Sasoon, *Picture-Show*

Several significant modernist techniques are effectively displayed in Camil Petrescu's *The Bed of Procrustes*, a novel emblematic of the century's sexual anxiety and anesthesia and of the uninhabitable, fractured landscape that evokes a Procrustean bed. The novel's parallel story lines animate male homosocial desire, a crisis of masculinity, and an acute dissociation of sensibility, akin to the 'hysteric' disposition of T. S. Eliot's poetry and corresponding to his broodings in the famous essay praising the Metaphysical poets. In Petrescu's novel, the two male protagonists – a poet whose cultural and personal anxieties both embody and perform male hysteria and his modernist double whose own sexual anxiety forges an hysteric identification with the poet that transcends male homosocial bonding – reflect modern man's aesthetic and cultural detachment and disembodiment that *The Bed of Procrustes*, following Baudelaire, Pound, and Eliot, ultimately delineates.

Published in 1933, Camil Petrescu's second novel, *The Bed of Procrustes*, is considered his masterpiece. With its highly unconventional style that merges narrative consciousness and traditional dialogue, it offers both an extension of the Proustian novelistic technique and a new modernist fiction in the Romanian literature of the interwar period.[1]

---

[1]   Space will not allow me to enumerate the great number of short, disparate articles from literary journals and newspapers that mention Camil Petrescu's indebtedness to Proust. As a synthesis of such views, mention needs to be made however of the respected critic Paul Georgescu's lengthy analysis in two essays, 'Frumuseţea adevărului' (*The Beauty of Truth*) and 'Clasicismul creator' (*Creative Classicism*), both included in his critical volume *Printre cărţi* (*Among Books*) (Bucureşti: Eminescu, 1973). After discussing the numerous similarities between the two novelists, Georgescu's commentary emphasizes the different scope of Petrescu's novel which, unlike the Proustian narratives, dramatizes first and foremost a panoramic view of the Romanian society between the two wars.

From the start, the author-narrator recommends himself as a simple go-between whose role is to put the readers in direct contact with the novel's characters – two pairs of lovers who narrate their lives either directly or through their disembodied voices echoed in their journals or private correspondences. Thus, although the journal and letter writing are a logical extension of the nineteenth-century novel's implicit promise of intimacy, as representations of consciousness they operate in *The Bed of Procrustes* beyond traditional novelistic depiction by simulating a perfect knowledge of other minds without recourse to speech and by simultaneously appropriating and abandoning the distinction between narrative and dialogue, interiority and exteriority.

The novel's first three chapters contain the letters of a strange Mrs. T to the nameless narrator, who had previously suggested to her that she should write down her interesting life. The bulk of the book includes the diary of young Fred Vasilescu, a dashing man-about-town, pilot, and wealthy heir to one of the country's greatest fortunes. He, too, has been encouraged by the narrator to put in writing his various exploits as a trendsetter on the party circuit of a very elegant 1930s Bucharest and his secret, consuming love for Mrs. T. The novel concludes with 'Epilogue I', recounted by Fred Vasilescu, and 'Epilogue II', written by the author-narrator who gives a final account of Fred's death.

Beyond detailing his two-year relationship with Mrs. T and the subsequent two years when he continued to love her mostly from a distance he imposes himself in spite, or maybe because, of her great love for him, Fred's diary also focuses on a particular afternoon spent in the bedroom of a quasi-prostitute and sometime actress, Emilia Răchitaru. It is here that Fred sees the letters she received from George Demetru Ladima, a journalist and poet friend of Fred, who had committed suicide four months prior to the time when Fred visits Emilia. Feigning indifference for the letters in order to deceive the unsuspecting Emilia, who thinks that she is entertaining her late afternoon lover, Fred is shocked to discover upon reading them Ladima's love for this vulgar and crude woman.

Fred's reading of Ladima's letters allows for side commentaries and insertion of stories that, while occasionally connected to Fred's own life and interactions with Mrs. T, expand primarily on the dead poet's thoughts, feelings, and epistolary accounts of his professional hardships and unwillingness to compromise his journalistic and social idealism in order to adapt to bourgeois (Procrustean) conformity and political compromise. The well synchronized episodes that merge Ladima's stories told in his letters to Emilia with events Fred remembers and recounts while reading Ladima's letters in Emilia's bedroom offer an ingeniously constructed narrative.

In modernist fashion, it enacts the parallel actions of the two couples, Fred/Mrs. T and Ladima/Emilia, and counterpoises them within the shifting terms of compulsory heterosexuality. As *The Bed of Procrustes* makes clear, in the twentieth-century Romanian society women had ultimate importance in the schema of man's gender construction – representing an absolute not only of exchange value, but also of being the ultimate victims of the painful contradictions in the gender system that regulates men and the male world.

In the novel's world, the two women appear to stand poised waiting for the men to separate themselves outside the feminine sphere and outside the women's lot. An especially incisive commentator, Fred appears as the socially empowered voice of a higher patriarchal utterance – so very high that it give him throughout the narrative a concrete and potent leverage over mere women. More importantly, his patriarchy is not just a monolithic mechanism for subordinating the female to the male; it is a web of valences and significations that commands women's surrender while asserting the intense and potent male patriarchal bonds and relations that regard women as a subaltern gender. Thus, in the novel's male-centered society, Fred's conception of women's role is integrated within the limits of homosociality – what Eve Kosofsky Sedgwick designates as 'the social bond between persons of the same sex; […] a neologism, obviously formed by analogy with "homosexual", and just as obviously meant to be distinguished from "homosexual" […] applied to such activities as "male bonding"'.[2]

Filtered through Fred's eyes, Emilia and Mrs. T are antagonistic types in relation both to their own sexuality and to male homosocial desire (or man's yearning for male bonding). Conducting his analysis of women as a form of male empowerment that concomitantly uncovers most assiduously the bond between the male protagonists, Fred considers Emilia, for instance, 'like a tool that conducts electricity badly or gives you the impression of a discharged battery, because it was initially damaged'; with similar condescendence, he finds 'Mrs. T. seems full of life, which makes her excessively sexual, even in the gestures that are inertial in other women (like laying a napkin on a small table when writing a letter; watching the tram leave)' (p. 241).[3] In the obligatory conservation of gendered roles and of male ascendancy, Fred's views gravitate in both instances around the woman's sexuality, which is meaningful in the novel chiefly within the context of woman representing symbolic goods between men. In those terms, vulgar femininity on display belongs to Emilia, the would-be actress and occasional prostitute, and reticent femininity is associated with Mrs. T. If the

---

[2]   Eve Kosofsky Sedgwick, *Between Men: English Literature and Male Homosocial Desire* (New York: Columbia University Press, 1985), p. 1.

[3]   All citations are from Camil Petrescu, *The Bed of Procrustes*, trans. by Ileana Orlich (Bucharest: Cultural Foundation Camil Petrescu Publishing, 2008).

coarse and vulgar Emilia sells her body and has no goals beyond wishing to be distributed in a good role on stage, Mrs. T is a model of beauty and refinement. Devoting her time to the shop where she works as a high-end interior designer, Mrs. T feels liberated from patriarchal control and indulges in the thought that her job is the source of her independence and power. 'This job', she tells Fred, 'is my independence, the money I earn give me the right to be myself, to buy nice books and things, not to be offended by the landlord and be kept safe from indecent proposals' (p. 225). But such self-empowering thoughts cannot enhance the status of women like Mrs. T within a prohibitive continuum structure of men-promoting-men. In the novel's male-dominated world, the schema of female sexuality, whether it be that of the virtuous or the whore, requires the banishment of the woman, in an affair between men in which the woman's role is intensely moralized and her treatment condescending at best.

In contrast with the two women, Fred and Ladima appear closely tied beyond the categorization of 'patriarchy' as mechanisms of the enduring inequality of power between women and men. To the narrative schism within femininity itself that Emilia and Mrs. T represent, Fred and Ladima appear as malleable and transitive bodies and sensibilities, mutating into both passive and active roles and an elaborate doubling and reversal of identities. Even though Fred has known Ladima only for the four years prior to the narrative present, their encounters during that period touch on the salient points of their entire lives. Further, no matter how different Ladima's reclusive spirit may appear next to Fred's mundane pursuits, such differences are predicated on fundamental similarities. For even though Fred is highly social, a loyal friend and ardent conversationalist who commands devoted friendships, those who know him well recognize his essential solitariness due to 'some loyalty and delicacy, a sort of sincerity of life' (p. 30) that also define Ladima's character.

In reading Ladima's letters while simultaneously listening to Emilia's stories, Fred discovers that he shares with the dead poet a symmetrical articulation of man's dependence on patriarchal heterosexuality as a sensitive register for making intelligible the play of desire and self-identification by which men negotiate their social and gender identity – an aspect Fred addresses unequivocally when he states that 'for about two years now I've been feeling the need to always be seen with one woman or another' (p. 54).

Concerning such issues, Emilia's interventions that are inserted between the readings to provide additional information or clarify the content of Ladima's letters serve two important purposes. First, they make warranted and explicit Ladima's jealousy and his threatened masculinity caused by his accurate perceptions of her numerous betrayals. Secondly, through Fred's perceptions of an alarming scarcity of love that Emilia can offer, they reveal indirectly both the mechanisms by which gender inequality is structured and the leap from the relation of heterosexual to male homosocial bonds. Specifically, since Emilia's sexual manipulations are her primary strategy for economic survival, Fred insinuates with apparently timeless authority the process by which in the schema of female sexuality woman and whore beget each other, taking their shape from the social dictates of gender difference. Further, since Fred visits Emilia to satisfy his natural quota of sexual discharge, sexuality is a highly charged signifier for differentials of power in which women, split between the virginal and the whorish, submit to men within the context of circulation and exchange prompting them to seek bonds of higher order and substance with other men.

With Fred enacting his double part as an investigative observer of the relationship between Ladima and Emilia and of his own relationship with Mrs. T, the couples' parallel stories draw on the complementary figures of the four lovers while building up a combination of tension and mystery, or a 'superior detective emotion'[4] haunting the lovers' lives and deaths: Ladima commits suicide after learning the truth about Emilia and her sexual dalliances and Fred dies, after rejecting all pleas of being reunited with Mrs. T, in a plane crash that has all the indications of a possible suicide.

For many years, I took Camil Petrescu at face value. As my analysis demonstrates, I've done exclusively straightforward readings of his characters and concentrated almost exclusively on homosociality without picking up on the warnings about missing the obvious with which *The Bed of Procrustes* is shot through in the case of the two male protagonists: Ladima fantastically unable to see that Emilia is a paid escort to wealthy and socially influential men and Fred incredibly unwilling to allow for the comfort of Mrs. T's love for him. As I've read Camil Petrescu more intensely since translating this novel, I've come to think that there is room in *The Bed of Procrustes* for discussing not only the dictates of the male protagonists' homosocial bond, but also, and perhaps more importantly, their ultimate inability or refusal of connection with women as a demonstration of a modernist crisis of masculinity – a crisis both willed and tragic.

Further, if it is true in this novel that both women characters, Emilia and Mrs. T, exist in some meaningful relation to the role of 'lady', their signifying relation with the two male characters grows more tortuous adding another Procrustean dimension to the men's stories. Since Mrs. T is a woman as she is a lady, and Emilia is a woman not in relation to her own desired role of 'lady', but only negatively, in a compensatory relation to Mrs. T, what is

---

[4]   George Călinescu, *Istoria literaturii române de la origini şi până în prezent* (*The History of Romanian Literature from the Origins to the Present*) (Bucureşti: Minerva, 1982), pp. 662-3.

clear is the centrality of sexuality in the novel, and of sex as an especially charged leverage-point, or point for the exchange of meanings between genders.

From such a perspective, and keeping in mind even a summary account of the novel's plot, *The Bed of Procrustes* strikingly echoes the efforts of modernists like Ezra Pound and T.S. Eliot to solidify the male's intellectual and sexual anxiety over the 'fermenting chaos' or unruly corporeal, often coded as the feminine. Pound explicitly formulates creativity as 'the phallus or spermatozoid charging head-on the female chaos'[5] while Eliot, somewhat less overtly, complains that Hamlet lacks an 'objective correlative' and suffers from 'the stuff that the writer could not drag to light'.[6] In discussing both Ladima and Fred in their relations to Emilia and Mrs. T, this 'stuff' is linked, as I propose to show, to an anxiety and crisis of masculinity (or male hysteria) that found their way in *The Bed of Procrustes* after being drawn from the two favorite sons of literary high modernism, Pound and Eliot, with whom Camil Petrescu was well acquainted from his engagement with the world of theatre and the literati.[7]

Grafted into the narrative much like Eliot's catalogued typology of women in the manuscript of *The Waste Land*,[8] the two women, Emilia and Mrs. T, stand for bad and, respectively, good womanhood. The choice of sexuality as a thematic emphasis for my discussion brings into salient focus at this point the degraded sex-scene between Fred and Emilia on which most of the narrative is centered. Carried out in Emilia's bedroom, this scene that also functions as the novel's primary setting is highly reminiscent of the carbuncular clerk and the typist's sordid encounter in the 'violet hour' of T.S. Eliot's *The Waste Land*. For although different in form from the poem, *The Bed of Procrustes* dramatizes, like the poem, the protagonists' experiences of sexual repression projected against an urban, decayed background and complicated by the pairing of unlikely lovers whose stories, feelings, and confessions trigger dislocated desire and sexual anxiety.

---

5   Remy de Gourmont, *Natural Philosophy of Love*, trans. with a postscript by Ezra Pound (New York: privately printed for Rarity Press, 1931), p. 169.

6   'Hamlet and His Problems', in *The Sacred Wood and Major Early Essays* (New York: Dover Publications, Inc., 1998), p. 58.

7   Camil Petrescu (1894-1957) was the director of the National Theatre in Bucharest (beginning in 1939) and became a member of the Romanian Academy a decade before his death in 1947.

8   Eliot's portraits of women, which suffered great changes after Ezra Pound's cuts in Eliot's manuscripts, include such 'types' as the 'plain simple bitch' and the 'strolling slattern in a tawdry gown'. For a detailed list, see T. S. Eliot, *The Waste Land: A Facsimile and Transcript of the Original Drafts*, ed. by Valerie Eliot (London: Faber and Faber, 1971), p. 27.

The evolution of male hysteria into a pronounced and even commonplace condition coincided with an array of historical and cultural shifts, of which the most well documented event in undoing social, gender, and sexual categories was the mass destruction of the First World War. Adding to the symptoms of 'shell-shock' and of the 'war neurotic' Freud articulates in *Beyond the Pleasure Principle*, Sandra Gilbert and Susan Gubar write that 'the unmanning terrors of combat lead not just to a generalized sexual anxiety but also to an anger directed specifically against the female'.[9] Beyond the mass destruction reverberating with a dissentegration or dissociation of body and soul, women appear as emblems of sexuality gone awry. Either as violated ingénues or neurasthenic vamps, women are demonized through mid-century modernism for their newly acquired liberties and targeted for the modern male's 'wounding', or even castration.

Like Eliot and Pound, who did not participate directly in war, Camil Petrescu was highly conscious of the male body's fragility and its potential resemblance to the female hysteric replicated away from the trenches as the less easily definable traumas of social angst. His first novel, *Last Night of Love, First Night of War* (1930), dealt primarily with the specter of sexual anxiety, the trauma men exhibit after being stuck in the trenches, and their overtly feminine responsiveness to shock translated into a crisis of masculinity. Petrescu's second novel, *The Bed of Procrustes*, continues and develops its characters' threatened masculinity by complicating their social and cultural circumstances and affective engagements and by delving further into the mechanisms and paradigms of masculinity in crisis.

Maximizing the veneer of respectability she possesses, Emilia secures Ladima's love by lying through calculated maneuvers about her scandalous sexual encounters carried out publicly. Located primarily at the crossroads of Emilia's observations and of Fred's readings of Ladima's own letters to Emilia, Ladima's character and sensibility are framed in Fred's consummate narrative. Its calculated cleverness stirs deep compassion for the betrayed and tormented Ladima and contempt for the promiscuous Emilia. Looking at a photograph attached to a pile of letters tied together with a ribbon in one of Emilia's drawers, Fred talks about Ladima's tall and thin looks, 'with round eyes and large, deep sockets [...] with a sergeant-major's moustache and a hairdresser's parting, with his black alpaca jacket and white shirt, the collar always too wide, starched, with big round cuffs, like rain pipes, pinned with pink cufflinks onto the shirt, while the other cufflinks were small sticks, of course in gold – who knows what souvenir [...] He would have had a beautiful head, if he hadn't been so old-fashioned [...] I don't think he was more than 35-40 years old (p. 67). Ladima's unhappiness is in the first place

---

9   Sandra M. Gilbert, and Susan Gubar, *No Man's Land: The Place of the Woman Writer in the Twentieth Century*, 2nd vol (New Haven: Yale University Press, 1989), p. 260.

about Emilia's depravity, i.e., her numerous erotic encounters that divide her
ever more completely from Ladima's purity and devotion. His most piercing
emotion seems attached to jealousy, and to the subsequent suppression or
concealment of sexual desire bound to turn Ladima into a disabled man, split
between erotic servitude to Emilia and an incorruptible political and artistic
engagement that makes him feared by the establishment (the corrupt political
scene of Nae Gheorghidiu and his friend, the wealthy Tănase Vasilescu,
Fred's father) and highly respected as a gifted poet and director of the
prestigious journal *Veacul* (*The Century*).

Ladima's naiveté regarding Emilia reveals a pattern of refusals,
suspending rather than negating the possibility of being duped and producing
an unlimited – because undefined – psychological potential, which is far from
ascetic, prude, or transparent. Although he is not, as the literary critics of
Communist Romania considered him, the exploited artist destroyed by the
pressures of capitalism and material deprivation,[10] Ladima exemplifies a
passing away of a certain type of artistic sensibility: his penchant for
chivalric posturing (he risks his life to defend Mrs. T from an insanely
jealous Fred), lengthy and passionate letters, and lyrical expression that once
connected an individual with tradition seem to be facing the endless vertigo
of modernity while his journal writing (an alien usurper of storytelling) is an
indication of his sustained effort to cope with the abbreviated nature of
modern life. But this gradual atrophy of narrative and lyric form required in
an age cut short by the shift to information can only partially justify Ladima's
isolation and lack of connection to his social circumstances, especially since
he continues to be highly regarded as a poet and feared as a journalist with a
poisonous pen.

The profound significance of Ladima's inwardness and of his
involvement with Emilia is best captured in Rimbaud's verse that Ladima
himself, painfully aware of his condition, writes to Emilia in one of his last
letters: '*Des serpents géants dévorés par des punaises*' (p. 273).[11] As each of
Ladima's letters addressed to Emilia that Fred reads is almost always
followed by Emilia's vulgar commentary, Ladima's disembodied voice
reverberates as that of the ideal poet constructed in Eliot's theory of

---

[10]   Once again, space will not allow me to mention the numerous names of critics who regarded
       Ladima as a victim of capitalism, a latter-day Bartleby of the journalistic world. Chief
       among such views is Sorin Arghir's commentary in his 'Preface' to the Year Edition of
       Patul lui Procust (*The Bed of Procrustes*) (București: Editura de Stat pentru Literatură și
       Artă, 1957). Arghir writes: 'Prin Ladima, Camil Petrescu înfățișează, de fapt, tipul
       proletarului intelectual, prezintă condiția de viață a acestuia în societatea burgheză'
       (*Through Ladima's character, Camil Petrescu portrays, in fact, the intellectual, proletarian
       type, presents his [the intellectual's] living conditions in a bourgeois society*).

[11]   'Huge snakes devoured by bed bugs.'

'dissociation of sensibility' and of a spectral Fisher-King whose sexual anxieties are coincident with Ladima's personal experiences of sexual repression. Focused on journalistic writing and his own poetry, Ladima has only once been involved sexually with Emilia and stubbornly saves their intimacy for a muffled and distant future of married bliss. Further, Ladima's sudden and impervious infatuation with Emilia on the one hand, and his social prominence on the other, reveal Ladima's double personality – a split pointing to the 'hysteric' relationship between mind and body that represents a dominant version of the crisis of masculinity in modernism.

According to Eliot, a 'dissociation' or split between intellect and emotion, a 'disparity between idea and image', reflects a 'progressive deterioration of poetry since the thirteenth century'.[12] In his famous essay praising the Metaphysical poets, Eliot broods: 'In the seventeenth century a dissociation of sensibility set in, from which we have never recovered'.[13] Such literary dissociation, which according to Eliot energizes innovation of the modern lyric, explains Ladima's superior creativity that even his detractors are forced to acknowledge. A prolific and talented poet, Ladima is the very embodiment of what Eliot hails when he proclaims the dissociated subject as the ideal poet: 'the more perfect the artist, the more completely separate in him will be the man who suffers and the mind which creates' (*Tradition and Individual Talent*, see note 13 above, p. 31). Inserted in the letters to Emilia, Ladima's poems provide an imaginary space where he articulates his brooding and anxieties over personal experiences. Hinging not upon his erotic desire for Emilia but upon the impossibility of his sexual self-identification through her, Ladima is an off-screen spectator who 'sees' but refuses to accept Emilia's promiscuity while seeking refuge in his regenerative verse. Detaching physical engagement from his consciousness, Ladima forges a hysterical identification with Emilia through a systematic corporeal self-mutilation and passive participation in his own sexual fantasy involving Emilia and their love relationship.

At the opposite end of the spectrum from Emilia's vulgarity and cheap sexuality, Mrs. T is the epitome of elegance and grace. Her strong sexual desire and erotic encounters with Fred speak of a woman trapped in the cage of her own passion. But her satisfaction of being understood is tainted because Fred, the man she desperately loves, does not wish to stoop to self-exposure. There is, in Fred's reticence and even in Mrs. T's behavior, a certain vacillation between two lovers' communication with each other and

---

[12] 'Lecture I: Toward a Definition of Metaphysical Poetry', in Ronald Schuchard, ed., *The Varieties of Metaphysical Poetry* (New York: Harcourt Brace and Company, 1993), p. 227.

[13] 'The Metaphysical Poets', in *The Sacred Wood and Major Early Essays* (New York: Dover Publications, Inc., 1998), p. 127.

an entrenched cynicism about the dishonesty of social signification. They always meet in remote locations in the country, to secure and protect the secrecy of their relationship from Bucharest's high society where both of them are highly visible personages. Swinging between a Romantic belief in psychological interiority and a Realist attention to the social significance of a couple, the relationship between Fred and Mrs. T evinces the characters' conflicted psychological self that wishes to be utterly transparent and yet resents the suggestion that his secrets are legible.

As Mrs. T cannot ultimately fulfill her lover's fantasy of silent communication and his attempt to reconcile the surface/depth dimension of his life, Fred appears broken and amputated emotionally like someone who both dissects and mutilates his own flesh. His feelings regarding Mrs. T reveal an acute discomfort with her body and a particular resistance to female corporeality that hinge upon his identification with hysteria. More often than not, Fred's reflections on Mrs. T, and especially his fragmented close-ups of Emilia half naked in her room, echo Eliot's portraits of women and the great poet's own discomforts with female corporeality fractured into multiple women in both *The Love Song of J. Alfred Prufrock* and *The Waste Land*. As in the two poems, *The Bed of Procrustes*'s thin plot pivots upon the tropes of sexual anesthesia and castration enacted by both Fred's and Ladima's characters.

While visiting Emilia, Fred acts and comports himself much like Prufrock when he confesses his essential fear and dissociation of women and shows his hysterical symptoms to be both etched upon his body's surface and projected elsewhere: 'I've never been married, I haven't even lived with a woman, and any woman that's ever undressed simply, for me, made me hold everything inside, astonished, the way one's breathing is held when waiting for something to happen' (p. 52). Like Prufrock, who is afraid to drown in the sensuality of the alluring mermaids 'in the chambers of the sea', Fred is afraid of Mrs. T's love even though he spies on her every move while letting his friends mock her for pursuing him. For much like Ladima's repudiation of his sexual needs and his glaring self-deception that perpetuate his excruciating pain, Fred's refusal to accept openly the real object of his desire (whether involving casual sex or particularly the obsession with Mrs. T), gives the most haunting portrait of the two men's essential loneliness, the longing or 'stuff' that they could not fully articulate even to themselves. This 'stuff' that even the writer could not drag explicitly to light, schematizes the two male characters' masculinity crisis, or the male hysteria, that *The Bed of Procrustes* ultimately delineates.

As a modern hysteric, Ladima corresponds to several of the type's characteristics enunciated in Pierre Janet's *Psychological Automatism* (1889) and *Mental State of Hysterics* (1892). The hysteric, according to Janet, was a victim of 'dissociation of personality' suffering from 'mental disaggregation', and 'psychic weakness'.[14] Whenever Emilia entertains her callers, Ladima plays cards in the room next door with her sister and, whenever Emilia is away from home with one of her many clients, he assumes that she is in her native town of Buzău to oversee family affairs. Even when he has occasional outbursts of jealous rage, Ladima ends up crawling back to Emilia and begging for her forgiveness, showing all the signs of an 'unassimilated second self, independent of our known one' (see note 14 above). By clinging to Emilia's promiscuity as cover over his castration, Ladima acts like a prototypical modern hysteric, whose body is neither fully under the control of consciousness nor entirely accountable by psychological discourse. His dissociated 'second self' gravitates in exclusively mechanical ways toward Emilia, whom he sees, in spite of all evidence pointing to the contrary, as an image of innocence and femininity, wronged by critics and jealous colleagues who refuse to admire her great talent as an actress.

Precisely because the possibility of loving a woman like Emilia is socially improbable, Fred is shocked to learn of Ladima's letters to her. As he cringes at Emilia's touches and panics at the thought of being found naked in her room by Emilia's sister, Valeria, whose voice he can hear on the other side of the door, Fred is actually projecting the habitual way in which he always retreats fearfully behind his circumspection from even the most tacit or intimate offers (notably Mrs. T's) to bridge the distance between himself and others. As an inactive lover following Emilia's body and movements whenever she hands him the letters or brings him coffee, Fred crafts himself into a disembodied observer enacting on an immediate level Baudelaire's dandy poet/spectator conceived as 'a kaleidoscope endowed with consciousness'.[15] Akin to Baudelaire's gaze in his paradigmatic poem *To a Red-Haired Beggar Girl*, Fred's camera eye objectifies Emilia's female body so that he himself can become what Pound, following Baudelaire, crafts: a spectator that is simultaneously a sexual agent ('enacting the copulation of images' [of Emilia's body]) and a disembodied observer.[16] Impelled by an intoxicating personal identification with Ladima while reading the poet's

---

[14] Qtd in Havelock Ellis, *Studies in the Psychology of Sex*, vol. I (Philadelphia: F. A. Davis Company, Publishers, 1913), p. 219.

[15] Charles Baudelaire, 'The Painter of Modern Life', in *Les Fleurs du Mal*, trans. by C. F. MacIntyre (Berkeley: University of California Press, 1947), p. 105.

[16] Fundamental to Pound's prototypical Imagist poem 'In a Station of the Metro', the compressed images result from the copulation of two depictable images in a visual metamorphosis that gives birth to a disembodied observer.

letters, Fred also offers himself as 'a contrasting disembodiment' while lying in Emilia's bed.[17]

Thus, although Fred visits Emilia on a sexual quest, he seems to extend his body through projection and displacement into a state of intense revulsion whenever she touches him. Fred's alienated body, which seems controlled by another master, performs the 'dissociation of sensibility' that structures many modernist works and that here, in Fred's case, underscores the male hysteric's paradoxical attraction to and disavowal of the corporeal by enacting the copulation of the juxtaposed images of Emilia's body for Fred as the disembodied observer. Sitting 'dryly' on her bed, Fred observes

> Emilia undress[es] in silence. Her arms stretched, she lifts her coffee-coloured dress over her head, then her chemise, and she remains naked, with a full midriff, with soft and a little smoky skin, only waiting for the body to bend to become thick lines. Her breasts are held, like those of a dancer in a shell, in the black net cups of her brassiere (nets which remind me of those used by men to hold their hair in place). A blue belt presses a little into her stomach, and from its sides hang the garters that stretch her stockings. Framed between the belt and the two garters which descend on the inside of her thighs, there's a little blond flower on a little flesh cushion, an equilateral triangle because of the width of the young belly, the centre of her woman's magic. This undressing seems unbelievably precise, for me it's like a threshold stepped over, as I know how long the way here can sometimes be, and how uncertain. [...] This strong white woman who sensed I like watching a naked woman, undoes her belt at the back, and it comes off with the entire apparatus of wide elastic bands, leaving the body naked, like the back of a young horse once its harness is off. The net caps on her breasts also come off. She sees me looking at her and asks surprised, the way you ask someone if they won't sit down, with big dull eyes, like stagnant green waters, 'Won't you undress?' She is waiting, thrown on the wide, king size bed, a corner of its green cover aside, after she cautiously put a small towel under the pillow. I feel her a stranger in my arms, a separate body, maybe because I am a little obsessed with the thought that her sister in the kitchen may discover the evolution of this visit (although it's certain that's exactly why she won't barge in, that they have an understanding), but also because Emilia lends something programmatic to this fact which, under these circumstances deserves its dictionary name, i.e. it is an 'act' (pp. 52-3).

Fred's fantasy of impersonating Ladima corresponds to another primary mechanism of hysterics – their capacity for identification. Although Freud sees this identification with the hysterics as their ability to 'express in their symptoms not only their own experiences but those of a large number of other people',[18] more crucially hysteric identification is suggested in *The Bed of Procrustes* in the hypnotism that hysterics exert over other hysterics, and it roughly translates into a hypnotism rooted in the fear of having the same kind

---

[17]   I am borrowing the term from Peter Nicholls, *Modernism: A Literary Guide* (Berkeley: University of California Press, 1995), p. 3.

[18]   Sigmund Freud, 'The Interpretation of Dreams' (1900) in *The Standard Edition of the Complete Psychological Works 4*, ed. by James Strachey (London: Vintage, 1991), p. 149.

of experiences. Memorably, in the novel, Fred meets and befriends Ladima when the latter stands up to Fred for insulting Mrs. T out of a jealous rage that overcomes him when she is in the company of other men to whom she appears to be attracted. Manifested as a tension between interior impulses and exterior control in a situation that places sexuality at its center, Fred's reaction partakes on an immediate level of the valences of the male hysteric. Later on, when Emilia gives Fred Ladima's letters, Fred's reading both elicits and dramatizes projection through permeability, the way 'exterior facts are continually transformed into interior elements and psychic events are exteriorized'.[19] In this way, the information conveyed from Ladima's letters is not only an accumulation of homosocial desire but appears to being continually transformed into Fred's own interiority that is in turn exteriorized as his own psychic outcome.

Thus, Fred's hypnotic attraction to Ladima's letters is not only an expression of his hysteric capacity for 'identification' but also reflects an unconscious tendency to inversion by which Fred fears, on an immediate level, that he too, not unlike Ladima, could be duped by a very stylish and much admired Mrs. T. By projecting his fears and hysteric identification with Ladima while in Emilia's room, Fred is overcome by a state of torpor. Passive and unable to move, he is disaggregated like Eliot's Prufrock who has been alternately attracted to a montage of 'arms, braceleted and white' and taken aback by a compulsive close-up of them 'downed with light brown hair'.[20] Staging Fred in a situation similar with Prufrock's, *The Bed of Procrustes* makes tangible once again the male hysteric's fear of identification with the female body. As Emilia attempts to smile and draw close to him, Fred takes pains to push her back and to create a desired distance from her:

> I smile gratuitously and coldly. She comes near me deceived by my smile and I feel her warm like a meal, her breath too heavy, her face too shiny from perspiration, and when she presses against me her skin is stuck to mine, so that any movement is like skinning. I avoid, disgusted, her attempt to kiss me (p. 56).

Spurred by the scapegoating of female sexuality, Fred's unconscious tendency to provoke unexpected identifications merges a fragmented Emilia into all the women, as in *The Waste Land* where in his note about the 'spectator' Tiresias, Eliot claims as well that 'all the women are one woman'.

---

[19] Lotte H. Eisner, *The Haunted Screen: Expressionism in the German Cinema and the Influence of Max Reinhardt*, trans. by Roger Greaves (London: Thames and Hudson, 1969), p. 15.

[20] T. S. Eliot, *The Complete Poems and Plays 1909-1950* (New York: Harcourt, Brace and Company, 1958), p. 19.

Here is Fred, in Emilia's room, invoking corporeal mutilation and psychic shock caused not only by the woman thrown on the bed, but by all women:

> I feel like waking up from a chaotic slumber... It feels like the link connecting me to this woman was interrupted and I become amorphous once again. It's all over. The former thought was associated with others, at the same time enhanced with blurring, subconscious plunges which were all designed to get this woman to bed... But now everything gets connected, within me, with smelly leeks; black bruised withered skin. Just like Emilia managed to become unique a moment ago, all women, are now just like the woman downstairs smelly leeks; black bruised withered skin (p. 199).

Although the invocation of women representing the male characters' anxiety over fleshiness in *The Bed of Procrustes* is limited to Emilia and Mrs. T who cannot measure up to the female chorus of women in *The Waste Land*, from the Philomel to mad Ophelia, the pub room Lil, or the typist, they are etched into the narrative and, in their own way replicate Eliot's personages. The hyacinth-girl, who elicits and manifests the most sensualized response in *The Waste Land* ('Your arms are full, and your hair wet/ I could not speak') and who potentially encapsulates and supersedes her own gender, is, like Mrs. T, the only mediator of male desire present in the poem as in the novel. Precisely because he feels attracted to her, Fred acts out a refusal to acknowledge openly his love for her or to admit his anxiety and insecurity toward a woman like Mrs. T, whose sexual freedom and financial independence secured through her job place her outside the patriarchal realm and Fred's control. Reduced to silence and forbidden to speak to or about Fred, Mrs. T is also a Philomel. With her tongue symbolically cut out, so that she is 'beyond speech', Mrs. T claims one of the novel's most powerful images that relate to male hysterics' response and reaction to female affection.

Although *The Bed of Procrustes* does not foreground the apocalyptic vision of a female chorus featured in *The Waste Land*, the novel details like the poem wide-angle views of Emilia's bed, body, undergarments, and toiletries – 'on her dressing table in front of the mirror..., next to the mascara brush, the tweezers, the shaving machine, the little blush box, a bottle of "Origan Coty" and the toilet water, all lined up' (p. 63). Even her behavior is reflective of several of the female characters in Eliot's poem. During the afternoon spent with Fred, Emilia echoes both the hyacinth girl and Maria in *The Waste Land* as 'she waves her hand in front of [his] eyes, like chasing a bee, as if she wanted to shred, physically, the canvass of [his] thoughts [before asking the absent minded Fred] "What are you thinking about?"' (p. 56). Her bed, where she receives her lovers, echo the typist's 'divan... (at night her bed) [piled with] stockings, slippers, camisoles, and stays' (see note 20 above, p. 45) catalogued in Eliot's poem. And, from Emilia's own stories, we may infer that her existence and mechanical sexual dalliances are patterned after the typist's modern, single life which allows for the sex-scene that will unfold with the arrival of her 'young man carbuncular' who 'assaults' and 'encounter(s) no defence'. But although Emilia's body canvasses the novel engaged in assaults and surrenders that involve occasional lovers, there is definite suppression of corporeality in her encounters with Ladima. With his shabby clothes and genteel inclinations resistant to the rabble and rubble of the mundane scene, Ladima's passivity evokes a sexual anesthesia reminiscent of the sexual wounding of the Fisher-King, glaring from the narrative in spite of Fred's skillful sexual plot built on Emilia's discredited body. Simultaneously hidden and omnipresent, much like the Fisher-King, Ladima is etched and constructed into the narrative as a castrated and vulnerable phantom. His only flickers of heroism appear consumed in futile encounters with the cultural establishment that lead to further isolation and 'hysterical' enervation reverberating with a dissociation or disintegration between Ladima's body and mind.

Fred's desire to enter and configure Ladima's past from the letters addressed to Emilia not only binds him over to the dead poet, but it also recommends him as the primary authority in digging out and interpreting Ladima's life. In the process of this psychic excavation, Fred opens up and embarks upon identifying with Ladima. As if hypnotized by Ladima's ghost while reading the letters, Fred responds hysterically by beginning to inhabit a hybrid consciousness that blurs the boundary between his own living body and the apparition which is Ladima's ghostly presence: 'I smoke, deep in thought. My own life stirs in me, summoned like you summon a spirit, and I suppress it with difficulty and sadness. When Emilia tries to kiss me on the lips even though I never allowed her to do that, I start reading again' (p. 77). Specifically, in the narrative context, as Fred and Ladima meet on shared grounds (Emilia's room) but never identically occupy it (their reactions to her are diametrically opposed), they merge into a familiar version of the modernist double articulated between the hypnotized body (Fred) and that of the projected and repressed (Ladima).

Sacrificing and then sublimating his own person, Fred's undergoing process of depersonalization takes away the feeling of Fred's own existence.

Submitting to this temporary depersonalization and denuded of energy, Fred's body becomes 'the body etherized on a table', a condition that, akin to Eliot's 'patient' in *The Love Song of J. Alfred Prufrock*, produces his sexual anesthesia and promotes not only his resolute distancing from Mrs. T but also engenders the in-between zone of his and Ladima's ghost-like bodies. Fred's continued inability to distance himself from identification with Ladima culminates in his radical separation from Mrs. T and his subsequent suicide that further enacts, as in Ladima's case, Fred's unsuccessful attempts to control the involuntary reflexes, dissociated bodies, and conditioned corporeality of male hysterics. The undepictable embodiment of both Ladima and Fred as modernism's male hysterics seems to belong to an uninhabitable landscape, a narrative *The Bed of Procrustes* that, like Tiresias's domain in *The Waste Land*, cuts into myths of cohesive embodiment and stable gender structures.

While both men's thoughts and emotions are made visible and tactile and their sex lives are deconstructed beyond the scope of male homosocial desire, their 'hysterical' masculinity draws us towards the characters as tropes of our own psychological haziness and sexual uncertainties. As the novel's characters urge the reactions of the readers for clues about ourselves, our curiosity about the characters' private lives and sexual crises is really symptomatic of a Procustean anxiety about the authenticity of our own.

WORKS CITED

Primary Sources

Petrescu, Camil, *The Bed of Procrustes* (Bucharest: Cultural Foundation Camil Petrescu Publishing, 2008)

Eliot, T. S., *The Complete Poems and Plays 1909-1950* (New York: Harcourt, Brace and Company, 1958)

—. 'Lecture I: Toward a Definition of Metaphysical Poetry', *The Varieties of Metaphysical Poetry*, ed. by Ronald Schuchard (New York: Harcourt Brace and Company, 1993)

—. 'Hamlet and His Problems', 'The Metaphysical Poets', 'Tradition and Individual Talent', *The Sacred Wood and Major Early Essays* (New York: Dover Publications, Inc., 1998)

Secondary Sources

Baudelaire, Charles, *Les Fleurs du Mal*, trans. by C. F. MacIntyre (Berkeley: University of California Press, 1947)

Călinescu, George, *Istoria literaturii române de la origini şi până în prezent* (*The History of Romanian Literature from the Origins to the Present*) (Bucureşti: Minerva, 1982)

Eisner, Lotte H., *The Haunted Screen: Expressionism in the German Cinema and the Influence of Max Reinhardt*, trans. by Roger Greaves (London: Thames and Hudson, 1969)

Ellis, Havelock, *Studies in the Psychology of Sex*, vol I (Philadelphia: F. A. Davis Company, Publishers, 1913)

Freud, Sigmund, *The Standard Edition of the Complete Psychological Works*, vol 4, ed. by James Strachey (London: Vintage, 1991)

Gilbert, Sandra M. and Susan Gubar, *No Man's Land: The Place of the Woman Writer in the Twentieth Century*, vol 2 (New Haven: Yale University Press, 1989)

Gourmont, Remy de, *Natural Philosophy of Love*, trans. with a postscript by Ezra Pound   (New York: privately printed for Rarity Press, 1931)

Nicholls, Peter, *Modernism: A Literary Guide* (Berkeley: University of California Press, 1995)

Sedgwick, Eve Kosofsky, *Between Men: English Literature and Male Homosocial Desire* (New York: Columbia University Press, 1985)

Roumiana L. Stantcheva

To Label, to Compare, to Appropriate…
As a Strategy of Foreign Literary Criticism

To label one writer, by comparing him to another – that happens and we can count it among the process of exchanging artistic valuables. In our case, since we are commenting the place of Eastern European literatures abroad, we could notice their complicated connection with the Western model. The inter-literary exchange today is a fact and exists practically and intensively, even though the inequality continues to be clearly visible in practice; it is expressed in the wish for a given writer to be presented through some established paradigm or hierarchical model, loaded with symbolic significance. What we do here is to comment on the positive and negative effects of such personified comparisons.

To label, to compare, and to appropriate a foreign literary text – these are strategies of literary criticism, when it presents to its reader a new piece of writing, by an unfamiliar writer, representing a vaguely known culture, which is never or almost never mentioned in the functioning domestic canon. The canonical writers, literary movements and genres in the context of the receiving country, end up being points of reference for the foreign text. The translated writer wakes up one lovely day, compared to ('named after') Maupassant, Baudelaire, or someone else, decorated with qualities, which he may not have suspected he possessed.

Then the question appears whether and to what extent the writer and his translated text will be able to be recognized under their new labels, among an unusual literary family and read through unexpected optical filters, sometimes deforming, other times differently tinted, and in all cases – simplifying. It is interesting to examine at what stage this phenomenon is today: primary, intermediate, or final. Does the process of globalization we find ourselves in today have any influence here?

The contemporary examples, selected randomly, come from the Romanian and Bulgarian literatures, translated into foreign languages. Examples from these two literatures will be drawn to illustrate our thoughts about this kind of dynamic, unsatisfactory, and provocative literary 'socialization' in the globalized world, and about the condition of national literatures.

The 'labeling' phenomenon certainly exists. It may be a sign of the underdeveloped perception of European literatures and, specifically, comparative literature, which studies literatures from different cultural environments, however belonging to the same wider community. Both the 'Western literatures', imagined as literatures of the Centre, and the literatures of Europe's peripheries, such as the Balkan ones, have adopted similar ideas for the evolution of the epochs and the corresponding literary movements. This apparent unity is not supported by real mutual knowledge of each other. The Western model has been accepted by the peripheries. The Centre, however, has not enriched its ideas of European symbolism or European Avant-gardes, for example, with representative names from the Peripheries.[1] The literary movements are muted if they are applied in an all-encompassing European framework. At times works are compared to or 'named' after canonical writers' names. In practice, nowadays, one may observe an interest in the dynamics of translations in a clear and recognizable crescendo still the question remains: how will the hurried 'namings' be overcome? Is there any hope of launching the names of writers from the peripheries into one common European usage? Will the symbolic ideas of hierarchy, which are contained in the generalization 'European literatures', be shaken? We will see later on that contrary to all contemporary dynamics, the breaches of old schemes are done by individual writers and texts, not by whole national literatures.

The writers who make up the literary canon receive, in other words, the status of literary categories. Being more internationally recognizable, Western writers – French, British, etc. – are used to function as literary models. Victor Hugo, Baudelaire, Emile Zola, Verlaine, Proust, Céline, Camus, Kafka, Shakespeare, William Blake, Ted Hughes, and others become emblems of different tendencies, movements, styles and identifying principles. To label one writer by comparing him to another – that happens and we can count it among the processes of exchanging artistic valuables. What is gained and what is lost when such comparisons are made? If we imagine the comparison as a winning strategy, does this bring about new labels and new identities? And if the answer is positive, is this new identity satisfactory or does it deform the author's image and his work to the degree

---

[1]   As Edward Shils points out: 'The central zone is not, as such, a spatially located phenomenon. […] The center, or the central zone, is a phenomenon of the realm of values and beliefs. […] The central zone partakes of the nature of the sacred', in Edward Shils, *Center and Periphery. Essays in Macrosociology* (Chicago and London: The University of Chicago Press, 1975), p. 3. Ivaylo Znepolski also reminds us that: 'Today, the center of culture is not geographically localized' (p. 119) but 'the problem "center of culture vs. periphery" continues to be current' (pp. 20-1), in Ivaylo Znepolski, 'Globalization: Cultural and Social identity of Peripheral Cultures' and in Jean Baudrillard, In memoriam, *Globalization as Cultural Shock* (Sofia: Ivaylo Znepolski, Dom na naukite za choveka i obshtestvoto, 2007).

of making him unrecognizable, lacking a connection to his starting position?[2] It is remarkable that the writers themselves can hardly oppose these types of maneuvers by the critics. They may conclude, to ponder the observer's point, eventually to express reservations, quietly to acquiesce or hide their disagreement, but not to stop the caravan.

One, though not the least, of the peculiarities of publishing policies nowadays is their more dynamic nature since the collapse of the Iron Curtain. During the last twenty years, the 'new' European democracies have most often conducted policies of extreme liberalism and have preferred not to involve themselves. They typically have mechanisms providing small-scale support for publishing houses, and never or rarely, for writers, translators, etc. However, the policy of non-interference has an effect in that it allows a hypertrophied role of the market in the cultural sphere. In this kind of vacuum, left by the government, cultural foundations work, in different formats – national, European, regional –, which interfere more or less successfully. However, it cannot be concluded as yet whether they artificially even out the literary field. At a given moment, a novel is in demand, later 'women's' literature, and still later poets or dramatists; it comes down to randomly filling empty bookshelves.

The 'labeling' phenomenon, which we are discussing, is not new. Even though this is a tactic of criticism, we cannot omit mentioning that nowadays, in 2008-2009, the translator's activity is multiplying in all directions, from different national literatures. The dynamism of the globalized world is also reflected upon the world of books. Programs and projects are engaged in facilitating literary exchanges in different formats. The bibliography of published foreign books is becoming quite rich. In this bounty, that 'labelling' game raises questions about the essence of dual identity, the accompanying deformations, and finally about the canonic images included in the game. Here we will ignore the purely economic dynamic, which is today additionally influenced by the global economic crisis. Even if some programs supporting book publishing ceased to function, publishers would not be able to stop all forms of activity in this direction and the issue of authentic representation of a given author remains open.

1. The example that stimulated this inquiry

---

[2]   The issue is additionally complicated since literary identity could be studied from different aspects: national, from the perspective of the literary movement, political-ideational position, stylistic, etc.

After Gallimard published the French translation of the novel *Wasted Morning*,[3] by the Romanian writer Gabriela Adameşteanu, in 2005[4], the French literary critic, along with other comments, launched the idea that there is an affinity between the Romanian writer's style and that of Louis-Ferdinand Céline:

> The morning in question is, no doubt, a symbol and quite a torturous one at that: of Romania which had been sacrificed for a whole century, first on the altar of wars, and then on that of Communism. These ominous apparitions haunt the novel writer, but she does not cease to attack them, by whirling the sarabande of her bright, intensive writing, as in Céline's work, which reinvents folk speech and the lyricism of the streets in a country where the clapper tongue has served as a coffin of the imagination: if Vica, Gabriela Adameşteanu's heroine, is a free woman, this is primarily because she rambles on like Bardamus...[5]

After reading this article, one's first reaction is: very well said! But then you begin to ask yourself if it is accurate. Is it appropriate? And additionally: What do the writer and Romanian literature acquire – comparability to French literature or lack of appropriate grounds for pointing to elements of the Romanian cultural identity? Let us trust a French literary dictionary to try to know what the French readers will understand from such a comparison: In the political sense, Céline is 'damned by literature', because of his far-right views; regarding the novel, the French writer, as the dictionary states, has brought about the apocalyptic view of society; and finally, this is one 'genius stylist'[6].

I have no doubts regarding the good intentions of Gabriela Adameşteanu's assessment. André Clavel's analysis accurately reflects the fact that her style is modulated, novel, and bright. The same goes for the fact that her novel marks an important moment in the development of contemporary Romanian literature. A. Clavel actually makes a 'presentation by analogy' in order to outline the significance of one Romanian writer, but

---

[3]   Three of her novels have been published in Bulgarian: Gabriela Adameşteanu, *The Meeting*, trans. by Roumiana L. Stantcheva (Sofia: Panorama, 2005); Gabriela Adameşteanu, *Wasted Morning*, trans. by Roumiana L. Stantcheva, Vasilka Aleksova (Sofia: Balkani, 2006); Gabriela Adameşteanu, *The Equal Way of Every Day*, trans. by Roumiana L. Stantcheva (Sofia: Balkani, 2007).

[4]   Gabriela Adameşteanu, *Une matinée perdue*, trans. by Alain Paruit (Paris: Gallimard, 2005).

[5]   André Clavel, 'Adamesteanu, la romancière qui lit dans les cœurs', *Lire*, novembre 2005, p. 144.

[6]   Evelyne Amon, Yves Bomati, *Les Auteurs de la littérature française* (Paris: Larousse, 1994), pp. 70-1.

in fact risks bending the identity of the translated writer, through the connotations, which inevitably come with the full understanding of Céline.

Such an instance of labeling one literary work in a new, foreign context, being founded on quite random associations, could entangle the author in unexpected connotations and deform his/ her presentation in a foreign cultural environment, which not only does not know anything else about his/ her work, but also often knows too little about the literature from which s/he originates.

2. The Circumstances before and after Globalization

Some aspects of Globalization concern the literary field, since the phenomenon is really quite large and could stimulate, spontaneously, the type of new labelling under discussion. The term 'globalization' is above all a term of economic policy that started in the 1980s partially in connection with free market ideas. The free market itself is a mechanism capable of regulating the exchange spontaneously and autonomously, including far outside the borders of national states.[7] For literature, the trans-border dynamic is an opportunity to acquire a larger readership. But the erasing of borders is problematic. Is the term 'glocalization', proposed by the sociologist Roland Robertson and not seldom used, according to which global and local interact to form new hybrids, appropriate in this case?

The processes of opening up are new only at first glance. This is a tendency which gained momentum in the countries of Central, South Eastern, and Eastern Europe after the breakup of the Communist Block. For the culture of a country which suffered from past isolation imposed by its totalitarian regime, such opening up appears quite favourable. The process allows for real and intensive exchanges. In fact Europe's peripheries and specifically the Balkan literatures have started an unequal dialogue with the West since their entering the modern tendencies during the 18th and 19th centuries. This inequality has been real both in the beginning, due to the conscious adoption of Western models and later, due to the lack of scale to enhance the authority of the periphery's literary market. Today, while I feel pleasantly allured by the possibilities of globalization and assess it not only as inescapable but also as useful and irreversible, some concomitant and often-appearing phenomena raise questions. This is so because they may lead to considerable changes in our attitudes toward notions such as 'national' and

---

[7]   Manfred B. Steger, *Globalization - a very short introduction* (USA: Oxford University Press, 2003).

'universal', with the corresponding reflections on the assessment of literary phenomena. What new things are being shaped up in this direction?   Of the new contexts in which the literatures of Southeastern Europe take part, the ones that directly interest me allow better exposure in the West to some texts from these literatures, but rarely open up the way for deeper understanding of these literatures in their entirety. We will notice that the translated writers are presented either on their own, and/or through sometimes very free analogies. The foreign critic faces a number of difficulties and most of all finds only a small number of works dealing with literary interferences in Europe. One edition like the *Brief Introduction to European Literature*, written by an authoritative group of authors, in 710 pages, tries to speak of a single 'European literature' and makes broad generalizations. The ever-forgotten peripheral European literatures have to look hard to find their authors and titles in one table at the end of the imposing volume, on top of that ridden with factual mistakes.[8]

The literary criticism of the receiving country does not easily find scholarly material to use in presenting the country and literature of origin of the writer. It has to simultaneously demonstrate the importance of the text in terms of its message to the original public; and also to find a code through which to include this little-known or completely unknown writer in the framework of works with which the new public is acquainted. Luckily there are enough generally valid theoretical literary concepts. Nonetheless the literary critic uses too often implicit comparisons to canonical works or writers' names, which would act as a bridge to the better understanding of a new writer's name.

Every hypothesis of Comparative Literature is based on knowing at least two national literary histories, but also experiences the necessity for a wider system of concepts, to build a whole, which we could call a model. A model makes it possible for the compared literatures to be drawn closer. In our case, since we are commenting on the place of Eastern European literatures abroad, we could notice their complicated connection with the Western model. This model functions as a common literary canon. The community of European literatures is real and works through the presence of 'shared values'. Precisely this allows for the literatures to be drawn closer and makes 'labeling', which we are commenting on and which can be more or less valid, possible.[9]

---

[8]   *Précis de Littérature européenne*, ed. by Béatrice Didier (Paris: Presses Universitaires de France, 1998).

[9]   Cf. Roumiana L. Stantcheva, 'Les littératures balkaniques et le modèle occidental', *Revue des études sud-est européennes*, 46 (2008), 277-84.

3. 'Labelling', reasonable or unreasonable?

Some of the following examples could amaze you. We could look at a somewhat new *Anthology of Modern and Contemporary Romanian Poetry*,[10] translated into English, published in the United States and aiming to present the connections of Romanian poets with the Western context.[11] The several commentaries in the anthology, in the beginning and end of the longer than 530-page volume, discuss, from different points of view, the peculiarities of modern Romanian poetry, seen in an international context, which is entirely logical in this case and is perfectly defended, both artistically and conceptually. The brief notes, which present every poet and introduce his texts are, however, what attracts the attention, with their numerous instances of 'labeling'. In a number of cases, the writers themselves have created in their work, implicitly or openly, such inter-textual cross references. In other case, the creation of international ties already exists in the ideas of the Romanian canon. Collected in one place in the anthology and only represented by very brief texts, such labeling sounds like parody. Tudor Arghezi, just 'Like Baudelaire', 'assembles worlds from *boils, yeasts and mud*' (see note 10 above, p. 6). The symbolist poetry of George Bacovia is 'influenced by Baudelaire's decadence and Verlaine's music' (p. 16). Along with other explanations: 'Urmuz's work anticipates that vision of the absurd that inspired Eugène Ionesco' (p. 23). Love motifs spring from Vasile Voiculescu's sonnets, 'inspired by Shakespeare' (p. 26). Ion Barbu's poetry 'involves his personal adaptation of Stéphane Mallarmé's hermetic aesthetics' (p. 33). Barbu Fundoianu/ Benjamin Fondane's masterpiece is 'similar to Baudelaire's poetry' (p. 58). Gherasim Luca's poetry contains 'metamorphosis and continuous surprise, close to Breton's *miraculous*' (p. 78). The poetry of Ştefan Augustin Doinaş involves a 'detached contemplation derived from Mallarmé by way of Valéry' (95). The mysticism of our contemporary Ileana Mălăncioiu 'like Blake's, is associated with ascension, flight and border crossing' (p. 150). The poems of Angela Marinescu, 'laconic and austere, [...] remind us of Blake's, marked by eroticism and sensuality' (p. 162). The poems of Ion Mureşan are 'written under the aegis of Rimbaud's rebellion' (p. 260). 'Discrete and melancholic, Vişniec evokes the absurd in the same direction as Ionesco' (p. 281).

---

[10] *Born in Utopia. An Anthology of Modern and Contemporary Romanian Poetry*, ed. by Carmen Firan and Paul Doru Mugur with Edward Foster (Jursey City, New Jersey: Talisman House Publishers, 2006).

[11] Already after the First World War and especially after the end of the Second, US literature began to function as part of the Western literary model and even to create influential paradigms.

Ironically speaking, perhaps it would be better to go straight to and read those emblematic writers like Baudelaire, Rimbaud, Blake, and so on, and not waste our time with the Romanian names, which we can sometimes hardly pronounce! The multiple instances of comparisons in the form of direct analogies or 'labeling' appear like an efficient approach to the brief presentation, within a few rows of text. This approach, however, moves us toward substitution and absurd simplification. Forwarding to another address sounds somehow comical. How will we understand that Tudor Arghezi is a great poet, not because he follows in Baudelaire's footsteps, but because he renews some of his themes in a different way, in a different epoch and context, and is a first-rate innovator within his literature? 'The Flowers of Evil' have become 'Flowers of Mildew' and the ugliness, mud, and marginalized person turn into a social and aesthetic fact through language, style, and verse, which enchant with their completeness and rich suggestions. We cannot however deny that Arghezi alone suggests the comparison to Baudelaire through the implicit dialogue with Baudelaire's title. Let us not forget that Baudelaire is not only a literary phenomenon. He is a symbol of the West, of Modernity, and of modern decadence. Besides, he symbolizes a number of prestigious notions: the specifically literary 'predecessor to Symbolism' or the Philosophical-Poetic 'aesthetics of ugliness', the transitive nature of what is modern, the 'correspondences' etc. The approach chosen for the anthology ensures a reading of Romanian literature that will create an image of connectedness to the West and with what is prestigious in our, already traditional, symbolic understanding. Whether that is the tendency that should be supported remains an open question.

By systematically tracing the application of analogies in the cited *Anthology*, we may conclude that as we proceed on to the pages with contemporary poets, the usage of comparison-'labeling' occurs more rarely. This reminds us that such 'christenings' are inherited from the literary understanding left from the time before Globalization: more traditional, dividing the world and literary world into a Centre and Periphery with clear geographical delineations. There could also be another reason however. Perhaps critical thought has not yet managed to work out the appropriate codes of clichés comparison for contemporary writers. From another perspective, there are known cases when such simplification of the message turned out to be quite efficient: let us mention just the example of Panait Istrati, who, during the 1920s, was introduced by Romain Rolland to literary Europe as the Balkan Gorki, setting in motion the beginning of a loud international literary and publicist career for the French-writing Romanian.

The possibilities of labeling are also confirmed by examples taken out of anthologies presenting Bulgarian writers to a foreign audience. Let us look closely at the selection of contemporary Bulgarian literary fragments, translated and discussed by the French specialist in Bulgarian literary studies

– Marie Vrinat-Nikolov. The book starts with the very successful idea to present Bulgarian literature through the prism of its attitude toward the issue of 'authority', which became quite topical after the fall of Communism.[12] The 'labeling' approach has not been used in the book's interpreting texts, but it is not entirely rejected. Yordan Yovkov is presented in the following way: 'Some of his stories, through their concentrated power, through the art of capturing character traits or some situation concisely, are close to Maupassant's stories' (see note 12 above, p. 12). As for Yordan Radichkov, the French author points out one possible comparison, even if she clearly states her reservations: 'All kinds of epithets have been stated for his work: satiric, grotesque, magical realism (something because of which he is often compared to Latin-American authors like Garcia Marquez), parodic and so on. It is very difficult to qualify him without narrowing the understanding of his work' (see note 12 above, p. 66). The French critic's reservations regarding the 'labeling' approach, which we are looking at here, actually supports the ambivalent position of contemporary criticism. To label or not to label? Is it possible to lock one literature up in itself? But if we rely on 'labeling', will the uniqueness of some literatures be erased until we find ourselves in a situation of worrisome vagueness?

It is valuable to also quote the choice made by one Bulgarian critic, drawn to examine 'the theme of authority in Bulgarian literature' in the same anthology, published in French. Georgi Tzankov, having in mind that he is writing for a French readership, feels obliged to highlight the universality of 19th century Bulgarian writers and to compare them to canonic Romantics like Hugo and Byron. When he points out the significance of Bulgarian writers like Hristo Botev, Ivan Vazov, and others, Georgi Tzankov, without 'labeling', points to certain models: '[...] the writers show an increasing curiosity regarding the mechanisms of the world order; they have been captivated by the rebellious romantic figures of Victor Hugo and Byron' (see note 12 above, p. 18). It turns out that "labeling" is not a trademark of the critic, situated outside the respective literary context.

One last example will provide new aspects on the issue of naming or 'labeling' one author through the name of another. Every critical assessment is focused toward a certain readership. Although Ana Blandiana is a writer with a very clearly distinguishable writing style, she also ends up being 'labeled' in the presentation of her book, translated in the Republic of Macedonia. In the postscript, the translator clarifies the active civic position which is evident in Blandiana's literary work, and comments on it in the following way: 'The ethical dimension of her poetry is ingrained in the

---

[12]   *Grandeur et dérision du pouvoir dans la littérature bulgare* (Choix de textes contemporains traduits et commentés), ed. by Marie Vrinat-Nikolov, *Cahiers Scientifiques de l'Université d'Artois* (Arras: Artois presses Université), 16 (2000).

lyrical tissue and this way her poetry is not socially-engaged in the sense of Mayakovski, but in the sense, formulated by Pasternak: reaching the natural (the internal) state of poetry and not the momentary (external)'.[13] Besides, the naming game, which for Romanian poets is most often oriented toward comparisons to French literature, turns out to be used in an unexpected way, even though it is likely to be efficient in the respective context. Here the significance of the readership and considering its points of reference comes to the forefront.

One of the explanations is indeed handy. We cannot forget the efforts to modernize most societies in South Eastern Europe from the moment of their actual synchronization to the modern time and formation of their national states during the 19th century. Their tardiness in comparison with the West poses a serious reason for some segments of these societies to strive toward the rhythm of Western Europe, while others kept traditional elements for a long time. From this situation derives the increased level of tension between tradition and modernity. The supporters of literary modernity manifested themselves already during this epoch and voluntarily entered the naming game. Later, the period between the two world wars, connected very categorically modern social views with literary modernism. Literary histories have spontaneously introduced analogies, because of their search for prestigious models.

*

The inter-literary exchange today is a fact and exists practically and intensively, even though the inequality continues to be clearly visible in practice; it is expressed in the wish for a given writer to be presented through some established paradigm or hierarchical model, loaded with symbolic significance.

What we could do is simply to comment on the positive and negative effects of such personified comparisons. Starting from the negative results, we could report a number of deformations, partially corrected by the rest of the commentary text or the work itself, which prove that labeling-comparisons are only conditionally valid. Actually the deformations relate to the difficulty of formulating, and in some cases to the insufficient care for the nuances. In addition to that, there is an almost certain loss of context, which has caused the work, and a difficulty to present the impulses, which have

---

[13]   Lidija Dimkovska, 'Pogovor'[v. Ana Blandiana, *Arhangel vo saghi* (Struga: Plejadi, 2004), p. 115.] (Лидија Димковска, 'Поговор', В: Ана Бландијана, *Архангел во саги*, Струга, Струшки вечери на поезијата, 2004, с. 115).

played a role in creating the work. National literature is eventually undermined by its indivisibility.

Positive aspects of the implicit comparisons, which are mentioned here, could also be seen. It is positive for a writer of a less-proliferated literature to end up at the level of an already canonized author. This way, a peculiar quiet initiation into a higher rank is carried out. A comparison pointed out only as an emblem could cause a future in-depth study of an author. Besides, such 'christenings' could serve to increase the understanding of a given widely-valid literary movement by adding new names from different literatures to the list of its adherents. Finally, let us comment on the notion of 'hybrid', which has arrived with the theory of globalization and with the notion of 'glocalization', which needs to be defined more accurately. In their position as literatures, considering themselves mostly within the concepts of the Western model, the Balkan literatures ended up in the naming trap from the moment they set out on the way to modernization. While the amalgamation of tendencies exists anyway, the notion of 'hybridity' becomes evident in the context of a given place, literature, or work. This hybrid nature is due to the social dynamic, which presupposes the more frequent appearance of bilingual writers, having dual citizenship, and this takes us toward doubting the clarity of the notion of 'national literature' nowadays.

The writer belongs mainly to his specific world, built upon the collection of contexts and traditions, which he wanted and finally succeeded to assimilate. Our attention is increasingly attracted by single phenomena and unique styles. With such expectations, the implicit comparisons, appropriations, and namings begin to lose their *raison d'être*. We are witnessing a kind of process of generalization. The literary movements of the 19th and first half of the 20th century have created essential notions which we recognize today as stylistic techniques, but in unusual combinations. For example, the surrealist gesture in poetry is recognizable today, without it being Surrealism.

Globalization gives new chances to the 'small' literatures to participate in the increased movement of spiritual values and to take advantage of the globalized epoch, which is spreading and imposing the notion of 'tolerance' around the world. In my opinion, it is not by chance that 'labeling' or 'christening' is ever more rarely seen as a good approach. The fact that the globalized world is watering down the geographic localization in the pair 'Centre-Periphery' gives good chances for every writer and every literature. 'Welcome, globalization' is what every 'small' literature ought to say.

Transl. from Bulgarian by Svetozar A. Dimitrov

WORKS CITED

Adameşteanu, Gabriela, *Une matinée perdue*, transl. by Alain Paruit (Paris: Gallimard, 2005)

—. *The Equal Way of Every Day*, trans. in Bulgarian by Roumiana L. Stantcheva (Sofia: Balkani, 2007) (Габриела Адамещяну, *Все същият път, ден след ден*)

—. *Wasted Morning*, transl. in Bulgarian by Roumiana L. Stantcheva, Vasilka Aleksova (Sofia: Balkani, 2006) (Габриела Адамещяну, *Изгубената сутрин*)

—. *The Meeting*, transl. in Bulgarian by Roumiana L. Stantcheva (Sofia: Panorama, 2005) (Габриела Адамещяну, *Пресрещане*)

Amon, Evelyne, Yves Bomati, *Les Auteurs de la littérature française* (Paris: Larousse, 1994), pp. 70-1

Clavel, André, 'Adameşteanu, la romancière qui lit dans les cœurs', *Lire*, novembre 2005, 144

Didier, Béatrice, ed., *Précis de Littérature européenne* (Paris: Presses Universitaires de France, 1998)

Dimkovska, Lidija, 'Pogovor' [v. Ana Blandiana, *Arhangel vo saghi* (Struga: Plejadi, 2004)] (Лидија Димковска, 'Поговор', В: Ана Бландијана, *Архангел во саги*, Струга, Струшки вечери на поезијата, 2004), pp. 111-116

Shils, Edward, *Center and Periphery. Essays in Macrosociology* (Chicago and London: The University of Chicago Press, 1975)

Steger, Manfred B., *Globalization – a very short introduction* (USA: Oxford University Press, 2003)

Vrinat-Nikolov, Marie, ed., *Grandeur et dérision du pouvoir dans la littérature bulgare* (Arras: Artois presses Université), *Cahiers Scientifiques de l'Université d'Artois*, 16 (2000)

Znepolski, Ivaylo, ed., *Jean Baudrillard, in memoriam. Globalization as Cultural Shock* (Dom na naukite za Choveka i obshtestvoto (Maison des Sciences de l'Homme et de la Société: Sofia, 2007), pp. 20-119

Cristina Balinte

National Enlisting / European Rallying. Access Criteria to the Continental Space for Romanian Literature

The contribution of Romanian literature to European and World Literature is insufficiently promoted, leading to 'an elusive Europe complex'. This study explores convenient and more efficient ways to make the Romanian literature clearly visible in the general European system. The aim of the research is to analyze a few spreading strategies: the participation at Mitteleurope ideology, the association with the 'Danubian literature', the distribution by means of multiculturalism

This paper tries to identify ways through which the relationship between Romania and Europe could become stable, rather than occasional, in a dialectics of integration and preservation of specific features. From the literary point of view, as well as from the political or economic point of view, the issue is not only to be present in Europe, but to become visible, to draw attention and to be acknowledged for one's contribution at continental level.

Firstly, it would be necessary to observe the number of books, written by Romanian authors, sold in the bookshops on the Western market or to review the elements pertaining to Romanian culture, the university academic libraries of the same space, in order to have an idea about the lack of knowledge about Romanian literature in the Western countries. After the collapse of the totalitarian regime, after successive years of cultural policies aimed at opening-up, in fact, a declared rather than actually supported opening-up, after the key-moment of the European Union accession and despite the blooming of local publishing, Romanian literature is still far from having a configuration at least coherent, if not correct, in the eyes of the foreign public.

Secondly, for most of the Western academics, since the Romanian literary field belongs to the initiated ones, to people following up a strict specialization or who have simply increased their general level by moving in marginal or 'exotic' circles, Romanian literature continues to be synonym with avant-garde writers (such as Gherasim Luca, considering that Tristan Tzara has undergone internationalization), the writers of the inter-war period (Mircea Eliade, E. M. Cioran, Eugène Ionesco), the novels of Panait Istrati, Constantin Virgil Gheorghiu, Dumitru Tsepeneag, and Paul Goma.

Besides, as late as the 3rd millennium, there is no Romanian literature for the common reader from abroad. We refer to the one who one day will be curious to read a piece of fiction written in this part of Europe and to discover its characteristic style. Equally, it is almost impossible to find the Romanian version of a poem, which would make the reader experience the emotions

Romanian readers usually experience when confronted with poetry. The selection was based on criteria related to the political attitude (Istrati, Gheorghiu, Tsepeneag, Goma), to the importance in the universal system (the avant-gardists, Eliade, Cioran, Ionesco), to relevance for the cultural life in Paris (Anna de Noailles, princess Brancovan). In the past, as well as nowadays, 'ideology precedes aesthetics', stresses Adrian Marino, when debating the 'internationalization' of national literature in the 5th volume of *The Biography of the Idea of Literature*.[1]

Next, we shall approach another Francophone situation. If one ran a search in the database of the library of Université Libre de Liège, one would be surprised to find miscellaneous studies belonging mainly to literary history: Emil Manu, *Istoria poeziei româneşti şi moderniste* (*The History of Romanian and Modernist Poetry*), Dan C. Mihăilescu, *Literatura română în postceauşism* (*Romanian Literature after Ceauşescu's Regime*), vol. 1, N. Manolescu, *Istoria critică a literaturii române* (*The Critical History of Romanian Literature*), vol. I, Perpessicius, *Eminesciana*, Angela Ion, *La littérature française dans l'espace culturel roumain* (*French Literature in the Romanian Cultural Space*), Ion Dodu Bălan, *A concise history of Romanian literature*, Adrian Marino, *Littérature roumaine-littératures occidentales : rencontres* (*Romanian Literature-Western Literatures: Encounters*), Alexandru Paleologu, *Spiritul şi litera, Liturghierul lui Coresi* (*Spirit and Letter: Coresi's Divine Liturgy*), Tudor Vianu, *La société littéraire 'Junimea'* (*The Junimea Literary Society*), Dumitru Micu, *Literatura română de azi* (*Romanian Literature Today*) ('azi' meaning 'today', i.e. 1965 !), L. Gáldi, *Stilul poetic al lui Eminescu* (*Eminescu's Poetical Style*). The above mentioned entries are supplemented only by two other entries recorded as 'Romanian literature – French translations', and this is the case for Virgil Gheorghiu's novel, *La tunique de peau* (*The Leather Jacket*), and for *Récits insolites* (*Out-of-the-ordinary Tales*) by Mihai Eminescu, with a preface by N. Manolescu.

At this point, we might ask which is the literary image of Romania in Europe and worldwide? Can we develop an image from isolated pieces?

1. The Elusive Europe Complex

---

[1]   Marino, Adrian. *Biografia ideii de literatură* [*The Biography of the Idea of Literature*], 7 vols (Cluj-Napoca: Dacia, 1998), V (1998), p. 29.

A difficult matter arises when speaking about Europe, because we do not know which Europe we are referring to. In the above quoted *Biography of the Idea of Literature*, Adrian Marino emphasizes this heterogeneous character, by saying that 'European literature has never made up an actual *unity*' (see note 1 above, p. 87). Béatrice Didier, the coordinator of a benchmarking anthology for the cultural studies, *Précis de littérature européenne* (*European Literature Synopsis*), also expresses doubts regarding global perception and she wonders about the action sphere of the 'European literature' concept. In her opinion, the syntagm is 'difficult to define', because usually the term 'European' turns out to be contradictory, and in addition to this, the other notion, 'literature', does not rely on a strict meaning, but covers an entire series of contextualizations.[2]

Moreover, in the integration process, the uncertainty related to the object of reference determines an elusive Europe complex, manifested by the 'insignificant literatures'. We cannot find a single type of discourse that would impress Europe. We mostly identify adapted discourses, to tempt any of the 'major' cultures and the 'literary imperialisms' of the continental space where we have to accede in the end.

In addition to this, the comparative study brought this dynamics of model-influences. In time, Romanian literature starting paying attention to the affinities with French literature, considered Europe's cultural centre, and then to the regional influences of the West and of the East, and to several degrees of cultural influences, most of them bookish. A literature trying to outline its originality for the first time during the national awakening is forced to look outside, aiming at positioning itself within the spirit of the age. Undergoing doctrinarian influences causing it to go backwards, Romanian literature finds out again that it is necessary to redefine itself as a creation formula in the current political and cultural profile.

In our opinion, the *tensed* relationship between the national and the universal should be replaced with an 'interaction' of the two elements, whose balance is always approximate. As there are no perfectly closed systems, the national and the universal do not exist as absolute values. If the contact between two nations through the agency of translations can be limited, with regards to extra-literary factors, the influence phenomenon is the most difficult to control. For example, Sorin Titel's novels, written during the communist regime, from the '60s until the '80s in the past century. The tetralogy, including *Ţara îndepărtată* (*The Far off Country*), *Pasărea şi umbra* (*The Bird and the Shadow*), *Clipa cea repede* (*The Furtive Instant*), *Femeie, iată fiul tău !* (*Woman, Behold Thy Son!*), seems external to the local

---

[2]   Béatrice Didier, *Étudier la littérature européenne* (*Studying the European literature*), in *Précis de literature européenne* (*European Literature Synopsis*) (Paris: Presses Universitaires de France, 1998), pp. 1-9.

history of its writing time. These are national productions, created under a totalitarian regime, speaking simultaneously the national language and the European language, which make visible the influences acquired imperceptibly, and not expressly, through the adherence to the imaginary of such a geographical and cultural region.

Back to the elusive Europe complex, we have to point out the reiterated sieges made by Romanian literature on the gates of this ideal fortress, by means of translations, by the presence in the European attribute-bearing contained space, by means of comprehension and written practice of its imaginary stereotypes. Reality shows us incoherent and partial results, of an amazing inefficiency, and cultural policies never pursued to the end. In terms of national pride, the situation would be settled once a Romanian writer (or a Romanian citizen) won the Nobel Prize. In basic terms, the situation could have a happy outcome the day a Romanian writer would be capable, by means of a book unassuming the wining of a prize, of a dialogue (therefore, no longer a monologue), a complete exchange (not only an offer) with the public from abroad, European or worldwide.

2. Western Space Integration Descriptors

A 'descriptor' is defined as an access key. We shall discuss further three modalities tested by Romanian literature after 1989, in order to open European gates. We maintain the idea of the diversified aspect of European literature as well as the 'influence spheres' theory, exercised by the 'large literary blocks'. Firstly, we shall look at the manifestations related to the recovery and to the incorporation into the ideology framework of Mitteleurope and the affirmation of an identity within a geographical structure. In the final part, we shall focus on the case of the intercultural manifestation called 'Les Belles Étrangères' ('The Beautiful Foreigners'), when a group of 12 Romanian writers belonging to different generations have been invited to France, on the occasion of a program of popularization of little known literatures, conducted by Centre National du Livre (the National Book Centre).

2.1. Joining an Ideology

The affinity with the Central European spirit becomes, after 1989, an essential point of the discourse promoted especially in the cultural centres in the Western part of Romania. First, in Timişoara, then in Oradea (*Aurora* magazine presenting in issue no. 2/1993 a report on the 'Identity of Central Europe') and Cluj-Napoca – in the order of their relevance. The echoes of this acclimatization to the European regime reach the Capital and Iaşi. Univers and, respectively, Polirom publishers edit the seminars of 'The Third Europe' Centre in Timişoara as well as field-reference studies, among which we note those of Jacques Le Rider, *La Mitteleurope* and Tony Judt, *A Great Illusion? An Essay on Europe*.

Theoretically speaking, depending on what we discover in a debate held by 'The Third Europe' Centre, published in the volume entitled *Europa Centrală sau paradoxul fragilităţii* (*Central Europe or the Fragility Paradox*), we draw a demarcation line between Mitteleurope, 'a geographical and historical notion, focused around a sort of German expansionism' and Central Europe, 'a socio-cultural concept, focused around Vienna'.[3] Keeping up with the same policy of understanding nuances, we identify, with regards to the Mitteleurope, a broad meaning of the concept, seen as an 'ideological notion [...], a mental map, a historical reality, a notion related to the history of culture' (see note 3 above) and a more refined, updated one, that of a nucleus persisting in showing interest in an age governed by the audiovisual and the multimedia, in 'the reconstruction of a cosmopolitan culture of the book' and in 'the literature (understood the same way as by Herder, as *Literatur*), as science, as source of ethical settlement and symbolic representation [...] of the spirit of a civilization' (see note 3 above, p. 136).

Effort for recovery, affirmation and promotion within a multicultural identity, this strategy does not require building a reality, but highlighting the specific features of a part in the unity of a historical reality. The collapse of the totalitarian system implies a decentralization in whose wake we notice the multiplicity of cultural sources, each of them possessing a contextualization of its particular discourse.

We may wonder why the first step of contemporary connection of the Romanian literature to the European one looks like joining a local ideology, but in a direction oriented towards the West. In an apparently constantly transitional period, as the '90s are, the configurations of the cultural institutions and market undergo fluctuations. Consequently, a manifested ideology is a point of stability, a rather solid anchorage to draw Europe's attention, even if this network of influence remains partial. Less productive when referring to the translations from the Romanian writers, this direction leads, first and foremost, to the results materialized in theories incorporated in anthologies or in collections in the West. The most important examples are the publications of 'Centre d'étude de l'Europe médiane' ('Middle Europe Study Centre'), thematic collective works coordinated by Maria Delaperrière and Antoine Marès, L'Harmattan de Paris Publishing Company – *Histoire et pouvoir en Europe médiane* (*History and Power in Middle Europe*) (1997), *(Post)modernisme en Europe Centrale* [*(Post)modernism in Central Europe*], *La crise des ideologies* (*The Crisis of Ideologies*) (1999).

---

[3] Jacques Le Rider, *Europa Centrală sau paradoxul fragilităţii* (*Central Europe or the fragility paradox*), ed. by Dana Chetrinescu and Ciprian Vălcan (Iaşi: Polirom, 2001), p. 20.

2.2. Incorporation Depending on the Geographical Position

Derivatives carrying on the concerns initially focused on the Mitteleurope issue, the discussions regarding the existence of a 'Danubian literature' enjoy a consistent developement at the beginning of this decade, continuing to be an element of constant reflection, reinforced by the Western debates on the 'culture focused around the Mediterranean Sea'. It is not now that we should dwell on the influence of the books by Claudio Magris, *Danubius* (translated into Romanian in 1994) and *A Different Sea* (translated into Romanian, 1999), both released by Univers Publishing House. These represent starting points for a geographical circumscription, doubled by a culture made up of cultures bearing similar features at the imaginary level. We perceive this as a way of grouping into an international literary network, a sort of 'magical realism' productions of the Danube plain in the south of Romania. It is an extension by means of cultural transfer propagated throughout the geography of the river in question. In order to be more explicit, we can find the elements of an imaginary link between the novelists Hermann Broch, Sorin Titel and Ştefan Bănulescu. More precisely, let us consider *The Tempter* (1953), *Pasărea şi umbra* (*The Bird and the Shadow*) (1977) and *Cartea Milionarului* (*The Millionaire's Book*) (1977). There is no influence of one writer upon the other, but a creative interpretative reception of a model in a junction region: thematic register, similar treatment of patterns, a role held by the symbolic metaphors of the story.

At the results level, this is always a modality to configure a European identity space and secondarily a modality of promoting the writers' works.

2.3. Intercultural Promotion

The past years are characterized by the development of publishing companies and by the building-up of a more focused picture of a national publishing market. The investment of these private institutions in 2005 made it possible for the popularization in France of the works of 12 Romanian writers belonging to different generations (from the '70s onwards), activity carried out within the annual project 'Les Belles Étrangères' ('The Beautiful Foreigners'), put into practice by Centre National du Livre (the National Book Centre).

Public readings in Paris and in several other cities in France, the broadcasting of a film about the participants at the event and a significant report in the monthly magazine *Lire*, entitled 'Spécial Roumanie' ('A Special Issue about Romania'), all these have been the tracks to cover towards the European interest finish point. Because, nowadays, just as before, winning France is equivalent, at least theoretically speaking, to winning Europe.

A publicity campaign was considered in Romania as a form of promoting Romanian authors, thus justifying the remark of Adrian Marino who warned against 'the instinctive tendency, the reflex gesture' of 'insignificant, exotic' literatures 'to proclaim themselves, at least potentially, competitive in comparison with all the world literatures' (see note 1 above, p. 33). On the verge of European integration, neither Romania nor France was quite ready to go beyond the commonplace of mutual politeness. If we look at the *Lire* report, we are amazed at the clichés it uses and especially at the failure to understand the writers' profiles, some of them already translated in France (Gheorghe Crăciun, at Maurice Nadeau, with *Composition aux parallèles inégales*, Gabriela Adameşteanu, at Gallimard, with *Matinée perdue*, Mircea Cărtărescu, at Austral, with *Lulu,* and at Denoël, with *L'oeil en feu* I, and others).

François Busnel, the editorialist, talks about Romanian literature in terms of 'mystery', therefore an unknown zone, which in the 'French imaginary comes down to the Carpathians mists, to fantastic vampire escapades, to the heavy burden of the communist years and to the abuses made by the Ceauşescu couple' (p. 140). Then, glancing through the presentations about the writers, one would be shocked by the information's lack of actual availability, which sometimes seems ridiculous. Let us note several titles of articles: *Adameşteanu, la romancière qui lit dans les cœurs* (*Adameşteanu, the Novelist Who Reads Hearts*), *Blandiana, l'Antigone de la poésie* (*Blandiana, the Antigone of Poetry*), *Zografi apostrophe les hommes et les dieux* (*Zografi Reprimands Humans and Gods*), and others. Along with the previously mentioned, there is one attempt to authentically place in the literary history: *Cărtărescu, une des figures montantes de la Génération 80* (*Cărtărescu, One of the Ascending Figures of the '80s Generation*), and a preconception – *Manea: une œuvre digne du Nobel* (*Manea: A Work Worthy of the Nobel Prize*).

So, what does literary Romania mean in the French space, taking into consideration the 'Belles Étrangères' team, made up of writers established in their native country and translated on a foreign land? The mysterious region of a writer worthy of a Nobel Prize (Manea), of a true benchmark author (Cărtărescu), of several picturesque creators – personages such as Ştefan Agopian and Dan Lungu.

3. Post-Integration. Several Observations as Conclusion

In an interview given by the theoretician Boris Groys and included at the end of the volume *Topologia aurei şi alte eseuri* (*Topology of Nimbus and Other Essays*), translated into Romanian in 2007 at the Idea Design&Print Publishing House in Cluj-Napoca, he speaks about a project initiated with the prospect of materializing Alterity, which could determine the specific difference between the cultural productions of the Eastern Europe and of Russia in relation with the Western area. One remark strikes us by its paradoxical contents: it is deemed that communism has strangled all cultural identity, all traditions in this region. But, nowadays, we notice that communism imposes itself in tradition and 'wrapped up in a sort of national serial design, […] it is then sold on the western post-colonial markets'.[4] (108).

With regards to the matter of interest to us, we note that, following the integration into the European Union, the product that sells well Romanian literature abroad is related to episodes dealing with life during the communist regime. This reconstruction of memory delights the Westerner who, as Groys says, has univocally linked the image of this cultural space to this political orientation. What makes the difference, awakening the Western public from its indifference towards the Romanian literature, in a rather unexpected manner, is the fiction discourse dealing with the communist period. Vacillating between the cultural stereotypes and the personality storytelling, some Romanian writers have well understood the 'stake'. Visibility cannot be attained by eroding the already established models. In this way, all one does is show one's readiness to obediently learn the lessons of the great masters.

To sum up, the active penetration on the European market means unity in diversity, specific difference within the framework of the proximity genre. For now, what matters is the distinctive voice within the main discourse, which is a fundamental element, constituted by landmarks that cannot be found anywhere but in this very region.

---

[4]   Boris Groys, *Topologia aurei și alte eseuri* (*Topologie der Kunst/ Topology of Nimbus and Other Essays*), trans. by Aurel Codoban, Lorin Ghiman and George State (Cluj-Napoca: Idea Design & Print, 2007), p. 108.

WORKS CITED

Didier, Béatrice, *Précis de literature européenne* (*European Literature Synopsis*) (Paris: Presses Universitaires de France, 1998), 1-9

Groys, Boris, *Topologia aurei și alte eseuri* (*Topologie der Kunst/ Topology of Nimbus and Other Essays*), trans. by Aurel Codoban, Lorin Ghiman and George State (Cluj-Napoca: Idea Design & Print, 2007)

Le Rider, Jacques, *Europa Centrală sau paradoxul fragilității* (*Central Europe or the Fragility Paradox*), ed. by Dana Chetrinescu and Ciprian Vălcan (Iași: Polirom, 2001)

Marino, Adrian, *Biografia ideii de literatură* (*The Biography of the Idea of Literature*), 7 vols (Cluj-Napoca: Dacia, 1998), V (1998)

Ioana Both

A Romanian Product Refused for Export: Mihai Eminescu, National Poet

This paper attempts to dwell upon the paradoxical situation of the 'major identitary figure' of the Romanian culture, that of the national poet Mihai Eminescu, in relation to strategies of integration of the Romanian literature in the European context. Although an extremely important figure for the Romanian identitary construction, Mihai Eminescu seems to be a hardly exportable cultural product. To blame exclusively a mythical 'untranslatableness' of his poetic genius, or to assert the 'fading' of his work – as well as of the entire European Romanticism, nowadays – both appear to us as reductive explanations. On the contrary, we believe that analysis of this 'failed export' is likely to point out interesting paradigmatic elements regarding the general strategies of the Romanian culture in terms of relating its national identity with a larger (European, Western, etc.) horizon. By reviewing some such flagrant episodes of the failure to export values represented by Eminescu's figure and work, we hope to challenge reflection upon the validity of certain strategies of cultural policy, Eminescu being, of course, just one privileged example of a more general situation of shortcomings in promoting Romanian culture outside the political borders of Romania itself.

For a few years now, I have been interested in the cultural (and political) construction of the Romanian national poet's figure (as it happens, Mihai Eminescu), trying to trace its history and its strategies, for more than a century of mystifying posterity.

This research has led me to the conclusion that, as the object of a tenacious and practically never-ending mystification ever since the year of his death, Mihai Eminescu has long since surpassed the limits of a 'writer's cult'.[1] If at the beginning of this process, as everywhere else in Europe, there is, within the Romanian frontiers, a connection 'between the state and popular cult of the great national writer, and the emergence of a literary history,' we are forced to admit that, soon afterwards, the national writer's cult becomes 'more than a particular form of the great men's cult or of the national memory construction process. It is invested with political games,

---

[1] We have studied this mystification process in *'Mihai Eminescu, poet naţional român'. Istoria şi anatomia unui mit cultural ('Mihai Eminescu, Romanian National Poet. The History and Anatomy of a Cultural Myth')*, ed. by Ioana Both (Cluj-Napoca: Dacia, 2001) and *Histoires littéraires (Literary Histories)*, ed. by Ioana Both (Cluj-Napoca: Centrul de Studii Transilvane, 2003), pp. 69-167.

bias conflicts, unanimity compromises...'[2] As an identitary figure – or, more likely as an identitary 'construction' – meant to represent an entire national culture, Eminescu sees himself transformed into a phenomenon that largely surpasses the precise area of literary studies.

Nowadays, we are faced with a revival of the discussions regarding a necessary 're-branding' of this representative figure of the Romanian culture, in order to export it as an identitary figure into a new Europe, if not into a (brave) new world seen as one. This type of debate does not, however, replace, with the help of a newspeak (that of Public Relations, of new institutions and of European politics), an ancient and well-known problem, which I will try to sum up by means of three guiding questions:

1. Eminescu and his work – are they exportable, and moreover – are they 'translatable' (both in the literal and figurative sense of this term)?

2. within the figure/effigy that Eminescu is censed to represent, does the attribute 'national' really serve the idea of export, in the sense that the figure (thus oriented from its construction) would become more accessible to a foreign public?

3. are we (the specialists in Romanian literature and in Eminescu in particular, together with the specialists in cultural politics and in 'branding') ready to critically consider the faults of our predecessors in this field, and to radically change our strategies?

The answers to these questions, as you might have already guessed, are more likely (although prudently) negative.

Certainly, nowadays we frequently speak with self-confidence about a necessary 'rebranding', in the European context, of this identitary figure of the Romanian nation. The latest articulate contribution in this regard is that of Iulian Costache, in the introductory part of his book *Eminescu, negocierea unei imagini (Eminescu: Negotiating the Image)* where the problem of a present 'rebranding' of the national poet's figure appears among the tasks which would motivate the advances of the scientific exegesis.[3] This would

[2]   Jean-Marie Goulemot, and Eric Walter, 'Les centennaires de Voltaire et Rousseau', in *Lieux de mémoire*, ed. by P. Nora, vol. I (Paris: Gallimard, 1997), p. 380.

[3]   *Eminescu, negocierea unei imagini (Eminescu: Negotiating the Image)* (Bucureşti: Cartea Românească, 2008), p. 9: 'how do the new European states that have joined, especially after 1990, intend to manage their own symbolic patrimony in the context of a European market of symbolic goods?'.

implicitly lead to applying a political perspective to science, and would take us back on the tracks of charted territories. The easiness with which the Romanian literary critique gives in, nowadays, to the tricks towards which the communist dictatorship experience should have turned us more skeptical, rests, in itself, an interesting point of reflection. The revival of the discourse of political activism in the field of the scientific competence, even though made in the name of a 'connection' between the Romanian culture and the new (united) Europe, is no less than a comeback of the genre.

Nevertheless, for the purpose of this paper, I will only focus on the development and the failure of the strategies meant to export worldwide the most important Romanian modern writer. In other words, the question is to determine why, in spite of Romanian culture's (concrete and long-lasting) efforts to transform Eminescu into an identitary key image, that is exportable and highly symbolic, 'Eminescu, Romanian national poet' does not pass, and, moreover, does not succeed in breaking the frontiers of a Romanian Studies specialists' circle, towards the Western academic environments.

Consequently, let us consider, through a classification whose schematic character I fully assume, some of the exporting strategies mentioned. (Given the nature of my academic experience abroad, most of the examples that I have chosen are French. For the benefit of the inventory, I ask you to trust me when I say that, most of the time, they are representative for all the others.)

1. The translations and the editions designed for export

The translations of Eminescu's work (above all – of his poetic work) are quite numerous, thanks to the promotion efforts which were a part of the communist cultural politics of the period between 1950 and 1989. Awards and special programs within the Romanian publishing houses constantly encouraged them. Nevertheless, their high number is not a guarantee either for the quality of the literary translations, or for their distribution in foreign libraries (I do, however, have a vivid memory of them piled up on the bookshelves that decorate our embassies abroad, which allegorically says a lot about the function that the communist régime had assigned to them...).

Still, translating Eminescu's poems faces one with other problems, some of them being, from my point of view, overwhelming. They are mainly related to 'the age of his language', which was not the one of other poets of his time, but one that preceded, in an impressive way, the language of 20th century Romanian poetry. For most of the European languages (and respective cultures), there is no similar linguistic mutation which a translator could rely upon. Therefore, the translator finds himself confronted with an initial restrictive choice: either he translates Eminescu into the language (let's say: French) of the mid-19th century (the result would be a poetry of an ancient taste, 'aulic', deprived of surprises and of major rhetoric innovations, but faithful to the historic moment), or he translates Eminescu into the French poetic language of the beginning of the 20th century, which would lead to a historic 'mistruth', but would respect the reality of his linguistic innovation in modern Romanian language.

Furthermore, there are in Eminescu's poetic language ambiguity effects, indecisive vibrations on the level of rhetoric figurality, which a translation has no other alternative but to reduce to silence.[4] This is definitely the reason why translators prefer the youth poems or the anthumous ones, much more limpid and less ambiguous. Yet, for the sensitivity of nowadays poetry readers, these texts are not the most interesting, on the contrary. Eminescu's poetics is constructed on the scaffold of an enormous fight against language, which the poet finally defeats, destroys and reduces to silence. This modernist critique of language is based on the elements of the romantic mythology of the logocentric universe. The discursive experiments of Eminescu's poetry are less obvious, but no less subversive. It is difficult, if not impossible, for any translator who is not a modernist innovator within his/her language to find the equivalents for something of the sort. Lost in translation, these language qualities entail within their disappearance a very rich poetic content – which explains the feeling of loss when reading Eminescu in a foreign language, as well as the foreigner's difficulty to perceive the main stakes of his poetics.

However, most of the translations' failures aren't this subtle, when it comes to their causes, but are rather due to wrong strategies, as I intend to prove with some subsequent examples.

Most of the time, translators supplied 'correct' translations (those of J.L. Courriol, Elisabeta Isanos – for French), settling the innovative poet for 'one of the last European romantics', a label that doesn't stimulate nowadays the interest of a non-specialised reader.

2. The presentation paratexts, designed for abroad, of the media's 'opinion makers' and of the Romanian cultural institutions

No matter how important they are among the export strategies, paratexts would leave a well-intentioned foreign reader, completely ignorant of the poet and of his native language, rather perplex. A particular category, that of exegesis made by foreigners or designed for foreigners, seems to have the advantage of a proper place and of an opening towards an ideal public. What is there to be considered, if we leave aside the few monographic studies that foreign Romanists dedicated to the poet? Eminescu conferences and symposiums have been occasionally organised in the Western academic

---

[4]   See M. Anghelescu's arguments in 'Eminescu în traduceri' ('Eminescu Translated'), *România literară* (*Literary Romania*), no. 20 (1990).

world, especially around an important commemorative date. Their proceedings have become, most frequently, reference volumes for the specialised bibliography. During communism, it was also possible that the main theme of a symposium would become the expression of the Romanian diaspora's anticommunist resistance, hence politicizing contributions to the extent of turning them irrelevant to the literature they were supposed to discuss (it is the case of a symposium held in Paris in 1950, the centenary year of Eminescu's birth). If that is not the case – as it happened with the Sorbonne symposium of March 1975 [published in the volume *Eminescu après Eminescu* (*Eminescu after Eminescu*) (Iassy: Junimea, 1978) – N.B.: again, edited in Romania!] –, we are talking about perfectly honorable scientific reunions, but with an impact that could not arouse an interest in Eminescu, beyond the limited circles of Romanists and of Romanians abroad.

The paratexts conceived by Romanians in order to present their national poet to foreigners suffer most often from a sterling opacity, which is, above all, hard to translate, given the highly tautological praises, such as: 'Eminescu is the homeland inhabited by words, he is the word born by our homeland, by the Romanian *dor*, by the national specific'.[5] The commemorative albums of the communist period, rich in photographs and in art reproductions, and intensely exported by the Romanian diplomatic services, seem to completely ignore the public they are meant to reach. The paratexts have the 'clarity' of: 'For the contemporary man, *Hyperion* can also take the significance of a pathetic appeal to reconciliation, of a new vital influx given to the complete man, the multidimensional man, the total man…'[6] With nothing to stir up the curiosity of a foreign reader; this para-literature does not exert any virtue of cultural mediation, on the contrary – it seems, this time as well, blocked within the logic of the untranslatable.

3. The presentation paratexts belonging to those who, foreigners themselves, are dedicated to the promotion of his work, or to the national poet identitary image – which are the effects?

3.1. A first category is that of translators who don't hesitate to sing his praise; certainly, Eminescu had his share of translators, good or bad, in many languages. His work's disposition to translation is in itself, as we have seen, a delicate chapter. This doesn't prevent him from being largely translated. But if we closely consider the published volumes, the publishers and the editions'

---

[5]   M. Popa, 'Ideea de Eminescu', in *Ideea de Eminescu* (*The Eminescu Idea*) (Sf. Gheorghe: Arcuş Publishing, 2000).

[6]   P.M. Gorcea, *Vesper – un mythe original*, in *Mihai Eminescu – Luceafărul*, commemorative album (Bucharest: Cartea Românească, 1984), p. 78.

circulation, we realise that, commonly, mostly after the Second World War (when we could actually speak of an increase in translations number), these works have been published in Romania. The publishing distribution followed rather a diplomatic network than a scientific one, which was an unsuitable strategy of cultural promotion. This is the reason why there is an abundance of those translations in libraries *en terre roumaine*, whereas numerous important scientific and popular libraries abroad have no such titles. We could rather be talking about an export inside Romania!

3.2. Eminescu is also presented by foreign writers, who speak Romanian, and who, most often, play the role of translators; they sometimes dedicated poems to Eminescu. The effect is actually minor, because it's usually the case of mediocre poets (perhaps with the exception of Iannis Ritsos or of Rafael Alberti), who give the impression of using the tribute to a foreign writer in order to include themselves 'in the consecrating picture', without being prestigious authors in their native cultures. They practice (without exception!) the encomiastic comparison, the analogy between absolute and incomparable values in themselves. Brenda Walker (English translator of the Romanian literature), for instance, declares without hesitation during an interview (addressed to the Romanian readers!) that Eminescu has the same value as Shakespeare, but her arguments don't go further than the limits of tautological praise.[7] Moreover, if they dedicate their original creations to Eminescu (which frequently happens), their poems abound in an intertextuality, opaque to any of those who are not already acquainted with the work of the Romanian poet; they are filled with Romanian cultural allusions, and, therefore, closed to any exploratory reading. This kind of mediation fallacy is not singular. Actually, this type of encomiastic literature is published especially in Romania, as a proof (reconforting for our self ego) of the national poet's worldwide prestige.[8]

3.3. Within the narrow frame of their field, specialists in Romanian Studies often situate our national poet in a comparative/universal perspective, but this perspective is always focused on Eminescu, and – in consequence – it is always enclosed upon him, as well as on the interests and on the competences of the specialised reader. Hence 'Eminescu's bibliography', for example,

---

[7]   In M. Cimpoi, *Spre un nou Eminescu* (*Towards a New Eminescu*) (Chişinău: Hyperion, 1993), pp. 190 sq.

[8]   See *Eminescu – pururi tînăr. Dedicaţii lirice* (*Eminescu, Forever Young. Lyrical Dedications*), ed. by C. Crăciun and V. Crăciun (Chişinău, Bucureşti: Litera, David, 1998). Among the foreigners who dedicate poetry (unsuccessful as literature) to Eminescu we could mention: Majtenyi Erik, Iannis Ritsos, Nikos Papas, Otar Şalamberidze, Bojena Maria Ha de Vernyj, Ungenda N'Sele.

notes studies consecrated to the relationship between this author's work and Schopenhauer, Shakespeare and Heine. On the contrary, he is absent from the (foreign) studies that sum up the impact of similar creators upon European literature in general...

Otherwise, there are also the studies on Eminescu signed by the Romanians from the diaspora. In this case, the scientific point of view is mixed with political bias, of no interest for the non-Romanian reader (besides, these studies are written in Romanian and usually published by the publishing houses of the Romanian diaspora). Their success belongs to a quite restricted circle, thus preventing us from talking about a real 'export' abroad [see Svetlana Paleologu-Matta, *Eminescu și abisul ontologic* (*Eminescu and the Onthological Abyss*) (Nord: Aarhus, 1988)]. Moreover, it is often the case that, despite their good intentions, such people mishandle literary theory and have dilettante or outdated specialised readings, which contributes to a decrease of their appeal in the eyes of a foreigner, in spite of their literary formation (Lucian Boz, Svetlana Paleologu-Matta, Ovidiu Vuia, etc.). The foreigners who deal with Eminescu's work enjoy a rather paradoxical fate: most of the time, they are well-known in Romania (Alain Guillermou, Jean-Louis Courriol, Brenda Walker), whereas in their own countries they are decently confided to the academic field of Romanian Studies, having little recognition and no aspiration for a large media acknowledgment. As the entire Romanian literature, Eminescu is a 'niche' specialisation abroad.

4. Eminescu in the contemporary encyclopaedias of universal/European culture

Statistics prove that, starting with the second decade of the last century, Eminescu is highly present, with richer and more exact references, in the most important encyclopaedias of universal literature: *Meyers Lexicon, Encyclopaedia Britannica, Brockhaus, Der Grosse Herder, Dizionario Universale della letteratura contemporanea, Uj magyar lexicon, Dizionario Enciclopedico Sansoni, Grand Larousse Encyclopédique en dix volumes, Dictionnaire universel des Lettres, The Penguin Companion to Literature,* etc.[9]. But there is an essential difference between being present in a 'cultural treasure-encyclopaedia' of the European or universal literature, and actually becoming a reference of universal literature, which is obviously not the case as far as Eminescu is concerned.

---

[9] See Gh. I. Florescu, 'Luceafărul în enciclopediile lumii' ('*Luceafărul* in World Encyclopaedias'), in *România literară*, no. 24 (1989).

5. Eminescu in nowadays new media

After a quick glance and search on Google, his presence on the internet reveals around 3.980.000 posts of his name in approximately 0,18 seconds of research (including fields such as www.eminescu.com and www.eminescu.net, bought and syrupy developed by a Romanian from the Nantucket Islands, Adrian George Săhlean, whose internet pseudonym is, well... Michael [sic!] Eminescu).

> N.B. None of the Romanian institutions officially designed to export this writer have manifested so far an interest in similar projects.

5.1. Online translations

Their great number doesn't represent an export success; these translations are either picked from previously published volumes, or done by the *expats* themselves, which is far from guaranteeing a literary accuracy. Besides, their author's intention is to provide a proof of patriotism 'against the geographic distance from the motherland', and not a proof of talent or of a good knowledge of the target-language. The most consulted sites are the following (and the selection is not very rich):

- http://www.agonia.net/index.php/poetry/86861/index.html

- http://www.antonia-dinsuflet.be/traductions.htm

- http://etoile-du-danube.com/litterature/poemes-dimitrie-grama-bastian-et-autres-confidances/classique/eminescu-poemes-traductions-de-constantin-frosin/

5.2. Sites dedicated to Eminescu (most of them are still written in Romanian, so the linguistic barrier actually stands)

5.2.1. Non-specialised sites: 1. bloggers whose pseudonym is 'Eminescu', sites in Romanian, focused on the Romanian latest news, nothing that would make them spectacular; 2. sites of the Romanian diaspora which integrate his poems in order to mark a symbolic communitarian belonging. The poet's image that they offer is sweetened, idyllic, either in a minor sentimental

rhetoric, or as a statement of high patriotism. In this last case, Eminescu functions as an ultimate reason for the political attitudes concerning Romania's current situation (they became very active since the scandal provoked by *Dilema* magazine in 1998, or due to H.R. Patapievici's texts: http://revista-ecoul.com/un-scandal-aparent-incheiat-dar-cu-ecouri-lungi-%E2%80%9D-eminescu-cadavrul-din-debara-%E2%80%9C/).

But most of them are in Romanian:

- http://www.aslrq.ro/ASLRQ_fichiers/eminescu.htm

- http://www.reper-romanesc.org/publicatie/0401/radacini.htm

- in French, there is an entire site (poor in information), which is dedicated to him, but it has been inactive ever since 2006 (http://jeanloup.roland.free.fr/)

- http://www.mihai-eminescu.net/ - this one, named after the national poet, is symptomatic for this genre of mixtures that we have mentioned above. It's a propagandistic site of the extreme-right Romanian movement, written entirely in Romanian. Actually, Eminescu is frequently present on the sites of the extreme-right Romanian groups, in the line of the political manipulations of his figure, inaugurated by the legionary ideologues of the '30s.

5.2.2. Specialised sites (having a rather restricted area of interest, they take us back to the problem of the limited target audience which is Roumanophone, especially because, with some exceptions, we are talking about sites written exclusively in Romanian). Furthermore, despite their scientific aspirations, these sites usually offer no guarantee in this regard – making us wonder if the term 'scientific' is actually the most adequate. They aren't numerous either:

- http://www.romanianvoice.com/poezii/poeti/eminescu.php – is the richest site in Romanian literature for foreign readers; yet, the poems posted are exclusively in Romanian, and they appear with no paratexts and with no philological indications concerning the original edition;

- http://www.mihaieminescu.eu/biografie.php; http://www.nouaromanie.ro/dictionar%20de%20personalitati%20ro manesti_files/index%20domenii/poeti/mihai%20eminescu.htm – the site contains biographies in Romanian, without indicating the source or the author of the posted texts;

- http://www.cimec.ro/Carte/Eminescu/ME.htm, http://eminescu.petar.ro/ – a good site presenting the work in Romanian, therefore – inaccessible to non-Roumanophones;

-   www.unifi.it/letrum – *Cronologia della letteratura rumena 1790-1914* (conceived as a didactic auxiliary, it would represent a good introduction, but it contains little information and a small number of texts; an Italian version is available, which opens the site to readers who do not understand or read Romanian).

5.3. Eminescu winds up on Youtube

Well, we can find him here! His poems appear as song lyrics, frequently out of nostalgia after the 'Flacăra' Folk Group of the revolutionary youth of the '70s-'80s. Therefore, Eminescu arrives on Youtube with a 'nostalgic' political meaning, which doesn't actually serve his export towards the foreign readers. The portal is charged with small films (with a soundtrack of romance or of kitsch extracts of the 19th century music), directed with a minor sentimentalism, and posted in the name of nationalism or of the identitary nostalgia of some exiles (the pseudonyms of those who posted them are transparent for a Romanian reader: *Zamolxis09, LonelyMoonRise, Wintermood, Spineshivers, Resistentza*, etc.). What is surprising is that there are little explanations on Eminescu and on the reasons of their choice. With a totally unjustified confidence, they prefer the tautologic strategy of 'Eminescu doesn't need any presentation, he's universally known' (n.I.B.: is he, really?).

Actually, Youtube's style involuntarily sums up what is most ineffective in all these export strategies: a (completely unjustified) confidence that 'Everybody knows who Eminescu is', nothing but a frail and fake gesture that highly calmed patriotism cannot save from incommunicability.

The attention of all these strategies is focused rather on the promotion of the identitary figure than on the reality of Eminescu's work, perpetuating a confusion which makes export always difficult, 'as it once used to be'…

Because the reading of Eminescu's work according to the patterns of a national (or nationalist) construction's identitary figure is forever banned to consider his work from a restrictive perspective, mainly anachronistic, nostalgically oriented, in short – improper. Furthermore, being a sort of patchwork for stakes unknown to Eminescu's work, the reading's logic remains (at most!) obscure for a foreign reader who is not a specialist in Romanian literature. I would like to mention, as a way of concluding, two of its reflexes, which are, in my opinion, the most recurrent and the most improper.

The most frequent strategy (and probably, the one with the strongest impact) consists in building the national representativeness of the national poet's figure with the help of de-contextualised (and mishandled) poetic images belonging to Eminescu's work. The mythic tree with the help of which Eminescu had imagined the birth of the Ottoman Empire (in *The 3rd Epistle*) becomes, with no hesitation from the part of the interpreter, 'The tree of Eminescu's genius [and the sign] of the Romanian genius's obvious creative power'.[10] In a logic that fictionalises on the work's margins and that is unfaithful to it, it is enough for an image to be attested in Eminescu's writings in order for it to function (in an identity constructing discourse) as the indicative of national particularity. The general impression given by these 'mythmakers' is that all the components of Eminescu's work can change their meaning in the name of the national representativeness imperative. Each one of them, down to the tragic accents of the last creative years, down to the blasphemies of the last phase of the *logos*'s poetic imagery,[11] because the stake is neither in the quality of the argumentation, nor in the faithfulness towards the texts, but in the image that the interpreters want to give of Eminescu: 'Eminescu is, above all, a Romanian poet; in no other work from our literature, the completeness of the Romanian soul is so well reflected; nobody has managed to reunite in other verse our ethnic components as Eminescu has' [Sextil Puşcariu, *Mihai Eminescu* (1909), see note 10 above, p. 88].[12] All these so-called arguments, when closely considered, do not stand for themselves.

Finally, the creation of 'Eminescu, a national poet (and an identitary figure)' coincides with a desynchronisation of our cultural evolution in comparison with the historic moment. Because, if Titu Maiorescu, as an opinion-maker, restores the literary canon of the Romanian modernity (rightly placing Eminescu's work at its peak), on the other hand, when it comes to winning the public opinion and forming an interpreting community according to his own taste, he chooses to perpetuate a messianic-

---

[10]   Constantinescu, Pompiliu, 'O catedră Eminescu' ('An Eminescu Literary Department'), in *Eminescu, poetul naţional* (*Eminescu, the National Poet*), ed. by Gh. Ciompec (Bucureşti: Eminescu, 1983), p. 255.

[11]   See Ioana Both, 'Imaginea patriei în poezia lui Mihai Eminescu faţă cu stereotipiile criticii' ('Homeland Images in Eminescu's Poetry Vs. the Critics' Stereotypes'), in *T(z)ara noastră. Stereotipii şi prejudecăţi* (*Our Country. Stereotypes and Prejudices*), ed. by R. Cesereanu (Bucureşti: Institutul Cultural Român, 2007), pp. 226-39. The over-interpretation of the romantic myth of Romanian's ethnogenesis, as it appears in Eminescu's poetic vision, and that the exegesis alters in the name of a more adequate perspective for the national imaginary constructions, in Ioana Both, 'Imaginea Romei antice în poezia patriotică a lui Mihai Eminescu' ('Ancient Rome's Image in Mihai Eminscu's Patriotic Poetry'), in *Cercetarea antropologică în România. Perspective istorice şi etnografice* (*Anthropological Research in Romania. Historical and Ethnographic Perspectives*), ed. by C. Papa, G. Pizza, and F.M. Zerilli (Cluj-Napoca: Clusium, 2004), pp. 63-75.

[12]   This same text carries on thereafter with unsustainable comments, by way of arguments, such as: 'Where Eminescu starts to speak, begins the loud speech of our literature's masculinity, it's with him that we cross the boundaries towards new times...' (p. 87).

revolutionary perspective of the writer, as a savior of the nation; the end of his article from 1889, *Eminescu and his poems*, is the prophetic outcome of this strategy. Many will hence follow Maiorescu in this 'mythmaker' undertaking, and none of them will find other objective proofs for their remarks, either in Eminescu's biography, or in his work. Responding to a collective and historic imagining context (so well characterised by Lucian Boia in his recent studies), the 'mythmakers' – which are also the creators of the Romanian modern national conscience – carry on, when it comes to the identitary construction, a residual perspective, dating back to 1848 (historically speaking, the period of the foundation the Romanian national institutions), and applied to a personality and to a work that are no longer a part of it. Yet, it seems obvious to us that this kind of conformity (which we could call "scientific") is of no interest. What the mythmakers aim at is to impose an identitary sense within this Trojan horse that is 'the national poet Eminescu'. We are talking about discursive strategies, whose essence is to make performative statements pass for constative ones.[13] Because the national poet is a word construction, a true masterpiece belonging to interpreting individuals, and to the interpreting communities they have educated.

With the risk of a lurking metaphor (but which is far from our intention), we could say that 'the national poet' has something to do with Mihai Eminescu, this great writer of the late Romanian romanticism, only in a weak and treacherous way. We could say that 'the national poet' is unknown to the one he should rely on, the same way that any discourse (or narration) is unknown to the reality – which explains its ontological weakness and its persuasive force.

Are there any solutions for this? Personally, I don't see many. Nevertheless, I will plead, as a matter of principle, for strategies concerning the work's opening to the contemporary public, without doing it by the bias of forever imperfect translations. Imposing him straightaway as a national figure threatens to drive away an 'innocent' (or at least a non-specialised) reader, who would be looking in those poems more likely for a subjective, empathic reading, rather than for some nation's symbolic constructions. But can we export him as a writer, without the weight of the political national imagery? Certainly, a possible way would be that of 'naturally' turning towards examples from his work, in comparative literary studies/ literary theory, which would put him in the company of established and accessible names from the universal literature. Often, our comparatists pass by his work, even when invoking him would be in the spirit of their approach. Of course,

---

[13]   In the sense given by J.L. Austin, *Quand dire c'est faire* (Paris: Seuil, 1970).

we are dealing with a strategy meant for literary specialists, but still it should be taken into consideration.

If not, Eminescu (his life, his work, his identitary representativeness) risks to remain confided to the narrow circle of Romanian academics. As far as I know, he is not among the writers proposed in the general or comparative literature curricula, alongside Baudelaire, Hölderlin, Ungaretti and Poe. *Inter pares*, as it would function in similar contexts, Eminescu would cease to be a self-enclosed, incomprehensible monad. Another way would be that of his historical person's 'de-tabooisation'. Far from the rumour of Eminescu's statues wars (statues which the diaspora puts up, for example, in order to mark a particular memorial site or an influence on the right to memory, that it hence claims), I rather think about the cinema's power, itself centenarian, as to an intelligent practice for memorial sites. Then, I will leave you to dream about a tourist circuit that would discover historical Transylvania to nowadays tourists, according to Eminescu's wanderings, or to another one that would revive him in Iaşi or Bucharest, with guides who are not driven by mythologizing and patriotic obsessions. In the same way I dare dream of a museum of everyday life in Iaşi, just as it used to be in Eminescu's times, counterbalancing, of course, in its approach, the museum complex from Ipoteşti, an exemplary self-enclosed space, trapped within the strategies of national mystification.

WORKS CITED

Ciompec, Gh., ed., *Eminescu, poetul naţional* (*Eminescu, the National Poet*) (Bucureşti: Eminescu, 1983)

Mihai Eminescu – Luceafărul, commemorative album (Bucharest: Cartea Românească, 1984)

Nora, Pierre, ed., *Lieux de mémoire*, vol. I (Paris: Gallimard, 1997)

Mădălina Vatcu

Openings of the Romanian Poetry Anthologies Translated into French.
Canonical Variations during the Communist Period

The present study examines the anthologies of Romanian poetry translated into French during the communist period, focusing on the configuration and the organization of the elements these books encompass – we will see up to what extent they are also canonical.

The presentations and excerpts chosen for representing a small, young literature or one that is not known abroad, such as the Romanian literature, are essential, especially since they are an externalization of literary information. The present study examines the anthologies of Romanian poetry translated into French during the communist period, focusing on the configuration and the organization of the elements these books encompass – we will see up to what extent they are also canonical.[1]

1. Ideal and practical implications of a (translated) anthology

Following the common conception, maintained by the large number of anthologies of chosen excerpts, an anthology requires mandatory filter value – a complex concept, subject to a number of assessment scales. Thus, the anthology is located at the junction of objectivity and subjectivity; it bears responsibility for something considered a representative selection of the highest degree, but in a richer, freer way than the volumes of a single author. With regard to literary anthologies, it is said that such books are all the more enjoyable, more diverse, while they retain cohesion, a required uniformity. Furthermore, an anthology demands either an effort of synthesis, an ability to discern, recognize, guess and isolate the value or, sometimes, a capacity to recycle and reassess.

An anthology requires the definition of clear composition criteria and consistency in complying with them. Their author's work is not mainly

---

[1] This study was made on the basis of documentation for a PhD research, *Les belles infidèles. Translations of Romanian literature into French, 1945-1949; a political-sociological perspective*, study coordinated by Professor Mircea Anghelescu (University of Bucharest).

creative, but it rather calls for qualities that define a literary critic and historian and an editor with a sense of the illustrative. The anthology also fulfills a didactical purpose for beginners, amateurs, being recommended as an initiation in an area and also broad enough to generate interest in it.

A genre with shifting borders, the anthology is sometimes associated with a certain vision; it is supposed to remove ignorance on a subject or theme; it is an opportunity to get closer to an unknown area. The purpose would be a complete capturing of the public; or, in the case of translated anthologies, they can stimulate translation, encouraging an appetite for a literature yet unknown, but deserving to be presented to foreign readerships and appreciated.

When speaking of anthologies that lay the ground of a literature, things get more complicated. Covering an entire literature is not only difficult, but also an ambitious project, with important consequences, that demand the finding of an appropriate summary, the appropriate recipe for putting together classic and contemporary authors. It requires careful weighing, since the translation of classics is also subject to significant losses. The anthologies, once translated, have to cope with this paradox: if they intend to be a carriers of the 'specificities' in a literature, during the translation many of these 'specificities' are lost or blurred; the demonstration intended as illustration will be, under these circumstances, only an attempt at a demonstration.

A translated anthology idea involves increasing relevance; it functions as a recommendation and must therefore be subjected to several influences: economic, political, aesthetic, pragmatic indicators of such an undertaking, worthy of the interest and involvement of the authorities. But 'representativity', as the coordinating principle, creates a smooth relationship between the anthology and the literary canon. The overlapping area of the two depends on the type of anthology; note that the anthology can follow the canon, that is rigid and retains only the masterpieces, but more often it is more than it, becoming an amount of canons. Now we will follow the limits of this expansion for the 11 anthologies of Romanian poetry translated into French, between 1945 and 1989.

The first noticeable curiosity is the average statistics recording an anthology being published every 4-5 years; what factors could justify the large numbers of works of this kind? Could it be because many of them have been a failure, defeating their purpose? But statistics are misleading, since at a closer analysis anthologies are less the result of hard work and more the result of circumstances.

2. Anthology types

2.1. Origin brands

Out of the 11 anthologies translated, two are devoted to folk literature: *Anthologie de la poésie populaire roumaine*, translated by Annie Bentoiu and Andreea Dobrescu-Warodin (Bucharest: Minerva, 1979), and *Ballades populaires roumaines* (bilingual edition), translated by Andrei Bucsan (Cluj-Napoca: Dacia, 1984). It is believed that these volumes are signs of reverence for model literature, pieces of treasury by default, pieces of heritage. The origins of these books that glorify peasants are relevant for an indirect way of conceiving restrictive and nationalistic literature.

With regards to other collections, we will analyze them grouped according to their features and we will see how much they are really related.

2.2. Anthology as official discourse

The first two anthologies, *Poèmes roumains, dès origines à nos jours* and *Introduction à la poésie roumaine* are published in France, both having the same editor, Hubert Juin. There are data that prevent us from separating them, but prior to an analysis, an overview of the period's customs is required.

The Romanian pride (or necessity) demanding to have anthologies translated and published abroad produced a real book-manufacturing system. In the late '50s and early '60s there was a real boom in anthologies of Romanian poetry translated; such volumes appeared in France, Spain, Brazil, Portugal, and the Netherlands, all with the cover name of some famous personalities in the country of origin. Could this be a success of the communist regime? It could be called so, because there was not a sudden interest of foreign countries in Romania and its literature, but the involvement of Bucharest authorities who were looking for acknowledged authors willing to adapt literal translations (in French or/and in English) made in Romania. The excessive centralization led to embarrassing results by similarity; the compared summaries of the anthologies clearly follow the 'canon', namely a common stock, at a rate of 80-90%, the variation being in the choice of titles, rarely changing the lot of authors. Actually, the foreign party's contribution is reduced to detailed comments on the summary, small changes or selection within the corpus of received translations. In conclusion, we have to do with a comfortable kind of anthology: the reproduced anthology. This being so, the question of 'how to make an anthology', based on the phrase 'how to set the summary of an anthology?' is summarized in terms of the foreign poet whose name appears under 'translation' and 'anthologized', in 'how to accept and sign a summary already set/chosen'.

To contract an anthology was not a personal mission, all materials being carefully studied by the Romanian state institutions, such as The Central Committee of the Communist Party, or the Ministry of Foreign Affairs. Moreover, in order to progress from the draft version of the anthology, money was required. The necessary amounts came along the official route, after the project had been seen and approved by the competent forums. It is easy to conclude that going against the official conception on poetry was impossible. However, one should keep in mind that the approval route was complex, including the Writers' Union, which sought to maintain a degree of aesthetics in the selected poems.

'Une anthologie est soumise à de nombreuses servitudes; [...] le choix, ici plus qu'ailleurs, trahit l'auteur.'[2] However, these anthologies had several authors, following successive approvals, and consequently we have avoided reconsidering the anthology as equivalent to a canon. In the first case, we speak of relevance and eligibility deriving from several sources; sometimes, foreigners received a list of recommendations from which to choose; sometimes, they did the presentations in the preface, starting from the critical articles or from Romanian dictionaries (all having the necessary approvals to be sent abroad). This process was the only solution, since foreigners with a passion for Romanian literature and able to compile an anthology were few and far between.

Going back to the selection indirectly signed by Hubert Juin in 1958 – dedicated to Veronica Porumbacu and Eugen Jebeleanu, politically engaged literary celebrities of the time – a quick glance is enough to realise that we are faced with an anthology with presentations and selections of poems made by someone very familiar with the Romanian literary and political discourse: 'L'histoire de la Roumanie est faite de souffrances, de trahisons et de sacrifices. Autour des trois principautés, les puissances étrangères veillent, comme des vautours.'[3] After folk poetry is praised as a specific Romanian excellence, this 'specificity' is exemplified by a passage from Cicerone Theodorescu's work, a prominent poet of the so-called 'proletcultist group', the fragment evoking a worker, victim in the uprising at the Grivița plants, 1933.

Three years later, the same Hubert Juin signed another anthology, *Introduction à la poésie roumaine*, (Paris: Club des amis du livre

---

[2]   'An anthology is subject to numerous constraints; [...] here, more than elsewhere, the selection betrays the author', in Georges Pompidou, *Anthologie de la poésie française*, Nouvelle édition suivie d'un post-scriptum (Paris: Hachette, 1989), pp. 527-528.

[3]   'Romanian history is made of suffering, betrayal and sacrifice; foreign powers were watching, like eagles, around the three Romanian provinces', in the preface signed by Hubert Juin, in *Poèmes roumains, dès origines à nos jours*, 1958, p. 10.

progressiste, 1961). The very short period of time from the first one is the most surprising feature. We could interpret this new anthology as related to a change of vision or a personal contribution. But this second collection is only a copy of the first – the same lyrics arrangements, with stanzas alternating with comments. With regards to the retained authors, if the first anthology contained a number of 19 poets, this one brings together 21 names; Dimitrie Bolintineanu was taken out from the first edition, while Nina Cassian, Miron Radu Paraschivescu and Veronica Porumbacu were added. Otherwise, it was almost the same synthesis of a history more or less literary, interpreted according to the times; both anthologies signed by Hubert Juin had politically induced selection criteria resulting in a weak composition method.

2.3. Permissive official anthologies

Anthologie de la poésie roumaine, coordinated by Alain Bosquet, with an introduction by Şerban Cioculescu, the last one signed by a French author, was released in 1968, the year of the liberalization. Its summary is an amazing mixture, for it to belong to a forum in Romania would have meant full liberalization; the secret of this collection can be understood by following the steps of the summary selection. We mention that the quoted data came from documents found in the archives of the Romanian Writers' Union.[4]

In late 1962, the consent of Alain Bosquet for the translation of an anthology of Romanian poetry had already been received, as proved by one of his letters to Veronica Porumbacu, head of the department for International Relations of the Writers' Union.

Je sais quel travail de titan ce doit être de réunir comme vous le faites une anthologie de poèmes roumains en traduction française. C'est probablement la meilleure formule étant donné que les connaissances en langues étrangères de nos poètes français sont, somme toute, inexistantes, et même assez rudimentaires dans des langues comme l'anglais ou l'allemand. Quand vous serez satisfaite de votre travail, je ne demande pas mieux que de relire l'ensemble, soit par moi-même, soit avec votre aide, s'il vous est possible de venir en France. Cela me permettrait de vous faire peut-être ici et là quelques suggestions de détail.[5]

---

[4]   I take the opportunity to thank the president of the Romanian Writers' Union, Mr. Nicolae Manolescu, who kindly gave me permission for consultation, and all those who facilitated my study of archival documents.

[5]   'I realize that the work you're involved in must be enormous, bringing Romanian poetry together, in order to create an anthology in French translation. It is, probably, the best formula, given the knowledge of languages by the French poets, non-existent and rudimentary regarding the other languages, even in terms of English or German. When you're satisfied with the result, I won't ask more than to read all the translations, either alone or with your participation, if you can come to France. So, I can make some suggestions of detail, here and there', in a letter of Alain Bosquet to Veronica Porumbacu.

So, this selection was also subject to control, the French poet having a strictly limited contribution. The anthology was to be published by Editions du Seuil, 1965; given the workload involved, the literal translations in Romania were done at short notice, so that the French poets Alain Bosquet and Eugène Guillevic (that contributed by the same method to the publication of an anthology of Hungarian poetry in French) could have enough time to review the text.[6] In 1964 and 1965, Alain Bosquet and Guillevic spent several weeks in Romania in order to finalize the translations.

Starting in April 1965, the negotiations on the summary were intensified; during this time, Seuil concluded an agreement with The Council for Freedom of Culture, which had begun to support editing such anthologies. The Council, through Pierre Emmanuel, its general secretary, came with an additional list of poets to be included suggested by Romanian dissidents, such as Paul Miron, Nicolae Caranica and Ioan Cuşa. Following the indications of the Romanian Embassy in Paris, Alain Bosquet accepted only a few of the listed names (Ovid Densusianu, Perpessicius, Camil Petrescu, Tudor Vianu, V. Voiculescu, I. Frunzetti, Al. Stamatiad, Dan and Emil Botta). Later, Pierre Emmanuel, probably growing tired of negotiating in parallel with the Romanians exiled in Paris (rejecting participation in a formal, imposed book), gave free hand to Bosquet to determine the final list of authors to be included in the anthology. Alain Bosquet also asked the Writers' Union for more texts, belonging mostly to poets of the early '60s (Ana Blandiana, Geo Dumitrescu, Ion Gheorghe, Emil Giurgiuca, Florin Mugur, Ştefan Aug. Doinaş, Ion Alexandru, Nichita Stănescu, Gabriela Melinescu). [7] Moreover, the final form of the anthology included exiled authors: Al. Busuioceanu and Aron Cotrus, long dead, and Jacques Costin, who had legally left the country, being also the one who helped Bosquet to put together his collection. Overall, the anthology included 82 Romanian poets, from the chronicler Miron Costin to the national poet, Mihai Eminescu, but also the 'discovery', with socialist roots Th. Dumitru Neculuţă, or some other poets, considered not minor, but

---

Date of correspondence, 29 November 1962, Romanian Writers' Union's archive, in *1962, England, Iceland, France* folder.

[6]   Address no. 1589/18.XI.1963, of Mihai Beniuc, for Pompiliu Macovei, deputy minister of Foreign Affairs, Romanian Writers' Union's archive, in *1963, External Relations, France* folder.

[7]   Document entitled 'Note: editing an anthology of Romanian poetry in France', unsigned, dated 16 April 1965. Romanian Writers' Union's archive, *1965. France and Congress, Dante and Provence, Avignon* folder.

almost unknown, such as Jacques Costin. Talking about the canon in relation to such a combination is superfluous. Meanwhile, this is the last anthology of Romanian poetry 'made' by a Frenchman during the communist period.

The second collection of the so-called 'official permissive' cathegory, *Anthologie de la poésie roumaine*, with a preface by George Macovescu (Paris: Editions Nagel, 1981), marked one last effort to encompass the entire Romanian literature, a huge effort resulting in a more than 1100 pages of a bilingual edition. We could say that this was the official anthology by definition, the outcome of the two presidents of the Romanian Writers' Union (Zaharia Stancu and George Macovescu). The content was more permissive than we would have expected from the transparently ideological introduction. There are 74 poets included, some appearing for the first time in an anthology translated into French; we can record an important step forward, consisting in the innovative, aesthetic style of the creations (Dimitrie Stelaru, Constant Tonegaru, Radu Stanca, Mircea Ivănescu, Grigore Hagiu, Emil Brumaru, but also Costache Conachi, Ion Heliade-Rădulescu, Mateiu Caragiale); in addition, some German and Hungarian poets can be found in this anthology.

2.4. In the absence of official obstacles

With one exception (the 1981 edition, published at Nagel), the anthologies translated into French after 1970 no longer have the ambition to cover a whole literature, they tend to focus on a period or theme instead, which were freer territories, protected from a mandatory list of authors required for demonstration. Such is the case of *Petite anthologie de poésie roumaine*, bilingual edition, published at Minerva Editions (Bucharest, 1975), in reality the work of a translation seminar entitled 'Mihai Eminescu' and held at Université de Provence, Aix-en-Provence, the selection belonging to the Romanian critic and coordinator of the seminar, Valeriu Rusu. Going through the summary, the proportions of poems in relation to their authors was strikingly different compared to the politically-dictated anthologies (for example, this anthology contains only a title from Eugen Jebeleanu's entire work, but 9 or 10 poems from Miron Radu Paraschivescu, Nichita Stănescu and Marin Sorescu).

In 1975, another anthology was released: *Poésis. Poètes roumains contemporains*, Editions Eminescu: the collection contained 122 poems belonging to 122 Romanian poets. Chronologically ordered, the contemporary poets series began with T. Arghezi (b. 1880) and ended with Carolina Ilinca (b. 1951). The mosaic of renowned authors and poets unknown even to the Romanian public (such as Franz Liebhard, Dragoş Vrânceanu, Vlaicu Bârna, Radu Cârneci, Alexandru Căprariu, Bodor Pal, Horia Zilieru, Ovidiu Genaru, Dimitrie Rachici, Mihai Negulescu, Dan Laurenţiu, Mircea Micu, Nicolae Dragoş, A.I. Zăinescu, Ion Crânguleanu,

George Chirilă, Mihai Duțescu, Marius Robescu, George Alboiu, Dan Mutașcu, Dorin Tudoran, and Dumitru M. Ion) customized the anthology, marking the transition from the 'classical' form of anthologies, which contain a limited number of authors, represented with more titles, to the refusal to submit the idea of focusing on the 'stars'. With its opening towards synchronism, the selection seemed to have abandoned the canonical principle.

A mixture of generations and styles, orientations and nationalities, marking the victory of the young poets, was the bilingual anthology, published in 1978 at "Cartea Românească" and entitled *30 poètes roumains*. Built under the spirit of tolerance, it confirms a trend towards a kind of artificial equality, since under an ambiguous title, no less than 60 poems are being collected, two for each poet. A relevant aspect is that the selection is not signed.

Unique in relation to other anthologies, *Florilège d'amour – poèmes, édition bilingue franco-romaine*, selection and translation by Aurel George Boeșteanu, Minerva Editions 1981, avoided the idea of canonical selection, preferring a thematic one. The book contained a series of poems, written by a wide range of Romanian poets (41), from the dawn of Romanian poetry to recent poets, from Alecu Văcărescu to Ileana Mălăncioiu and Mircea Dinescu, going through Zaharia Stancu, Dumitru Popescu and G. Călinescu and without neglecting folk poetry.

Original in terms of composition is *Jeunes poètes roumains*, with texts selected and translated into French by Dan Ion Nasta, published by Editura Eminescu, Bucharest, 1985, the last one released before 1989. Being acclaimed as the book of a generation, it was intended by the editor (also an aesthetician by orientation) to give an international audience to the generation of Romanian poets from the '80s, who were promoted by the same Eminescu Publishing House. An ingenious method meant to promote the 22 young people, most of them at the first publication in an anthology translated into French (Daniel Turcea, Ioana Ieronim, Adrian Popescu, Dinu Flămând, Dan Verona, Ion Mircea, Ioana Diaconescu, Grete Tartler, Mircea Florin Șandru, Liliana Ursu, Daniela Crăsnaru, Doina Uricariu, Paul Balahur, Denisa Comănescu, Gabriel Chifu, Cornelia Maria Savu, Traian T. Coșovei, Matei Vișniec, and Mircea Cărtărescu). Creating such an anthology is first and foremost a bet that required intuition and that defied the idea of a 'canon', of a writer who could earn his place among the chosen ones only after death. If other anthologies included contemporary poets in addition to classic ones, it was time to have an anthology dedicated solely to the youth of Romanian poetry.

3. Anthologies and the relative legitimacy

As a conclusion on the Romanian poetry anthologies translated into French, we can speak of legitimacy only in the areas covered by such collections, depending both on the purpose of the work and on what it was supposed to demonstrate. On the other hand, this type of anthology only allowed a slim chance for the authors to be later published in a volume, which was possible only if they were supported by other means, because the anthology by itself could not work as a launching pad for the author's volume. Also, if we compare the aesthetic charge and the historic weight, we will find that the first anthologies, chronologically speaking, are nothing but windows to the past, avoiding contemporary poets. As we approach the end of the '60s, through Alain Bosquet's anthology, the composition rules seem to change: the poems containing 'progressive', communist messages are avoided, even if authors who made a career in that period weren't excluded from the summary. The number of authors increased, the poets' Pantheon evolving in order to accomodate them. Once the Romanian poetic wave of the '60s arrived, the anthology included new entries, whilst maintaining the poets with literary activity prior to 1945 and proceeding to a selection of the '50s so-called 'court poets'. Dispersal, rather than diversity would be a more appropriate description for the selection of an anthology, avoiding a strict canonical formula. Therefore, rather than analyzing the canonical character of an anthology, a discussion on its permissiveness would seem more relevant.

WORKS CITED

Anthologie de la poésie française, ed. by. Georges Pompidou, Nouvelle édition suivie d'un post-scriptum (Paris: Hachette, 1989)

Anthologie de la poesie populaire roumaine, trans. by Annie Bentoiu and Andreea Dobrescu-Warodin (Bucharest: Minerva, 1979)

Anthologie de la poésie roumaine, ed. by Alain Bosquet (Paris: Seuil, 1968)

Anthologie de la poésie roumaine, with a preface by George Macovescu (Paris: Editions Nagel, 1981)

Ballades populaires roumaines, bilingual edition, trans. by Andrei Bucsan (Cluj-Napoca: Dacia, 1984)

Florilège d'amour – poèmes, édition bilingue franco-romaine, selection and trans. by Aurel George Boeşteanu, (Bucharest: Minerva, 1981)

Introduction à la poésie roumaine, ed. by Hubert Juin (Paris: Club des Amis du Livre Progressiste, 1961)

Jeunes poètes roumains, with texts selected and trans. by Dan Ion Nasta (Bucharest: Eminescu, 1985)

Petite anthologie de poésie roumaine, bilingual edition (Bucharest: Minerva, 1975)

Poèmes roumains, dès origines à nos jours, ed. by Hubert Juin (Paris: Éditions Hautefeuille, 1958)

Poésis. Poètes roumains contemporains (Bucharest: Eminescu, 1975)

30 poètes roumains (Bucharest: Cartea Românească, 1978)

ABOUT THE AUTHORS

CRISTINA BALINTE, PhD in Comparative literature, researcher at 'G. Călinescu' Institute of History and Literary Theory of Bucharest (Romania). She co-authored various volumes notably some treating iconology and ekphrasis, signed several articles in Romanian cultural reviews (*Synthesis, Cultura, Adevărul literar şi artistic*), and edited the novels and the movie screenplays of the Romanian prose writer Sorin Titel. Research fellow at the University of Liège (Belgium), at the University of Caen (France) and at the National Library of France.

IOANA BOTH is Professor at the Department of Romanian Literature, literary theory and ethnology, Faculty of Letters, University 'Babeş-Bolyai' of Cluj-Napoca. Visiting professor of Romanian Literature at universities in Rome ('La Sapienza'), Florence, Geneva, Fribourg, Zürich, St. Gallen. During the last 10 years, she participated at several international research projects, dedicated to the European contextualization of the history of Romanian Literature (see *Cronologia della letteratura rumena moderna, 1790-1914*, Ioana Both & Angela Tarantino, www.unifi.it/letrum). Interests in historical poetics, concretized in the volumes *Histoires littéraires. Littérature et idéologie dans l'histoire de la littérature roumaine* (*Literary Histories. Literature and Ideology in Romanian Literary History*) (Cluj, 2003) and *Sensuri ale perfecţiunii. Literatura cu formă fixă ca încercare asupra limitelor limbajului* (*Senses of Perfection. Questioning the Language's Limites through Fixed Form Literature*) (Cluj, 2006).

FRÉDÉRIC CANOVAS is an art critic and associate professor of French studies at Arizona State University. He has published extensively on André Gide, Jean Cocteau, Paul Valéry and other literary figures of the late 19th century (Gourmont, Schwob, Léautaud, Huysmans, Rimbaud) and of the 20th century (Crevel, Barthes, Renaud Camus, Michel Tournier). His study on dreams in modern French narrative *L'Ecriture rêvée* was published by L'Harmattan in 2000. He is currently completing a book-length study on illustrated books by the post-impressionist painter Maurice Denis which received the support of the National Endowment for the Humanities.

ADINA CIUGUREANU is Professor of English and American Literature at Ovidius University Constanţa, Romania. She is currently Dean of the Faculty of Letters. Since 2008 she has served as President of the Romanian Association for American Studies. Her research area is British and American culture of late nineteenth to mid-twentieth century. Her publications include: *High Modernist Poetic Discourse* (1997), based on her PhD dissertation, *Modernism and the Idea of Modernity* (2004, 2008), *Victorian Selves* (2005, 2008), and *Post-War Anxieties* (2006). After a Fulbright research grant in the

USA, she published *The Boomerang Effect* (2002), a study on American popular culture viewed as remodeling European cultural patterns. The study was translated into Romanian and published by Editura Institutul European, Iaşi, 2008. She is also editor of the conference volumes following the international conferences she organizes at her home university.

THEO D'HAEN is Professor of English and Comparative Literature at the University of Leuven (Louvain) in Belgium. Earlier he was Chair of English and American Literature at Leyden University, and before that taught at Utrecht University, both in The Netherlands. Visiting Professor at the Sorbonne III (2004) and Harvard (2007); Fulbright Researcher at Harvard (2010). He holds a PhD in Comparative Literature from the University of Massachusetts at Amherst. Recent book-length publications (as co-author and/or co-editor) in English include: *Contemporary American Crime Writing, Configuring Romanticism, How Far is America From Here, Cultural Identity and Postmodern Writing, International don Quixote,* and *Literature for Europe?.* Present or past editor or advisory editor of numerous scholarly series and journals in the fields of Comparative, English and American, and Dutch Literature. Editor-in-chief of the *European Review.* Present or past board member of, and organizer of world congresses for, the International Comparative Literature Association and the International American Studies Association. Currently President of FILLM (Fédération Internationale de Langues et Littératures Modernes). Member of the Academia Europaea.

DAVID DAMROSCH is Professor and Chair of Comparative Literature at Harvard University, and is a past president of the American Comparative Literature Association. He has written widely on world literature from antiquity to the present. His books include *The Narrative Covenant* (1987), *What Is World Literature?* (2003), *The Buried Book: The Loss and Rediscovery of the Great Epic of Gilgamesh* (2007), and *How to Read World Literature* (2009). He is the general editor of the six-volume *Longman Anthology of World Literature* (2004) and the editor of *Teaching World Literature* (Modern Language Association, 2009) and co-editor of *The Princeton Sourcebook in Comparative Literature* (2009).

CAIUS DOBRESCU is Professor at the University of Bucharest (Literary Theory Department). Among other research interests, he authored books on literature and politics in the Communist and post-Communist social environments (*Modernitatea ultimă* [*The Ultimate Modernity*], 1998; *Inamicul impresonal* [*The Impersonal Enemy*], 2001), and on the interaction between the conflicting understandings of the notion of 'bourgeois culture' and the evolutions of the literary modernity, in a comparative perspective and at a global scale (*Semizei şi rentieri* [*Demigods and Rent-seekers*], 2000;

About the Authors 351

Revoluția radială [*The Radial Revolution*], 2008). He was granted a Herder scholarship at Vienna University and was a Fellow of New Europe College in Bucharest and of Budapest Collegium. As a Fulbright scholar affiliated with the Committee on Social Thought of the University of Chicago he conducted research on terrorism and literary modernity.

SIMONA DRĂGAN, PhD, is a teaching assistant at the Department of European Studies, Faculty of Letters, University of Bucharest. Individual volumes: *Creație și putere. Concepte discursive în poststructuralism* (*Creation and Power. Discursive Concepts in Post-Structuralism*) (Bucharest: Ideea Europeană, 2009) (awarded the Prize for literary theory in 2009, by the Romanian Association of General and Comparative Literature). Collective volumes: M. Constantinescu (ed.), *Cultura în epoca post-umanismelor* (*Culture in the Post-Humanist Age*) (Bucharest: Univers Enciclopedic, 2006). She published articles, reviews, and scientific papers in Romanian and foreign cultural journals, on subjects of literary theory, philosophy, comparative literature, art history, and gender studies. Two studies on E. M. Cioran were translated in Spanish and published by M. Liliana Herrera (*Paradoxa. Revista de filosofía. Cioran. 10 Años*, no. 9, 2005, Universidad Tecnológica de Pereira, Colombia, and *Cioran. Ensayos Críticos*, Universidad Tecnológica de Pereira, Colombia, 2008).

ZAKARIA FATIH is interested in the discourse on broader modernity in general and the clash of tradition and modernity in the Francophone novel of North Africa in particular. His first book: *L'âge des Lumière entre vérité et altérité* (*The Enlightenment Age between Truth and Alterity*) deals with the relationship of truth and alterity in the Enlightenment. He has also published articles on Proust, Benjamin, and Tahar Ben Jelloun and is currently revising a book-length manuscript on the clash of tradition and modernity in the Maghreb. He teaches at the University of Maryland, Baltimore County in Baltimore.

OANA FOTACHE is assistant professor of literary theory at the University of Bucharest (Romania). PhD in literary theory (2006). Publications: *Divanul criticii. Discursuri asupra metodei în critica românească postbelică* (*Discourses on Method in Postwar Romanian Literary Criticism*), 2009; coeditor (with Anca Băicoianu) of the anthology *Teoria literaturii. Orientări în teoria și critica literară contemporană* (*Literary Theory. Directions in Contemporary Literary Theory and Criticism*), 2005; articles, reviews, papers in Romanian and foreign literary and cultural journals (*Euresis. Cahiers roumains d'études littéraires et culturelles, New International Journal of Romanian Studies, Literary Research/ Recherche littéraire, Annals of the University of Bucharest*, etc.).

WILLIAM FRANKE is Professor of Comparative Literature and Religious Studies at Vanderbilt University. He is the author of *Poetry and Apocalypse: Theological Disclosures of Poetic Language* (Stanford University Press, 2009) and *Dante's Interpretive Journey* (University of Chicago Press, 1996), as well as of the two-volume anthology-cum-theory-and-history *On What Cannot Be Said: Apophatic Discourses in Philosophy, Religion, Literature and the Arts* (University of Notre Dame Press, 2007). He has been Fulbright-University of Salzburg Distinguished Chair in Intercultural Theology and Study of Religions (Spring 2007) and has held visiting appointments or international fellowships at the University of Hong Kong, the University of Potsdam (Alexander von Humboldt-Stiftung), the Camargo Foundation (France), and the Bogliasco Foundation (Italy).

MIHAELA IRIMIA, Professor, Director of Studies of the British Cultural Studies Centre and Director of the Centre of Excellence for the Study of Cultural Identity, University of Bucharest, teaches C 18 and Romantic British Culture, Cultural Theory, and History of Ideas. Her professional affiliations comprise ESSE, BSECS, ISECS. She has signed more than 30 individual and co-authored volumes and almost 200 articles and studies published in Europe and the USA. Among her recent publications are: 'Romanian Romanticism', in St. Prickett (ed.), *European Romanticism: A Reader*, London & New York: Continuum International Publishing Group, Limited, 2010; 'The Ineffectual Angel of Political Hijacking', in M. Rossington & S. Schmid (eds), *The Reception of Shelley in Europe*, London & New York: Continuum, 2008; 'A Walpolian Anecdote: The Garden of Alcinous', in T.G. Rapatzikou (ed.), *Anglo-American Perceptions of Hellenism*, Newcastle: Cambridge Scholars Publishing, 2008; 'Colonial London in the Eighteenth Century', in É. Hanquart-Turner (ed.), *Urbs et Orbis: Métropoles et villes provinciales dans le monde Anglophone,* Paris & Ivry/Seine: Éditions A3, 2007.

ION MANOLESCU is PhD Associate Professor of Romanian Literature at the University of Bucharest. Education: Advanced Study Fellow, *New Europe College*, Bucharest, 1996-97; *Netherlands Institute for Advanced Study*, Wassenaar, 1998; *New Europe College-LINK*, Bucharest, 2005-06. Publications (selection): *Notions for the Study of Virtual Texts* (Bucureşti: Ars Docendi, 2002); *Videology. A Techno-Cultural Theory of Global Imagery* (Iaşi: Polirom, 2003). Areas of specialization: 20th century Romanian literature, postmodern literary canons, techno-culture. Current research interests: communist literature and ideology, cognitive psychology and philosophy, cyberpunk literature.

ELAINE MARTIN is professor of German and Women's Studies at the University of Alabama in the US, where she also directs the Program in

Comparative and World Literature. She has written on German-speaking women's writings on World War II, on representations of food/eating in literature and film, and on comparative literature in the context of cultural studies. She is currently preparing an annotated bibliography and filmography of works on terrorism and is working on a book of essays concerning terrorism in literature and film.

RODICA MIHĂILĂ is Professor of Literature and American Studies and Director of the Center for American Studies at the University of Bucharest. Her publications include *Aspects of American Literary Modernism. A Study of Tensions in the Poetry of Hart Crane* (1975), *The American Challenge* (1993), *Turning the Wheel. The Construction of Power Relations in Contemporary American Women's Poetry* (1995), *Spaces of the Real in American Fiction* (2000) and *The Re-Usable Past* (2002), several anthologies of American literature as well as articles and studies in scholarly journals and the literary press. She is co-editor of a series of volumes of literary and cultural studies *Transatlantic Connections* (2001), *America in/ from Romania* (2003), *Our America: People, Places, Times* (2005), *New/ Old Worlds. Spaces of Transition (*2007), *The Sense of America. Histories into Text* (2009) and *Transatlantic Dialogues* (2009) and she is also a well-known translator of English and American literature.

ILEANA ALEXANDRA ORLICH is Professor of Comparative Literature and Director of Romanian Studies and the Central European Cultural Collaborative in the School of International Letters and Cultures at Arizona State University. Her books include *Silent Bodies: (Re)Discovering the Women of Romanian Short Fiction* (2002), *Articulating Gender, Narrating the Nation: Allegorical Femininity in Romanian Fiction* (2005), *Myth and Modernity in the Twentieth-Century Romanian Novel* (2009), and *Avantgardism, Politics, and the Limits of Interpretation: Reading Gellu Naum's* Zenobia (2010). She is also a well-known translator of Romanian and English literature and has published extensively in scholarly journals.

LIVIU PAPADIMA is Professor and Dean of the Faculty of Letters, University of Bucharest. Research scholarships in Romania (New Europe College, Bucharest) and abroad (University of Vienna and Vrije Universiteit, Amsterdam). Visiting Lecturer and Visiting Professor at the University of Vienna (1991-1994, 2000-2002) and at the University of Amsterdam (1996-1997). Executive secretary of the Romanian Association of General and Comparative Literature, affiliated to the International Comparative Literature Association (ICLA) (1997-2004). Publications: individual volumes of literary studies: *Caragiale, firește* (*Caragiale, Obviously*), 1999; *Literatură și comunicare. Relația autor - cititor în proza pașoptistă și postpașoptistă*

(*Literature and Communication. The Author-Reader Relation in (post)1848 Literature*), 2000; *Mai are timpul răbdare?* (*Is Time Still Patient?*), 2007.

D.R. POPA (Dumitru Radu Popa) holds an MA from the University of Bucharest (1972) and an MS from Columbia University in New York. His literary works in Romanian include five collections of short stories, and two novels. He also translated Romanian poetry into English and wrote literary criticism. In 2007 his first book in English *Lady V. and Other Stories* was published at Spuyten Duyvil, in New York. D.R. Popa is an Assistant Dean and Director of the Law Library at New York University School of Law. He has been teaching in the field of International Legal Research in the United States, Russia, Armenia, China, and South Africa. D.R. Popa is a Member of the Society of Romanian Writers, American Association of International Law, IFLA, IALL. Featured in *Who's Who in American Law* and *Who's Who in America*.

MAGDA RĂDUŢĂ is a teaching assistant in the Romanian Literary History Department, Faculty of Letters, University of Bucharest. Her PhD thesis, *The Romanian Literary Pamphlet in the Interwar Period* (2009), makes use of an interdisciplinary approach (poetics, literary history, socio-critics) on this genre of Romanian literature. She is currently working on a second thesis on literary sociology (*Avant-garde consacrée et consacrante: la génération littéraire 80 pendant et après le communisme roumain* [*Consecrated and Consacring Avant-garde: the '80s Literary Generation during and after Romanian Communism*], coordinated by Prof. Rose-Marie Lagrave, EHESS, France).

ROUMIANA L. STANTCHEVA is an Associate Professor, Dr. Sc., and Director of Balkan Studies at Sofia University 'St. Kliment Ohridsky'. Areas of research: Comparative Literature, Balkan Literatures (Romanian and Bulgarian), French Literature, Modernism – 19th-20th centuries. She is president of the Bulgarian Academic Circle for Comparative Literature, member of the ICLA and of its Committee for the Study of the South-East European Literatures; officer of the Executive Committee of REELC; *Doctor Honoris Causa* of the University of Artois, France. Main publications: *Modern Rumanian Poetry through a Comparative Approach* (Modernata rumanska poezia), Sofia, 1994; *Reception of the European Literatures in Bulgaria, XIX-XX s.* (Prevodna retzeptzia) (In collab.). Vol. 6. Sofia, Academic Publishing House, 2004. Editor for : *L'oublié et l'interdit. Littérature, résistance, dissidence et résilience en Europe Centrale et Orientale (1947-1989).* (En collab. avec Alain Vuillemin). Ed. de l'Institut d'Etudes balkaniques, Ed. Limes, Ed. Rafael de Surtis, 2009, *The Blending of Literatures or What Comparative Literature Compares?* (Goliamoto vpisvane), Sofia University ed., 2009.

STEFAN H. UHLIG is Lecturer in English Literature at the University of Cambridge. He has published on the idea of world literature, eighteenth-century conversation, and the value of ordinary life in Gray and Wordsworth. He is writing a study of the conceptual resources of literary studies, and is co-editor of *Aesthetics and the Work of Art: Adorno, Kafka, Richter* (2009) and of *Wordsworth's Poetic Theory: Knowledge, Language, Experience* (2010).

DELIA UNGUREANU is a seminar tutor in the Theory of Literature Department, Faculty of Letters, University of Bucharest. She is a collaborator of Polirom and Art Publishing and a contributor to *Observator cultural* magazine. She translated Harold Bloom's *The Western Canon* (*Canonul occidental*, Bucharest: Art, 2007) and Terry Eagleton's *Literary Theory: an Introduction* (*Teoria literară. O introducere*, Iaşi: Polirom, 2008). She works on her PhD study, *The Disequilibria of the Literary Field and the Beginnings of Dictated Ideology in Romanian Literary Magazines (1944-1947)* [*Dezechilibrele câmpului literar şi începuturile ideologizării în revistele literare româneşti (1944-1947)*].

MĂDĂLINA VATCU is a PhD candidate at the University of Bucharest. Her research is a continuation of her M.A. thesis, *A Geography of the Communist Thaw. Translations from Romanian Literature in France and Italy*. Her current focus is on the political and sociological aspects of French translations from Romanian during the communist period.

ALEXANDRA VRÂNCEANU teaches comparative literature at the University of Bucharest since 1992. She published her PhD thesis in 2002 (*Applying Literary Models to Visual Narratives. How to Read a Visual Story*) and she published many articles in the field of interart studies in Romania, Italy, France, and the US. She also taught at l'Université Jean Monnet, Saint Etienne, France (2001-2005). Alexandra Vrânceanu's recent scientific interests are the study of *ekphrasis* in the contemporary novel and the analysis of the role played by the migrant writer in world and national literature.